CHARLES H. FLEI

THE SHRM ESSENTIAL GUIDE TO EMPLOYMENT LAW

A Handbook for HR Professionals, Managers, Businesses, and Organizations

CHARLES H. FLEISCHER, ESQ.

THE SHRM ESSENTIAL GUIDE TO EMPLOYMENT LAW

A Handbook for HR Professionals, Managers, Businesses, and Organizations

SOCIETY FOR HUMAN RESOURCE MANAGEMENT
Alexandria, Virginia • www.shrm.org

STRATEGIC HUMAN RESOURCE MANAGEMENT INDIA
Mumbai, India • www.shrmindia.org

SOCIETY FOR HUMAN RESOURCE MANAGEMENT
Haidian District Beijing, China • www.shrm.org/cn

SOCIETY FOR HUMAN RESOURCE MANAGEMENT,
MIDDLE EAST AND AFRICA OFFICE
Dubai, UAE • www.shrm.org/pages/mena.aspx

This publication is designed to provide accurate and authoritative information regarding the subject matter covered. It is sold with the understanding that neither the publisher nor the author is engaged in rendering legal or other professional service. If legal advice or other expert assistance is required, the services of a competent, licensed professional should be sought. The federal and state laws discussed in this book are subject to frequent revision and interpretation by amendments or judicial revisions that may significantly affect employer or employee rights and obligations. Readers are encouraged to seek legal counsel regarding specific policies and practices in their organizations.

This book is published by the Society for Human Resource Management (SHRM). The interpretations, conclusions, and recommendations in this book are those of the author and do not necessarily represent those of the publisher.

This publication may not be reproduced, stored in a retrieval system, or transmitted in whole or in part, in any form or by any means, electronic, mechanical, photocopying, recording, or otherwise, without the prior written permission of the publisher, or authorization through payment of the appropriate per-copy fee to the Copyright Clearance Center, Inc., 222 Rosewood Drive, Danvers, MA 01923, 978-750-8600, fax 978-646-8600, or on the Web at www.copyright.com. Requests to the publisher for permission should be addressed to SHRM Book Permissions, 1800 Duke Street, Alexandria, VA 22314, or online at http://www.shrm.org/about-shrm/pages/copyright--permissions.aspx.

SHRM books and products are available on most online bookstores and through the SHRMStore at www.shrmstore.org.

The Society for Human Resource Management is the world's largest HR professional society, representing 285,000 members in more than 165 countries. For nearly seven decades, the Society has been the leading provider of resources serving the needs of HR professionals and advancing the practice of human resource management. SHRM has more than 575 affiliated chapters within the United States and subsidiary offices in China, India, and United Arab Emirates. Please visit us at www.shrm.org.

Interior & Cover Design	Shirley Raybuck
Manager, Creative Services	James McGinnis
Manager, Book Publishing	Matthew Davis
Vice President, Editorial	Tony Lee

Library of Congress Cataloging-in-Publication Data has been applied for and is on file with the Library of Congress. ISBN (pbk): 978-1-586-44470-9; ISBN (PDF): 978-1-586-44471-6; ISBN (EPUB): 978-1-586-44472-3; ISBN (MOBI): 978-1-586-44473-0

Printed in the United States of America   FIRST EDITION

PB PRINTING   10 9 8 7 6 5 4 3 2 1

61.11003 17-0820

Contents

While every attempt has been made to provide accurate, authoritative, and current information regarding the subject matter covered, this book is for general information only and is not intended as legal, tax, accounting, or other professional advice. The reader should consult an attorney, accountant, human resource professional, or other appropriate expert regarding specific questions or problems. Neither the author nor the publisher is liable for any errors or omissions.

Introduction

Not too many years ago, managing employer-employee relations was relatively simple. Little more was required than meeting pay-roll and remembering to deposit withholding taxes on time. Since then, life has become infinitely more complicated and uncertain. Employment practices that easily passed muster yesterday now expose employers to substantial risk and expense. At the same time, employees have become more knowledgeable about their rights and much less bashful about exercising them.

It is easy to cite examples of practices that may once have been common, but now, depending on the circumstances, could give rise to civil lawsuits and even criminal prosecutions. Do any of these sound like good ideas?

- *I'll just call my staff independent contractors and avoid the hassles that come with employees.*
- *Bob worked overtime all day Saturday copying and stapling the proposal, so I'll give him a day off next week.*
- *Nancy quit on me in the middle of her project. There's no way I'm going to pay her for the two weeks' vacation she had coming.*

- *If I hire through a temp agency, I can tell them to send me men for the sales positions and women for secretaries without having to worry about sex discrimination.*
- *Becky in Accounting has been dating her assistant. I hear they're having problems, but they're just going to have to work things out.*
- *The next person who gets his salary garnished is out of here!*

If any of these strikes a familiar chord, this book is for you!

Employment is, fundamentally, an *economic relationship*. The employer seeks an employee who will work competently and dependably in furtherance of the employer's business. The employee seeks regular work at reasonable compensation.

At the same time, the employment relationship is awash in powerful, psychodynamic currents. Employers, having risked their personal capital to keep their businesses afloat, may have unreasonable expectations of loyalty and devotion from their workforce. Employees, on the other hand, may feel at sea when subjected to seemingly arbitrary and unexplained decisions by their bosses. Both sides often define themselves and derive their sense of self-worth from the employment relationship, so stormy encounters can be treacherous.

Employment is also a highly regulated relationship. Since employers have historically held greater economic power than individual employees, federal, state, and even local governments have felt it necessary to intervene. As a result, employers do not have freedom to dictate (or even negotiate) many terms and conditions of employment. They must pay minimum wages and time-and-a-half for overtime. They must comply with detailed workplace safety standards. They must conform their employee benefit plans to complicated legal requirements. And they are forbidden from making employment decisions based on a host of prohibited criteria.

Employers are also easy targets for the imposition of requirements that otherwise have little to do with the employment relationship. In the income tax area, for example, employers enforce their employees' obligations to the Internal Revenue Service (IRS) and to state taxing authorities by withholding an array of items from employee paychecks. Employers also finance government social policy embodied in workers' compensation and unemployment compensation laws. They must even assist the government in collecting certain debts and locating parents who ignore their child support obligations.

This book is intended as an overview of U.S. workplace laws, regulations, and court decisions that employers, large or small, are likely to face. Some chapters explore the employment relationship primarily as it is affected by the common law—the law we inherited from England and are developing by judicial decisions in this country. Other chapters deal with federal and state statutes that bear directly on the employment relationship or that impose obligations on employers. The goal in each case is to present general principles, to highlight hot issues, and to offer specific examples and suggestions to make the employer-employee relationship run more smoothly.

For readability, statutory and case citations have largely been omitted, no footnotes have been used, and wherever possible, technical legal terms have been avoided. Employment issues are often technical, however, so an extensive glossary has been included.

The employment relationship involves a wide range of complex issues and is also subject to frequent change. Congress, state legislatures, federal and state regulatory agencies, local governments, and courts at all levels have a say in the relationship. Any one of these bodies can make illegal tomorrow what is thought to be perfectly legal today. It would be impossible, therefore, to write a fully comprehensive, this-is-all-you'll-ever-need-to-know treatise.

Reading this book will not make you an employment lawyer or a tax expert. You will not be well equipped to respond to an Equal Employment Opportunity Commission charge, to set up a pension plan, or to deal with a union-organizing campaign. But you will gain a broad understanding of employer-employee relations, know where most of the dangers lurk, and be alert to situations in which professional advice is needed.

While there is no substitute for familiarity with the intricacies of the employment relationship, we dare to offer, at the outset, three rules of conduct for employers. Adopt them now, follow them faithfully, and you will avoid many of the pitfalls discussed here.

1. *Treat your employees reasonably.* They are not indentured servants, nor are they part of your extended family. They usually respond best when treated like reasonable adults, and they may quit (or worse, sue) if they feel unfairly treated.

2. *Focus your personnel policies and decisions directly on accomplishing your business mission.* Leave your biases, prejudices, and social agendas at home.

3. *Keep detailed, current, written records of all personnel actions.* If it is not in writing, it did not happen.

CHAPTER 1

The Employment Relationship

- Overview
- Employees, Independent Contractors, and Agents
- Statutory Employees and Nonemployees
- Joint Employers
- The Employment-at-Will Doctrine
- Employment Contracts
- Indemnity Obligations
- Arbitration Agreements
- Business Owners' Employment Status

OVERVIEW

The employment relationship is a mutual, voluntary arrangement between two parties. The *employer*—which may be a corporation, some other entity, or an individual—voluntarily agrees to pay the employee in exchange for the employee's work.

The employee—who is always an individual—voluntarily agrees to work for the employer in exchange for pay.

The relationship is *voluntary* in the sense that the law does not force anyone to work for a particular employer. The 13th Amendment to the U.S. Constitution declares that "neither slavery nor involuntary servitude ... shall exist within the United States." As implemented by the Congress, the 13th Amendment prohibits forced labor through use of physical restraints, threats of physical harm, or threats of legal action. The prohibitions against forced labor also protect persons from compulsory work to pay off a debt—sometimes called *peonage* or *indentured servitude*.

The United Nations International Labour Organization (ILO) has adopted the *ILO Declaration on Fundamental Principles and Rights at Work*, to which the United States subscribes. The declaration states that all member nations have an obligation to respect four fundamental rights:

- "freedom of association and the effective recognition of the right to collective bargaining;
- the elimination of all forms of forced or compulsory labour;
- the effective abolition of child labour; and
- the elimination of discrimination in respect of employment and occupation."

Although the employment relationship is voluntary from the employer's viewpoint, in that the employer usually has no obligation to employ anyone in particular, in limited circumstances an employer can be forced to hire or re-employ a particular individual as a remedy for discriminating against that individual or violating that individual's rights under a protected leave law, such as the Family and Medical Leave Act (FMLA).

The employment relationship is often thought of as a *contract* between employer and employee. However, it usually does not take the form of a typical bilateral (or mutual) contract, in which each party makes a promise to the other, such as, "I promise to deliver goods to you next week if you promise to pay me $1,000 in 30 days." Instead, the employment relationship usually takes the form of a unilateral contract, in which only one party (the employer) makes a promise, such as, "If you come work for me, I will pay you $12 per hour." The employee usually does not promise to work. He or she just shows up, works, and becomes entitled to the promised pay. Mutual employment contracts are discussed in more detail on the following pages.

EMPLOYEES, INDEPENDENT CONTRACTORS, AND AGENTS

An employer's workforce can be classified broadly as employees and independent contractors. An employee and an independent contractor may or may not be an agent of the employer, depending on the authority given by the employer to obligate the employer to contracts.

Employees

An *employee* is someone whose manner of work the employer has a *right to control*, even if the employer does not actually exercise that control. An entry-level file clerk will likely be subject to close, daily, or even hour-by-hour supervision and is therefore an employee. So, too, is the president of a large corporation, not because he or she is closely supervised, but because the corporation's board of directors has the right to control his or her work. This right to control is illustrated by the outdated legal terms *master* and *servant* used historically to describe the employment relationship.

True employees (as distinguished from independent contractors) are sometimes known as *W-2 employees*, referring to the Forms W-2 issued to them for federal income tax purposes.

Vicarious Liability

As a matter of public policy, the courts hold employers *vicariously liable* for injuries or property damage caused by their employees if the injury or damage occurred during the course and scope of the employee's employment. This is sometimes referred to as the doctrine of *respondeat superior*—a doctrine requiring the superior (the employer) to respond (by paying damages) for the conduct of its employee.

Normally, such liability is imposed when the employee acts negligently, such a causing a car accident while driving on the job. But vicarious liability may be imposed even if the employee intentionally causes the injury, so long as the employee acted with the intention to benefit his or her employer and the employment relationship enabled the employee to cause the injury. An example might be a store clerk who physically restrains a customer wrongfully suspected of shoplifting.

Negligence and intentional misconduct that cause injury or damage are referred to in the law as *torts*—French for *wrongs*.

Independent Contractors

An *independent contractor*, in contrast to an employee, is someone you engage to perform a certain task, but whose manner of work you do not have a right to control. Good examples are professionals, such as outside lawyers or accountants, and trades persons such as electricians and plumbers. In each of these examples, the independent contractor's work is governed by professional standards, state and county codes, and the like, with which you are probably not familiar. Your lack of familiarity is precisely why you engage an independent contractor instead of doing the work yourself or having one of your employees do it.

Certainly you can tell your independent contractor what it is you want done, and you remain free to dismiss him or her if you do not like the work. But it is the result you are interested in; the manner in which that result is accomplished is up to the independent contractor and is not subject to your control.

Unlike an employee, an independent contractor generally cannot impose vicarious (tort) liability on his or her employer.

⚠ **ALERT!**

Whenever a worker's status as an independent contractor could reasonably be questioned, the safest course is to treat that worker as an employee.

Independent contractors are issued *Forms 1099* to report income for federal tax purposes, as opposed to Forms W-2 issued to employees. Unlike employees, independent contractors are not subject to income and payroll tax withholding.

Employers sometimes try to classify their workforce as independent contractors, rather than employees, in an effort to avoid being subject to laws and regulations that apply to employees. In response, the various regulatory agencies, such as the Internal Revenue Service (IRS), the U.S. Department of Labor (DOL), the Equal Employment Opportunity Commission (EEOC), the Occupational Safety and Health Administration (OSHA), state wage and hour departments, workers' compensation commissions, and unemployment insurance administrators, have adopted complex tests—that differ from agency to agency—to distinguish employees from independent contractors. These tests tend to be biased in favor of an employer-employee relationship—that is, in favor of finding that the person is covered by the particular employment law or regulation the agency is charged with enforcing. (Tax issues relating to independent contractors are discussed in Chapter 7. See "Contingent Workers" in Chapter 20 for more details about the independent contractor relationship.)

The consequences of misclassifying an employee or a group of employees as independent contractors can be expensive. For example, the employer might be held liable for income taxes that should have been withheld, but were not, wage and hour violations, retroactive coverage under employee benefit plans, back pay, penalties, statutory damages, and interest.

☞ QUICK TIP

Some workers are required by law to work under another's supervision. This is true, for example, in various health care professions. Even though the worker may otherwise qualify as an independent contractor, the duty to be supervised may convert the worker into an employee.

Agents

An *agent* is someone you authorize to make contracts on your behalf and to bind you to those contracts. Employees can be agents, but employees do not automatically become agents; it depends on what, if any, additional authority you give them. For example, if you told your employee to take a computer to the shop and make arrangements to have it repaired, you have given your employee authority to act as your agent. When he or she signs a work order in your name, you as the principal, not the employee, will have to pay the repair bill.

Similarly, an independent contractor can be, but is not necessarily, an agent. When you engage a landscape architect to prepare a design for the grounds around your new office building, the architect is an independent contractor but not an agent. However, when you then authorize the architect to buy plantings, he or she becomes your agent as well and has the power to obligate you in contract to the nursery.

STATUTORY EMPLOYEES AND NONEMPLOYEES

Some laws classify workers as employees or independent contractors regardless of the employer's right of control or lack of control over the manner in which the work is done.

For payroll tax purposes, the Internal Revenue Code classifies the following four categories of individuals as *statutory employees* even though they could be independent contractors under the common-law test:

- a delivery driver (other than one who delivers milk)
- a full-time life insurance agent
- an individual who works at home on materials or goods supplied by the employer

- a full-time salesperson who sells merchandise for resale or for use in the buyer's business operation

The Internal Revenue Code classifies the following individuals as *statutory nonemployees* for all federal tax purposes:
- direct sellers of consumer products in the home or a place of business other than a permanent retail establishment
- licensed real estate agents
- companion sitters who are not employed by a companion sitter placement service

Workers' compensation statutes, unemployment insurance statutes, and other laws also state who does or does not qualify as an employee for purposes of the statute.

JOINT EMPLOYERS

In a number of situations the law considers an employee to be jointly employed by two or more employers. As a result, both employers may be liable for discrimination or unfair labor practices, obligated to pay overtime and withhold and remit payroll taxes, or provide workers' compensation or other benefits.

A common example of joint employment is the staffing firm that leases an employee to another business. If the business directs the staffing firm to replace the leased employee based on the employee's race or age and the staffing firm does so, both the business and the staffing firm will be liable for discrimination.

In another example, suppose a nurse's aide works for two separate nursing homes that are owned in part by the same individuals. The total hours she works for both nursing homes may be aggregated in determining whether she is entitled to overtime.

In the construction industry, a prime contractor may engage a subcontractor, who in turn provides employees to the job site. If those employees perform work both for the subcontractor and the prime contractor, they may be deemed jointly employed by both entities. Similarly, franchisers may be considered as joint employers of their franchisees' employees.

In the 2015 decision in *Browning-Ferris Industries of California, Inc.*, the National Labor Relations Board (NLRB) expanded its definition of joint employment in determining what constitutes an appropriate bargaining unit for union representation purposes. According to the NLRB, in evaluating whether an employer possesses sufficient control over employees to qualify as a joint employer, the board considers whether an employer has exercised control over terms and conditions of employment indirectly through an intermediary or whether it has reserved the authority to do so. As of this writing, the case is on appeal to the U.S. Court of Appeals for the D.C. Circuit. (Unions and labor relations are discussed in more detail in Chapter 24.)

In *Salinas v. Commercial Interiors, Inc.*, the U.S. Court of Appeals for the 4th Circuit (headquartered in Richmond, Va.) ruled that joint employment exists when two or more entities "share, agree to allocate responsibility for, or otherwise co-determine—formally or informally, directly or indirectly—the essential terms and conditions of a worker's employment." The Court went on to list a number of factors to be considered in determining that question.

As these cases indicate, joint employment remains a developing legal area and is becoming more common given the growing variety of business models and labor arrangements. It should also be noted, however, that the DOL under the Trump administration has withdrawn a 2015 administrator's interpretations that offered an expansive view of joint employment.

THE EMPLOYMENT-AT-WILL DOCTRINE

Most employment is *at will*. That means there is no fixed period of time that the employment relationship will last, and either party is free to terminate the relationship at any time, with or without cause. In other words, the employer may fire, or the employee may quit, for any reason or for no reason at all.

In almost all states, there is a presumption that any particular employment relationship is at will. The presumption applies unless it is shown that employment for a specific period of time, such as two years, was intended. The fact that the employer and the employee intended the relationship to last a long time or for an indefinite period does not overcome the presumption of at-will employment, since in almost all cases the parties hope (at least at the outset) that the relationship will last a long time or indefinitely. An employer's promise of work for as long as the job exists and for as long as the employee wants it is nothing more than indefinite, at-will employment. Even so-called *permanent employment* is still employment at will (although employers should not use the term *permanent* when intending only an at-will relationship).

An important corollary of the at-will doctrine is the implied covenant of good faith and fair dealing. In most states, every contract is presumed to contain that implied covenant, requiring parties to the contract to act reasonably toward each other. However, the covenant is generally not implied in the normal at-will employment arrangement, since the covenant depends on the existence of an employment contract with a definite term. (A handful of states do recognize the covenant in an at-will employment relationship.) It follows, at least in theory, that an employer may treat at-will employees unreasonably and may fire them without cause, although it is seldom good practice to do so.

The at-will employment doctrine has five important exceptions:

- the employment contract exception (discussed later in this chapter)
- the abusive discharge exception (see Chapter 4)
- the exception for protected leave (see Chapter 8)
- the discrimination/retaliation exception (see Chapters 14 through 17)
- the exception for collective bargaining agreements (see Chapter 24)

When one of these exceptions applies, discharging an at-will employee may result in a lawsuit, an award of money damages against the employer, or an order that the employer reinstate the employee.

EMPLOYMENT CONTRACTS

An *employment contract* (more accurately, a *mutual* employment contract) is an agreement between the employer and the employee that the employment relationship will last for a fixed, definite period of time or that the relationship can be terminated only for cause or under specified conditions. Employment contracts should be in writing, since oral contracts that cannot be performed within one year are generally unenforceable according to the *statute of frauds*. Even if an oral contract of employment is enforceable, it can give rise to misunderstandings, and its provisions are difficult to prove.

The contents of any particular employment contract depend on the circumstances. A typical contract might include provisions dealing with the following:

- job description, including employee duties and authority
- whether the position is exempt or nonexempt under the Fair Labor Standards Act
- beginning date and term of the contract and any extensions
- compensation arrangements
- bonuses and equity, such as stock options
- health and other benefit plans
- other fringe benefits, such as a company car or an expense account
- exclusivity, such as no moonlighting or no conflicts of interest during term
- vacation and sick leave arrangements
- grounds for early termination, such as death, disability, revocation of a required license, or dishonesty
- confidentiality and trade secrets
- ownership of intellectual property, such as copyrightable and patentable works or inventions

- noncompetition and nonsolicitation of customers and fellow employees after termination
- liquidated damages for breach by employee
- waiver of jury trial or arbitration of disputes, along with prohibition on participating in class or collective actions
- indemnification
- choice-of-law provision
- choice-of-forum provision
- abbreviated statute of limitations

In most cases, the employer wants to preserve an at-will employment relationship and avoid being bound by an employment contract or by any implied covenant of good faith and fair dealing. This would be true, for example, in the case of lower-level employees who can be replaced fairly easily. However, in a tight labor market in which qualified employees are difficult to find, the employer may want the protection of an employment contract. The employer might also want contract protection for employees in whom costly training is being invested, for employees who have access to closely guarded company secrets, or for employees who have unusual or complicated compensation arrangements.

An employee may want the security of a contract when, for example, the employee is resigning from a stable position to take a job with a start-up company or making a costly move to the new employer's headquarters. Whether the employer gives a contract in those circumstances depends on the employee's bargaining power and worth to the new employer.

Choice-of-law and *choice-of-forum* provisions are particularly helpful to large, multistate employers, which might otherwise be subject to conflicting state laws. They allow the employer to specify which state law will govern the employment contract and which court will hear any disputes that arise under the contract. The employer might, for example, specify the law of the state and the courts of the state where its headquarters are located or where most of its employees work. So long as the employer's choices are reasonable and do not impose an undue burden on the employee, most courts uphold these provisions.

Some employment contracts also seek to shorten the time within which an employee may bring suit against the employer. If state law specifies a three-year statute of limitations, the contract might shorten that time limit to, say, 18 months. While these types of provisions are controversial, some courts have upheld them.

Fill-in-the-blank contract forms are available from commercial publishers. Electronic forms can even be purchased or downloaded from the Internet. But if the employment relationship is important enough to justify a contract in the first place, it should be important enough to justify a consultation with employment counsel to be sure the contract fits the particular circumstances and conforms with state and local law.

Implied Contracts

Although the parties may not have explicitly intended to enter into an employment contract, the employer's actions can inadvertently bind the employer to the same extent as if there were a written, signed agreement. Some courts have found, for example, that an employee handbook amounts to an employment contract, even though no contract was actually intended. Even the wording of a simple employment letter can create a contract if it implies that a specific time period is contemplated. Consider this letter:

> We are pleased to offer you the position of sales manager beginning January 1. Your base salary will be $50,000 per year, increasing to $60,000 your second year, and $70,000 your third year. You will also earn an override commission of 2.5 percent on all sales.
>
> We have already made definite plans to expand our market into the southeastern states over the next three years. By the end of the third year, sales should reach $1.5 million, which translates to a commission to you of $37,500. We are counting on you to take the lead

in these expansion plans, and we have every confidence that, with you at the helm of our sales department, we will reach our goal.

While the letter does not exactly promise a three-year arrangement, it certainly implies that the sales manager should expect to stay that long. Couple that with the sales manager's own testimony that he was indeed promised three years, and the employer might find itself bound to such a contract.

Breach of Contract

When employer and employee have agreed that the employment will last a fixed period of time, or that the employment can be terminated only for specified reasons, the courts generally enforce such an agreement by awarding money damages for its breach. If the *employer* breaches, it may be liable not only for the compensation the employee would have earned but also for fringe benefits such as health insurance, pension plan contributions, and stock options.

If the *employee* breaches, damages are more difficult to measure, since it is not easy to quantify just how a particular employee's performance would have affected future profitability. Absent a *liquidated damages* provision (a provision that specifies in advance the amount of damages to be recovered), the employer's claim might be limited to employment agency fees, employee relocation costs covered by the employer, and any license or similar fees paid by the employer on the employee's behalf. Remember that a court will not order the employee back to work since such an order would violate the Constitution's involuntary servitude clause.

⚠ ALERT!

Even in employment-at-will situations, the employer may be held liable for misrepresentation if an employee is induced to accept work based on false or incomplete representations as to the conditions of employment. (See Chapter 2 for more on fraud and misrepresentation during the hiring process.)

INDEMNITY OBLIGATIONS

In an indemnity agreement, one party agrees to protect the other party from claims by third parties. For example, a physician employed by a hospital might agree to indemnify the hospital from malpractice claims by the physician's patient. Or a business corporation might agree to indemnify its senior management from claims by shareholders or other employees. Such an agreement serves, in effect, as private insurance between the parties.

Whether an indemnity provision will be included in an employment contract and, if so, who will be indemnifying whom, are matters of negotiation between the parties. A highly desired candidate, for example, might insist on being indemnified as a condition to accepting a job offer. On the other hand, a candidate with little bargaining power may have no choice but to agree to indemnify his or her employer to get the job.

Even absent an indemnity provision in an employment contract, the employer may have an indemnity obligation to some or all of its employees under state corporation law or under provisions of its corporate charter or bylaws.

⚠ ALERT!

An indemnity provision in an employment contract or in corporate documents exposes the employer to a risk of substantial liability. The employer should therefore carry adequate liability insurance and be sure that the potential indemnity obligation is covered by the policy.

ARBITRATION AGREEMENTS

Arbitration of disputes is often viewed as preferable to litigation. Arbitration is generally faster and cheaper; it involves only limited pretrial discovery, the proceedings take place in private, and the results are usually final and unappealable. Since arbitration means no jury trial, an employer that fears a runaway jury and a runaway damage award may view arbitration as a highly desirable alternative to litigation.

Both the *Federal Arbitration Act* (FAA) and its state counterparts say that a contract provision for resolution of future disputes by arbitration is valid and enforceable. The courts have gone so far as to rule that the law favors arbitration and that when a contract contains an arbitration clause, a presumption arises that all disputes relating to the contract must be arbitrated. These principles have been applied to labor disputes under collective bargaining agreements and to employment disputes in the securities industry, in which arbitration clauses have been common for years. Arbitration provisions are now finding their way into more and more contracts, including routine employment agreements.

☞ **QUICK TIP**

A *pre-dispute* arbitration agreement—that is, an agreement to arbitrate made at the outset of employment or at some other time before a dispute has arisen—should be distinguished from an agreement to arbitrate made after a dispute has arisen. Courts almost always enforce a post-dispute arbitration agreement that is entered into knowingly and voluntarily. Enforcement of a pre-dispute arbitration agreement, however, may be open to a variety of objections, such as unfairness or lack of true consent.

For some time, there was a question whether an employee could be forced to submit federal statutory claims to arbitration. Suppose an employer routinely requires employees, as a condition of employment, to sign an agreement that subjects all future employment-related disputes to binding arbitration, including discrimination claims based on the various federal nondiscrimination statutes. Under the principle that statutory rights cannot be waived in advance, some federal courts initially ruled that an employee would not be bound by such an agreement, made in advance of any dispute.

The Supreme Court, which is the ultimate authority on interpretation of federal law, resolved the question in March 2001. In a decision involving an employee of an electronics store in California, the court ruled that an agreement to arbitrate discrimination claims was valid and enforceable under the FAA. The court went on to praise arbitration agreements in the employment context, because of the smaller sums of money normally involved.

The EEOC, which opposes binding arbitration of discrimination claims, will not stay its own hand in investigating or attempting to resolve a discrimination charge just because the parties have entered into an arbitration agreement. In a 2002 case, an employee of a chain restaurant was fired from his short-order cook job when the restaurant learned he suffered from seizures. In response to the EEOC's suit for violations of the Americans with Disabilities Act (ADA), the restaurant argued that the employee had signed a pre-dispute arbitration agreement that barred the EEOC's suit. The Supreme Court upheld the EEOC's suit, saying the EEOC has an independent statutory right to pursue whatever remedies it feels appropriate that included not only injunctions against future violations but also victim-specific relief such as reinstatement and back pay.

Nor can an arbitration agreement, or any other agreement for that matter, prevent an employee or former employee from filing a charge of discrimination with the EEOC or a state fair employment practices agency.

Arbitration may not always be cheaper than litigation. There are often significant filing fees just to initiate arbitration. And while judges are provided by the government without charge, arbitrators typically charge substantial hourly rates payable by the parties.

Some employers have tried to shift the burden of arbitration costs to the employee, so that the employee ends up paying far more to arbitrate than he or she would in a court suit. Other employers have drafted arbitration agreements that are so one-sided in favor of the employer as to be fundamentally unfair to the employee. Decisions by a number of federal appellate courts have refused to enforce such agreements, ruling that any attempt to burden an employee with excessive costs or to give employers unfair procedural advantages is a denial of the employee's statutory rights.

☞ **QUICK TIP**

For companies that require employees to sign *noncompetition* or *nonsolicitation con-tracts*, an arbitration agreement should have an exception allowing the employer to go to court for an injunction to bar an employee's or former employee's violation of the contract.

Arbitration provisions should not be placed in the employee handbook, since the employee handbook is not intended to be a contract of employment. (However, the handbook may mention the fact that an employer has an arbitration-of-disputes policy.) For those employees with whom the employer has a formal contract of employment, the arbitration provision would be included there. For at-will employees, the employer should use a separate written document, dated and signed by the employee, that contains both the desired arbitration provision and a disclaimer to the effect that the arbitration provision is not a contract of employment and does not change the at-will status of the employee.

Despite the Supreme Court's blessing, legal issues involving pre-dispute arbitration agreements continue to arise, particularly in the area of fairness and cost-shifting. To help ensure their validity, arbitration agreements should do the following:

- contain a clear and unmistakable waiver of the employee's right to go to court and specify that arbitration is final and binding
- specifically identify the types of potential claims that the employer intends to submit to arbitration—claims under Title VII of the Civil Rights Act, the ADA, the Age Discrimination in Employment Act (ADEA), the FMLA, state human rights and fair employment practices acts, county and local nondiscrimination laws, claims for abusive discharge, pay disputes, etc.
- provide for a neutral arbitrator, not one who is affiliated with the employer or who regularly hears disputes involving the employer
- allow at least minimal discovery
- not burden the employee with costs in excess of those he or she would incur in court

- be balanced, fair to both sides, and not attempt to give the employer any procedural advantages
- be binding on the employer as well as the employee (that is, it should not obligate the employee to arbitrate while giving the employer the option of arbitrating or not)
- not attempt to take away any of the employee's substantive statutory rights or limit an employee's statutory remedies
- require the arbitrator to issue a written award

With increasing frequency, employers are including class- and collective-action waivers in arbitration agreements in an effort to prevent employees from participating with a large group of plaintiffs. Class and collective actions allow individual plaintiffs to aggregate their claims into one lawsuit or arbitration proceeding when each individual claim may be economically too small to pursue.

In *AT&T Mobility LLC v. Concepcion,* the U.S. Supreme Court held that class-action waivers are enforceable in the context of a dispute between a business and a consumer. However, the National Labor Relations Board takes the view that in the employer-employee context, such waivers violate employees' rights under the National Labor Relations Act (NLRA). (See Chapter 24 for more on the NLRA.) As of this writing, the issue is before the U.S. Supreme Court in *NLRB v. Murphy Oil USA, Inc.*

BUSINESS OWNERS' EMPLOYMENT STATUS

Business can be conducted in a variety of forms, from the sole proprietorship to the publicly held, multinational corporation. In between are general partnerships; small or closely held corporations that have elected S status for federal income tax purposes (S corps), limited liability partnerships (LLPs), limited liability companies (LLCs), and professional corporations (PCs).

The right choice of business entity goes beyond the scope of this book. This section is concerned with the status of business owners who also work for the entity they own. Are they considered employees of the entity? And what liability do they have for entity obligations or the negligence of other employees? The answers depend on the specific type of entity involved and on certain tax elections available to those entities.

Sole Proprietorships

A *sole proprietorship* is a business owned by a single individual in his or her individual name. While a sole proprietor can have employees, he or she is considered *self-employed* and can never be an employee of the business. Sole proprietors report their business income and expenses on Schedule C of Form 1040 for federal income tax purposes.

Sole proprietors are personally liable for their own negligence, and, as employers, they are vicariously liable for the work-related negligence of their employees. They are also personally liable for the business' obligations, such as wages, lease payments, business loans, and vendor invoices. For liability reasons, a sole proprietorship is usually not a recommended form for doing business.

General Partnerships

A *general partnership* is a group of individuals who share profits and losses of the partnership's business. Partnerships are treated as separate entities for some purposes and as pass-through entities for other purposes. For example, a partnership can have employees (other than the partners themselves), and it files its own income tax returns. However, partnerships generally do not pay any income tax. Instead, any net income or loss shown on the partnership return is allocated to the partners according to the partnership agreement. Partners pay tax on their allocated share (as shown on Schedule K-1 (Form 1065) that the partnership issues to them) whether or not net income has actually been distributed to them in cash. Partners are considered to be self-employed.

Partners are personally liable for partnership obligations, just like sole proprietors. Also, each partner is considered the agent of each other partner and is personally liable for the negligence and contractual obligations of each partner. (Think of a partner as a sole proprietor with multiple personalities.) This is the main reason for the popularity of S corps and, more recently, LLPs and LLCs.

S Corporations

An *S corporation*, or *S corp*, is just like any other corporation formed under state law, but it has elected S status for federal income tax purposes. (The *S* refers to the Internal Revenue Code subchapter that permits the election.) As a result, it is treated much like a partnership for federal income tax purposes, yet it retains the limited liability features of a corporation. An owner of an S corp is considered self-employed and gets a Form K-1, just like a partner in a partnership. However, there is no personal liability for corporate obligations or for the negligence of other employees or co-owners. Because they have characteristics of both corporations and partnerships, S corps (along with LLPs and LLCs) are sometimes called *hybrids*.

S corp status is available only to small business corporations with one class of stock and fewer than 100 shareholders. Only individuals, decedent's estates, and some types of trusts can be shareholders. Partnerships and other corporations cannot own stock in an S corp.

Limited Liability Partnerships and Limited Liability Companies

Owners of an LLP (who are called *partners*) and owners of an LLC (who are called *members*) are the equivalent of partners in a general partnership for tax purposes. Therefore, they are normally considered self-employed and they get year-end K-1 forms showing their taxable shares of LLP or LLC profits. However, LLPs and LLCs (or any other entity treated as a partnership under state law) may take advantage of the IRS's check-the-box rule and elect to be taxed as corporations. Worker-owners would then be treated as employees, as with any other corporation.

Regardless of an LLP's or LLC's status for tax purposes, its partners or members have no personal liability for obligations of the LLP or LLC, or for the negligence of other partners, members, or employees.

☞ **QUICK TIP**
Small businesses with only a few owners may find it advantageous to organize as LLCs and then elect to be taxed as S corps. This arrangement enjoys simplicity of organization, pass-through tax status, and protection of owners from personal liability. In addition, it allows an income tax deduction for the employer's portion of FICA due on compensation paid to owner-employees. Had the LLC not elected corporate taxation status, all compensation to owner-employees would have been subject to self-employment tax for which *no deduction is available.*

Professional Corporations

Traditionally, professionals like doctors, lawyers, and accountants were only permitted to practice as sole proprietors or as partnerships. The fear was that if they practiced in corporate form, their professional judgment would be compromised by being subjected to the wishes of a corporate board of directors. At the same time, however, federal income tax law (particularly regarding pension plans) strongly favored corporations over partnerships. So professionals brought pressure on state legislators and licensing boards to allow them to incorporate. The result was the *professional corporation* (PC).

☞ **QUICK TIP**
Depending on a variety of factors, owners of a professional corporation may or may not be counted as employees for federal nondiscrimination law purposes. In *Clackamas Gastroenterology Associates, P.C. v. Wells,* the Supreme Court applied the common-law test of whether the employer controls the means and manner of the workers' performance in determining whether the physician-shareholders in a medical practice should be counted as employees.

PCs are in every respect true corporations under state law. An owner who works for the PC is usually classified as an employee for tax purposes and receives a Form W-2 at year-end, just like employees of other corporations. (PCs can elect S corp status in which case owners are treated as self-employed for federal tax purposes.) However, only licensed members of the particular profession for which the PC was organized can be shareholders, directors, and officers.

Professionals who work for a PC are personally liable to their clients for professional negligence, regardless of their status as employees for other purposes. But the good news is that they are not personally liable for the negligence of their fellow professionals—a liability they would have if they had organized in partnership form.

C Corporations

Large businesses have little choice in their type of entity. To participate effectively in capital markets they must organize in corporate form. They also cannot qualify as S corps under the Internal Revenue Code because they have a broad shareholder base, and perhaps several classes of stock. *C corp* shareholders may work for the corporation but they have no special status as shareholder-employees. Both the president who owns 10,000 shares and the janitor who owns 10 shares get Forms W-2, and neither is generally liable for corporate obligations or the negligence of fellow employees.

☞ QUICK TIP

Although sole proprietors and partners are considered self-employed, many workers' compensation statutes allow them to opt in and obtain coverage. Conversely, while members of LLCs and corporate officers are covered by workers' comp statutes, they are often permitted to opt out of coverage. (Workers' compensation insurance is discussed in Chapter 11.)

CHAPTER 2
The Hiring Process

- Job Descriptions
- Advertising the Opening
- Applications
- Interviews
- Background Checks and Consumer Reports
- Pre-Employment Testing
- Employment Offers
- Medical Exams
- New-Employee Procedures
- Fraud and Misrepresentation in Hiring
- Interference with Contractual Relations
- Negligent Employment

Employers and employees have numerous interactions during the employment relationship. While any of these interactions can give rise to liability, those involving hiring (discussed here), evaluating (discussed in Chapter 3), and terminating (see Chapter 4) stand out as particularly critical.

The hiring process has one purpose: to exchange enough information so that the parties can make an informed decision about whether to enter into an employment relationship. Good hiring practice involves the collection of appropriate information untainted by information that should not be the basis for a hiring decision. The hiring procedure usually involves the steps discussed below.

JOB DESCRIPTIONS

To focus on job qualifications, the employer should first prepare a clear, written description of the job being offered. The description should include at least the following:

- essential functions of the job—the critical functions that go to the heart of the job and that the person holding the job must, unquestionably, be able to do
- less critical functions that the employee may be called on to perform from time to time or that could be done by others if necessary
- special skills required, such as ability to operate complex equipment
- special education, licenses, or certificates required
- title or position of the person to whom the employee reports
- number and classification of persons who report to the employee
- whether the employee is exempt or nonexempt under the Fair Labor Standards Act
- date the description was prepared or most recently revised

The job description should *not* include any employee characteristics that the employer is prohibited from considering, such as age, gender, and race.

The job description should be prepared *before* the job is advertised and *before* any candidates are considered. That way, the employer will have a much easier time defending its decision to reject a candidate on grounds that he or she could not perform the essential functions of the job despite reasonable accommodation.

ADVERTISING THE OPENING

Any want ads the employer runs or notices it posts should describe the job being offered, not the person the employer thinks it is looking for. Expressions such as *recent graduate*, *energetic person*, or *digital native* could provide evidence of age discrimination if the position is filled by a younger candidate after an older candidate has been turned down. Expressions that indicate a gender preference, such as *waitress*, should also be avoided. (Discrimination is discussed in detail in Chapters 14 through 17.)

Use of only a single method for recruiting unduly restricts the candidate pool and discourages workplace diversity. Word-of-mouth recruiting, for example, has been attacked by the Equal Employment Opportunity Commission (EEOC) as potentially discriminatory: if your current workforce consists mostly of white, middle-age males, word-of-mouth recruiting is likely to produce candidates who are mostly white, middle-aged males.

Internet Recruiting

Advertising job openings via the Internet is a convenient, relatively inexpensive way to attract resumes—and that is the problem. An employer can be overwhelmed with the number of responses and lack sufficient staff time to screen them effectively. Screening software, while effective, may inadvertently discriminate if the wrong keywords are used to do the screening. Employers that limit their recruitment to this medium should also be alert to possible disability discrimination claims if their website lacks accessibility.

☞ **QUICK TIP**

Some employers report that electronic applications, particularly those with attachments purporting to be resumes or supporting documents, contain ransomware or other destructive code.

APPLICATIONS

A written application form should be developed for initial screening purposes. The application form should obviously not ask for information that the employer is prohibited from considering as part of the hiring process.

Some seemingly innocuous inquiries can also cause trouble. For example, the applicant should not be asked to attach a photograph. Age or birthdate questions should be saved until after the applicant has been hired (although for child labor purposes, the employer should ask whether the applicant is at least 18). Similarly, immigration status questions should be saved for later, and the application should be limited to the question, "Are you legally eligible to work in the United States?" Even a question about whom to contact in an emergency should be avoided in the initial application, since it could reveal marital status or family information.

In the past, application forms routinely asked about a candidate's criminal history. The EEOC has weighed in on this practice, asserting that basing employment decisions on such information could discriminate against groups that, statistically, suffer higher conviction rates than the general population.

According to the EEOC, arrest records alone should never be considered, because an arrest does not establish guilt. And instead of a blanket policy excluding every applicant who has a conviction record, the employer should consider, on a case-by-case basis, the following:

- the nature and gravity of the criminal offense
- the time that has passed since the offense and/or completion of sentence
- the nature of the job

In short, the employer must be able to show that its criminal history policy accurately distinguishes between applicants who pose an unacceptable risk and those who do not.

Complicating the issue, states and even counties and cities have begun adopting *ban-the-box* rules that prohibit or restrict employers from asking about a candidate's criminal history. In one local jurisdiction, for example, employers can ask about criminal history, but only after the initial interview. These social policies may be well intended, but to the extent they limit an employer's ability to obtain information relevant to the hiring decision, they could expose the employer, fellow employees, and the public generally to avoidable risks.

Further complicating matters, a few jurisdictions have adopted or are considering the adoption of laws prohibiting employers from asking about compensation history (on the theory that this perpetuates pay disparities suffered by women and minorities) and from discriminating against persons who are currently unemployed.

☞ **QUICK TIP**

When hiring a former U.S. government employee, it is important to know whether the employee is restricted in the type of work he or she may engage in. Either by law or by executive order, many former government employees are prohibited for specific time periods, and in some cases forever, from working on matters that would create a conflict of interest or the appearance of a conflict.

INTERVIEWS

Interviews should be conducted by experienced personnel using a standard written interview form. The interview form should be limited to questions or topics directly relevant to job performance, and the interviewer should stick to the form, noting the applicant's responses. By having and following a standard written form, the employer can more easily show that it did not inquire about any prohibited matters and that no particular applicant was singled out for special questioning.

It is difficult to get a feel for an applicant's personality and communications skills if all that is asked are yes-or-no questions, so interviewers naturally like to ask open-ended questions, such as "Why do you want to work here?" or "Tell me what you like and don't like about your current job." There are risks to open-ended questions, however, particularly when they are not strictly job-related, because they may elicit personal information that can later form the basis of a discrimination claim.

Another common pitfall in the hiring process is family status. Suppose an interviewer asks, "Do you have any family responsibilities that could keep you from getting to the office?" The applicant responds, "I'm a single parent and my son has special needs, but I have day care arrangements that work pretty well." Later, when checking with the applicant's previous employer, the interviewer learns of a tardiness problem. If the applicant is rejected, the employer is open to charges of violating the Americans with Disabilities Act (ADA) or other nondiscrimination laws.

An employer may not ask, "Are you disabled?" or "Do you have any medical conditions that could interfere with your performance?" However, an employer may inquire, "Can you do this job?"—provided the question is asked of every applicant and not just those who may appear to have disabilities.

BACKGROUND CHECKS AND CONSUMER REPORTS

Once you have a short list of candidates, or have tentatively chosen a single candidate, it is time for background checking. This could include, as appropriate, calls to references and previous employers, ordering a consumer or credit report (see below), ordering a criminal convictions check (if warranted by the nature of the job and permitted by state law), and obtaining a copy of the candidate's driving record. It may even include a drug test. Background checking will *not* include a lie detector test, and until you have actually made a conditional offer to the candidate, it will *not* include a medical exam. (Chapter 17 discusses medical examinations.)

Federal law regulates the use by employers of credit and investigative reports prepared by consumer reporting agencies. The federal *Fair Credit Reporting Act* (FCRA) defines a *consumer reporting agency* (CRA) as a person or entity that, for a fee, assembles or evaluates credit information or other information on *consumers* (defined to include employees and candidates for employment) for the purpose of regularly furnishing consumer reports to third parties (such as employers). Even an online search engine that assembles personal data from public sources may qualify as a CRA.

In general, employers may obtain consumer reports from CRAs, including investigative reports, to assess character and general reputation for purposes of evaluating, promoting, reassigning, or retaining an applicant or employee. The law places limits on how far back the credit reporting agency may search for various types of information, but those limits do not apply when highly compensated positions are being filled.

When requesting a consumer report, the employer must disclose to the applicant or employee in writing that it is requesting such a report and must obtain the applicant's or employee's written authorization to obtain the report. The disclosure and authorization must be a separate, stand-alone document and not be embedded in the employment application or some other form. The applicant may in turn make a written request to be informed of the full nature and scope of the report being requested, and the employer must then furnish that information.

If the employer intends to make an adverse employment decision based wholly or partly on the consumer report, the employer must first inform the applicant of this intention. In addition, the employer must supply the applicant or employee with the name and address of the CRA that made the report, a copy of the report, and a statement explaining the applicant's rights under federal law to challenge the accuracy of the report. The federal Consumer Financial Protection Bureau, which enforces the FCRA, has developed a form statement of employee rights under federal law that satisfies the employer's FCRA obligations, available on the bureau's website.

CASE STUDY:
EXTRANEOUS TEXT IN FCRA DISCLOSURES

An employer obtained a consumer report on its applicants, using a disclosure form that also contained a waiver of liability in connection with the use and dissemination of any information contained in the consumer report. In a 2017 case, the U.S. Court of Appeals for the 9th Circuit (headquartered in San Francisco) held that inclusion of the liability waiver violated the FCRA requirement that the disclosure be a stand-alone document. The court also held that, since the stand-alone requirement is so clear, the employer's conduct amounted to a willful violation of the law.

Pursuant to a 2003 amendment to the FCRA known as the Fair and Accurate Credit Transactions Act (FACT Act), the Federal Trade Commission (FTC) adopted regulations governing the disposal of consumer information. The FTC's *Disposal Rule* requires employers and others that have such information to properly dispose of it when no longer needed by taking reasonable measures to protect against unauthorized access or use. Examples of reasonable measures include burning, pulverizing, or shredding papers containing consumer information and implementing and enforcing policies for erasure of electronic media containing consumer information.

⚠ ALERT!
Some states flatly prohibit employers, with limited exceptions, from obtaining an applicant's or employee's credit information for employment purposes, even though the employer has fully complied with the FCRA. Other states permit the obtaining of credit information, but they regulate the process.

Should employers search social media as part of a background investigation? There are dangers in doing so, since so much personal information—such as family status, recreational activities, and religious affiliations—is posted online. One solution is to have someone who is not the decision-maker screen social media content, delete irrelevant personal information, and report only job-relevant data to the decision-maker. (Social media policies are discussed in more detail in Chapter 18.) Employers that decide to include a social media search in their background investigations should develop a standard list of media to search, so that all applicants are treated similarly.

Some states prohibit employers from requesting applicants or current employees to provide social media passwords. And of course, it is illegal for an employer to hack another's social media account.

PRE-EMPLOYMENT TESTING

Title VII of the federal Civil Rights Act makes it unlawful for an employer, when selecting candidates for employment, to adjust the scores of, use different cutoff scores for, or otherwise alter the results of employment-related tests on the basis of race, color, religion, sex, or national origin. Even short of such blatant discrimination as using different cutoff scores, tests that have the unintended effect of excluding certain groups could result in *disparate impact discrimination*. For enforcement purposes, the EEOC has adopted a four-fifths rule—if a particular test (or any other selection procedure, for that matter) results in a selection rate for any race, sex, or ethnic group that is less than four-fifths (80 percent) of the rate for the group with the highest selection rate, the procedure will generally be regarded as evidence of adverse discriminatory impact.

Tests also need to be validated—that is, shown by statistical or other evidence to be good predictors of job performance. The EEOC has adopted detailed regulations on validation requirements, which go beyond the scope of this book. The regulations also require employers to keep records on the impact of their testing procedures, classified by gender, race, and ethnic group.

EMPLOYMENT OFFERS

When you have finally identified a single candidate, the next step is to make an offer. A *written* offer is recommended to avoid any misunderstandings and reduce the possibility of disputes down the road. For at-will employees, the offer will usually be in the form of a simple letter. Figure 2.1 is an example of a written offer.

FIGURE 2.1: AT-WILL OFFER LETTER

Dear [candidate name]:

We are pleased to offer you the full-time exempt position of [job title] at a starting salary of $[amount] per year, beginning [date]. This offer is subject to your furnishing sufficient evidence that you are eligible to work in the United States [and to completion of a background check, drug test, and medical exam at the company's expense].

Vacation and sick leave policies, benefit plans, and other company policies and procedures are explained in our employee handbook, a copy of which will be provided on your start date. You are expected to read and be familiar with the employee handbook and to sign a receipt for the handbook. [As part of the hiring process you will be required to sign [company name]'s standard forms of Noncompetition Agreement and Arbitration Agreement, copies of which have previously been provided to you.]

This letter is not intended to be a contract of employment or a promise of employment for a specific period of time. You will be an at-will employee of [company name], meaning that either you or [company name] can terminate the employment relationship at any time for any reason, with or without cause, and meaning that [company name] can change the terms and conditions of your employment at any time.

If you accept this offer, please sign and return the enclosed copy of this letter no later than [date].

You should report to [employee name] at [time] on your first day of work to complete the hiring process.

All previous discussions and negotiations are merged in and superseded by this letter.

Very truly yours,
[company name]

By _____
[employee name], [title]

I accept this offer of employment:

Signature: _____ Date: _____

MEDICAL EXAMS

Medical exams (but not tests for illegal drugs) are governed by the ADA, discussed in Chapter 17. Before actually offering employment, an employer may *never* require an applicant to undergo a medical exam. When the employer actually offers employment, the offer may be conditioned on the results of a medical exam if the following apply:

- all entering employees in the job category are subject to examination
- the exam requirement can be shown to be job-related and consistent with business necessity
- the resulting medical information is separately maintained and treated as confidential
- the results are not used to discriminate against persons with disabilities

If the offer is subject to any conditions in addition to the medical exam, the medical exam will violate the ADA.

NEW-EMPLOYEE PROCEDURES

The employer should take the following steps when the employee actually starts work:

- Obtain evidence of the employee's eligibility to work in the U.S. and complete Form I-9 (discussed in Chapter 21).
- Check the employee's work eligibility status using E-Verify (if the employer participates in the E-Verify system).
- Have the employee complete Internal Revenue Service Form W-4 and the appropriate state counterpart (see Chapter 7).
- Obtain any additional personal information not given on the application, such as birthdate and emergency contact.
- Collect information as to the employee's race, sex, and national origin if required to file an EEO-1 report (see Chapter 14).
- Give the employee copies of the employee handbook and other applicable work rules and policies, and obtain signed receipts.

- Give the employee a copy of his or her job description and obtain a signed receipt.
- Have the employee sign an arbitration agreement, if appropriate (see Chapter 1).
- Have the employee sign a confidentiality, noncompete, and non-solicitation agreement, if appropriate (discussed in Chapter 19).
- Have the employee enroll in any benefit plans for which he or she is then eligible.
- Notify the appropriate state agency of the new hire within 20 days after the employee begins employment.

National Directory of New Hires Database

Federal law requires each state to establish a *National Directory of New Hires database* that is then shared with other states to track persons who have child-support obligations. The information is also used to detect fraud or abuse in welfare and unemployment programs. The states, in turn, have passed laws to establish the directory and to require in-state employers to report new hires within 20 days after hiring. The one-page form can be mailed or faxed. Forms can be obtained, and in some cases completed, online.

Multistate employers (employers with employees in more than one state) have two reporting options: they may report each newly hired employee to the state where the employee is working, following the new-hire reporting regulations of that particular state, or they may select one state where they have employees working and report all new hires electronically to that state. Employers must choose between the two options; they cannot use both. Employers that choose the second option must register with the U.S. Department of Health and Human Services (HHS) as a multistate employer.

More information on new-hire reporting and forms for registering as a multistate employer are available online at the Office of Child Support Enforcement of the HHS.

Probationary Periods

Many employers consider the first 90 or 180 days of employment as a probationary period, during which a new employee is under close scrutiny and can be summarily discharged if not performing to expectation. Such a policy may make sense in a union setting, in which employees enjoy job protections after expiration of the probationary period, but the policy makes little sense in an at-will employment situation. If an employee is at will, what is his or her status after successfully completing probation? It is still at will, as far as the employer is concerned, but the employee might reasonably expect that he or she can now be fired only for cause. In a true at-will situation, everyone is always on probation!

FRAUD AND MISREPRESENTATION IN HIRING

Resume Fraud

Prospective employees sometimes lie on their job applications. When the position being applied for involves risk to the public, the employer should take reasonable steps to verify the information. Even when no obvious risk is involved, the employer may wish to verify education or past experience that bears on the applicant's qualifications for the job.

While ferreting out these lies is becoming increasingly burdensome, employers can take steps to ensure they obtain an accurate picture of the candidate:
- Check each reference.
- Ask each reference to furnish the name of another person who knows the candidate and check with that person as well.
- Require the candidate to complete a standard written employment application and check the application against the resume for inconsistencies.
- If the candidate claims knowledge or experience in a particular technical field, have one of the company's technicians participate in interviewing the candidate.

- Require candidates to present original documentation in support of resume claims (for example, degrees, certifications, drivers' licenses).
- Obtain official transcripts directly from schools the candidate attended.
- Obtain driving records from state motor vehicle authorities.
- Search the Internet for publicly available information (but see the discussion above and in Chapter 18 about social media).
- Contract with companies to obtain background investigations, criminal conviction checks, and credit checks (but be sure to comply with FCRA requirements, discussed above).
- Hire candidates provided by employment agencies that prescreen their referrals.

Suppose a falsified resume slips past the employer and is not discovered until months or years down the road. What rights and remedies does the employer then have?

At-will employees may, of course, be discharged for any reason (except an illegal reason) or for no reason. As for those employees with employment contracts, if the resume contains a false statement about a *material matter* (that is, about a matter that a reasonable person would find significant), and the employer actually relied on the statement in offering employment, then the employment contract is the product of the employee's fraud. The employer may avoid the contract and discharge the employee so long as the employer acts promptly after discovering the fraud. However, if the false statement is an obvious typographical error (say, inversion of two digits in the date for previous employment), it is trivial, or it is so inherently improbable that the employer could not reasonably have relied on it, then the contract of employment remains enforceable.

☞ **QUICK TIP**

For both contract and at-will positions, it is a good idea to include in the employment application a certification by the applicant that the application is truthful and that all supporting items such as transcripts and reference letters are genuine and unaltered.

Employer Misrepresentations

Suppose an employer makes an offer of at-will employment and, in the process, makes certain statements to the prospective employee about, for example, the nature of the job or working conditions. The applicant relies on those statements, accepts the job, turns down other offers, and begins work. Then, for the first time, the employee learns that the employer's prehiring statements were untrue and that actual job conditions are much less favorable than as represented.

It could be argued that the employee has no basis to complain about the employer's false prehiring statements, since in an at-will relationship the employer has the absolute right to change working conditions at any time and to fire an employee whenever the employer feels like doing so. However, several courts have ruled that an at-will employee who, in reliance on an employer's false statements, resigns from another job, turns down other offers, or incurs relocation expenses, can sue the employer for fraud, deceit, and negligent misrepresentation.

CASE STUDY:
EMPLOYER LIABLE FOR MISREPRESENTATION

When an applicant for a physical therapist position at a hospital was interviewed, the hospital's CEO represented that the hospital's contract with an outside therapy provider would be ending and that the hospital would be bringing physical therapy services in-house. However, the CEO lacked authority to make those changes on his own. He also lacked authority to hire without approval by certain other officials. Nevertheless, the CEO made a firm offer to the therapist.

The therapist accepted the offer and turned down another opportunity. Only then did he learn that the offer had not been authorized and that, in fact, the offered position was not available. In the therapist's suit against the hospital for negligent misrepresentation, the hospital argued that, since the offer was only for at-will employment, the hospital could have gone through with the hiring, then fired the therapist the next day. The court answered that argument by saying that while the at-will nature of the offer would affect the amount of damages that could be awarded, that factor had no bearing on whether the therapist could bring suit for negligent misrepresentation in the first place.

Employers can protect themselves from negligent misrepresentation suits brought by disappointed applicants by doing the following:
- describing the job accurately and furnishing a written job description that is complete and up-to-date, without overselling the position
- giving accurate estimates of job features that are likely to be of interest or concern to an employee, such as overtime requirements and travel
- allowing the applicant an opportunity to review the employee handbook and all documents the applicant will be required to sign upon hiring, such as arbitration and noncompete agreements
- describing the hiring process, including who makes the decision to offer a job and what further approvals, if any, are necessary
- stating clearly and explicitly that the offer is conditioned on approval by the company's board of directors or by some other official, if that is the case
- disclosing other relevant facts, such as that the company is about to move its facilities, is considering a possible bankruptcy, or is facing the loss of an important contract that could significantly affect the applicant's job
- giving the applicant a firm date by which the company will make a decision and, if the company has not made a decision by that deadline, contacting the applicant, informing him or her that the decision is still pending, and asking whether the applicant wishes to continue being considered
- informing the applicant promptly once a decision is made
- if the applicant is being rejected, sending a note confirming the rejection, thanking the applicant for his or her interest, and making clear that the applicant is no longer under consideration

INTERFERENCE WITH CONTRACTUAL RELATIONS

One of the questions every applicant should be asked, both in the application and during the interview, is whether the applicant is bound by any restrictive covenants (such as a confidentiality, nonsolicitation, or noncompete agreement) from previous employment. If the applicant says yes, a copy of the document should be obtained and reviewed by employment counsel to determine whether the applicant can be hired at all and, if so, whether his or her job duties need to be restricted. If the applicant says no, the applicant should be required to certify that fact in writing.

An employer that hires a candidate with knowledge that the employment violates a restrictive covenant with a previous employer is exposed to possible suit by the previous employer for *interference with contractual relations*.

NEGLIGENT EMPLOYMENT

Chapter 1 discusses an employer's vicarious liability under the doctrine of *respondeat superior*—an employer will generally be held liable for torts committed by its employees in the course and scope of employment. But even if the employee's negligent or willful conduct is outside the course and scope of employment, the employer might still be liable for injury or damages to third parties under the doctrine of *negligent employment*.

Take, for example, an apartment building owner who hires a resident manager and provides him with a passkey to all the units. The manager later uses the passkey to enter units whose tenants are on vacation and steal jewelry and electronics. Many courts would conclude that such criminal activity is outside the course and scope of the manager's employment and that therefore the building owner is not vicariously liable for the thefts. But if it turns out that the manager had several recent convictions for theft, which the building owner could easily have discovered but did not, the building owner may be directly liable under the doctrine of negligent hiring.

The negligent hiring doctrine is based on the notion that the employer has a duty to use reasonable care to select employees competent and fit for the work assigned to them and to refrain from retaining the services of an unfit employee. Particularly in positions in which an employee is expected to come into contact with the public, the employer must make some reasonable inquiry before hiring or retaining the employee to ascertain his or her fitness. (Chapter 18 discusses criminal records checks in more detail.)

⚠ **ALERT!**

The negligent employment doctrine is not limited to hiring. An employer that learns about the dangerous propensities of an existing employee but who takes no action to protect the public can be sued for negligent retention.

Ban-the-box rules, discrimination concerns, and possible invasions of privacy all work to restrict an employer's ability to make inquiries about criminal history or perform criminal records checks. On the other hand, the doctrine of negligent employment holds an employer liable for its employee's criminal conduct if the employee's propensity for misconduct could reasonably have been discovered. So what should an employer do in the face of this dilemma? Unfortunately, there is no easy answer.

Obviously, the employer must comply with any state and local restrictions. To the extent those restrictions allow inquiries or a records check, the employer should do so only if a criminal history would be relevant to the position being filled, such as involving contact with the public or access to company finances. And if a criminal history is discovered, the employer should disregard crimes that are old or otherwise irrelevant to the position being filled.

CHAPTER 3
Evaluations, Work Rules, and Discipline

- Reasons for Evaluating
- Legal Considerations
- Employee Handbooks
- Dress Codes
- Personnel Files
- Required Posters
- Corporate Ethics and the Sarbanes-Oxley Act
- Disciplinary Actions

REASONS FOR EVALUATING

Employers have good reasons to perform evaluations if they are done properly. They provide a rational basis on which to promote, discipline, and terminate. And they provide powerful evidence to meet a claim that adverse action was taken for discriminatory or other improper reasons. Employees, particularly newer employees who may be uncertain of their performance, like them. If not done properly, however, they do more harm than good.

Evaluating an employee is a whole lot easier if a history of open communication and regular feedback exists. In short, the process should not be full of surprises.

Some employers have their employees fill out a self-evaluation form that the evaluator then reviews and comments on. While that approach may ease the evaluator's burden, it seems less direct. The employee may end up feeling not only that his or her work habits need improvement, but also that his or her character, honesty, and self-insight are under attack as well.

Some organizations use what are known as *360-degree evaluations* (also called *360-degree assessments* or *multirater feedback systems*). These involve evaluations not only by an employee's supervisor, but also by peers, direct reports, and in some cases, internal or outside customers and clients. Employers need to plan 360-degree evaluation programs with particular care and understand and clearly communicate to employees the procedures and objectives. Follow-up is also critical; otherwise, substantial time will have been wasted collecting useless or unused data.

☞ **QUICK TIP**

Since evaluations themselves are not usually considered adverse actions, a bad evaluation will normally not justify a claim of discrimination or retaliation. However, imposing discipline or terminating an employee based on a discriminatory evaluation can give rise to a claim.

LEGAL CONSIDERATIONS

Below are a few suggestions for evaluating employees. Figure 3.1 is an evaluation disclaimer that should also be considered.

- If you have an evaluation policy, follow it. Nothing looks more suspicious than a negative evaluation done just before taking adverse action, especially when the employer's past evaluation procedures have been haphazard and intermittent.
- Use a written form containing a standard set of objective criteria.
- Be truthful and candid. An effort to spare an employee's feelings is bound to backfire should the employee eventually be let go.
- Avoid vague, subjective comments, like "unprofessional," "bad attitude," or "poor work habits." Such comments offer little guidance.
- Avoid comments that could be construed as discriminatory, such as "Your approach to the job is stale" (age discrimination), "You need a softer, less aggressive demeanor with clients" (sex discrimination when directed to a female employee), or "I know your husband's health has been a distraction for you" (disability discrimination).
- Keep job descriptions up-to-date. Employees will feel unfairly treated if they are criticized on aspects of their jobs for which they did not know they were responsible.
- Tie comments on job performance—whether positive or negative—to the job description.
- Tie comments on behavioral problems to the employee handbook or other written policy statements.
- Give specific examples to support comments: "Jane's report last May on production problems in the York, Pa., plant was prompt and thorough and contained many good suggestions. This is typical of her high-quality work."
- If you evaluate annually, be sure the evaluation considers the entire past year and not just the last few months.

- Discuss your evaluation with the employee and offer him or her an opportunity to comment in a private, confidential setting. Transcribe the employee's comments to writing and include them in the employee's personnel file.
- Follow up on any specific deficiencies noted in the evaluation and make a record of your follow-up in the employee's personnel file.
- Provide regular feedback—particularly, positive feedback—between evaluations.

FIGURE 3.1: EVALUATION DISCLAIMER

An evaluation that is misleadingly favorable might convince an employee that he or she has long-term prospects with the company, when in fact that is not true. Therefore, an evaluation that is shared with the affected employee might contain the following disclaimer:

This evaluation is solely for the company's benefit. Nothing in this evaluation is intended to change or affect in any way the at-will employment relationship between the company and the employee or to limit or affect the company's or the employee's right to terminate the employment relationship at any time for any reason.

EMPLOYEE HANDBOOKS

While there is no obligation for an employer to have a written employee handbook, many employers find them to be a valuable management tool.

Advantages

Handbooks promote uniformity in treatment of employees, particularly for larger employers with several layers of management. That in turn improves morale and frees the employer from a stream of requests for special treatment.

Handbooks are also a convenient source of information for job applicants and new hires, as well as existing employees. They promote efficiency and help establish an institutional culture. They set out guides for workplace behavior that, if willfully violated and result in termination, provide the employer with a defense to an unemployment insurance claim or an abusive discharge suit.

Finally, they provide evidence of employer compliance with law in areas such as workers' compensation, equal employment, and sexual harassment.

Employers that choose to have an employee handbook should not overlook the requirement that if the handbook describes leave policies and the employer is covered by the Family and Medical Leave Act (FMLA), the handbook *must* include a description of extended leave benefits under the FMLA. (See Chapter 8 for details.) And since an employer *must* have a written sexual harassment policy to be able to defend against sexual harassment charges (discussed in Chapter 15), the handbook is the obvious place to set out that policy.

When distributing employee handbooks or updates to employees, have each employee sign an acknowledgment that he or she has received the handbook and will read it. Such acknowledgments are helpful in meeting an employee's claim that he or she was unaware of a particular policy or procedure contained in the handbook.

☞ **QUICK TIP**
Handbooks can be distributed online via a company intranet, and employees can be alerted to updates via email. When an employee accesses the handbook or an update, he or she should be required to check an electronic acknowledgment in lieu of a paper acknowledgment.

Disadvantages
The down side to having an employee handbook or similar statement of policy is that it might be considered a *unilateral contract*— that is, a one-sided offer by the employer to abide by the provisions of the handbook that the employee accepts simply by working for the employer. In other words, courts may treat a poorly worded handbook as converting an at-will employment relationship to a contractual relationship that limits an employer's right to fire or discipline.

When adopting an employee handbook, consider the following steps to reduce, if not eliminate, the risk of contractual liability:

- Include prominent disclaimers that the handbook is not a contract of employment and is not intended to change the at-will status of any employee.
- State that the handbook is intended only as a convenient source of information about the company and its current practices and procedures, which are subject to change at any time without prior notice.
- State that employees are free to resign at any time and that the company is free to discharge an employee at any time, with or without cause.
- State that the company is not bound to follow any particular disciplinary procedures and that the company need not be consistent in imposing discipline.
- Avoid statements such as the company *promises* or *guarantees* or *will take* specified action in certain circumstances.
- Avoid any requirement that employees sign an agreement to comply with or be bound by the handbook.
- Follow the policies specified in the handbook.

In addition to an employee handbook, some companies have a *managers-only manual*, distributed only to managers, setting out required procedures for them to follow for discrimination complaints, discipline, termination, and so on, involving their subordinates. Placing procedural requirements in a managers-only manual, rather than the employee handbook, makes it more difficult for rank-and-file employees to claim that the company is contractually obligated to follow the procedures. Even these manuals, however, must be drafted with care and include disclaimers that nothing in the manual is intended to change any employee's at-will status.

⚠ **ALERT!**

The National Labor Relations Board has attacked numerous handbook provisions, claiming they tend to chill employees' rights to engage in concerted activities protected by the National Labor Relations Act (see Chapter 24).

DRESS CODES

An employer may generally impose a dress code or grooming code on employees, so long as doing so has a legitimate business reason and so long as the code is not discriminatory on the basis or gender, race, religion, or other protected criteria. (Dress codes as a form of sex discrimination are discussed in Chapter 15. Also see Chapter 14 regarding dress codes and religious discrimination.)

⚠ **ALERT!**

Relaxing dress code standards may be a required reasonable accommodation for an employee suffering from a medical condition covered by the Americans with Disabilities Act (ADA).

Dress codes are nothing new. For example, safety considerations may warrant banning long sleeves or flowing skirts. Companies often require their delivery personnel to wear identifying uniforms sporting the corporate colors. Physicians wear white lab coats. Lawyers wear conservative suits and carry briefcases. In office settings, suit jackets, ties, and appropriate slacks for men and suits, dresses, and skirts and blouses for women have long been the unofficial uniforms. The only exceptions might be casual, summertime Fridays, or special allowances for persons with medical conditions or temporary injuries.

Casual, summertime Fridays are giving way to casual everyday all year. *Casual* can mean anything from a comfortable old sports jacket with leather elbow patches to a beer-stained T-shirt and torn jeans, from a blouse and slacks to a bare midriff.

If you decide to go casual, keep the following points in mind:

- Your dress policy should be in writing (such as in the employee handbook) and well publicized.

- The policy should contain a clear definition of *business casual.* For example: "Dress and grooming should be neat and consistent with a professional office atmosphere. Clothing should be clean and without rips or excessive wear. Women may wear dresses, blouses, sweaters, slacks, skirts, blazers, and dress sandals; men may wear shirts with collars, polo shirts, sweaters, chino slacks, jackets, and dress sandals."
- The policy should also contain a clear statement of what is *not permitted.* For example: "The following are examples of items that do not qualify as 'business casual' and are not permitted at any time: T-shirts; tank tops; halters; jeans; shorts; sweats or similar athletic clothing; "athleisure" ware, yoga pants, or see-through clothing; clothing that exposes areas normally covered by business attire; clothing that exposes underwear; work boots; and flip-flops and sneakers."
- Managers should have the authority to determine that casual dress for their immediate staff is inappropriate on particular days, such as when customers or visitors are expected.
- Since not everyone is comfortable wearing casual clothes to work, those who would prefer to dress more formally should feel free to do so.
- The consequences of inappropriate dress should be spelled out. For example: "Employees who report to work unacceptably dressed may be required to return home to change and will be charged with leave during their absence."
- The policy should be consistently and evenhandedly enforced.

PERSONNEL FILES

The employment relationship generates a vast array of documents. Some of them are required by law and must be retained for specified time periods. Good examples are Forms I-9 forms and wage and hour records. Other documents, though perhaps not legally required to be retained, provide evidence of legal compliance. A copy of the *new-hire report* form submitted to the State Directory of New Hires falls in this category. Finally, there are documents that management needs, like job descriptions, evaluations, and disciplinary actions to make sound employment decisions.

Employers should maintain a separate *personnel file* for each employee. The file should not be a waste basket containing everything related to the employee. Instead, management should determine in advance which documents are, and are not, to be kept in the file. In addition, the file should be organized into sections so that particular items can be located easily. A checklist placed on top of each section avoids misfiling and enables management to see, at a glance, whether it is complete and current. Files should be reviewed periodically to ensure compliance with established requirements and procedures.

A typical personnel file might include the following:

- employment application, along with supporting materials such as resume, transcripts, and interview notes
- recommendation letters and reference checks
- copies of restrictive covenants with the employee's previous employers
- offer letter and any contractual documents, such as restrictive covenants and arbitration agreements
- Form I-9 (note that some employers prefer to keep all Forms I-9 together in a separate file for ease of updating and reverifying)
- copy of new-hire report form
- tax withholding forms (W-4, W-5, and state equivalents)
- job description
- copies of any required licenses or certificates required for the position
- signed receipt for employee handbook
- testing materials, if the employee was required to take any tests as part of the application process
- training records relating to job competency, safety, sexual harassment policies, etc.
- evaluations
- commendations and disciplinary actions

- personal information—such as home address, home telephone, and name of spouse—and emergency contact (but see Chapter 18 about employee privacy)
- benefit plan participation records (for example, application, beneficiary designation)
- exit interview notes
- recommendation letters and notes of references given to prospective employers

Personnel files should *not* contain medical information that the employer may have received in connection with an ADA accommodation request or an FMLA leave request, and they should *not* contain data collected to complete the EEO-1 report to submit to the Equal Employment Opportunity Commission (EEOC).

Employers should also establish a *records retention policy*. When particular documents are required by law, the law usually specifies how long they need to be retained. In the absence of a specific requirement, the applicable statute of limitations should be the guide. (A statute of limitations says that a claim may be barred unless suit on the claim is filed within a specified time period, such as three years.) Convenience also plays a role. For example, if the employer commonly receives reference inquiries up to two years after an employee leaves, then the employer may want to retain relevant records at least that long to respond.

Employers also need to establish rules for who has access to personnel files and who may add, remove, or change file contents. Access restrictions also need to be in place for files that are maintained electronically. Backup information should be kept offsite to protect against disasters and sabotage.

Litigation Hold

With the explosion of employment-related lawsuits, just about every organization can expect to get sued sooner or later by a disgruntled employee. Once a suit is pending, a process known as *discov-*

ery begins, during which the employee's attorney can require the employer to answer written questions under oath, furnish personnel files and a variety of other documents, and attend depositions at which the attorney takes testimony with a court reporter present.

When an employer receives a subpoena or a formal request for documents from opposing counsel, the employer cannot simply destroy the documents and then claim they do not exist. (Whether or not the employer actually has to produce all the requested documents is another issue, but destruction is not an option.)

However, the duty to preserve evidence, known as a *litigation hold*, begins long before receipt of a formal request. The courts generally take the view that a party has a duty to preserve evidence when the party is on notice that the evidence is relevant to pending litigation or an administrative charge, or when the party should have known that the evidence may become relevant to future proceedings. Destruction of evidence in these circumstances, known as *spoliation*, can expose the party to significant court-ordered sanctions.

The litigation hold applies not only to paper documents but to email and other electronic data as well. Therefore, when litigation has begun or appears likely, the employer should suspend existing policies for automatic deletion of electronic data and preserve electronic media such as backup tapes.

Employee Access

A number of states have statutes affording an employee the right to see his or her personnel file, copy it, and rebut any negative evaluations or comments contained in the file. However, absent a statute affording such rights or a contract or collective bargaining agreement in which the employer has agreed to grant access, the employer does not have to allow an employee access to his or her file.

Even in the absence of a statute or agreement, it is probably a good idea to allow employees access to their personnel files. One approach is to allow an employee to inspect the file generally, but only receive copies of documents he or she has signed. So if an employee wants a copy of a disciplinary notice, for example, he or she first has to sign it, which places the employer in the desirable position of having a receipted copy of the notice.

Another advantage of a policy allowing an employee access to his or her personnel files is that it promotes open communication and a healthier, less secretive work environment. Yet another advantage is that if an employee has access but fails to dispute unfavorable information, he or she is in a poor position to complain about subsequent personnel actions or references that are based on the information. Perhaps most important, under an open access policy managers and supervisors are likely to be more disciplined in how they keep personnel files and what they put in them.

REQUIRED POSTERS

The various federal agencies charged with implementing federal employment statutes require employers to post notices in the workplace summarizing the provisions of the statutes the agencies enforce. These include the following:

- the EEOC's "Equal Employment Opportunity Is the Law" poster, covering discrimination under Title VII, the ADA, the Age Discrimination in Employment Act (ADEA), genetics, the Equal Pay Act, and retaliation
- the U.S. Department of Labor's (DOL's) "Employee Rights under the Fair Labor Standards Act" poster, covering minimum wage and overtime requirements, child labor, tip credit, and break time for nursing mothers
- the DOL's "Employee Rights under the Family and Medical Leave Act" poster
- the DOL's "Employee Rights on Government Contracts" poster, applicable to U.S. government contractors
- the DOL's "EEO is the Law" poster supplement, covering equal employment opportunity for U.S. government contractors

- the DOL's "Migrant and Seasonal Agricultural Worker Protection Act" poster
- the DOL's "Employee Polygraph Protection Act" poster
- the DOL's "Your Rights Under USERRA" poster
- the Occupational Safety and Health Administration's (OSHA's) "Job Safety and Health" poster

These posters are available on each agency's website in English, Spanish, and in some instances other languages. States and some local jurisdictions have their own poster requirements typically covering *nondiscrimination, wage and hour rules, workers' compensation, unemployment insurance,* and *smoking.* Private publishers have put together for sale comprehensive posters covering federal, state, and local requirements for most jurisdictions.

CORPORATE ETHICS AND THE SARBANES-OXLEY ACT

The rash of corporate scandals by publicly traded companies prompted Congress to pass the *Sarbanes-Oxley Act of 2002.* Although the act focuses primarily on accounting oversight and corporate governance, it also contains a number of provisions that directly affect high-level, and in some cases, lower-echelon, employees of publicly traded companies. Highlights of the act include the following:

- *Certification of financial statements.* The act requires the Securities and Exchange Commission (SEC) to issue rules requiring a company's principal executive and financial officers to certify the company's financial statements as true and complete. In the event of any failure to comply with reporting requirements such that financial statements have to be restated, those same officers must forfeit their bonuses and incentive compensation for a 12-month period.
- *Blackouts.* Whenever a company imposes a blackout by prohibiting pension plan participants from trading in company stock, company directors and executive officers are also prohibited from selling any stock they may have acquired through their

employment with the company. Plan administrators must give advance notice of the blackout to plan participants and beneficiaries, including a statement of the reason for the blackout.

- *Loans.* Subject to certain narrow exceptions, companies are prohibited from making personal loans or extending credit to their directors and executive officers.
- *Code of ethics.* Companies must report to the SEC whether they have adopted a code of ethics for their senior financial officers and, if they have not, why they have not.
- *Document retention.* The act requires the SEC to adopt rules governing companies' retention of documents relating to financial audits and reviews. Knowing and willful violation of the rules is a criminal offense.
- *Fitness to serve.* The SEC is authorized by the act to prohibit persons who are deemed unfit from serving as officers or directors if they have violated rules governing deception or fraud.
- *Whistle-blowing.* It is also criminal for a company to retaliate against an employee who assists in any investigation by federal regulators, Congress, or company supervisors, or who provides information to federal law enforcement officers. Any person who suffers unlawful retaliation may also initiate a civil proceeding for reinstatement, back pay, and other damages.

Even if your company is not publicly traded and subject to the Sarbanes-Oxley Act, it is a good idea to have a corporate code of ethics for employees covering the president on down. Prohibited activities, many of which are illegal as well as unethical, might include the following:

- hiring relatives
- carrying phantom employees
- borrowing money from subordinate employees, vendors, or customers
- accepting bribes, kickbacks, expensive gifts, or lavish entertainment from vendors or customers

- accepting discounts on purchases from vendors or customers that are not offered to the general public
- falsifying business records, tax returns, or reports to government agencies
- carrying off-the-books employees, accounts, or funds
- performing paid services for customers on a personal basis outside normal company channels
- blacklisting employees, customers, or vendors
- fixing bids or sharing pricing or cost information with competitors
- requiring customers to buy unwanted products to get products they do want

DISCIPLINARY ACTIONS

Assuming you have made the decision to issue an employee handbook, to what extent should you spell out in the handbook how and when you will take disciplinary action? Probably the less specific the handbook is in this regard, the better, so that management retains discretion to impose discipline as the circumstances warrant. Figure 3.2 contains a suggested handbook provision on discipline.

FIGURE 3.2: DISCIPLINARY ACTION

Failure to observe established rules and practices can, in the company's sole discretion, lead to disciplinary action, including an oral reprimand, a written reprimand, probation, suspension without pay, demotion, reassignment, and discharge.

For minor infractions, the company generally follows a progressive discipline approach, beginning with an oral reprimand and proceeding with more severe discipline if the matter is not corrected. However, the company is not obligated to follow a progressive discipline approach and may take more severe action, including dismissal, in its discretion. Disciplinary action may be taken whether or not it is set out in this handbook, with or without prior warning, and whether or not such disciplinary action is consistent with other actions directed to the employee involved or to other employees.

Every disciplinary action should be accompanied by a concurrent, written, dated, and signed entry in the employee's personnel file describing the offense and the action taken.

🔔 **ALERT!**

In suspending without pay, the employee must be paid for all past work. Loss of pay can occur only for the period the employee is suspended. For exempt employees, suspension without pay must be consistent with the salary basis regulations of the DOL. (See Chapter 5.)

Offenses meriting a multistep approach might include tardiness, excessive absenteeism, minor neglect of work, violation of company parking regulations, violation of smoking regulations, or frequent personal phone calls. More serious offenses justifying immediate suspension, demotion, or termination might include insubordination, theft or unauthorized use of company property or property of fellow employees, use or possession of illegal substances, possession of a firearm (unless permitted under state law), gambling on company premises, use of company facilities to transmit obscene material, violence or threats of violence against supervisors, racial or sexual harassment, other forms of intentional discrimination, falsifying records or reports, and willful disregard of important company policies such as workplace safety procedures.

🔔 **ALERT!**

Currently, illegal drug use is not protected by the ADA. However, drug addiction and alcoholism are disabilities that can trigger company obligations under the ADA.

This list of offenses is not, of course, complete. Discipline needs to be tailored to each employer's circumstances. A restaurant, for example, will be far more concerned about the failure of its kitchen staff to report communicable diseases than will a computer software company whose programmers work at home.

Even when conduct would otherwise justify immediate termination, it is often better to suspend the employee first. This approach allows tempers to cool and provides an opportunity for a more objective assessment of the situation.

Performance Improvement Plans

A *performance improvement plan* (PIP) may be a better way to accomplish management's objectives than simply imposing discipline. A PIP should be in writing and should contain at least these features:

- identification of the employee's specific performance or behavioral issues that need improvement
- a plan of action, developed collaboratively between management and the employee, to address the issues, such as providing additional training in deficient areas
- specific goals and deadlines by which to achieve them

Once the deadlines have been reached, a follow-up assessment is needed to determine whether the goals have been achieved. If they have been achieved, the employee should be released from the PIP. If they have not been achieved, management needs to decide whether to extend the PIP or take other action, such as termination.

Last Chance Contracts

Depending on the seriousness of the offense, some employers use a *last chance contract* in which the employee agrees, in writing, that he or she is being given one final opportunity to correct the problem and will be terminated if it is not corrected. Then, if the problem later recurs, the employer is on solid ground in following through with termination.

CHAPTER 4
Terminating the Relationship

- Decision to Terminate
- Termination Procedures
- Final Pay and Accrued Leave
- Termination for Cause
- Severance Payments and Releases
- Constructive Discharge
- Retaliation
- Whistle-Blower Regulations
- Abusive Discharge
- Defamation Liability
- Intentional Infliction of Emotional Distress
- Employee Due Process
- Downsizing and Mass Layoffs

DECISION TO TERMINATE

Under the employment-at-will doctrine, recognized in almost all states, employers can fire employees for any reason or for no reason at all (just not an illegal reason). But it rarely makes sense to do so. Instead, the decision to fire should be for a well-documented reason tied directly to the employer's business needs.

When an employer exercises its business judgment in terminating an at-will employee, courts have no right to substitute their own judgment and second-guess the employer's decision. But if the employer cannot explain and support a business-related reason for the termination, such as poor performance or repeated misconduct, the fired employee, and the Equal Employment Opportunity Commission (EEOC), may assume the decision was improperly motivated, such as by discriminatory animus.

Even with a good business reason, it still may not be in the employer's interest to fire. An involuntary termination will likely disrupt the workplace, possibly having a negative impact on morale. And if the departing employee is not bound by a noncompete agreement (discussed in Chapter 19), he or she may take valued customers or clients. Worse, disgruntled former employees with time on their hands may decide to sue or complain to the EEOC. (If you have never had to answer written interrogatories propounded by your former employee's attorney, produce box loads of personnel records, or suffer through depositions of half your workforce, you are in for an unpleasant surprise.) There is also the risk that a fired employee will become a whistle-blower or even resort to sabotage or violence. Consider, finally, the effect of a termination on your unemployment insurance rate. In short, getting rid of a troublesome employee may cause more harm than good.

Finally, such decisions should rarely be made on the spot. Even in the face of egregious misconduct, a temporary suspension usually works best, allowing tempers to cool and providing time for a thoughtful, rather than a heat-of-the-moment, decision and time to consult with HR or outside counsel.

Answering the following questions will help guide the decision to fire:

- Does the company have a good, business-related, well-documented reason to terminate that it can clearly articulate if challenged?
- Is the employee at will, or is he or she protected by an employment contract or a collective bargaining agreement?
- If there is a contract, is the firing permitted by the contract, and have all required preliminary steps been taken?
- Is the employee in a protected status, such as on Family and Medical Leave Act (FMLA) leave?
- Has the employee recently complained about working conditions, discrimination, or other matters, such that firing him or her could be considered retaliatory?

TERMINATION PROCEDURES

When the decision has been made to terminate an employee, the actual process should be carefully planned. A face-to-face termination meeting is generally recommended as more respectful than a phone call or an email. A face-to-face meeting also allows the employee to vent and allows management an opportunity to observe and assess the employee's reaction.

The meeting should take place behind closed doors and away from other employees. Scheduling the meeting for before or after normal working hours means fewer fellow employees will be present and may spare the employee some embarrassment.

Normally, two representatives of management will be present—one to conduct the meeting and the other to observe. This arrangement also conveys to the employee that the decision to terminate is firm. The speaker should prepare in advance what he or she is going to say. Ideally, a lengthy explanation of the reasons for the decision should be unnecessary, since there will be a history of previous counseling or discipline. However, the speaker should be truthful and specific about the performance or behavioral issues that warrant termination. A vague reference to the employee's not being a "good fit" or that "things are just not working out" will leave the employee uncertain and suspicious of the real reason.

The employee may argue that the company is mistaken on its facts or that the reason given does not justify termination. Presumably, the company has already considered these matters in reaching its decision. In any event, this is not the time to engage in a debate with the employee. The response to the employee's objections should be brief and clear: "I'm sorry, Bob, but the decision is final."

Management also needs to consider the following:

- whether a severance payment should be offered in exchange for a release of claims
- if security personnel should be available to escort the employee from the worksite and provide ongoing security
- whether state law requires immediate delivery of a final paycheck
- whether to inform the employee that he or she is prohibited from returning to the employer's premises and will be considered a trespasser if he or she returns

⚠ ALERT!

Giving a false or ambiguous reason for termination may seem less painful, but it can make defending an unemployment insurance claim or a suit for abusive discharge or discrimination more difficult.

When an employee voluntarily quits, the employee should normally be interviewed by a senior member of management just before departure. The employee should be asked about the reasons for quitting. Often the employer can gain valuable insight at this juncture into morale or other problems such as a hostile sexual or racial environment.

The following matters, as applicable, should be accomplished during the termination meeting or exit interview:

- Collect keys, security passcards, ID badges, cellphones, laptops, and other property belonging to the employer.

- Confirm the employee's current address and phone number.
- Instruct the employee to remove all personal belongings.
- Inform the employee as to when a final paycheck will be available and determine the employee's wishes as to whether the check should be mailed or held for pickup.
- Provide any notices required by state law, such as a notice regarding the availability of unemployment insurance benefits.
- Remind the employee of any continuing confidentiality, non-compete, and nonsolicitation obligations.
- Remind the employee of the employer's policy on references.

Immediately after the termination meeting or exit interview, the interviewers should prepare a file memo summarizing the interview, including any reasons given by the employee for a voluntary quit. If not previously accomplished, the employee's access to the company's computer network should be terminated. This is also a good time to change other employees' passwords, since employees often know each other's passwords.

Promptly after the interview, the employer should (as applicable) do the following:

- Notify human resources and payroll of the employee's status change and request a final paycheck.
- Give a COBRA notice to the employee.
- Provide the employee with notice of any conversion privileges available under health, life, disability, or other insurance plans maintained by the employer.
- Provide notice of any rights or obligations regarding retirement plan participation and benefits.
- Terminate any signature authority the employee has over employer bank accounts or other financial accounts.
- Notify insurers and retirement plan managers of the employee's status change.
- Notify affected employees of the termination (without discussing the reason).

- Notify others of the termination, such as security personnel, customers, vendors, and financial institutions, with whom the employee had contact (again, without discussing the reason).
- Notify persons receiving garnishment or withholding order payments from the employee's wages of the employee's status change.
- Arrange for issuance of a final Form W-2 at year's end (or within 30 days if the employee requests it sooner).

FINAL PAY AND ACCRUED LEAVE

A departing employee is entitled to be paid at the agreed rate for all work actually performed up to the time of termination. The employer cannot withhold wages on the ground that the employee failed to give two weeks' or some other specified notice before quitting. Nor can the employer dock the wages of a fired employee on the theory that the employee's work quality was unacceptable (but see the discussion of the faithless servant doctrine in Chapter 19).

State law also specifies *when* a departing employee must be paid. In some states, the final paycheck does not need to be issued until the next regular payday. In others, the departing employee must be paid immediately or within a few days of termination, depending on the circumstances of termination.

The employer may deduct from the employee's paycheck any claims the employer has against the employee, so long as the employee has agreed in writing to the deduction. Suppose, for example, that the employee borrowed money from the company, to be repaid out of future paychecks. Or suppose the employer advanced unearned leave on the understanding that, in the event of an early termination, the employee would make reimbursement out of final wages. In these examples, an appropriate setoff against the employee's paycheck is permitted. However, the employer should not deduct the amount of a disputed claim or any other amount not agreed to by the employee, since doing so may violate wage and hour laws. Nor should any deductions reduce the employee's pay below the minimum wage.

Is a terminating employee entitled to have his or her accrued but unused leave cashed out on termination? In many states the employer may adopt a policy of not cashing out accrued leave, or cashing it out only under certain circumstances. For example, the employee handbook might say that accrued leave is not cashed out if the employee quits without giving specified advance notice, or if the employee is fired for cause. Absent such a policy, however, state law may treat accrued leave as part of the employee's compensation and require that it be cashed out.

The question of cashing out accrued leave is limited to vacation or paid-time-off accruals. Other forms of paid leave—such as sick leave and bereavement leave—are normally not cashed out on termination.

Garden Leave

Many companies have a policy requiring employees to give at least two weeks' advance notice of quitting. Of course, if an employee quits without giving the notice, he or she cannot be forced to work for the two-week period. (A policy of forfeiting accrued leave for failure to give the requisite notice, if permitted by state law, may well reduce instances of abrupt termination.) But what if the employee does give two weeks' notice? Must the employer keep the employee on for the entire notice period?

At-will employees may be fired at any time without cause. So in theory, on receipt of two weeks' notice, the employer could in turn fire the employee immediately. Doing so, however, will undermine the employer's notice requirement by discouraging other employees from complying. A better policy is to place the employee on so-called *garden leave*—keeping the employee on the payroll for the full two weeks, but relieving him or her of all duties and telling him or her not to report to work. Figure 4.1 contains a suggested handbook provision for garden leave.

FIGURE 4.1: GARDEN LEAVE PROVISION

> Upon giving or receiving notice of termination, the company reserves the right to relieve the employee of all duties and place him or her on garden leave during the notice period.

TERMINATION FOR CAUSE

Sometimes an employer is willing to give up the right to terminate an employee at will and offer job security in the form of an employment contract. For example, the labor market may be tight, and the employer may be having trouble attracting qualified candidates, a particular position may just be difficult to fill, or a desirable candidate may be of interest to the competition.

One way to promise job security is to offer employment for a specified period of time as long as the employee's performance remains satisfactory or to agree that employment can be terminated only for *cause* or *good cause*. When an employer makes such an offer to a prospective employee, and the employee accepts the offer and begins work, the employer is bound by the arrangement. The employee is no longer at will, and he or she cannot be dismissed except as stated in the contract.

⚠ **ALERT!**

An employer may unintentionally be limited to terminating only for cause as a result of statements inadvertently made in the employee handbook. (See Chapter 3 for tips on drafting employee handbooks to reduce this risk.)

What does *cause* or *good cause* mean in this context? The parties to a contractual arrangement are free to spell out in their contract exactly what they mean by the term. For example, if the employee needs a particular license to work (such as a plumbing license), suspension or revocation of the license might be listed as a cause for termination. Convictions for certain types of crimes, insubordination, drunkenness, and physical assaults on customers or fellow employees might also be on the list. There may also be explicit do's and don'ts set out in an employee handbook or job description.

The employment relationship itself implies certain duties on the part of the employee, including a duty to show up for work in reasonably fit condition, a duty to have and exercise reasonable skill in performing the job, a duty of loyalty and honesty, and a duty to refrain from insubordinate and threatening behavior. A substantial breach of any of these implied duties is cause for termination.

In the absence of a definition or clear indication of the meaning of cause in a contract of employment or an employee handbook, the courts have defined the term along the following lines: "Fair and honest reasons, regulated by good faith on the part of the employer, that are not trivial, arbitrary, or capricious, unrelated to business needs, goals, or pretextual. A reasoned conclusion, in short, supported by substantial evidence gathered through an adequate investigation that includes notice of the claimed misconduct and a chance for the employee to respond."

In a Wyoming case, the court adopted a definition similar to the above. The court went on to say that, in determining whether an employer had cause for termination, the question is not, "Did the employee in fact commit the act leading to termination?" Rather, the question is, "Was the factual basis on which the employer concluded a dischargeable act had been committed reached honestly, after an appropriate investigation and for reasons that are not arbitrary or pretextual?" In other words, the courts are not going to second-guess an employer's business judgment so long as the decision to terminate is reached honestly and fairly.

⚠ ALERT!

If the employer is unionized, the definition of *cause* is in the collective bargaining agreement and termination procedures may be different.

SEVERANCE PAYMENTS AND RELEASES

Some employment contracts, particularly those with higher-paid executives, provide for *severance payments* on termination. The payment may be conditioned on the employee's being terminated without cause or quitting with good reason, or it may be triggered by a change in ownership or control of the company. The payment should also be conditioned on the employee's signing a general release of claims. (Severance payments to high-level executives are sometimes called *golden parachutes.*) Absent such a contractual obligation, employers are not required to pay severance, even to long-time, faithful employees.

In a reduction-in-force termination, the employer might nevertheless pay severance voluntarily as a reward for many years of service or to maintain morale among remaining employees. In an effort to reduce labor costs, an employer might also use an offer of severance as an incentive for employees to voluntarily quit or retire.

An employer's offer of severance is typically accompanied by a request that the employee release any claims he or she might have against the employer. A release in these circumstances would be unenforceable if the employee derives no additional benefit beyond what he or she is already entitled to, so the severance serves as consideration in exchange for the release.

A release is typically broadly worded to cover any possible claims that might arise out of the employment relationship and its termination, including claims under federal and state discrimination laws, possible violations of mandatory leave laws, defamation, and invasion of privacy. To be effective under the Age Discrimination in Employment Act (ADEA), the release must comply with detailed statutory requirements, including giving the employee 21 days to consider the release and an additional seven days after signing to change his or her mind. When the release is part of an exit incentive package offered to a number of employees, the 21 days extends to 45, and the employer must provide additional information about the ages and job categories of employees who are and who are not being offered the exit incentive. (See Chapter 16 for more on age discrimination and the ADEA.)

Certain provisions *should not* be included in releases, would be unenforceable if included, and might even be considered retaliatory. For example, the employee should not be asked to waive his or her right to file a charge with the EEOC, state or local human rights agencies, or the National Labor Relations Board. Nor should a release prohibit the employee of a public company from filing a whistle-blower complaint with the Securities and Exchange Commission (SEC). Employees of U.S. government contractors and federal grant recipients have a right to report waste, fraud, and abuse. A nondisparagement provision (by which the employee agrees not to make negative statements about his or her employer) or a confidentiality provision may be so broadly worded as to interfere with these statutory rights.

A release *should* specify how the severance payment is to be treated and reported for tax purposes. Since the payment is normally in consideration of the employee's previous work, it will be treated as wages subject to withholding and payroll taxes and reported as W-2 income. But in limited circumstances, when a claim of discrimination or other law violation has actually been made, the parties may agree that a portion of the severance is in settlement of an emotional distress claim—a taxable payment reported on Form 1099, but not subject to withholding or payroll taxes.

⚠ ALERT!

Depending on how they are structured, severance payments could be deemed *nonqualified deferred compensation* under Internal Revenue Code §409A, triggering unintended tax consequences for the departing employee and a claim of misrepresentation or breach of contract against the employer. (Nonqualified deferred compensation plans are discussed in Chapter 9.)

CONSTRUCTIVE DISCHARGE

When the law looks behind the form of a transaction to discover its true substance, it uses the strange term *constructive*. In a *constructive discharge*, it may appear that the employee quit, but because of the underlying circumstances, the law concludes that he or she was fired.

Take, for example, employees who are told that unless they quit, they will be fired. It is easy to see why the law would view that as an involuntary termination. An employer's request for a resignation will be treated the same way.

But the concept of constructive discharge goes beyond the quit-or-be-fired scenario. When an employer permits working conditions to become so intolerable that a reasonable person would quit, an employee who actually does quit rather than suffer the conditions will be deemed to have been fired. To illustrate, suppose serious safety hazards exist at the workplace that the employer knows about but refuses to fix. Or suppose a minority employee is subjected to severe and pervasive racial harassment by supervisors and fellow employees.

Under certain circumstances, a change in title or duties could amount to a constructive discharge. For example, the president of a company, whose contract specifies that he or she is the chief executive officer, might be able to claim constructive discharge on being required to report to the newly appointed chair or being stripped of some of his or her executive authority, even though the president's salary remains the same.

The point of a constructive discharge is that an employer will be held liable to the same extent as if it had directly fired the employee. If there was a contract of employment and insufficient grounds for termination, the employer will be answerable for breach of contract. And in the racial harassment example given above, the employer can be charged with illegal racial discrimination.

⚠ **ALERT!**
Employer liability for harassment is not dependent on the employee actually quitting. Merely subjecting an employee to severe and pervasive harassment can constitute illegal discrimination. (See Chapter 15 for more on harassment.)

RETALIATION

Most federal and state laws that grant statutory rights to employees go on to prohibit employers from *retaliating* against their employees for exercising those rights. Examples of rights include the following:

- federal and state nondiscrimination laws
- federal and state wage and hour laws
- employee benefit plans governed by the Employee Retirement Income Security Act
- federal labor laws
- federal and state workplace safety laws
- federal and state protected leave laws
- state workers' compensation laws
- whistle-blower laws, such as the False Claims Act that encourages employees to report government fraud
- federal corporate ethics laws, such as the Sarbanes-Oxley Act

These statutes effectively modify the at-will employment relationship by prohibiting an employer from terminating or otherwise retaliating against an employee, despite the employee's at-will status.

Retaliation claims sometimes become the tail wagging the dog. In the discrimination arena, for example, an employee may have a weak or improbable claim of race or sex discrimination, but when the employee complains, the employer responds by firing the employee. In effect, the employer has converted a weak discrimination claim that the employee would probably have lost into a strong claim of retaliation that the employee will likely win.

While the acts constituting retaliation must be sufficiently adverse to dissuade a reasonable employee from pursuing a claim of discrimination, they do not need to be employment-related. That is, the retaliation need not involve firing, demotion, undesirable transfer, or similar job-related punishment, so long as it would likely discourage the ordinary employee from exercising his or her legal rights. As the Supreme Court said in *Burlington Northern & Santa Fe Railway Co. v. White*, "An employer can effectively retaliate against an employee by taking actions not directly related to his employment or by causing him harm outside the workplace."

CASE STUDY:
RETALIATION

In a federal appeals court case, a father and son were both employed by the same organization. When the father complained of discrimination, the employer retaliated by firing the son. The court said that form of retaliation is also illegal under federal nondiscrimination laws, pointing out that to retaliate against a man by hurting a member of his family is an ancient method of revenge and is not unknown in the field of labor relations.

WHISTLE-BLOWER REGULATIONS

Persons who go public with violations of law by their employers, particularly violations involving fraud against the government, are known as *whistle-blowers*. In the absence of specific statutory protections, whistle-blowers may find themselves out of a job with little right to complain. A number of jurisdictions have decided, however, that whistle-blowers should receive some limited protection.

A Civil War-era federal statute known as the *False Claims Act* permits anyone who learns about fraud against the U.S. government to file a lawsuit in the name of the government. For example, suppose a computer company that has a contract to provide programming services to the U.S. Department of Treasury overbills for time spent in writing a software program. If a disgruntled company employee learns of the overbilling and files suit against the company under the False Claims Act, a provision of the act prohibits the company from firing or otherwise retaliating against the employee. The act provides the employee with an incentive to sue by allowing him or her to collect a percentage of any recovery from the suit.

Some states have enacted their own whistle-blower laws protecting employees who disclose fraud at the state level.

The *Dodd-Frank Act* authorizes the SEC to pay rewards to individuals who provide original information that leads to successful SEC enforcement action. Employees of public companies who voluntarily provide information of securities violations and who are not otherwise required by law to report such violations may recover substantial whistle-blower rewards. (Press reports say that between 2011 and 2016, the SEC awarded approximately $149 million to some 41 whistle-blowers under this program.) When an employee makes such a report under the reasonable belief that the information relates to a possible securities law violation, the employer is prohibited from retaliating against the employee or otherwise interfering with communications between the employee and the SEC.

Employees of U.S. government contractors, subcontractors, and grantees are also protected by federal law when reporting waste, fraud, and abuse both to government officials and internally to company officials. (See Chapter 22.)

ABUSIVE DISCHARGE

An important variation on the retaliation theme arises when no statute expressly prohibits retaliation, but when a significant, well-established public policy is involved. When a firing tends to undercut such a policy, courts may characterize the discharge as *abusive* or *wrongful* and allow the employee to recover damages against the employer despite an at-will employment relationship.

To illustrate, suppose an employee is instructed to make a delivery using the company truck. The employee points out that the truck's safety inspection sticker has expired and that it is illegal to drive a truck with an expired sticker. In addition, brake repairs are needed for the truck to pass reinspection. The employer's supervisor insists that the delivery be made anyway, and when the employee refuses, he is fired. Many states would view that as an abusive discharge, because it undercuts an important state highway safety policy.

There is no clear answer as to what public policies will override the at-will employment doctrine. The doctrine of abusive discharge has been developed (and is still developing) on a case-by-case basis as suits come before the courts. In addition, judges' views of what is and what is not important and well-established public policy differ from state to state and over time.

One consistent theme has emerged from the cases: firing an employee for refusing to commit an illegal act or for fulfilling a duty required by law is abusive and will provide grounds for a wrongful discharge suit in most states. Another theme involves an employee's exercise of rights granted or protected by law. For example, employees covered by workers' compensation statutes have a right to file claims for work-related injuries and cannot be fired (or otherwise disciplined) for doing so. Refusal to take a lie detector test is also not grounds for firing, since in most circumstances administering the test would be illegal.

Things become less clear when the employee is engaged in conduct that is permitted by law or seen as socially desirable but is not necessarily protected by law.

CASE STUDY:
RIGHT TO CONSULT WITH COUNSEL

Suppose a dispute arises between employer and employee, and when the employee threatens to contact a lawyer for advice regarding the dispute, he or she is fired. Is the right to consult with counsel so fundamental that termination for exercising that right violates public policy?

A 1994 federal case applying Iowa law concluded that termination under those circumstances did violate Iowa public policy. An Ohio state court reached the same conclusion. But a decision by Maryland's highest court in 2003 ruled otherwise, saying that while access to counsel may be favored, there is no violation of any clear mandate of

Maryland public policy in firing an employee for involving counsel in an employment dispute.

Knowing how to proceed in the face of uncertain and changing rules can be difficult for an employer. At the least, a prudent employer should hesitate to fire an at-will employee for engaging in an activity that is protected or encouraged by the law or that is usually considered of value to society, or for refusing to engage in illegal conduct or conduct that is usually considered immoral or otherwise improper.

⚠ ALERT!

In a number of states it is illegal to fire or discipline an employee for his or her lawful, off-duty conduct. In Washington, D.C., for example, an employer cannot discriminate against an employee who smokes (although the employer has no obligation to allow smoke breaks during working hours).

DEFAMATION LIABILITY

It may be surprising to learn that one of the more significant liabilities an employer faces is *defamation*. In fact many abusive discharge cases include claims of defamation.

To defame someone is to make a false statement of fact that injures the person's reputation. A written defamatory statement is *libelous*; a spoken defamatory statement is known as *slander*. In order for a person to have a good claim of defamation, the false statement must be *published*—communicated either in writing or orally to a third person. Generally, to be defamatory the statement must be one of fact, such as, "John stole office supplies for his personal use." Mere statements of opinion, such as, "John does not use office supplies efficiently," are not usually defamatory.

Conduct can also amount to defamation. Suppose that after being informed of a termination, an employee is escorted off the employer's premises by senior management. Even though the employee may feel embarrassed, that conduct alone probably does not constitute a defamatory publication. But suppose that instead of being escorted by management, the company uses its security guards who, in the process, search the employee and question him or her at length about suspected stealing, all in front of co-workers. That conduct could give rise to a good defamation claim.

Privileged Statements

A statement that might otherwise be defamatory can sometimes be *privileged* or protected by law from a claim of defamation. Privileges come in two types: absolute and conditional (sometimes called qualified). When a member of Congress makes a speech on the House floor, for example, the statements are absolutely privileged, meaning that he or she can never be sued for defamation, no matter how offensive the words might be. In contrast, employers that give references for former employees, that issue warnings and termination letters, and that offer candid employee evaluations are entitled only to a conditional privilege.

The employer's privilege is conditional because it can be lost if the employer handles the communication in any of the following ways:

• issues it without any legitimate business purpose
• issues it with knowledge of its falsity or with a reckless disregard for its truth or falsity
• issues it with malice, spite, or ill will toward the employee
• disseminates it beyond those who have a business need to know

To illustrate, suppose an employee is terminated, finds a new position, and after starting work at the new job, the old employer contacts the new employer and, without being asked, relates derogatory information about the new employee. This *blacklisting* of a former employee will be compelling evidence of malice and will also void any privilege defense.

Unfortunately for the employer, issues of legitimate business purpose, malice, spite, ill will, and excessive dissemination usually turn on the specific facts of each case. As a result, even weak defamation claims may result in protracted and expensive court proceedings.

Job References

Job references present a special problem. On the one hand, if the employer provides highly detailed information about a former employee, including factual statements and opinions that go beyond what the prospective new employer specifically asked, the employer runs a substantial risk of a defamation or an invasion-of-privacy claim. On the other hand, if the employer undertakes to provide a reference but then provides a skimpy or inaccurate one, or leaves out favorable information, a defamation claim may loom as well.

⚠ ALERT!

Giving a bad reference for a former employee in retaliation for the employee's filing a discrimination claim is itself illegal discrimination under Title VII. (See Chapter 14.)

Rather than run these risks, some employers have adopted a *neutral reference* or *no-comment* policy under which they do no more than confirm dates of employment and perhaps title and salary. While such a policy may be the safest for individual employers, it has a social cost in restricting the amount of pertinent information available to prospective employers. Less qualified workers may get jobs that more qualified applicants would have received had full information been available. Worse, persons who would otherwise be rejected because of the danger they pose to the public may not be weeded out in the application process.

A middle ground is to adopt a no-comment policy but to make an exception when the employee or former employee approves in writing the content of a proposed reference letter, authorizes its issuance, and releases the employer from liability for issuing the letter.

Whatever policy you adopt, be sure it is communicated to all employees and that it is faithfully followed. The policy should also identify those persons within the company who are authorized to give out reference information, and it should prohibit everyone else within the company from doing so.

Some states offer a measure of protection for employers that provide information to prospective employers about an employee's or former employee's job performance or reason for termination. In these states, by statute, mere negligence in providing an erroneous reference is not sufficient to support a defamation suit. Instead, the unhappy employee must show that the employer acted maliciously or intentionally in disclosing false reference information.

Compelled Self-Publication

A bizarre twist on the law of defamation deserves mention. Suppose an employer terminates an unsatisfactory employee and tells the employee the reason for the termination. Further, suppose the employer tells no one else about the reason and, consistent with the employer's no-comment policy, confirms only the dates of employment, job title, and salary to a prospective new employer. No defamation claim could possibly be brought, right?

Unfortunately, no. Some courts have adopted a doctrine known as *compelled self-publication*, which holds that since the employee must honestly tell a prospective employer about the reason given for the termination, the employee has no choice but to defame himself or herself and may therefore sue the former employer. Fortunately, the doctrine of compelled self-publication is not widely recognized.

⚠ ALERT!

Giving a favorable but inaccurate reference may expose an employer to third-party liability. For example, if a former employer is asked for a reference by a subsequent employer but fails to mention the employee's dangerous propensities, and the employee later causes injury or damage, the former employer may be liable for the injury or damage.

CASE STUDY:
LIABILITY FOR MISLEADING REFERENCE

An anesthesiologist in Louisiana had a drug problem. After he failed to answer a page while on duty, he was fired. When the anesthesiologist later sought hospital privileges in Washington state, his former colleague wrote a glowing letter of recommendation, saying he was an excellent anesthesiologist and was capable in all fields of anesthesiology. The letter concluded, "I highly recommend him." No mention was made of the drug problem. After being hired by the hospital and while working under the influence of drugs, the anesthesiologist permanently injured his patient. The hospital's insurance company paid millions to the patient and then successfully sued the former colleague who had given the misleading recommendation.

INTENTIONAL INFLICTION OF EMOTIONAL DISTRESS

Another ground on which an employer can be held liable is intentional infliction of emotional distress. In general, if an employer (or anyone else, for that matter) acts in an extreme or outrageous way and either intentionally or recklessly causes someone else to suffer severe emotional distress, the victim of such conduct can recover damages in court. Claims for intentional infliction of emotional distress are sometimes coupled with charges of harassment based on sex, race, or other protected categories.

CASE STUDY:
EMPLOYER POTENTIALLY LIABLE
FOR INTENTIONAL INFLICTION

In a strange case involving Georgetown University in Washington, D.C., an employee of the university claimed that her supervisor placed two electrically operated noisemakers outside the supervisor's door aimed at the employee's workplace. According to the employee, the devices emitted an unbearably loud, static-sounding, piercing, humming, and droning noise every hour of the workday for some nine months, causing the employee extreme emotional distress. Despite her complaints, the university did nothing. The U.S. Court of Appeals for the D.C. Circuit ruled that the employee stated a good claim for intentional infliction of emotional distress and that the case should not have been dismissed before trial.

EMPLOYEE DUE PROCESS

We so often hear terms like *due process, freedom of speech, freedom of the press*, and *freedom of information* that we may be tempted to think these rights apply in all our relationships. Not so. The constitutional right of due process limits the ways in which the *government* can deal with us. Our free speech right only prevents government censorship. Federal and state freedom-of-information acts and sunshine laws guarantee us access only to certain government information and proceedings.

Except for government employees, the employment relationship generally does not include employee due process rights. An at-will employee can be arbitrarily disciplined or fired without any right to a hearing, without any opportunity to explain or justify the supposedly offending conduct, and without any opportunity to confront the person who supposedly reported any offending conduct. (Of course, arbitrariness is seldom the best way to manage employees.)

There are a few limited exceptions to an employer's ability to act out of sheer arbitrariness. An employer cannot, for example, discriminate on the basis of race, ethnicity, gender, or other irrelevant characteristics; an employer cannot discharge an employee in violation of a protected leave law or public policy; and an employer cannot act contrary to its contractual obligations.

When an employee does have an employment contract, or when an employee is a member of a union that has a collective bargaining agreement, an employer's right to discipline or discharge the employee is typically limited by the contract to *for cause* terminations. The contract may also provide a grievance procedure, leading to binding arbitration, should an employee dispute the employer's personnel action. Even absent an employment contract, statements in an employee handbook dealing with disciplinary procedures may rise to the level of a contractual obligation.

Fifth Amendment

The *Fifth Amendment* to the U.S. Constitution grants each person the right against being "compelled in any criminal case to be a witness against himself." In other words, no one may be compelled, under threat of being held in contempt of court, to answer questions under oath when the answers might help convict the person of a crime. Although the amendment is limited to compelled testimony in criminal cases, the Supreme Court has held that the protection applies in a range of situations in which testimony is coerced, including civil cases, grand jury proceedings, depositions, and appearances before Congress.

The privilege is limited to testimony and does not extend to compelled production of physical evidence such as handwriting exemplars and blood specimens. Nor does the privilege protect documents from compelled disclosure, unless by the very act of producing the document the person is admitting the existence or possession of the document and thereby incriminating himself or herself. (The Fourth Amendment's right against unreasonable searches and seizures is discussed in Chapter 18.)

Corporations and other organizations have no Fifth Amendment privilege. So if a corporation is served with a subpoena for records, it has no basis, at least under the Fifth Amendment, to resist the subpoena and refuse to produce the records. While corporate officials can claim the privilege to protect themselves from incrimination, they cannot claim privilege to protect their corporate employer.

If employees are invited or required to testify, an employer cannot in any way encourage employees to claim the privilege, threaten them should they fail to do so, or promise rewards for doing so. This type of conduct could amount to an *obstruction of justice*—a serious crime that will likely get the prosecutor's attention. Employers also need to avoid indirect encouragement. This can arise, for example, when the employer urges employees to be represented by the same attorney who represents the company, and the attorney, in turn, advises the employees to claim the privilege.

Employers are generally free, however, to require their employees to testify, and to discipline them if they refuse and claim the privilege. Remember that the Fifth Amendment is designed to protect against government, not private, coercion.

🔔 **ALERT!**

In jurisdictions in which the abusive discharge exception to the at-will employment doctrine is unsettled, employers should be cautious in firing an employee for claiming the privilege. It is conceivable that a court would find a public policy protecting an employees' Fifth Amendment rights.

DOWNSIZING AND MASS LAYOFFS

Terminating an employee is among the most difficult tasks facing any employer. When a decision is made to lay off a significant portion of the workforce, the difficulty and the legal risks are multiplied. Particularly in tough economic times, laid-off employees will have a more difficult time finding new employment, so their incentive to sue is even greater.

☞ **QUICK TIP**

When an exit incentive program is made available to a class or group of employees, coupled with a severance agreement and release, the Older Workers Benefit Protection Act requirements may be triggered. (See Chapter 16 for more details.)

While the legal risks associated with a mass layoff can never be entirely eliminated, employers can take steps to reduce their exposure by doing the following:
- considering other cost-saving alternatives to a layoff, such as offering wage rate or hour reductions to employees
- developing and documenting the business reasons for the layoff

- focusing on positions, not people, to be eliminated
- hiring an outside expert to help decide what positions to eliminate
- making sure that layoff decisions are not influenced in any way by discriminatory factors, such as race, gender, or age
- using an outside expert to review the unintended impact along race, gender, and age lines once tentative layoff decisions have been made
- offering severance packages, early retirement packages, or other exit incentives in exchange for a release of all claims
- following customary exit interviews and procedures for each individual being laid off

Worker Adjustment and Retraining Notification

The federal *Worker Adjustment and Retraining Notification Act* (WARN Act) requires an employer with 100 or more employees to provide notification 60 days in advance of a planned plant closing or mass layoff. In determining whether an employer meets the 100-employee floor, only full-time employees are counted, unless part-time employees in the aggregate work at least 4,000 hours per week, in which case part-time employees are counted as well.

A *mass layoff* for WARN Act purposes is a layoff of at least 50 employees at a single site that amounts to at least 33 percent of the employees at that site. So, if an employer has 1,000 employees at a given site and lays off 100, that would not be a mass layoff.

The 60-day notice must be given to the affected employees, to the state dislocated worker unit, and to the chief elected official of the local government where the plant closing or layoff is to occur.

The WARN Act recognizes that in some circumstances employers may not be able to give the requisite notice. The act's unforeseeable business circumstances exception is applicable when a similarly situated employer exercising commercially reasonable business judgment would not have foreseen the closing. So long as an employer is exercising reasonable business judgment, the employer will not be held liable under the WARN Act for failing to predict economic conditions that may affect demand for the organization's products or services.

CHAPTER 5
Wage and Hour Requirements

- Minimum Wages

- Overtime

- Alternatives to Overtime

- Exemptions from Overtime

- Settling FLSA Wage Disputes

- Other Wage Regulations

- Child Labor

- Priority of Wages and Benefits in Bankruptcy

- Anti-Trust Considerations

Wage and hour requirements are a mix of federal and state law. The principal federal law is the *Fair Labor Standards Act* (FLSA) enacted in 1938.

In general, and subject to the exemptions discussed later in this chapter, the FLSA applies to all employees of a business or organization (referred to in the law as an *enterprise*) that meets any of the following descriptions:

• has an annual dollar volume of sales or business of at least $500,000
• is a hospital, a business providing medical or nursing care for residents, or a school or preschool
• is a government agency

In addition to enterprise coverage, the FLSA applies to employees who are engaged in interstate commerce or in the production of goods for interstate commerce, even if they are not employed by an enterprise.

Employees cannot waive their right to the minimum wage and overtime guaranties of the FLSA because, according to the Supreme Court, allowing them to do so "would nullify the purposes of the FLSA and thwart the legislative policies it was designed to effectuate." So a private agreement that an employee will be paid and will accept less than the minimum wage, or will not be paid an overtime premium to which he or she would otherwise be entitled, is unenforceable.

MINIMUM WAGES

The FLSA requires every employer to pay each covered employee a minimum wage at this writing of $7.25 per hour. The minimum rate for newly hired employees who are under 20 years of age is currently $4.25 per hour, but that rate is applicable only during the first 90 days of employment. Although an employee need not receive the minimum wage for every hour worked, the employer must average the minimum wage every workweek.

There is a long list of occupations that are exempt from minimum wage requirements. The exceptions are narrowly drawn, however, and apply only in limited circumstances. Employers should assume that they owe the minimum wage to each of their employees unless they have obtained competent advice to the contrary.

Volunteer Employees

Among the potential pitfalls for an employer is the *volunteer employee* or *unpaid intern*.

The FLSA allows individuals to volunteer their services, without pay, to state or local government agencies and to nonprofit food banks for humanitarian purposes. U.S. Department of Labor (DOL) guidance goes a bit further, expanding humanitarian purposes to include individuals who volunteer their time, freely and without anticipation of compensation, for religious, charitable, civic, or humanitarian purposes to nonprofit organizations.

Despite the DOL's somewhat expanded view of humanitarian purposes, however, an unpaid intern may volunteer at a for-profit, private-sector employer only if each of the following six criteria is satisfied (according to the DOL):

- The internship, even though it includes actual operation of the facilities of the employer, is similar to training that would be given in an educational environment.
- The internship experience is for the benefit of the intern.
- The intern does not displace regular employees, but works under close supervision of existing staff.
- The employer that provides the training derives no immediate advantage from the activities of the intern, and on occasion its operations may actually be impeded.
- The intern is not necessarily entitled to a job at the conclusion of the internship.
- The employer and the intern understand that the intern is not entitled to wages for the time spent in the internship.

EXAMPLE: A for-profit architectural firm receives an inquiry for summer employment from a third-year architecture major at a local university. She says that job opportunities are extremely tight and, to gain experience and build her resume, she is willing to work for free helping existing employees with drafting and other duties. Since the proposed arrangement would be of direct benefit to the employer and since the student would be performing work for free that the employer normally has to pay for, the FLSA's minimum wage requirement applies.

In *Glatt v. Fox Searchlight Pictures*, a 2016 decision by the U.S. Court of Appeals for the 2nd Circuit (headquartered in New York City), the court rejected the DOL's six-factor test in favor of a *primary beneficiary test*—whether the intern or the employer is the primary beneficiary of the relationship. Ironically, the court then proceeded to list not six, but seven, factors to be considered in applying the primary beneficiary test, many of which sound similar to the DOL's list.

Eventually the Supreme Court will need to resolve the question of when an unpaid intern may volunteer services to a for-profit employer. In the meantime, for-profit employers should seek competent counsel when considering an unpaid internship program.

Meals and Lodging

The FLSA allows employers to credit against their minimum wage obligation the fair value of meals and lodging provided by the employer. The credit for lodging will be allowed only if the following conditions apply:

• The lodging is regularly provided.
• The employee voluntarily accepts the lodging.
• The lodging is furnished in compliance with all applicable laws.
• The lodging is provided primarily for the benefit of the employee rather than the employer.
• The employer maintains accurate records of the cost of the lodging.

⚠ ALERT!

The value of meals and lodging provided in partial satisfaction of the employer's minimum wage obligation is taxable income to employee. Meals and lodging provided for the employer's convenience are not taxable to the employee, but they also do not count against the employer's minimum wage obligation.

Tips

Special rules apply to employees who receive tips. Tips may be counted against the minimum wage, but only up to $5.12 per hour at this writing. The employer must pay at least $2.13 in cash wages and, if actual tips combined with cash wages do not equal the minimum wage, the employer must make up the difference. (Some state minimum wage laws do not count tips or count tips only up to a lesser dollar amount.)

Tips are subject to withholding and other tax requirements just like regular compensation. (See Chapter 7 for more specific information regarding tax requirements.)

Breaks

Except for nursing mothers (discussed below in this chapter), the FLSA does not require employers to grant rest breaks. Nevertheless, many employers provide brief morning and afternoon breaks to their nonexempt employees. When those rest breaks are no longer than 20 minutes, they must be accounted and paid for as hours worked. However, according to the DOL's *Field Operations Handbook*, when an employee extends his or her break past 20 minutes without authorization, the employer need not compensate the employee for the unauthorized extension if the employer has expressly and unambiguously communicated to its employees that the authorized break may last only a specified length of time and that any extension of the break is against the employer's rules and will be punished.

State and Local Laws

States and local jurisdictions are free to adopt higher minimum wages, and some have done so. Some state and local governments have also adopted *living wage* or *prevailing wage* laws that require government contractors doing business with those jurisdictions to pay their employees a minimum wage substantially in excess of the federal floor. Aside from the economic debate over the effect of minimum wages, this lack of federal uniformity imposes substantial compliance burdens on multistate employers and encourages them to move their workforces to more business-friendly states.

🔔 ALERT!

Pay differentials based on gender or on any other prohibited consideration such as race or national origin are illegal under nondiscrimination laws. (See Chapter 15.)

Penalties

Penalties for violating the FLSA and state laws are substantial, including liquidated damages, attorneys' fees payable to the employee involved, criminal fines, and even prison sentences.

CASE STUDY:
MANAGERS' PERSONAL LIABILITY FOR AN FLSA VIOLATION

After Castaways Casino filed for bankruptcy protection, a former employee sued Castaways' individual managers under the FLSA for unpaid wages. The employee claimed that the managers qualified as his "employer," which the FLSA defines as "any person acting directly or indirectly in the interest of the employer in relation to an employee." The federal appeals court for the 9th Circuit ruled that when an individual exercises control over the nature and structure of the employment relationship or economic control over the relationship, that individual is an employer within the meaning of the FLSA.

OVERTIME

Overtime requirements under the FLSA give rise to issues of how much to pay and when to pay. The basic rules for nonexempt, private-sector employees are the following:

- The maximum number of hours an employee may work in any workweek without receiving overtime compensation is 40.
- Overtime compensation is one and one-half times the employee's regular hourly rate of pay.
- Overtime compensation must be paid on the next regular payday (or as soon thereafter as practical if the amount due cannot be computed by that payday).

⚠ ALERT!

The FLSA imposes a time-and-a-half overtime premium on work in excess of 40 hours in any workweek. Some state laws require overtime for work in excess of eight hours per day and impose a double-time premium for overtime work. Collective bargaining agreements in union shops may also impose additional overtime requirements.

Calculating Work Time

The *workweek* is a period of 168 hours (24 hours per day times seven days per week). It is up to the employer to establish when the workweek begins and ends, and it need not coincide with pay periods. When the two do not coincide (for example, when the employer's pay period is semimonthly, or 24 paydays per year), each paycheck includes regular pay for 13, 14, 15, or 16 days and includes overtime pay for one, two, or three workweeks, depending on how many workweeks end during the particular pay period involved. An employer may establish different workweeks for different employees, but the employer cannot repeatedly change the workweek to manipulate overtime obligations.

Overtime must be paid at one and one-half times the employee's *regular hourly rate*. In general, the regular hourly rate is the hourly rate actually paid the employee for the normal, nonovertime workweek for which the employee is employed. Employers are not required to compensate their employees on an hourly rate basis, however. They may, for example, compensate on piece-rate, salary, commission, or other basis, but in such cases a regular hourly rate must be computed to determine what the overtime rate should be. In computing the regular hourly rate, all remuneration for employment must be included, such as commissions and production bonuses. However, the FLSA specifies that the following items are *not* included in computing the regular hourly rate:

- gifts, so long as they are not measured by or dependent on hours worked, production, or efficiency
- payments made while the employee is on leave
- expense reimbursements
- bonuses paid at the sole discretion of the employer and not pursuant to any previous contract or promise
- profit-sharing payments
- employer contributions to employee benefit plans
- premium payments for work on weekends and holidays, so long as the premium rate is at least one and one-half times the rate for regular work

As the above list suggests, bonuses that are tied to productivity *are* included in computing the employee's regular pay rate for overtime purposes. So if an employer pays a quarterly or year-end productivity bonus to nonexempt employees, the employer must recalculate the employees' regular pay rate for the period covered by the bonus and pay any additional overtime that may result.

EXAMPLE: A company's normal workday is 9:00 a.m. to 5:30 p.m. with an hour for lunch. That equates to 37.5 hours of work per workweek. If an hourly employee works 39.5 hours in a particular week, at what rate should he or she be paid for the extra two hours? The company is free to pay overtime at one and one-half times the normal rate after 37.5 hours, but it is not required to do so. The company is in full compliance with the FLSA if it pays only straight time for the two hours, since the FLSA's overtime obligations kick in only after 40 hours.

Employers should not overlook the effect of holidays, vacations, and other time off on their overtime obligations. For time to be counted toward overtime, the employee must actually be at work. Even though an employee may be on paid leave, if he or she is not actually working, the time is not included in computing overtime. For that reason, overtime is usually not a problem during periods such as the Christmas week, when many employees take time off.

Wage and hour violations can occur unintentionally. Employers should be alert to the following pitfalls:

- "Would you mind running an errand for me on your lunch hour?" "I'd appreciate your taking the late mail to the post office when you leave today." "Could you drop off this package on your way in tomorrow?" If these favors take more than a few minutes of an employee's time, they need to be counted for pay and overtime purposes.

- "Company policy prohibits overtime unless explicitly approved by your supervisor." If the time actually required to complete the assigned job is more than the standard workday, an official policy limiting overtime will not excuse the employer from paying time-and-a-half.

- "I need you to carry a beeper." "In your job, you're on call 24 hours a day." "You can't drink on your off hours, since I may need you in on short notice." "I want you at home where I can reach you." Restrictions on off hours can trigger pay and overtime obligations if they substantially limit the employee's freedom. The you're-on-call-24-hours-a-day dictate, without more, is probably not a substantial restriction, nor is the alcohol prohibition. But the beeper requirement could be, if the beeper's range is very limited. The stay-at-home requirement definitely would need to be counted as work time.

- "You can eat lunch at your desk if you like, but that's unpaid time." Unless the employee is entirely free from work responsibilities during a so-called lunch break, the time is compensable.

- "The company encourages you to get involved in civic and charitable activities in the community." Truly volunteer activities, performed after working hours, are not compensable. However, activities performed during normal working hours with the approval of the employer are compensable and need to be counted for overtime purposes. Even after-hours activities can be compensable if they are done at the employer's specific request or direction, or if the employer coerces or pressures the employee into volunteering.

Portal-to-Portal Act

Another risk involves activities immediately before and immediately after regular work periods. The *Portal-to-Portal Act* (an amendment to the FLSA) makes clear that an employee's *commuting time*—time walking, riding, or traveling to and from the actual place of performance of the principal activity or activities that the employee is employed to perform—is not compensable for minimum wage or overtime purposes. Similarly, activities that are *preliminary* or *postliminary* to principal activities are not compensable.

On the other hand, an activity *is* compensable if it is primarily for the employer's benefit, if there is an express written or oral contract that the employer will pay for the activity, or if it is compensable by custom or practice. Examples of activities that may or may not be compensable, depending on the circumstances, include changing into or out of a work uniform, punching a time clock, waiting in line to punch a time clock, settling up a cash register drawer at the end of a shift, cleaning or repairing tools, showering after working with hazardous or toxic materials, and inspecting a motor vehicle before or after driving a delivery route.

ALTERNATIVES TO OVERTIME

Overtime obligations significantly increase an employer's payroll costs. In addition to time-and-a-half, other costs such as payroll taxes, workers' compensation premiums, and retirement plan contributions may increase as well. So it is usually in an employer's interest to avoid overtime when possible. The following alternatives to overtime may be available, depending on the employer's specific circumstances.

Compensatory Time

If an employee who normally works an 8-hour day happens to work 9 or 10 hours on a particular day, he or she may be offered the opportunity (or may even be required) to work fewer hours on another day, so long as it is in the same 168-hour workweek. However, with few exceptions overtime may not be taken as *compensatory time* (or *comp time*) in another workweek. If overtime is not offset by time off within the same 168-hour workweek, wages at the overtime rate must be paid. This rule applies regardless of the pay periods established by the employer. For example, even though the pay period may be every two weeks, 45 hours of work in week 1 cannot be offset by 35 hours in week 2.

The rule also applies even if the employee is perfectly willing to waive overtime pay and take comp time the following week. Suppose an employee wants to take an extended vacation later in the year and offers to build up comp time so that regular paychecks will continue during vacation. The request cannot be honored, since neither the employer nor the employee can agree to an arrangement different from the overtime requirements of federal and state law.

On a number of occasions, Congress has considered amending the FLSA to permit comp time in the private sector. (Comp time has long been allowed for federal government employees.) Organized labor has generally opposed any such change, however, and the proposed amendments have all died without passage.

Time-Off Plan

There is one exception to the rule that comp time in workweek 2 does not satisfy the employer's obligation for overtime in workweek 1—the so-called *time-off plan*. Suppose an employer pays every other week. If a nonexempt salaried employee works overtime in workweek 1, the employer can give the employee time off in workweek 2 at the rate of 1.5 hours for each hour of overtime worked in workweek 1. By paying the employee the regular salary for both workweeks, the employer fully satisfies its overtime obligation.

EXAMPLE: Suppose an employee normally works 40 hours per workweek and is paid a biweekly salary of $800 ($400 per week or $10 per hour). If the employee works 50 hours in workweek 1, the employee can take (or be ordered to take) 15 hours off in workweek 2, since 1.5 times the 10 hours of overtime worked in workweek 1 equals 15 hours. In this example, the employee has worked a total of 75 hours over both workweeks, but will be paid his or her regular biweekly salary of $800. In effect, the employer satisfies its overtime obligation by paying comp time at a premium rate instead of paying a cash premium.

A time-off plan for salaried employees works only if the employer's pay period is longer than one workweek and if overtime occurs in the first workweek. In the above example, if the overtime occurred in workweek 2, the employer would have to pay the overtime premium in cash.

Belo Plan

Belo plans (from a Supreme Court case of that name) are available only for employees whose duties necessitate irregular hours because of the nature of the work. Examples might include on-call service workers and emergency repair crews. Under a Belo plan, the employer enters into a contract with the employee that guarantees the employee a fixed salary regardless of the number of hours worked. The contract specifies a regular hourly rate for the normal 40 hours and 1.5 times that regular hourly rate for guaranteed overtime (so long as total time covered by the plan is no more than 60 hours per workweek).

EXAMPLE: A power company employee's job is to restore electrical service following outages caused by storms, traffic accidents, construction mishaps, and the like. The amount of work needed is unpredictable, typically varying anywhere from 30 to 50 hours per workweek, so the employer enters into a contract guaranteeing the employee a fixed weekly salary of $550, representing 40 hours at $10 per hour and 10 hours at a $15 overtime rate. In other words, the contract guarantees the employee 10 hours of overtime each week. Then, regardless of the number of hours worked (up to the agreed total of 50 hours in this example), the employer has no additional overtime obligation. Of course, if the employee works fewer than 50 hours, he or she still gets paid $550.

In the above example, any time worked in excess of 50 hours would have to be compensated at $15 per hour. While the parties could have agreed to guarantee more than 10 hours of overtime, their agreement could not go beyond 20 hours of overtime under a Belo plan.

Half-Time Plan
Belo plans are available only when the inherent nature of the work necessitates irregular hours and when the number of hours per workweek vary both above and below a normal 40-hour workweek. In contrast, under a *half-time plan* (sometimes called a *fluctuating workweek plan*), the fluctuation can be subject to the employer's control, and hours worked can routinely exceed 40.

Under a fluctuating workweek plan, the employer and employee agree that the employee will be paid a fixed salary covering all time worked in the workweek. This should be a written agreement by which the employee clearly acknowledges that the fixed salary covers the straight-time component of all hours worked even if they exceed 40. For any given workweek, the employee's regular hourly rate is computed by dividing the fixed salary by the number of hours actually worked in that workweek. If the number of hours worked exceeds 40, the employer pays the employee half (not one and one-half) of his or her regular hourly rate for the hours exceeding 40. The reason the employer pays only half-time for the overtime is that the straight-time component is already covered by the fixed salary.

EXAMPLE: Employer and employee agree to a fixed salary of $400 per week. If, in a particular workweek, the employee works 50 hours, then the employee's regular hourly rate for that workweek is $8 ($400 / 50). Therefore, the employer's overtime obligation for that workweek is $40 (.5 x $8 x 10 hours), and total compensation due the employee for that workweek is $440. Now suppose the employee works 55 hours. His or her regular hourly rate would then be approximately $7.27 ($400 / 55), and the total compensation due would be $454.53 ($400 + (.5 x $7.27 x 15 hours)).

As the above example shows, as overtime increases, both the regular hourly rate and the overtime rate decrease. If the employee worked 80 hours in a particular workweek, his or her regular hourly rate would then drop to $5.00 per hour, which is below the minimum wage and which would therefore violate federal law. The fixed salary under a half-time plan must be high enough to guarantee at least the minimum wage.

EXEMPTIONS FROM OVERTIME

Overtime requirements are subject to a long list of exemptions under both federal and state law. Although the federal and state exemptions often overlap, they are not identical. An employee (or position) covered by one of these exemptions is referred to as *exempt* and is not entitled to time-and-a-half for overtime. In contrast, an employee (or position) not covered by any exemption is referred to as *nonexempt* and is entitled to overtime.

☞ **QUICK TIP**
Even though an employee is exempt from minimum wage or overtime requirements, the employer must still comply with the FLSA's equal pay provisions, which prohibit gender-based wage discrimination. (See Chapter 14 for more information.)

White-Collar Exemptions

Probably the most significant exemptions for most businesses are for salaried employees employed in a bona fide executive, administrative, or professional capacity. These exemptions, together with the exemption for outside salespersons, are sometimes called the *white-collar exemptions*. For an employee to qualify as exempt in one of these categories, his or her position must meet one of the duties tests specified in DOL regulations and described below. In most cases, a salary test applies as well, requiring that the employee be paid on a salary basis of at least $455 per week.

⚠ **ALERT!**
In May 2016, the DOL (then under President Obama) issued final regulations raising the $455-per-week salary basis requirement to $913 per week, effective December 1, 2016. A Texas federal court temporarily enjoined enforcement of the new regulation. In August 2017 the same court issued a final ruling that the new regulation is invalid. As a result, the existing $455-per-week salary requirement continues in effect. The current administration has solicited public comment on the matter but, as of this writing, has not proposed any changes to the existing regulation.

An *executive* is an employee whose primary duty is management of the enterprise in which he or she is employed (or a customarily recognized department or subdivision thereof). An executive customarily and regularly directs the work of two or more other employees and has the authority to hire or fire other employees (or whose suggestions and recommendations as to the hiring, firing, advancement, promotion, or any other change of status of other employees are given particular weight).

A *business owner* falls under the executive exemption if he or she owns at least a 20 percent bona fide equity interest in the enterprise in which he or she is employed and qualifies as an executive for overtime exemption purposes, even if he or she does not satisfy the salary test of $455 per week.

An *administrator* is an employee whose primary duty is the performance of office or nonmanual work directly related to the management or general business operations of the employer or the employer's customers. His or her primary duty must include the exercise of discretion and independent judgment with respect to matters of significance.

A *professional* is an employee whose primary duty is the performance of work requiring either of the following:

- knowledge of an advanced type in a field of science or learning customarily acquired by a prolonged course of specialized intellectual instruction, such as an accountant, nurse, medical technologist, dental hygienist, or chef (a *learned professional*)
- invention, imagination, originality, or talent in a recognized field of artistic or creative endeavor (a *creative professional*)

Employees who are licensed to practice law or medicine qualify as exempt professionals whether or not they meet the $455-per-week salary requirements. (For these purposes, medical practitioners include not only physicians but also osteopaths, podiatrists, dentists, optometrists, and veterinarians.) Teachers also qualify as exempt professionals whether or not they meet the $455-per-week salary requirement.

Computer programmers and others with highly specialized knowledge of computers qualify as professionals so long as they are paid either on a salary basis of at least $455 per week or on an hourly basis of at least $27.63 per hour.

Highly compensated employees—employees who earn at least $100,000 per year—are exempt so long as at least some of their duties (but not necessarily their primary duties) are executive, administrative, or professional. In addition to the $100,000-per-year requirement, they must also be compensated on a salary basis of at least $455 per week. (The $100,000 amount was raised to $134,004 under DOL regulations due to be effective December 1, 2016, but a Texas federal court has since ruled the new regulations invalid.)

Executives, administrators, and professionals will not lose their exemption by being temporarily assigned to nonexempt work, even for assignments lasting several weeks, so long as their primary duties fall within the definitions of executive, administrative, or professional.

An *outside salesperson* is an employee whose primary duty is making sales or obtaining orders and who is customarily and regularly engaged away from the employer's place of business (in other words, out in the field at the customers' places of business or homes). A person who works from his or her own home does not qualify as an outside salesperson. Since outside salespersons are typically paid by commission, the salary basis requirement does not apply.

DOL regulations say that the determination of an employee's *primary duty*

> must be based on all the facts in a particular case, with the major emphasis on the character of the employee's job as a whole. Factors to consider when determining the primary duty of an employee include, but are not limited to, the relative importance of the exempt duties as compared with other types of duties; the amount of time spent performing exempt work; the employee's relative freedom from direct supervision; and the relationship between the employee's salary and the wages paid to other employees for the kind of nonexempt work performed by the employee.

Salary Basis

As previously stated, for an executive, administrator, or professional to be exempt, he or she must generally be paid on a salary basis of at least $455 per week. DOL regulations provide that an employee will be considered as paid on a salary basis if he or she "regularly receives each pay period on a weekly, or less frequent basis, a predetermined amount constituting all, or part, of his or her compensation, which amount is not subject to reduction because of variations in the quality or quantity of the work performed."

Under this definition, an employee must generally be paid a full week's compensation for any workweek in which he or she performs any work, without regard to the number of days or hours worked. In other words, so long as the employee is ready, willing, and able to work a full workweek, the employer cannot reduce the compensation for the week just because the employer does not have any work available.

An employee will not qualify as salaried under DOL regulations if the employer docks wages for jury duty, temporary military leave, or attendance as a witness in court lasting less than a full workweek. However, the employer may reduce an employee's salary by the amount the employee is paid as a juror or witness or for military service.

If an employee fails to report to work for a day or more for personal reasons (other than sickness or accident), the employer may dock his or her salary for each full day (but not for a partial day) the employee is absent without affecting the employee's exempt status. (Deductions for absences of a day or more relating to sickness or accident are also permitted if the employer has a plan, policy, or practice of providing alternative compensation under those circumstances.) But if the employee is absent for less than a day, no deduction is allowed. In short, if an employer treats exempt employees as if they were hourly instead of salaried, they will cease being exempt.

DOL regulations provide a few additional exceptions to the general rule that an exempt employee must be paid a full week's compensation for any week in which he or she performs any work. When a new employee works less than a full week on initial hire or a departing employee works less than a full week on termination, he or she need to be paid only for the days actually worked. In addition, an employer may penalize employees by making deductions from pay in good faith for infractions of safety rules of major significance (such as smoking in an explosives plant) and may suspend employees without pay for one or more full days for infractions of written, generally applicable workplace conduct rules (such as rules prohibiting sexual harassment).

The DOL's definition of salary basis says that all or part of an employee's compensation must be *predetermined*. This means that an employee will be considered salaried even if some portion of his or her compensation is paid in the form of commissions or bonuses that vary depending on productivity or other factors. However, the predetermined amount must satisfy the minimum salary requirements—$455 per week as of this writing—for most white-collar exemptions.

⚠ **ALERT!**

Some employers mistakenly think that all salaried employees are automatically exempt. To the contrary, while being salaried is one of the requirements for most white-collar exemptions, the employee must also satisfy the *duties test*—that is, qualify as an executive, administrator, or professional as defined in DOL regulations.

Although the FLSA does not regulate an employer's vacation policies, those policies can sometimes trigger FLSA concerns. Say, for example, that an employer advances four hours of paid vacation time to an exempt employee who has used all his or her accrued leave. If the employee quits before earning back the four hours, and the employer then deducts the four hours from the employee's final pay, the employer has in effect docked the employee for a partial day of personal leave, contrary to the salary basis requirement.

Improper Deductions

Improper deductions from an otherwise exempt employee's salary will convert that employee, and other employees in the same job classification who work under the manager who made the improper deduction, to nonexempt status. Any overtime worked while the improper deductions were being made will then have to be paid at time-and-a-half.

Under the *window of correction* rule, isolated or inadvertent deductions will not cause loss of exemption. However, the employer must have a policy in place that prohibits improper pay deductions and includes a mechanism for employees to complain about a deduction. (See Figure 5.1 for an example of such a policy.) Once an improper deduction is brought to the employer's attention, the employer must reimburse the employee and must make a commitment to comply in the future.

FIGURE 5.1: WINDOW-OF-CORRECTION POLICY

The following policy will help ensure that inadvertent deductions from a salaried exempt employee do not convert the employee to nonexempt:

The company prohibits deductions from the compensation of exempt employees that could result in loss of exempt status. Any exempt employee who believes an improper deduction has been made from his or her compensation is encouraged to submit a complaint, preferably in writing, to the company's payroll officer. The company will promptly investigate the complaint. If the company determines that the deduction was improper, the company will promptly refund the deduction to the employee. The company commits itself to compliance with applicable wage and hour laws, including those governing exemptions from overtime pay.

Other Exemptions

Other exemptions may be significant for some employers. Unlike executives, administrators, and professionals, a few exemptions do not require payment of a fixed salary. In addition to outside salespersons, these include *drivers, drivers' helpers, loaders,* and *mechanics* for motor carriers whose duties affect safe operation of commercial motor vehicles in interstate commerce and who are subject to regulation by the U.S. Department of Transportation.

Employees of a *seasonal establishment* that is an amusement or recreational establishment, organized camp, or religious or nonprofit educational conference center are exempt in either of the following situations:

- the establishment does not operate for more than seven months in any calendar year
- during the preceding calendar year, the establishment's average receipts for any six months of such year were not more than 33 and one-third of its average receipts for the other six months of such year

Even if an employee is not entitled to premium overtime pay under the FLSA, he or she may be entitled to premium pay under state law. While state law is similar to the FLSA, states often have different exemptions from overtime. Different exemptions also apply to work performed under government contracts. (See Chapter 22 for more on government contractors.)

SETTLING FLSA WAGE DISPUTES

When an employer underpays an employee in violation of the FLSA, the employee may recover not only the balance of wages owed but also additional liquidated damages equal to the unpaid amount, and the attorneys' fees incurred in pursuing the claim. In cases of underpayment, the employer and employee generally cannot enter a binding settlement agreement in which the employer agrees to pay something less than the full amount due.

A 1945 Supreme Court decision invalidated a settlement agreement between an employer and an employee that did not provide for payment of liquidated damages to the employee. The court reasoned that the FLSA affords statutory rights that simply cannot be waived. A year later the court ruled that even when there was a bona fide dispute between the parties as to the employer's overtime obligation, a settlement agreement would not be enforceable. However, in that case the dispute involved a *legal issue* of whether the employer was engaged in interstate commerce and, therefore, whether the FLSA applied. The court left open the question whether a bona fide dispute over a *factual issue*, such as how many hours of overtime the employee actually worked, might support a settlement agreement in which an employee agrees to compromise his or her FLSA claim.

The question left open by the court in 1946 remains unanswered today. So, as a practical matter, an employer should not enter into a private settlement of a wage and hour dispute under the FLSA, because the employee's release of his or her claims in exchange for a cash payment is likely to be invalid and unenforceable. To resolve such disputes, the employer should request the DOL to participate in and supervise a settlement or, alternatively, file a law suit in court and ask the court to approve a proposed settlement.

OTHER WAGE REGULATIONS

The states regulate many other aspects of wage and hour requirements. Typical requirements are that employers do the following:
- establish regular pay periods
- pay hourly workers at least twice a month and pay salaried employees at least monthly
- pay in U.S. currency
- pay terminated employees within a specified time period after termination

If bonuses and commissions are part of an employee's regular compensation package, they must be paid just like other wages.

⚠ ALERT!

Most states prohibit employers from including Social Security numbers on employee paychecks.

Direct Deposit

As an alternative to issuing paper paychecks, *direct deposit* of employee compensation into their bank accounts is a great convenience to employer and employee alike. Recognizing that some employees may not have, or qualify for, a bank account, many states require individual employee consent before paying via direct deposit.

Payroll Cards

Payroll cards are another alternative to paper checks. A payroll card is a reloadable, prepaid card that can be used for purchases and at participating ATMs, much like a debit card. Under a payroll card program, funds are delivered electronically and are quickly available to employees. This avoids the delay of depositing a paper check and waiting for it to clear or cashing a paper check at a check-cashing store and paying the associated fee. But like a debit card, the payroll card can be lost or stolen.

Payroll cards are also subject to Regulation E of the Consumer Financial Protection Bureau. Under that regulation, card issuers (employers) must disclose any fees associated with use of the card, any liability limitations to which the card is subject, and the types of transactions that may be made with the card. Further, employers must make account history available and must respond to reports of errors regarding the cards. Cards may also be subject to regulation under state law.

Deductions

All employers are *required* to deduct taxes and related items from employee paychecks and amounts subject to garnishment. (Chapters 6 and 7 give more details regarding deductions from an employee's paycheck.) Employers *may* deduct other amounts agreed to by the employee, such as voluntary contributions to a retirement plan and the employee's contributory portion of health insurance premiums. Employers are generally *prohibited* from deducting amounts on account of workers' compensation benefits, unemployment insurance, or other amounts claimed due from the employee, like reimbursement for breakage or for mistakes on customer accounts.

Record-Keeping Requirements

Federal and state laws also impose certain record-keeping requirements. In general, employers must keep records for at least three years showing the name, address, Social Security number, and occupation of each employee; the employee's rate of pay; the amount actually paid each pay period; and, for non-exempt employees, the hours worked each day and each workweek. The records are subject to onsite inspection by wage and hour officials.

Nursing Mothers

Although the FLSA does not generally impose leave or break-time requirements, it does require employers with 50 or more employees to provide reasonable break times for a nursing mother to express breast milk for up to one year after the child's birth. In addition, the employer must provide a place, other than a bathroom, that is shielded from view and free from intrusion from co-workers and the public. The break time is not compensable unless the employee uses a paid break period to express milk. Employers with fewer than 50 employees are also subject to these requirements unless the requirements would impose an undue hardship.

⚠ ALERT!

The Patient Protection and Affordable Care Act (PPACA), discussed in Chapter 10, added a provision to the FLSA prohibiting employers from discriminating against an employee because he or she received a *premium tax credit* under the PPACA.

Scheduling Protection Laws

A number of local jurisdictions have adopted, or are considering, ordinances that prohibit *on-call scheduling*—calling an employee to work a shift on only a few hours' advance notice. Particularly in the retail industries, this practice can be extremely disruptive to, say, a single parent with child-care responsibilities who must on short notice make costly coverage arrangements or risk losing his or her job. As of this writing, San Francisco and Seattle have laws requiring more reasonable notice, and New York City and Washington, D.C., are considering similar laws. State attorneys general have also co-signed letters to major retailers asking them to halt the practice.

CHILD LABOR

Both federal and state laws regulate child labor. On the federal side, the FLSA prohibits *oppressive child labor*, which is defined as employment of any child who is under the age of 16, regardless of the occupation, and employment of a child who is between the ages of 16 and 18 in mining, manufacturing, or any other industry the secretary of labor finds particularly hazardous.

Excluded from the definition are the following:

- employment in a family business, so long as the employment is not in mining, manufacturing, or other particularly hazardous industries
- agricultural employment (with parental consent if the child is under 14 and only when school is not in session if the child is under 16)
- employment as an actor or performer in movies, the theater, and radio and television productions
- delivering newspapers to consumers
- making wreaths at home and harvesting forest products to be used in wreath-making

☞ **QUICK TIP**

Specific work, such as serving alcoholic beverages or driving commercial vehicles, may be subject to additional age restrictions under state law. For a child working in the entertainment industry, some states require that a portion of his or her pay be set aside for the child's later benefit.

State regulation of child labor differs from jurisdiction to jurisdiction. The definition of *minor* may vary, for example. Each state also has its own list of exclusions reflective of prominent local industries or regional customs.

Minors need a *work permit*, typically issued through the school system, before being able to work. Employers must keep permits on file and available for inspection. Even when a minor is properly permitted to work, additional restrictions may apply, such as when and how many hours a minor may work. These time restrictions vary depending on whether school is in session.

The illegal employment of minors exposes the employer to substantial criminal and civil penalties.

PRIORITY OF WAGES AND BENEFITS IN BANKRUPTCY

At any given time, an employer usually owes wages to employees. Depending on the frequency of pay periods and the lag between the end of a pay period and the date checks are issued, nonexempt employees could be owed as little as a few days' pay or as much as a few weeks' pay. Exempt employees and employees who are due commissions may be owed substantially more. Similarly, at any particular time employers with pension or other benefit plans usually have an unfunded obligation to those plans.

When an employer's assets are being administered in bankruptcy court, the U.S. Bankruptcy Code specifies an order of priority for payment of claims against the employer. High on the priority list are amounts due to employees and to employee benefit plans. Under the Bankruptcy Code, the items that come before claims of the employer's other unsecured creditors include wages, salaries, and commissions (including vacation, severance, and sick leave pay) earned during the 180-day period before the filing of the bankruptcy petition, capped at $12,850 per employee as of this writing, and contributions due to employee benefit plans arising from services rendered during the 180-day period before the filing of the bankruptcy petition, also capped at $12,850 per employee as of this writing.

In a 2017 case called *Czyzewski v. Jevic Holding Corp.*, the Supreme Court confirmed that bankruptcy courts cannot disregard the priority of wages and benefits without the consent of the employees involved, regardless of how the bankruptcy court disposes of the case.

ANTI-TRUST CONSIDERATIONS

Federal anti-trust laws generally prohibit contracts, combinations, and conspiracies in *restraint of trade*. It would be illegal, for example, for a group of service station operators in a particular region to fix prices by reaching agreement among themselves not to sell gasoline below $3.40 a gallon.

Likewise, employers may not engage in *wage-fixing* agreements. Suppose a particular industry faces a labor shortage so that employers in that industry are unable to attract all the employees they need. Rather than engage in a bidding war (that the employers perceive as just running up everyone's labor costs without solving the problem), they decide to impose a cap on wages by mutual agreement. This is illegal.

It is perfectly legal for employees, whether unionized or not, to conspire among themselves in an effort to better their wages, benefits, and working conditions. However, they lose this ability when they conspire with employers outside the scope of legitimate employee objectives. The Supreme Court ruled, for example, that an agreement between a coal miner's union and one set of mine owners—that the union would insist on specified wage standards in its negotiations with other mine owners—violated the anti-trust laws. (Chapter 24 covers unions and labor relations.)

Predatory Hiring

Wholly apart from contracts, combinations, and conspiracies, an employer might well have liability under the anti-trust laws if, without regard to its own business needs, it targets a competitor's employees (called *predatory hiring*) to harm the competitor's business. The risks here can be reduced if the new employer can demonstrate a genuine business need for the employees and if it can show that a particular competitor was not targeted, but that qualified employees were sought from a range of sources.

No-Poaching Agreements

Some years ago, a number of high-tech Silicon Valley companies entered into *no-poaching agreements* with each other, agreeing not to cold-call the other's employees. The U.S. Department of Justice (DOJ) filed civil enforcement actions against the companies, resulting in consent judgments.

More recently, in October 2016 the DOJ and the Federal Trade Commission—the two federal agencies charged with enforcing federal anti-trust laws—issued their *Antitrust Guidance for Human Resource Professionals* in which they make clear that such no-poaching agreements, as well as other agreements among competitors to fix wages or other terms of compensation, are illegal and will result in criminal prosecutions and civil suits. The guidance cautions that companies should take care not to communicate their labor policies to other companies competing for the same types of employees, nor ask other companies to go along with those labor policies.

CHAPTER 6
Wage Attachments and Assignments

- Garnishments
- Withholding Orders
- Tax Levies
- Debtors in Bankruptcy
- Department of Education Garnishments
- Wage Assignments

The obligations an employer owes its employees under wage and hour laws (discussed in Chapter 5) are trumped by a variety of court-ordered garnishments and wage attachments. When an employee's wages are garnished or attached, the employer satisfies its wage-payment obligations by paying a portion of the employee's wages to a third party to whom the employee is indebted.

GARNISHMENTS

When an employee's creditor sues your employee on an unpaid debt and obtains a court judgment, the creditor is authorized to *execute* on the judgment, meaning the creditor can try to collect the judgment out of assets belonging to the employee or income due or to become due the employee. Collecting a judgment out of an employee's wages is known as a *garnishment*. The cast of characters in that arrangement is the *judgment debtor* (your employee), the *judgment creditor* or *garnisher*, and you, the *garnishee*.

An employer usually first finds out about a garnishment when served with a court *writ*. (When the garnishment relates to family support obligations in a domestic relations case, it is called a *withholding order*.) The employer must respond by filing an answer in court within the time limit specified in the writ, stating whether the judgment debtor is in fact an employee and, if so, what his or her wages are. If the employer states that the judgment debtor is not an employee, that usually ends the matter, unless the judgment creditor requests a hearing to explore the issue further.

While the employer can assert defenses to the garnishment, including defenses the employee may have, it should be up to the employee, not the employer, to litigate the lawfulness of the garnishment. Employers may wish to include in their handbooks a disclaimer like the one in Figure 6.1.

FIGURE 6.1: GARNISHMENT DISCLAIMER

Garnishments, withholding orders and tax levies, are orders attaching a portion of an employee's compensation to satisfy a court judgment, support obligation, or tax obligation of the employee. As required by law, the company will honor all garnishments, withholding orders and tax levies that appear to be lawful and proper. The company has no obligation to dispute the lawfulness of any garnishment, withholding order, or tax levy. An employee who wishes to dispute a garnishment, withholding order, or tax levy does so at his or her own expense, without involving the company.

⚠ ALERT!

Some employers may be tempted to help their employees evade garnishments and withholding orders by falsifying information about compensation or by paying employees off the books. Doing so exposes the employer to criminal prosecution as well as civil liability.

Attachable Wages

Assuming the judgment debtor is an employee, the employer is required to withhold the *attachable wages* of the employee and remit them periodically to the garnisher (the judgment creditor) until the judgment is paid or the employment ends. The garnishment applies to any wages that are unpaid at the time of the attachment, as well as wages that become due in the future. The attachable wages are limited by the federal Consumer Credit Protection Act to the lesser of (a) 25 percent of the employee's disposable earnings (after deducting tax and similar withholdings and after deducting the employee's portion of any medical insurance premiums) or (b) the amount by which the weekly disposable earnings exceed 30 times the federal minimum hourly wage. The writ of attachment will say exactly how to compute the amount to be withheld.

Even though an employer is making payments to a garnisher, the employer must treat the payments as part of the employee's compensation for purposes of computing income tax withholding, FICA, etc. (See Chapter 7 for more details.)

Penalties

Penalties for ignoring a garnishment can be substantial. In some circumstances, the employer might be held in contempt or might be
required to cover the costs and attorneys' fees incurred by the garnisher to enforce the garnishment. The employer might even have to
pay double wages—once to the employee and again to the garnisher.
In other words, it is a good idea to take garnishments seriously.

If the employee quits or is fired while the garnishment is in effect,
the employer's obligation to remit attachable wages ends. (In some
states, rehiring an employee within a short time period automatically revives the garnishment.) If several garnishments for the same
employee are received, the employer must honor the garnishments
in the order they are served, paying off the first one completely
before starting payments on the next one.

Federal law prohibits an employer from firing an employee
because the employee's wages are subjected to attachment for any
one indebtedness within a calendar year. Many states have similar
laws protecting the jobs of garnished employees.

Wages Subject to Garnishment

State law defines what constitutes *wages* for garnishment purposes.
The definition generally covers bonuses and commissions, as well as
regular compensation. In some states, employee tips may also have
to be included.

Contributions to a pension plan that is subject to the Employee Retirement Income Security Act (ERISA) are exempt from garnishment, even when state law seems to provide otherwise. ERISA
requires plan documents to contain a provision protecting benefits
from an employee's creditors, and ERISA preempts (supersedes)
state law relating to pension plans. (ERISA is covered in Chapter 9.)

WITHHOLDING ORDERS

A *withholding order* is a special kind of wage attachment issued in a
domestic relations case in connection with spousal or child support.

Alimony and child support used to be the exclusive concerns of state courts. With enactment of amendments to the Social Security Act in 1975, which established the child support enforcement program (Title IV-D of the act), the federal government got involved in a big way. Under Title IV-D, each state must develop a formal program, which is subject to approval by the secretary of health and human services, for locating noncustodial parents and obtaining child support and support for the spouse (or former spouse) with whom the noncustodial parent's child is living. Child support must include health care coverage whenever it is available to the noncustodial parent at a reasonable cost, without regard to enrollment or open season restrictions.

Each state has a Directory of New Hires (discussed in Chapter 2) along with support guidelines and collection procedures, in accordance with the program.

When a current employee who is obligated to make support payments becomes more than 30 days delinquent, the delinquency usually results in issuance of a withholding order directing the employer to withhold the support payments from the employee's wages. Within 20 days after an employer hires a new employee, the employer must submit the employee's name, Social Security number, and other identifying information for inclusion in the state's Directory of New Hires. If that information matches with an outstanding withholding order, then the state sends a notice directing the employer to withhold the required amount from the employee's wages.

As with garnishments, the federal Consumer Credit Protection Act also sets limits on the amount of wages that may be withheld pursuant to a withholding order. However, the limit may be as high as 65 percent of disposable earnings if the employee is in arrears in support payments and has no new spouse or dependent children to support.

Pursuant to the a state's Title IV-D program, withholding orders will direct the employer to remit withheld payments not to the employee's child or to the parent who has custody of the child, but instead to the state agency or court that monitors enforcement of such orders.

Employers are prohibited from retaliating in any way, such as by firing or disciplining an employee who is the subject of a withholding order. States may, however, permit employers to charge a fee for processing withholding orders.

(See also *Qualified Medical Child Support Orders* in Chapter 10.)

TAX LEVIES

When your employee fails to pay his or her federal income taxes, the Internal Revenue Service (IRS) can collect the unpaid taxes from you, the employer, by serving you with a *levy*. Levies, like garnishments, require the employer to pay to a third party (in this case, the U.S. Department of Treasury) some portion of the wages otherwise due the employee to extinguish the employee's debt to that party. Corporate officials who are responsible for payroll matters can have *personal liability* for disregarding a tax levy.

State law also provides means for collecting delinquent taxes through garnishment of salary or wages. The procedures and exemptions differ from state to state.

If your employee disputes the validity of the levy and sues you for unpaid wages, you are discharged from any obligation or liability to the employee because you made payments in accordance with an IRS levy.

⚠ ALERT!

Under a 2015 amendment to the Internal Revenue Code, a taxpayer who has a seriously delinquent tax debt can have his or her passport revoked or limited. A *seriously delinquent* tax debt is a debt greater than $50,000 and as to which the IRS has filed a lien or issued a levy. The impact on employees who travel internationally for a living could obviously be substantial.

DEBTORS IN BANKRUPTCY

Chapter 13 of the federal Bankruptcy Code is titled "Adjustment of Debts of an Individual with Regular Income." Under Chapter 13, a debtor with a regular income may ask a bankruptcy court to prohibit creditors from suing him or her or otherwise attempting to collect debts. In exchange, the debtor must propose a plan to pay down the debts out of ongoing disposable income (generally defined as income not reasonably necessary for the support of the debtor). The plan can last no more than three years, and it must be designed so that the creditors receive at least as much under the plan as they would have received had the debtor simply brought all assets into court in a Chapter 7 liquidation.

⚠ **ALERT!**

Federal law prohibits discrimination against persons who have filed for bankruptcy.

If the bankruptcy court confirms (approves) the plan, then the court will issue an order directing the debtor's employer to pay specified amounts to a Chapter 13 trustee. The trustee, in turn, makes periodic payments to the creditors. Bankruptcy orders are exempt from the limitations imposed by the Consumer Credit Protection Act.

DEPARTMENT OF EDUCATION GARNISHMENTS

Under the federal *Higher Education Act*, the U.S. Department of Education (DOE) may garnish the disposable pay of individuals who are delinquent in repaying *student loans* made, insured, or guaranteed by the federal government. Under the garnishment procedure, the department issues a withholding order to the employer. If the employer fails to withhold in accordance with the order, the employer can be sued both for the amount that was not withheld and for attorneys' fees and punitive damages. The term *disposable pay* is defined as compensation remaining after deduction of any amounts required by law to be withheld.

Employers may not retaliate by discharging or disciplining an employee whose pay is subject to a DOE withholding order. Employers are also prohibited from refusing to hire a prospective employee because he or she is the subject of a DOE withholding order.

WAGE ASSIGNMENTS

An *assignment* of wages is different from a garnishment. Garnishments are government orders with which the employer must comply. Assignments, on the other hand, are private agreements between an employee and a third person—usually a creditor to whom the employee owes money—that may or may not be valid, depending on whether they comply with state law.

State law often restricts the ability of an employee to make a voluntary assignment of wages. It may also impose specific requirements and procedures to make a valid assignment. The safest practice is for an employer to adopt a uniform policy and distribute it to all employees, such as through the employee handbook, stating that the employer will not honor any wage assignments and—except as otherwise required by law—will pay all wages directly to the employee without regard to any assignment. See Figure 6.2 for a suggested handbook provision.

FIGURE 6.2: ASSIGNMENT OF WAGES PROVISION

Except for garnishments and similar government orders, all net wages earned by an employee are payable to the employee only. Employees are prohibited from making any assignments of their wages. The company considers any attempted assignment of wages to be void and will not honor any attempted assignment.

CHAPTER 7
Tax Considerations

Tax considerations drive, or at least help shape, any number of transactions in the business world. The same is true for the employer-employee relationship. With combined federal and state income tax rates at or above 40 percent, the deductibility of employer expenditures becomes a critical factor in a business's survival. At the same time, employees look to limit or defer tax on their employment-related benefits. The result is a complex web of employer opportunities and requirements.

DEDUCTIBILITY OF WAGES AND BENEFITS

Wages and benefits paid to employees are deductible from the employer's gross income for purposes of computing the employer's federal and state income tax, so long as the amounts are reasonable, ordinary, and necessary. This means, for example, that for a corporate employer that is in the 39 percent marginal federal tax bracket and the 7 percent state tax bracket, 46 cents of each additional dollar in wages and benefits are effectively paid by federal and state governments in the form of reduced tax liabilities.

☞ **QUICK TIP**

As an alternative to taking a deduction for wages, an employer may claim a *work opportunity tax credit* (WOTC) against its income tax for a portion of the first- and second-year wages paid to targeted groups of hard-to-employ individuals, such as those receiving benefits under the Temporary Aid for Needy Families (TANF) program or the Supplemental Nutrition Assistance Program (SNAP), long-term unemployed individuals, summer youth employees, and certain veterans and ex-offenders. The individuals must be certified as qualified for the credit through the employer's State Workforce Agency. The amount of the credit varies, depending on which targeted group the specific individual is a member of and the number of hours the individual was employed during the year for which the credit is being claimed. See Internal Revenue Service (IRS) Forms 8850 and 5884 and instructions. As of this writing, the WOTC is scheduled to expire in December 2019.

As a general rule, whenever the employer takes a deduction for a wage or benefits payment, the employee who receives the payment must include it in his or her own gross income for federal and state tax purposes. The IRS keeps track of these shifting tax burdens by requiring employers to report employee payments on Form W-2 and payments to independent contractors on Form 1099.

However, the general rule has important exceptions. One exception is for items of *deferred compensation*—compensation that the employee cannot immediately enjoy, such as qualified retirement plan contributions. It may make little difference to an employer whether compensation to employees is in the form of wages or partly in wages and partly in the form of a qualified retirement plan contribution, since both are fully deductible if they are within the limits imposed by law. But it can make a big difference to the employee because of the time value of money.

Take, for example, an employee whose marginal tax bracket for federal and state tax purposes is 40 percent. For each additional dollar received in wages, 40 cents is paid to the government, and only 60 cents is left to save or spend. (The employee's portion of FICA and Medicare reduce even more the amount left to save or spend.) And if that 60 cents is invested, any investment income is subject to additional taxation.

In contrast, a dollar of deferred compensation is not subject to immediate tax, so the full dollar can be invested without reduction for taxes. In addition, earnings on that dollar—called inside build-up—are not subject to immediate tax either. In the end, the employee should have a greater nest egg than if he or she had received and invested after-tax wages. Of course, that nest egg is subject to income tax as it is withdrawn during retirement, but in most cases, the employee is still better off, particularly since his or her tax bracket in retirement is probably lower than when actively working.

There are other important exceptions to the general rule that whatever the employer deducts, the employee must report. For example, employer contributions to group health insurance, health savings accounts, and group term life insurance up to $50,000 in coverage (all discussed in Chapter 10) are generally deductible by the employer but not includable in the employee's income.

Some noncash *fringe benefits* may be deductible for the employer but, subject to specified limits and conditions, not includable in the employee's gross income (see IRS Publication 15-B). These include the following:

- no-additional-cost service, which is a service to an employee that the employer normally provides to its customers, as long as doing so is without substantial additional cost to the employer
- employee discounts on goods (provided that the discount does not exceed the employer's profit margin) and on services (provided that the discount does not exceed 20 percent of the retail price)
- working condition benefits, such as upscale office appointments and use of a company car for business purposes
- de minimis benefits, such as use of the copying machine or office supplies for personal purposes and such as eating facilities at or near the employer's premises (so long as the facility is operated on at least a break-even basis and the employer does not discriminate in favor of highly compensated employees)
- transportation benefits, including a transit pass, parking, bicycle expenses, or cash reimbursements for those items (up to specified statutory limits)
- cellphones provided primarily for business reasons, even though employees may use their phones for personal purposes as well

Federal tax law allows companies to deduct all *ordinary and necessary expenses* of carrying on a trade or business. These include reimbursements to employees who have incurred expenses on behalf of their employers. But special rules apply to transportation and travel expenses. For example, while companies can reimburse their employees for, and then deduct, actual expenses incurred in operating an automobile for business, IRS regulations have long allowed use of standard mileage rates in lieu of providing substantiation for actual expenses. (For 2017, the standard rate for business use of an automobile is 53.5 cents per mile.)

The IRS takes a similar approach to *per diem* business travel expenses (meals, lodging, and incidental expenses), allowing standard reimbursement/deduction rates instead of requiring substantiation of actual expenses. Employers may use one of two methods to reimburse employees, either of which satisfies the substantiation requirement. One, called the *high-low method* (available only for travel within the continental U.S.), allows a deduction of $282 per day for specified high-cost areas, and $189 for all other areas for 2017. See *Internal Revenue Bulletin 2016-41*, available on the IRS's website. Alternatively, employers may use the *federal per diem rates* method, based on location-specific rates established by the federal government for cities within the continental U.S. (the CONUS rates) and outside the continental U.S. (the OCONUS rates). The U.S. Government Services Administration (GSA) establishes and publishes these rates.

The deduction for food, beverages, and entertainment (but not lodging) is limited to 50 percent of the otherwise deductible amount, subject to a number of exceptions. Amounts paid to employees in excess of deductible amounts constitute income to the employees and are subject to withholding requirements and payroll taxes.

LIMITATIONS ON DEDUCTIBILITY

Most business corporations are classified as *C corporations* (C corps) for federal income tax purposes. C corps are separate taxable entities whose taxable income is determined by starting with the corporation's gross revenue and deducting the cost of goods sold, salaries, rent, and other expenses. After paying tax on the resulting net income, the corporation may choose to distribute some or all of what is left to its shareholders in the form of a *dividend*. Dividends represent taxable income to the shareholders.

Because a C corp is a taxable entity, income is taxed twice on its way through the corporation to its shareholders: one tax is paid at the corporate level, and a second tax is paid at the individual shareholder level. Particularly in the case of small, closely held corporations, in which the shareholder-owners are also the directors, officers, and employees, this double taxation burden is problematic.

One way to avoid double taxation is to accumulate earnings inside the corporation and not pay dividends. But if the corporation accumulates earnings beyond its reasonable business needs, the corporation may end up owing an accumulated earnings tax that is designed to stop that very practice.

Another way to avoid double taxation is to elect *S corporation* (S corp) status. (This is discussed in more depth in Chapter 1.) Although S corps are generally not subject to tax as separate entities, there are restrictions on who may elect S status. There may also be undesirable tax consequences to S corp owners.

Yet another way is to pay year-end bonuses to owner-employees. Through careful calculation, the bonuses can be set so that the corporation has virtually zero taxable income, and it pays almost no tax. (It is usually not possible to reach exactly zero, since some cash expenditures during the year, such as equipment purchases and meals, may not be fully deductible, but they reduce the amount of cash available to pay bonuses.) The owner-employees, of course, will owe tax on the bonuses along with whatever other compensation they receive, but that is still just one tax, not two.

The taxpayer corporation has the burden of proving that its compensation payments are reasonable under Internal Revenue Code §162. And particularly when the taxpayer corporation is controlled by the employees receiving the compensation, the payments are subject to careful scrutiny by the IRS to be sure that they truly represent (deductible) compensation for services rendered, rather than disguised (nondeductible) dividends. In determining whether compensation is reasonable, the courts look at a number of factors, including the following:

• the employee's qualifications
• the nature, extent, and scope of the employee's work

- the size and complexity of the employer's business
- a comparison of salaries paid with the employer's income
- prevailing rates of compensation for comparable positions in comparable companies
- the amount of compensation paid to the employee in previous years
- whether the employer offers pension and profit-sharing plans to its employees

These factors are applied on an individual employee basis, rather than in the aggregate to a group of employees. In other words, that the company's overall deduction for compensation is reasonable does not matter; each individual employee's compensation must be reasonable as well.

☞ **QUICK TIP**

Payments to partners in a partnership and to members of a limited liability company are generally treated as nondeductible distributions rather than deductible wages and salaries. This occurs even when the partner or member works for the partnership or limited liability company.

Public Companies

Under Internal Revenue Code §162(m), publicly held corporations also face limits on the amount they can deduct. In general, the code places a $1 million-per-year cap on deductions for remuneration paid to *covered employees*—defined as the chief executive officer and the four highest-paid officers other than the CEO—unless the board of directors takes special steps to authorize higher compensation.

Closely related to these income tax caps are several executive compensation disclosure requirements. The Securities and Exchange Commission (SEC) requires each publicly held company to disclose in its annual proxy statement the amount of compensation paid to its *high-level executives*—its chief executive officer, chief financial officer, and its three other most highly compensated executive officers. The company also must disclose the criteria used in reaching executive compensation decisions and the relationship between the company's executive compensation practices and corporate performance.

And a 2010 amendment to the Dodd-Frank Act, known as the *say-on-pay rule*, requires public companies periodically to disclose in its proxy statements, and give shareholders a vote on, executive compensation and any golden parachute payments, although the vote in not binding on the company.

Dodd-Frank also requires the SEC to issue a pay-ratio rule, under which most public companies would have to disclose the following:
- the median of the total annual compensation of all employees (except the CEO)
- the CEO's total annual compensation
- the ratio of the above two numbers

In 2015 the SEC issued final rules as required by Dodd-Frank, and in September 2017, the SEC issued further interpretive guidance on the rules.

INDEPENDENT CONTRACTORS

As pointed out in Chapter 1, employers sometimes try to classify their workers as independent contractors to avoid the laws and regulations that apply to employees. When a worker is misclassified as an independent contractor, the results can be financially ruinous for the employer. For example, employees (but not independent contractors) are subject to federal and state income tax withholding, they are entitled to have employer FICA contributions made on their behalf, they are covered by workers' compensation and unemployment insurance for which the employer must pay premiums, and they are entitled to participate in the employer's various benefit plans. So if an employer wrongly treats a group of employees as independent contractors over a period of years, the total cost of remedying the error can be substantial.

Traditionally, the question whether a worker is an employee or an independent contractor turns on whether the employer has a *right to control* the manner in which the worker does his or her job. This is sometimes known as the *common-law test*. To determine whether there is a right of control, a number of subsidiary factors are considered, such as who sets the worker's hours, whether the worker works for one or several employers, whether the worker or the employer provides necessary tools and workspace, whether the worker has specialized knowledge or requires a license or a professional degree to do the job, and so on. The problem with the common-law test is its lack of certainty. If the employer guesses wrong, disaster can strike.

In an effort to resolve this uncertainty, Congress enacted legislation to provide a *safe harbor* for employers. Under these safe harbor provisions, an employer's treatment of a worker as an independent contractor is relatively safe from IRS challenge if the employer meets the following criteria:

- It has never treated the worker as an employee.
- It filed all required tax reports and returns relating to the worker on a timely and consistent basis.
- It had a reasonable basis for treating the worker as an independent contractor.

The employer will be considered to have a reasonable basis for treating the worker as an independent contractor if the employer relied on a court decision involving facts similar to the employer's own or if the employer relied on rulings or technical advice from the IRS. The employer can also demonstrate a reasonable basis if a significant segment of the industry in which the worker is engaged has a long-standing recognized practice of treating such workers as independent contractors. A *significant segment* of the industry is 25 percent. However, the employer will not have a reasonable basis for treating a particular worker as an independent contractor if the employer has other workers doing similar jobs who are treated as employees.

While the IRS can still challenge a safe harbor classification, the burden of proving that the classification is wrong falls on the IRS. To ensure that the safe harbor provisions are fully effective, the IRS must provide the employer with a written notice of the provisions when it audits an employer in connection with a worker classification issue. The IRS is also prohibited from issuing regulations or rulings dealing with the safe harbor provisions.

CASE STUDY:
SAFE HARBOR PROVISION APPLIED

A company licensed as a residential service agency wants to provide nonskilled, home health aides for the elderly in the Washington, D.C., area. Before opening for business, the company conducts a survey of some 20 to 30 local competitors. It finds that approximately 80 percent of the agencies surveyed treat their aides as independent contractors, while only 10 percent treat them as employees. (The other 10 percent did not respond.) Upon opening additional offices in Baltimore and Richmond, the company conducts similar surveys in those areas and obtains similar results. Based on these surveys, the company classifies its workers as independent contractors. The company's reliance on its surveys is reasonable, and the company's classification of its aides is accepted by the court.

Another approach to resolving the employee/independent contractor issue for federal tax and withholding purposes is to ask the IRS to decide. Upon filing Form SS-8 (either by the employer or by the worker whose status is in doubt), the IRS will determine whether the worker is an employee or an independent contractor. The determination can then be relied on for safe harbor purposes. It is probably fair to assume that the IRS resolves close questions by concluding that the worker is an employee, not an independent contractor. So as a practical matter, the SS-8 route may not be very helpful to employers.

Yet another solution is to participate in the IRS's *Voluntary Classification Settlement Program.* Employers that want to voluntarily change the prospective classification of a worker or group of workers from independent contractors to employees file IRS Form 8952 and enter into a closing agreement with the IRS. Under the closing agreement, the employer agrees to treat the workers as employees for future tax periods. The IRS in turn limits the employer's previous tax liability to 10 percent of what would have been due on compensation paid to the workers for the most recent tax year. In addition, the IRS waives penalties and interest, and it agrees not to conduct an employment tax audit with respect to those workers.

Suppose an employer incorrectly classifies a worker as an independent contractor when, in reality, the worker should have been treated as an employee. As an independent contractor, for 2017 the worker pays a self-employment tax equal to 15.3 percent of earnings up to $127,200 (which equals $19,461.60), plus an additional Medicare tax of 2.9 percent on any earnings above $127,200. Had the worker been properly classified as an employee, however, the employee would have paid only half the $19,461.60 as the employee's share of FICA, and the employer would have paid the other half. So the question arises whether, as a result of misclassification, the worker has a claim against the employer for the $9,730.80 that the employer should have matched but did not.

In a case from the U.S. 11th Circuit Court of Appeals (headquartered in Atlanta), the court ruled that FICA is a tax statute that only the federal government can enforce and that it does not create a private right of action. In other words, so far as FICA is concerned, an employer may be liable to the government for misclassification, but the employer is not liable to the misclassified employee.

FEDERAL WITHHOLDING REQUIREMENTS

We are all used to seeing a long list of deductions and withholdings on our pay stubs. Some of them are voluntary, like the employee portions of retirement plan contributions and health insurance premiums. Others are required by law.

How does the employer know how much to withhold? And what is done with the money? The first step in the process is for the employer to obtain an *Employer Identification Number* (EIN). The number has nine digits, as do Social Security numbers, but instead of being in the format 123-45-6789, an EIN is formatted 12-3456789. EINs are obtained by filing Form SS-4 with the IRS and may also be obtained by phone or fax or by completing an online application.

The next step is for the employee to submit IRS Form W-4 and the applicable state equivalent to the employer. This must be done at hiring time and whenever the employee's tax withholdings need to be changed. Form W-4 calls for basic information, such as the employee's name, address, Social Security number, and marital status. It also contains a worksheet for figuring the number of exemptions to be claimed on the employee's tax return and various other factors that affect the employee's tax liability. These factors, known as *allowances*, are then totaled and entered on the form. Finally, Form W-4 permits the employee to claim a complete exemption from federal income tax withholding under certain conditions.

⚠ ALERT!

While an employer cannot challenge the allowances claimed by the employee, the IRS certainly can. The IRS may request an employer to provide copies of Forms W-4 for specific employees. If the IRS concludes that an employee is not entitled to claim married status or is not entitled to the allowances he or she claimed on the W-4, the IRS will instruct the employer (by what is commonly known called a *lock-in letter*) as to how to withhold for the future.

When is an employee considered married? According to the IRS's Publication 15 (also known as Circular E), a marriage of two individuals is recognized for federal tax purposes if the marriage is recognized by the state, possession, or territory of the United States in which the marriage is entered into. As a result of the Supreme Court's 2015 decision in *Obergefell v. Hodges*, states no longer have a choice about recognizing same-sex marriages.

The employer has four basic federal tax obligations relating to employees:

- federal income tax
- Social Security tax (FICA)
- Medicare tax
- unemployment insurance contributions

The first three are discussed below. Unemployment insurance is covered in Chapter 12.

Federal Income Tax

With Form W-4 in hand, the employer turns to a set of tables issued by the IRS in Publication 15 to determine how much to withhold from each paycheck. The tables are based on four variables:

- the frequency of paydays (for example, weekly, biweekly)
- the employee's marital status as shown on Form W-4
- the amount of the wage payment
- the number of allowances claimed by the employee

Publication 15 (updated annually) is really the employer's bible when it comes to federal employment tax matters. It can be viewed and downloaded from the IRS's website.

Social Security (FICA) Tax

The tax rate for an employee is 6.2 percent on a maximum wage base of $128,400 for calendar year 2018, which translates to a maximum withholding of $7,960.80. The employer must match whatever amount is withheld from the employee. So for an employee whose annual salary is at least $128,400, the total payment on account of Social Security is $15,921.60, half of which is withheld from the employee and half of which is the employer's own matching contribution. The amount to be withheld from each paycheck is simply 6.2 percent of the gross payment until the maximum amount $7,960.80 has been withheld. These rates and the wage base are subject to periodic change.

Medicare Tax

The Medicare tax rate is 1.45 percent of all wages for the employee and a matching amount of 1.45 percent for the employer. There is no wage base cap—the Medicare tax applies to all wages. The amount to be withheld from each paycheck is 1.45 percent of the gross payment.

⚠ ALERT!

Owner-employees of S corporations engaged in personal services (for example, doctors, lawyers, accountants) may try to reduce their payroll tax obligations by paying themselves unreasonably small salaries (which are subject to payroll taxes) and treating the remaining corporate profits as shareholder income (which is not subject to payroll taxes). When this scheme comes to the IRS's attention, it will recharacterize all or most of the corporate profits as salary.

Exceptions

In general, all employees who are U.S. citizens or resident aliens are subject to withholding for federal income tax, FICA, and Medicare. Publication 15 contains a list of situations in which special rules apply, including the following:
- nonresident aliens
- household employees
- clergy
- disabled workers
- deceased workers

Independent contractors are also exempt from withholding requirements. However, a few, limited types of workers called *statutory employees* are required by law to be treated as employees, even though they might otherwise qualify as independent contractors. (See Chapter 1 for more information.)

☞ **QUICK TIP**

Workers' compensation benefits (discussed in Chapter 11) are exempt from income tax.

Irregular Pay

Questions sometimes arise regarding withholding on back wages paid to an employee for some earlier year. Suppose, for example, that the employer and employee are in dispute over the exact amount due, and the dispute gets resolved in court, years after the employee did the work. Or suppose back pay is awarded in connection with a discrimination suit or an unfair labor practice complaint. Should the employer treat the wages as paid when they were *originally due* or as paid in the year they were *actually paid*? (The answer can make a big difference if the tax rates or FICA cap changed.) The IRS has long taken the position that the wages should be treated as paid currently, and the Supreme Court affirmed that position in a 2001 case involving the Cleveland Indians baseball club.

Other taxable benefits subject to withholding include bonuses, commissions, expense reimbursements (unless the reimbursement is pursuant to an arrangement that requires the employee to verify expenses), payments in kind, meals, and lodging (unless provided for the employer's convenience on the employer's premises).

TIPS

In addition to withholding for wages, the employer must withhold on account of *tips*. Employees are required to report tips to their employer no later than the 10th of the month after the month the tips are received, unless tips for the month are less than $20. The report should include not only cash tips the employee receives directly from customers but also tips received in a sharing arrangement with other employees and tips paid by credit card. Employees may use Form 4070 (contained in IRS Publication 1244) or a similar statement to report tips to their employers.

The employer then must figure tax withholdings, payroll taxes, and garnishments just as if the tips were wages paid by the employer.

However, the employer is not liable to taxing authorities or garnishers for more money than actually comes into the employer's hands. Employers that operate *large food and beverage establishments* (defined as employing more than 10 people who work more than 80 hours per week in the aggregate) must file Form 8027 annually with the IRS showing total tips.

The IRS has developed a Tip Rate Determination and Education Program in which employers may participate. The program primarily consists of two voluntary agreements developed to improve tip income reporting: the Tip Rate Determination Agreement and the Tip Reporting Alternative Commitment. For more information, see IRS Publication 3144.

OTHER TAXABLE PAYMENTS

Suppose an employee is laid off under circumstances that could give rise to a claim of abusive discharge. Fearing a claim, the employer obtains a written release of claims from the employee and, as consideration for the release, makes a lump sum payment to the employee. Or suppose the employee refuses to sign a release and instead files a lawsuit that results in a money judgment against the employer. Are those payments deductible by the employer and taxable to the employee? Are they subject to withholding and reporting requirements? To payroll taxes?

It has long been the rule that the proceeds of a personal injury action (a suit claiming injury to the body or person of the suing party) are *excluded* from taxation and from any withholding or reporting requirements. In the past, the parties to an employment dispute often characterized payments in settlement of the dispute as damages for emotional distress, injury to reputation, and so on to avoid tax obligations.

In 1996, the Internal Revenue Code was amended to narrow the exclusion. The code now states that gross income does not include damages received on account of personal *physical* injuries or *physical* sickness. A private letter ruling by the IRS defines personal physical injuries as "direct unwanted or uninvited physical contacts resulting in observable bodily harms such as bruises, cuts, swelling, and bleeding."

As a result of the 1996 amendment, most payments in employment dispute situations will be includable in the recipient's gross income for federal income tax purposes. At the same time, the payments will be deductible by the employer. In addition, since damages in an employment dispute are usually based on *lost wages*, the payments are generally viewed as the equivalent of employee compensation and therefore subject to wage withholding and FICA requirements.

When an employer and employee settle an employment dispute, they may agree to treat only a portion of the settlement payment as wages and allocate the remainder to *emotional distress*. The IRS will respect such an allocation for wage withholding and FICA purposes, so long as the allocation is reasonable, but the IRS will nevertheless view the entire payment as taxable income to the employee. Therefore, the employer should report the portion allocated to wages as Form W-2 income subject to withholding and payroll taxes, and the portion allocated to emotional distress as Form 1099 income not subject to withholding or payroll taxes.

Sometimes the employer agrees to pay the employee's attorney's fees as part of a settlement. Before the *American Jobs Creation Act of 2004*, most courts took the view that the attorney's fee portion of the settlement was taxable income to the employee, even when the attorney's fee portion was paid directly to the employee's lawyer. The American Jobs Creation Act now provides that, in most employment disputes, the attorney's fee portion is *not* taxable income to the employee, although it *is* taxable, of course, to the lawyer.

When negotiating a settlement agreement, a prudent employer should insist that the agreement explicitly state how all payments are being allocated and how they will be reported for tax purposes. If the agreement attempts to characterize any portion of the payment as nontaxable (a risky arrangement), the agreement should at least contain a provision requiring the employee to indemnify the employer should the IRS later recharacterize the payment as taxable.

☞ **QUICK TIP**

The settlement of an employment dispute should be in writing and include a provision by which the employee, former employee, or applicant for employment clearly releases all employment-related claims against the employer. If the release is intended to cover an actual or potential age discrimination claim, the release must conform to special rules contained in the Age Discrimination in Employment Act. (See Chapter 16 for specifics on age discrimination.)

Garnishments

When an employer satisfies a garnishment by paying a portion of the employee's salary to the employee's creditor, the employer is discharging a debt the employee owes. Economically, it is as if the employer paid wages to the employee and the employee, in turn, paid down the debt. So for tax withholding and reporting purposes, a garnishment payment is treated just like a wage payment to the employee.

STATE WITHHOLDING REQUIREMENTS

Most states impose their own taxes on income and require employers to withhold against that tax. State withholding requirements can get confusing, particularly for employees who commute to work from out of state. For each employee, the first step is to determine the state or states in which the employee *may* have to file a state income tax return. If the employee both lives and works in the same state, then only that state's withholding requirements apply. If the employee lives in one state but commutes to work in another state, then *both* states' withholding requirements need to be considered, since the employee potentially has tax filing obligations in both states. (Those few states that do not have any income tax at all can be ignored.)

Even though an employee may have a tax filing obligation in a particular state, the employer might not be required to withhold under that state's law. This situation could occur if the employer itself is not subject to the jurisdiction of that particular state, because the employer has no office in that state and does not do business in that state. Take, for example, a Maryland company whose employees all work in Maryland, but some of whom live in Virginia. Virginia might like the company to withhold from its Virginia employees, but if the company is not subject to Virginia's jurisdiction, Virginia has no power to compel the company to do so. At the same time, Maryland, where the company *is* subject to jurisdiction, has no interest in enforcing Virginia's tax laws.

The company could withhold Maryland income tax from all its employees. But this would mean that its Virginia employees would face a big Virginia tax bill not covered by withholdings, plus they would need to deal with Maryland to get back some or all of their Maryland withholdings. To resolve this situation, Maryland and Virginia have entered into *reciprocal agreements* with each other. Under these agreements, the Maryland company in the example above withholds Maryland tax from its Maryland employees and Virginia tax from its Virginia employees.

Many other states that have common borders have entered into reciprocal agreements similar to those between Maryland and Virginia. Contact your state employment tax office for details.

☞ **QUICK TIP**

At least one state (New Jersey) takes the view that a company that has no offices in the state but that employs a teleworker there is subject to New Jersey's jurisdiction for tax and corporate purposes. (See Chapter 20 for details.)

EARNED INCOME TAX CREDIT

The *Earned Income Tax Credit* (EITC) is a tax credit available to low- and moderate-income employees. The amount of the credit ranges from a few hundred dollars for an employee with no dependent children up to $6,318 for an employee with three or more dependent children. The credit is *refundable*, meaning that if the credit reduces the employee's tax liability below zero, the employee owes no tax and the government pays the amount of the *negative tax* to the employee.

Employers must notify their employees who have no federal income tax withheld that they may be able to claim a tax refund because of the EITC. The back of copy B of Form W-2 contains the required notice.

DEPOSIT AND REPORTING REQUIREMENTS

All employment-related federal tax payments—taxes withheld from employees, and employers' and employees' Social Security and Medicare taxes—must be deposited using *electronic funds transfer* (EFT). Deposits are made using either the IRS's Electronic Federal Tax Payment System (EFTPS) or by having a third party, such as the employer's tax professional, financial institution or payroll service, make the deposit. Employers must enroll in EFTPS to use that system.

The frequency of deposits depends on the amount of taxes involved. In general, if the annual amount is less than $50,000, the deposits are made monthly, and if the amount is $50,000 or more, the deposits are made semiweekly. However, if an employer accumulates a tax liability of $100,000 or more on any day during a deposit period, the deposit must be made by the next banking day. An employer owing less than $2,500 in employment taxes per quarter may remit those taxes with its quarterly return, rather than depositing the taxes separately.

The rules governing employment taxes under the Federal Unemployment Tax Act (FUTA) are covered in Chapter 12.

Trust Fund Penalty

Taxes withheld from employees are considered to be held by the employer in trust. Rather than just owing the money to the IRS, the employer is treated as having a fiduciary duty to ensure that deposits get made as required by law. If the employer fails to do so, the IRS may impose a *trust fund penalty* equal to the amount of the undeposited tax in addition to collecting the tax itself.

The corporate shield offers no protection when it comes to the trust fund penalty, since any person responsible for collecting, accounting for, or depositing the tax will have personal liability for the penalty. Responsible persons can include corporate officers, employees, directors, anyone who signs checks or has authority for spending business funds, and even volunteers of nonprofit organizations. (Volunteers of tax-exempt organizations are relieved of personal liability if they are serving in an honorary capacity, if they do not participate in the day-to-day or financial operations of the organization, and if they had no actual knowledge of the failure to withhold or make the required deposit—so long as there are at least some remaining responsible persons left to pay the taxes.) Liability for withholding taxes and for trust fund penalties is *not* dischargeable in bankruptcy.

☞ QUICK TIP

Even though a single-member limited liability company is considered a *disregarded entity* so that its owner is treated as a sole proprietorship for federal income tax purposes, under IRS regulations the owner of the LLC is not liable for the *LLC's share* of employment taxes (although he or she would be liable for taxes withheld from employees).

W-2s, 1099s and K-1s

No later than January 31 of each year, employers must issue IRS Form W-2 to each employee, reporting the employee's compensation for the previous calendar year. Copies of the Forms W-2 are then transmitted to the Social Security Administration using IRS Form W-3. If an employee quits or is terminated during the year, the employer must, if so requested by the employee, issue a W-2 within 30 days. Forms W-2 may also be filed electronically.

Independent contractors that have been paid more than $600 during the previous calendar year are issued Form 1099-MISC by January 31. Although corporate independent contractors (including limited liability companies that have elected to be taxed as corporations) do not have to be issued Forms 1099, payments to *attorneys*, regardless of their corporate status, do have to be reported on Forms 1099.

Partners in general partnerships, members of LLCs that have not elected to be taxed as corporations, and shareholders of corporations that have elected S corporation status are issued Schedule K-1 (Form 1065) at the time the partnership, LLC, or S corp files its own tax return. (See Chapter 1 for more information.)

Payroll Services

For very modest charges, a commercial payroll service provides the following:

- calculates each employee's deductions and withholdings
- issues net checks to employees using the employer's preprinted check stock (or makes deposits directly to the employees' bank accounts)
- provides a paper or electronic check stub to each employee showing current and year-to-date earnings, deductions, withholdings, and leave accruals
- makes all required federal and state tax deposits
- prepares all federal and state reports
- prepares Forms W-2 and appropriate transmittal forms

Particularly for smaller employers, this service is difficult to beat. Be cautioned, however, that the employer will be held responsible if the payroll service fails to make required tax deposits. For that reason, it is a good idea to check with the IRS periodically to be sure no deficiencies exist. The address on file with the IRS for mailing deficiency notices should be the employer's address, not that of the payroll service.

CHAPTER 8
Leave Policies

- Vacation and Sick Leave
- Paid Time Off
- Mandatory Paid Leave
- Family and Medical Leave
- Americans with Disabilities Act Leave
- Military Leave
- Other Leave

With a few exceptions discussed later in this chapter, there is no obligation for an employer to offer any leave at all. Of course, most employers do so because it is customary, it is humane, and not doing so could place the employer at a competitive disadvantage.

VACATION AND SICK LEAVE

A typical vacation formula for regular, full-time employees might give 10 days (two weeks) per year for the first two or three years of employment and 15 days (three weeks) per year after the third or fourth year. Limitations are commonly placed on the amount of vacation that can be carried forward—a *use-it-or-lose-it policy*. This encourages employees to take regular vacations, which in turn improves morale. It also avoids the disruption of extra-long absences.

Sick leave may be 5 or 10 days per year. Employers need to specify in their employee handbooks what is covered by sick leave and what is not. For example, must the actual employee be sick, or does a sick child or spouse also qualify? How about routine, nonemergency medical and dental visits for the employee or for the employee's child? And believe it or not, the policy should address sick pets as well.

☞ **QUICK TIP**

For employers covered by Title VII of the federal Civil Rights Act or equivalent state law, a temporary disability caused by pregnancy or childbirth must be treated the same under the employer's sick leave policy as a temporary disability caused by other medical conditions. (See Chapter 15 for more details.)

When time off for an injury or illness extends more than a few days, employers may want to require written verification from the employee's health care practitioner. After a serious illness or injury, the employer may require a *certification of fitness for duty* on the employee's return. These policies, too, should be spelled out in the employee handbook and applied uniformly to avoid claims of favoritism or discrimination.

⚠ ALERT!

A diagnosis of the condition that gave rise to the absence might reveal an underlying disability or genetic disorder. Therefore, an employer requirement that certification of fitness for duty include a diagnosis may violate the Americans with Disabilities Act (ADA), discussed in Chapter 17, or the Genetic Information Nondiscrimination Act, covered in Chapter 14.

☞ QUICK TIP

To eliminate any implication that employees are hired for a year period, it is good practice to express vacation and sick leave as the number of hours accrued per pay period or per hours worked, rather than the number of days accrued per year. For example, for an employer that pays semimonthly (24 times a year), 10 days of vacation per year translates to 3.33 hours per pay period. For the same reason, the terms *vacation* or *paid leave* are preferred over *annual leave*.

⚠ ALERT!

Vacation and sick leave benefits that an employer provides out of its general assets are exempt from Employee Retirement Income Security Act (ERISA) requirements. However, if the employer establishes a dedicated fund to cover those benefits, ERISA may apply. (ERISA is discussed in Chapter 9.)

PAID TIME OFF

Some employers have abandoned the various forms of voluntary leave—such as vacation, sick leave, emergency leave, bereavement leave, hazard leave, and personal leave—and replaced them with a *paid-time-off* (PTO) plan.

Suppose, for example, that a company's policy grants 10 days of paid vacation per year, 5 days of paid sick leave per year, 3 days of leave without pay for a death in the immediate family, 3 days of personal leave without pay, and up to 3 days of hazard leave with pay for weather-related absences. Keeping track of all these categories is an administrative nightmare for the company. Worse, determining in which category a particular day off falls imposes a substantial burden on supervisors and may engender hard feelings among employees.

And having to justify sick leave by providing personal medical information may feel like an invasion of the employee's privacy.

After switching to a PTO plan, the company now grants 20 paid days off per year (6.67 hours each semimonthly pay period) that employees can use for any purpose. In addition to reducing administrative burdens and morale problems, the PTO plan discourages employees from taking sick leave, because doing so uses up vacation time. Instead, employees now schedule most of their leave in advance, giving the employer an opportunity to arrange for coverage or an opportunity to require that the leave be taken at a time more convenient for the employer.

PTO plans can be fine-tuned, depending on a particular employer's experience and needs. For example, a day of scheduled leave might cost the employee only six hours out of his or her PTO bank, but unscheduled leave might cost the full eight hours. The employer might also impose a cap on the amount of PTO that can be accumulated in the PTO bank. Allowing employees to draw prescribed amounts of PTO in cash in lieu of leave time tends to limit overall absences. PTO time can also be cashed out with pretax dollars in the form of employer contributions to a *401(k) retirement plan* or *cafeteria plan*.

And under carefully prescribed conditions, an employee may be permitted to give a portion of his or her accumulated PTO to another employee who faces a serious illness or family emergency but whose PTO is exhausted.

Other details need to be considered in implementing a PTO plan. For example, what happens to accumulated PTO at termination of employment—is it forfeited or cashed out? How is PTO coordinated with leave under the Family and Medical Leave Act (FMLA)—is the employee required to exhaust PTO before taking FMLA leave, or may he or she take FMLA leave first? Of course, these same questions arise with any leave policy the employer may have.

PTO plans seem to have many advantages over traditional leave arrangements: they are simpler to administer; they are more flexible;

they can be fine-tuned to meet the employer's specific needs; they eliminate, or at least reduce, the need to examine personal medical information; and they discourage unscheduled sick leave. PTO plans deserve consideration.

But there are disadvantages of PTO plans as well. In those states that require accrued vacation to be cashed out at termination, converting sick leave to PTO effectively means that accrued sick leave as well as vacation will now have to be cashed out. And in those jurisdictions that have adopted mandatory leave laws (discussed below), integrating a PTO plan and mandatory leave may result in paid vacation time for employees who would not otherwise earn vacation.

MANDATORY PAID LEAVE

A growing number of states and local governments have adopted or are considering imposing paid leave requirements on employers within their jurisdictions. (See Chapter 22 for paid leave requirements applicable to U.S. government contractors.) These mandatory paid leave laws may require employers to grant, say, one hour of paid leave for every 30 or 40 hours worked. The rate of accrual sometimes varies, depending on the size of the employer, with larger employers required to grant more paid leave than their smaller counterparts. Very small employers may be entirely exempt.

Typically, the leave is available for the employee's own illness, for illness of a family member, and for the birth of a child or the placement of a child for adoption or foster care. Leave may also be available for a variety of other purposes, such as to obtain preventive medical care and for victims of domestic abuse to seek legal services or to temporarily relocate. So far, the laws prescribing mandatory paid leave have not included vacation as one of the authorized leave purposes, but that may be changing as well.

The laws also address other issues of which employers must be aware: whether part-time employees qualify for leave, when leave begins to accrue, whether there is a waiting period before taking accrued leave, the amount of leave that may be taken in a given period, the amount that may be carried over, and how accrued but unused leave is treated on termination of employment.

For multistate employers, this mix of requirements and refinements poses a substantial record-keeping and compliance burden. One solution would be to enact a uniform federal law, but unless that law expressly supersedes any state or local laws (not likely in the present political climate), there would be no guaranty of uniformity. Another, somewhat less effective, solution would be for each state to adopt a uniform state law for employers within its jurisdiction and, at the same time, bar cities and counties in the state from legislating on the topic. That would ensure at least statewide uniformity.

Without any uniformity on the horizon, employers must decide how best to integrate mandatory leave laws with existing leave policies. One approach might be to adopt a PTO plan that is at least as generous as the most generous applicable leave law and that allows employees to use leave essentially for *any purpose*, including the purposes specified in the mandatory leave laws. This approach allows easier tracking of leave, since each employee has only one PTO "bank account" instead of multiple bank accounts for each of the various mandatory and voluntary leave purposes. Other advantages and disadvantages of PTO plans are discussed above.

FAMILY AND MEDICAL LEAVE

Some employers consider the FMLA, the ADA, and workers' compensation laws to be a three-legged stool upon which employees rest while milking their employer. It is true that before those laws, an employer could fire an employee for taking extended leave, no matter how good the reason, and had no obligation to offer a returning employee his or her old job, or any job at all. It is also true that under certain circumstances, an employee could now be entitled to the protections of all three laws *at the same time*. The real problem for employers, however, is not so much that these laws give employees too many rights, but that the laws are complex and compliance can be tricky.

When leave qualifies under FMLA, a covered employer must do the following:

- grant an eligible employee up to 12 weeks of unpaid leave (26 weeks to care for a service member), including intermittent leave when medically necessary, within a 12-month period
- restore the employee to his or her former job upon return to work, or to an equivalent job
- maintain group health insurance coverage for the employee, including family coverage, on the same basis as if the employee had continued to work

⌂ ALERT!

Every employer covered by the FMLA is required to post a notice explaining the act's provisions and providing information concerning the procedures for filing complaints of violations with the Wage and Hour Division of the U.S. Department of Labor (DOL). If the employer has any eligible employees and has an employee handbook, it must also include the notice in its employee handbook. See *The Employer's Guide to the Family and Medical Leave Act,* available on the DOL's website.

Coverage and Eligibility

Employers are covered under the FMLA if they have 50 or more employees (including part-time employees and employees who are on leave) for at least 20 weeks during the current or preceding calendar year. An employee is potentially eligible for FMLA leave if each one of the following conditions is met:

- The employee works for a covered employer.
- The employee has been employed for at least 12 months (which need not be consecutive).
- The employee has worked at least 1,250 hours during the previous year.

- At least 50 employees work at the location where the employee works or within 75 miles of that location (as measured by the shortest route using service transportation).

Use of Leave

An eligible employee is entitled to FMLA leave in the following circumstances:

- The employee has a serious health condition (including incapacity due to pregnancy and for prenatal medical care).
- The employee needs to care for a spouse, child, or parent with a serious health condition.
- The employee is caring for a newborn child within one year of birth.
- The employee adopts a son or daughter or has a child placed with the employee for adoption or foster care within one year of placement.
- A qualifying exigency arises involving a family member who is called to active military duty.
- The employee needs to care for a spouse, parent, child, or next of kin who is a service member or recent veteran undergoing medical treatment, recuperation, or therapy in an outpatient status, or who is on the temporary disability retired list for a serious injury or illness that is service-related or that was aggravated in the line of duty.

Serious health condition is defined as an illness, injury, impairment, or physical or mental condition that involves any of the following:

- treatment as an in-patient in a hospital, hospice, or residential medical care facility
- a period of incapacity requiring absence of more than three days from work, school, or other regular activity and that involves continuing treatment by a health care provider
- any period of incapacity due to pregnancy or prenatal care

- any period of incapacity due to a chronic, serious health condition
- a period of incapacity that is permanent or long term, even if there is no effective treatment
- absences to receive multiple treatment in which the underlying condition, if left untreated, would likely result in incapacity of more than three consecutive days

DOL regulations expand on the statutory definition of serious health condition. DOL regulations say that a condition qualifies as serious if the employee is incapacitated for more than three consecutive calendar days and the condition requires treatment two or more times by a health care practitioner.

A *qualifying exigency* is one of the following events arising from the employee's spouse, child, or parent being called to active military duty:

- short-notice deployment in which a member of the military is called to active duty on less than seven days' notice
- military events and related activities, such as attending family support or assistance programs related to the active duty status of the service member
- child care and school activities, including arranging for alternative child care when a call to active duty necessitates a change in child care arrangements or providing child care on an urgent, immediate need basis
- financial and legal arrangements to address the member's absence for active duty
- counseling by someone other than a health care provider for oneself, for the service member, or for a child of the service member
- rest and recuperation, including spending time with a service member who is on short-term, temporary rest and recuperation—limited to 15 days
- post-deployment activities during the 90-day period following termination of the member's active duty status, including attend-

ing arrival ceremonies and events sponsored by the military or addressing issues arising from the death of the member while on active duty

- parental care to care for the parent of a service member who is incapable of self-care
- additional activities to address other events that arise out of the service member's call to active duty as the employer and employee agree

☞ **QUICK TIP**

For employers covered by the FMLA, unexplained or undocumented leave should never result in automatic discipline. The employer should first make an effort to determine whether the leave qualifies as FMLA leave and, if so, whether the employee wishes to take FMLA leave.

Medical Certification

The FMLA requires employers to respond promptly to employee requests for FMLA leave. Employers may require a *medical certification* from a health care provider if the leave is based on a serious health condition. The employer must allow the employee 15 days to obtain the certification. The employer may, at its own expense, obtain a second opinion from another health care provider of the employer's own choosing, so long as the health care provider is not under contract with, or regularly used by, the employer. If the two opinions differ, the employer and employee together choose a third health care provider, whose opinion is final and binding. Optional Form WH-380 (available on the DOL's website) may be used for these medical certifications.

An employer may also develop its own medical form, but it may not request information beyond what is allowed by the FMLA and implementing regulations.

The list of health care providers whose medical certifications can trigger FMLA leave is long and somewhat surprising. As might be expected, it includes doctors of medicine and osteopathy, but they need to be licensed only in the state in which they practice, not necessarily in the state where the employer or employee is located. The list also includes podiatrists, dentists, clinical psychologists, optometrists, chiropractors, nurse practitioners, nurse midwives, clinical social workers (as long as they are practicing within the scope of their licenses), Christian Science practitioners, and any health care provider recognized by the employer's health care benefits manager. Foreign as well as U.S.-licensed health care providers are included.

Employers must maintain the confidentiality of all medical information received in support of an FMLA leave request. Failure to do so could be deemed interference with the employee's FMLA rights or retaliation against the employee for requesting FMLA leave.

⌂ ALERT!

For disabilities covered by the ADA (or its state counterpart), the employer may be required to offer leave as a reasonable accommodation, provided doing so does not cause an undue hardship. A requirement to offer ADA leave is separate from FMLA leave requirements and may even extend beyond the 12-week FMLA obligation.

Benefits

An employee on FMLA leave is entitled to no more than 12 weeks' leave within a 12-month period (26 weeks in the case of certain service members). The employer has some options in determining when the 12-month period begins and ends:

- the calendar year
- the employer's fiscal year
- an employment year based on the employee's start date
- a rolling 12-month period that looks back from when the leave is to begin
- a rolling 12-month period that looks forward from when the leave is to begin

Using a fixed year, such as a calendar year, has the disadvantage that an employee could take 12 weeks' leave at the end of year

1 and another 12 weeks' leave at the beginning of year 2, for a total of 26 consecutive weeks. Therefore, some employers prefer the backward-looking, rolling 12-month period method. Under that method, the employer may deny a new FMLA leave request if, during the immediately preceding 12-months, the employee took the full 12-week entitlement.

Whatever option the employer chooses must be applied consistently to all employees.

⚐ ALERT!

When the leave is taken to care for a service member, only a 12-month period measured forward from the date the employee's FMLA leave is to begin may be used.

The employer must continue group health insurance coverage during FMLA leave on the same basis as if the employee had continued to work. This means that if the plan is *noncontributory* (meaning the employer pays 100 percent of the premium), the employer must continue to do so for employees under FMLA leave. On the other hand, if the plan is *contributory* (that is, if the employees pay some portion of their premiums), the employer may require an employee on FMLA leave to continue contributing on the same basis. The employer has a right to recover the employer's portion of the premiums if the employee does not return to work when FMLA leave ends, unless the employee's failure to return results from circumstances reasonably beyond the employee's control. If the employer has no group health plan, the employer does not have to provide health insurance during FMLA leave. The employer may, but is not required to, continue other benefits for employees on FMLA leave.

☞ QUICK TIP

When a husband and wife are employed by the same employer, they are entitled only to a combined total of 12 weeks' FMLA leave if the leave is based on the birth of a child or the placement with them of a child for adoption or foster care.

Among the most difficult FMLA issues facing employers are *intermittent leave* and *reduced work schedules* because of the possibility of abuse. DOL regulations make clear that intermittent leave (leave taken in separate blocks due to a single qualifying reason) and a reduced schedule (such as temporarily switching from full time to part time) are both available under the FMLA. When the qualifying reason is a serious health condition, there must be a medical need for the leave that can best be accommodated through intermittent leave or a reduced schedule. When the leave is to care for a healthy newborn, the employer need not agree to such a leave arrangement. In charging intermittent leave against an employee, the employer must use the smallest time increment the employer uses in charging other forms of leave, but in no event more than one hour.

Although FMLA leave is generally unpaid, the employee may choose to substitute any accrued paid leave he or she might have. If the employee does not choose to do so, the employer may require the employee to substitute paid leave. When either the employee or the employer makes the choice to substitute paid leave, the leave is still charged against both the employee's FMLA entitlement and the employee's accrued leave. In other words, in this situation FMLA leave and paid leave run concurrently.

☞ **QUICK TIP**

Under the Fair Labor Standards Act, an employee who is exempt under one of the white-collar exemptions must generally be paid a full week's salary for any workweek in which he or she does any work. (See Chapter 5.) However, when an exempt employee takes unpaid FMLA leave for part of a week, the employer may reduce the employee's salary to reflect his or her absence without affecting the employee's exempt status.

When FMLA leave ends, the employer is required to restore the returning employee to the same or an equivalent position. DOL regulations define *equivalent position* as one that is virtually identical to the employee's former position in terms of pay, benefits, and working conditions, including privileges, perquisites, and status. Assignment of an employee to a different shift on return from FMLA leave could violate the equivalent position requirement.

Compliance

Employers that are covered by the FMLA should follow these guidelines:

- Post the FMLA notice (WH Publication 1420) required by the DOL.
- Adopt an FMLA policy and publicize it to employees (see Fact Sheet No. 28 of DOL's Employment Standards Administration, available on the DOL's website).
- If the employer has an employee handbook or a collective bargaining agreement, set out the FMLA policy in those documents.
- Be alert to leave that may qualify under the FMLA and make inquiry to determine whether the FMLA might apply whenever an employee requests any type of leave—whether or not the employee even mentions the FMLA.
- Never discipline an employee for unauthorized absence without first determining whether the FMLA might apply.
- When an employee requests FMLA leave, notify the employee within five business days whether the leave will qualify under the FMLA, whether a medical certification or other documentation in support of the leave is required, and what the employee's rights and responsibilities are while on FMLA leave (DOL Form WH-381 satisfies the employer's notice requirements).
- Maintain group health insurance for the employee during FMLA leave on the same basis as if the employee had continued to work.
- Upon termination of FMLA leave, restore the employee to the same or an equivalent position.

The only exception to the duty to restore the employee to the same or equivalent position is for *key employees* whose absence would cause substantial and grievous economic injury to the operations of the employer—a tough standard to say the least. If the employer intends to deny restoration on this basis, the employer must first notify the affected employee and give the employee an opportunity to change his or her mind about taking FMLA leave.

FMLA leave may be terminated for an employee who states, unequivocally, that he or she does not intend to return to work or who fails to comply with the employer's requirement to furnish periodic reports justifying continued leave.

The question whether an employer may discipline an employee while on FMLA leave does not arise frequently. But it can arise when, for example, the employee's misconduct occurs before he or she takes FMLA leave. It is clear that an employer cannot discipline an employee *because* he or she is on FMLA leave, but nothing in the law prevents an employer from pursuing disciplinary action unrelated to the FMLA *while* an employee is on leave.

CASE STUDY:
MISCONDUCT WHILE ON FMLA LEAVE

In a 6th Circuit Court of Appeals case (the 6th Circuit is headquartered in Cincinnati), the employer had a policy prohibiting employees from performing outside work without the employer's permission. The employee in that case requested and was granted four weeks' FMLA leave in connection with his wife's childbirth, but while on leave he managed a restaurant that his wife had recently purchased. The employer fired the employee when he returned from leave, and the court upheld the firing. The court pointed out that the right to reinstatement under FMLA is not absolute, since an employer need not reinstate an employee who would have lost his job even if he had not taken FMLA leave. That was exactly the case here—the employee was fired for violating the company's outside work rule, not because he took FMLA leave.

The 6th Circuit decision relied on the DOL's FMLA regulations that list a number of principles governing the requirement that the employee be reinstated to the same or equivalent position on return to work:

- If an employee fails to provide a requested fitness-for-duty certification to return to work, an employer may delay restoration until the employee submits the certificate.
- An employee has no greater right to reinstatement or to other benefits and conditions of employment than if the employee had been continuously employed during the FMLA leave period.
- An employer may require an employee on FMLA leave to report periodically on the employee's status and intention to return to work.
- An employee who fraudulently obtains FMLA leave from an employer is not protected by the FMLA's job restoration or health benefits provisions.
- If the employer has a uniformly applied policy governing outside or supplemental employment, such a policy may continue to apply to an employee while on FMLA leave.

DOL regulations prohibit employers from discriminating or retaliating against employees and applicants who have taken FMLA leave. So an employer may not base a job decision on the fact that an existing employee, or a former employee who is reapplying, exercised rights under the FMLA. Similarly, if a job applicant took FMLA leave while with a *different* employer, the new employer cannot use that fact in deciding whether to hire.

Nor can an employer interfere with an employee's exercise of his or her FMLA rights. One way an employer might interfere is asking an employee on FMLA leave to do work. Continually pestering an employee about work issues could amount to interference. On the other hand, occasional, brief inquiries as to the location of a file or the status of a pending matter probably does not amount to interference.

CASE STUDY:
NO INTERFERENCE OR RETALIATION UNDER THE FMLA

In a case decided by the U.S. Court of Appeals for the 3rd Circuit (headquartered in Philadelphia), an employee took FMLA leave, claiming an inability to work because of leg pain. While on leave he went drinking with friends and on his way home was arrested and charged with DUI. The DUI was reported in the local paper, and when the employer saw the report, it realized that the drinking incident occurred while the employee was on leave. The employer fired its employee under the company's dishonesty policy. The court decided for the company, saying that the company acted on the honest belief that the employee violated company policy and misused FMLA leave.

An employer does not interfere with an employee's FMLA rights by requiring him or her to comply with a reasonable call-in policy in the event of an emergency or other unforeseeable need for leave. But a violation of the policy should not result in automatic discipline; instead, the employer should inquire whether unusual circumstances prevented the employee from complying with the policy.

AMERICANS WITH DISABILITIES ACT LEAVE

Granting leave may be a reasonable accommodation under the ADA. (The ADA is covered in depth in Chapter 17.) The Equal Employment Opportunity Commission (EEOC) offers the following examples of when ADA leave may be appropriate:

- obtaining medical treatment (for example, surgery, psychotherapy, substance abuse treatment, or dialysis), rehabilitation services, or physical or occupational therapy
- recuperating from an illness or an episodic manifestation of the disability
- obtaining repairs on a wheelchair, accessible van, or prosthetic device
- avoiding temporary adverse conditions in the work environment (for example, an air-conditioning breakdown causing unusually

warm temperatures that could seriously harm an employee with multiple sclerosis)
- training a service animal
- receiving training in the use of braille or to learn sign language

The courts have ruled, however, that an employer generally need not grant *indefinite leave* under the ADA, since an employee on indefinite leave is not able to perform the essential functions of his or her job. However, the employer should not deny leave just because the return date is uncertain; instead, the employer should consider the likely duration of the leave given the nature of the disability and whether accommodating such leave would be an undue hardship.

It should be noted that a *disability* under the ADA is not the same as a *serious health condition* under the FMLA. An employee may qualify for temporary leave under the ADA because he or she is disabled, but at the same time not qualify for FMLA leave because the disability does not amount to a serious health condition. The reverse is also true. For example:
- noncomplicated pregnancy, routine broken bone, appendectomy, chicken pox, mild hernia, flu—*covered only by the FMLA*
- vision or hearing impairment, physical abnormalities that do not require inpatient care or a continuing course of treatment—*covered only by the ADA*

MILITARY LEAVE

The *Uniformed Services Employment and Redeployment Rights Act* (USERRA) requires employers to carry service members on leave status for benefit and seniority purposes while on active duty and to re-employ them when they return. USERRA also prohibits employers from discriminating against veterans and persons in the uniformed services. USERRA applies to all service members except those who receive dishonorable or bad conduct discharges, or who are discharged under less than honorable conditions. It protects employees who volunteer for service as well as those ordered to active duty.

To be eligible for USERRA protection, the service member must notify the employer that he or she has been called to active duty, unless he or she is precluded from doing so by military necessity, or unless it is otherwise impossible or unreasonable to do so.

Employees on active duty are considered to be on furlough or leave of absence. As such, they are entitled to whatever benefits other similarly situated employees receive. In addition, the following conditions apply for employees on active duty:

- They may (but cannot be required to) use any accrued vacation or other paid leave.
- They may elect to continue any employer-sponsored health insurance coverage for up to 18 months. (For employees on active duty for less than 31 days, the employee can only be required to pay the portion of the premium normally charged to employees. For employees on active duty for more than 30 days, the employee can be charged up to 102 percent of the full premium.)
- They may continue to contribute to any retirement plan to which they were contributing before active duty.
- They must be treated as continuing to work for the employer for purposes of computing the employer's pension plan funding obligation and benefits under any pension plan in which they participated. (This would be significant for defined benefit plans using a formula that includes a years-of-service component.)

A returning service member is entitled to be re-employed unless the employer can show that the employer's circumstances have so changed as to make re-employment impossible or unreasonable or that re-employment would impose an undue hardship. This right applies to service members who have been on active duty for as long as five years, and, in some cases, even longer.

The returning service member is entitled to be placed in the position in which he or she would have been employed but for the call to active duty (or in a position with equivalent seniority, status, and pay). Under this *escalator* provision, the employer must take into consideration any promotions or advancements the member would have received if he or she had continued to work.

If a member who has been on active duty for more than 90 days is not qualified for an escalated position, the employer must make reasonable efforts to help the member become qualified. For returning service members who became disabled while on active duty, the employer must make reasonable efforts to accommodate the disability.

To be eligible for re-employment, the returning service member must, after release from active duty, notify the employer of his or her intent to return to work. Strict time limits apply to this notice requirement:

• If the period of active duty was less than 31 days, the returning member must report to work on the first regular workday after release from duty (after allowing for an eight-hour rest period and safe transportation home).

• If the period of active duty was between 31 and 181 days, the returning member must apply for re-employment within 14 days after release from duty.

• If the period of active duty was more than 180 days, the returning member must apply for re-employment within 90 days after release from duty.

These time limits can be extended for up to two years or more in the case of a returning service member who is hospitalized or convalescing from an illness or injury suffered while on active duty.

Once the employer has re-employed a returning service member, the employer is restricted in its ability to discharge the member. Except for discharges for cause, members who have been on active duty for 180 days or less cannot be fired for a period of 180 days after re-employment. Members who have been on active duty for more than 180 days cannot be fired for one year.

⏏ **ALERT!**

Docking the salary of exempt employees who are on temporary military leave of less than a full workweek will cause loss of the exemption for FLSA purposes. However, an employer may offset any compensation received by the employee for military service. (See Chapter 5 for more details.)

OTHER LEAVE

State laws frequently have their own provisions regarding required leave. Be alert to the following possibilities in your state.

Extended Leave

State FMLA laws are becoming increasingly popular, although eligibility and leave periods do not necessarily coincide with federal law.

Jury Duty

Federal law protects the jobs of employees who are serving as jurors in federal courts, and most states provide similar protection for employees serving at the state level. Some states even require salary continuation during periods of jury service. Even when salary continuation is not required, it is common for employers to pay full salary or at least make up the difference between juror fees and regular salary. Docking the salary of exempt employees who are on jury service of less than five days will cause loss of the exemption for FLSA purposes, although an employer may offset any juror fees received by the employee.

Figure 8.1 contains a provision recommended for inclusion in employee handbooks regarding jury duty.

FIGURE 8.1: JURY DUTY

The company encourages employees to fulfill their civic obligation to serve as jurors when summoned. The company will not discharge, threaten to discharge, intimidate, or coerce any employee by reason of such employee's jury service, or the attendance or scheduled attendance in connection with such service.

🔔 **ALERT!**
Asking an employee to lie about his or her availability for jury duty is a criminal offense.

Maternity and Paternity Leave
See Chapter 15.

Testimony
Some states protect the jobs of employees who are subpoenaed to appear in court as *witnesses* or who are attending court under a *victim's right* law. Docking the salary of exempt employees in these circumstances will cause loss of the exemption for FLSA purposes, although an employer may offset any witness fees received by the employee.

Election Day Leave
Some states require employers to grant time off for employees to vote on election day.

School Activities
Some states require that time off be granted for a parent to attend his or her child's school activities.

CHAPTER 9
Deferred Compensation and ERISA

- Qualified Plans
- Plans for Small Businesses
- ERISA
- Spousal Rights to Pension Benefits
- Other Deferred Compensation Arrangements

For a typical employer, the cost of employee benefits—together with other payroll costs like FICA and workers' compensation insurance—may be 25 percent or more of payroll. So, for every salary dollar promised an employee, the employer actually incurs at least $1.25—a significant factor when considering hiring an additional employee or raising salaries.

On the other hand, benefit plans help an employer attract and keep quality employees. Their costs are generally tax deductible by the employer, like wage and salary payments. Some benefit plans enjoy especially favorable tax treatment: even though the employer gets a current tax deduction for the cost of providing a benefit, the employee need not include the value of the benefit in current gross income for tax purposes. In other words, the benefit has a tax postponement feature. When taxation of earnings on benefit contributions—called *inside build-up*—is postponed, the benefit fund can grow more rapidly than the employee's other after-tax investments. Many deferred compensation arrangements qualify for this favorable tax treatment.

If properly designed and administered, some plans give the employer a current tax deduction for the cost of providing the benefit, but the benefit is *never* taxed to the employee. Group health insurance and certain life insurance plans fall in this category.

⚠ ALERT!

One of the risks of classifying workers as independent contractors is that if the Internal Revenue Service (IRS) disagrees and reclassifies them as employees, these new employees may demand benefit plan contributions for previous years. Worse, if a plan fails to include workers who should have been covered, the plan may lose its tax-qualified status.

These tax morsels come at a price. Employee benefit plans are highly regulated under tax and labor laws administered by the IRS and the U.S. Department of Labor (DOL). For example, a qualified plan cannot discriminate in favor of highly compensated individuals—it cannot give all the benefits to the boss and leave little or nothing for the rank and file. Qualified retirement plans must also meet strict funding and vesting requirements, so that the promised benefit is not illusory.

The design and operation of benefit plans are among the most complex tasks you are likely to face as an employer. It is best to hire an experienced *benefits consultant* who is familiar with the range of available options. A benefits consultant can project your future costs in managing and funding various plans, guide you through tax and labor law requirements, and help with plan administration.

QUALIFIED PLANS

A *qualified plan* is a benefit plan that is described in (and qualifies under) §401(a) of the Internal Revenue Code. Various types of plans qualify under §401(a), including the following:

- retirement plans
- profit-sharing plans
- employee stock ownership plans (ESOPs)

Some common characteristics of each of these plans are that contributions to the plan within specified limits are deductible for tax purposes by the employer, but are not immediately includable in the employee's gross income; that the accumulated benefits must *vest* (become nonforfeitable) within a specified time period; and that the plan itself is exempt from taxation of its income. In the case of qualified retirement plans, the right to withdraw funds from the plan is restricted before retirement, which can be as early as age 59½. Withdrawals become mandatory when the plan participant reaches age 70½ or later retires. (Retirement plan participants who hold a 5 percent or greater ownership interest in the sponsoring employer must begin mandatory withdrawals at age 70½ even if they keep working.)

Retirement plans generally fall into two broad categories—defined contribution plans and defined benefit plans.

Defined Contribution (Money Purchase) Plan

In a *defined contribution plan*, a separate account is established for each participating employee, into which the employer (and sometimes the employee) make regular contributions according to an established formula such as a percentage of salary. When an employee retires, the employee's retirement benefit is whatever has been contributed to his or her account, plus any income the account has earned through investments (but minus any investment losses the account has suffered). 401(k) plans and profit-sharing plans are defined contribution plans.

Defined Benefit Plan

In a *defined benefit plan*, there are no separate accounts for employees. Instead, there is simply a *common fund* out of which each retiring employee is entitled to a specified monthly benefit. The amount of the monthly benefit is usually based on a formula, such as years of service times the highest annual income, times some factor such as 1.5 percent, divided by 12. So for an employee earning $50,000 who retires after 30 years, the monthly benefit might be 30 x 50,000 x .015 / 12 = $,1875. The employer is obligated to keep sufficient assets in the fund based on actuarial computations to enable payment of the benefits when they come due.

The major differences between defined contribution and defined benefit plans are the following:

- *Separate account.* In a defined contribution plan, each employee has a separate account, whereas in a defined benefit plan there are no separate accounts but only a common fund.
- *Investment risk.* In a defined contribution plan, the employee wins if the market goes up and loses if the market goes down. In a defined benefit plan, the employer bears the investment risk.
- *Mortality risk.* If the employee lives for many years after retirement, he or she may use up all the funds in the defined contribution account. But if he or she had a defined benefit plan, the monthly annuity continues for life. In short, the employer bears

the mortality risk in a defined benefit plan; the employee usually bears that risk in a defined contribution plan.

- *Insurance.* Defined benefit plans are insured by the federal Pension Benefit Guaranty Corporation, for which the employer pays an insurance premium. Defined contribution plans are not insured because there is no guaranteed benefit at retirement.
- *Settlement options.* Defined benefit plans simply pay the prescribed monthly benefit. In a defined contribution plan, the retiring employee can usually use the amount in his or her account to purchase an annuity, optionally (and subject to spousal consent, as discussed later) take the account in a lump sum, or roll it over to an individual retirement account from which he or she may make periodic withdrawals.
- *Funding.* Defined contribution plans are always fully funded (assuming the employer actually makes the promised contribution), because the benefit is based on whatever is in the account. Defined benefit plans may become underfunded if investments do not turn out as expected or if retirees live longer than their life expectancies. For that reason, the employer must do an annual actuarial study of the plan and cover any shortfalls. Of course, if investments have performed better than expected, the employer's funding obligation in a defined benefit plan will be reduced.
- *Loading.* Defined benefit plans that use a years-of-service/highest-pay formula to determine benefits are said to be back-loaded because the size of the benefit produced by the formula tends to increase significantly in the last few years of employment. Defined contribution plans tend to be more front-loaded because the benefit amount grows at a more even rate.

Cash Balance Plans

Another item in the plan menagerie is the *cash balance plan.* Technically classified as a defined benefit plan, a cash balance plan has characteristics of both defined benefit and defined contribution plans. For that reason, cash balance plans are sometimes called *hybrids.*

☞ **QUICK TIP**

When an employer converts from a defined benefit plan to a cash balance plan, employees lose the back-loaded boost they had anticipated from their defined benefit plan.

In a cash balance plan, the employee establishes a hypothetical account for each employee. The account is hypothetical because there are no actual specific assets that belong to the employee; instead, all plan assets are in a common fund, as in a defined benefit plan.

The employer credits each hypothetical account with a specific dollar amount each year, usually based on a percentage of the employee's salary. In addition, the employer credits the account with interest earned on the account balance—either a fixed interest rate or a rate tied to treasury bills or some other index.

EXAMPLE: An employer establishes a cash balance plan under which it credits 8 percent of salary and which is deemed to earn interest at 7 percent per year compounded annually. For an employee who earns $35,000 per year, the balance in the hypothetical account will be $2,800 at the end of the first year (8 percent of $35,000). At the end of the second year, the balance in the account will be $5,796: the original $2,800, plus 7 percent interest on that amount ($196), plus another $2,800 credited at the end of the second year. When the employee retires, his or her benefit is based on whatever is then in the hypothetical account.

Because each employee has an account—albeit hypothetical—and because the amount of the ultimate benefit depends on what is in the account at retirement, cash balance plans look like defined contribution plans. Other characteristics, however, make them look like defined benefit plans. For example, if the fund earns more than the interest rate promised to employees (7 percent in the above example), the employer's funding obligation is reduced, and therefore the employer bears the investment risk.

Profit Sharing Plans

Profit sharing plans allow an employer to share company profits with employees. At the same time, they give the employer some flexibility in determining how much to contribute to the plan. Although the employer's contribution must be substantial and recurring to maintain the plan, the employer can change the contribution from year to year to track business cycles. Profit sharing plans are defined contribution plans, since each employee has an individual account and the ultimate benefit is a function of what is in the account. They are often used as retirement plans or at least as a component of a retirement plan, but they can also provide benefit payments at other times, such as after a fixed period of years, without regard to retirement.

401(k) Plans

401(k) plans (so called because they are authorized by §401(k) of the Internal Revenue Code) are a special type of defined contribution plan. Typically, the employee makes an election each year to contribute a certain percentage of salary. The employer then matches that election in some ratio, such as 100 percent of the employee's contribution up to 3 percent of the employee's salary and 50 percent of the employee's contribution that is between 3 percent and 5 percent of salary. Neither the employee's contribution nor the employer's match is subject to tax. In addition, 401(k) plans include a profit sharing component, by which the employer agrees to pay an additional percentage of employee salaries that the employee can elect to take in cash (which is taxable to the employee) or in the form of an additional contribution to the plan (which is nontaxable). The elective component of the plan is sometimes called a *cash or deferral arrangement* or CODA.

403(b) Plans

403(b) plans (also called tax-sheltered annuities) are only available to organizations that are exempt from income tax under §501(c)(3) of the Internal Revenue Code, such as educational organizations, churches, and public and private schools. (See Chapter 23 for more on exempt organizations.)

Employee Stock Ownership Plans

Employee stock ownership plans (ESOPs) are discussed in Chapter 10.

PLANS FOR SMALL BUSINESSES

Small businesses that are unwilling to incur the cost of establishing and maintaining a traditional pension plan have several attractive alternatives: a SIMPLE IRA plan, a SEP-IRA plan, and a payroll deduction IRA. These plans are easy and inexpensive to establish and operate, and they have no employer reporting requirements. Employees are always 100 percent vested.

SIMPLE IRA Plans

Under a *SIMPLE IRA plan* (SIMPLE stands for Savings Incentive Match Plan for Employees), each participating employee establishes an individual retirement account (IRA) with a financial institution either of his or her own choosing or one designated by the employer. The employer may allow all employees to participate, or it may limit participation to employees who earn at least $5,000 annually. These plans are generally limited to businesses with 100 or fewer employees.

Employees may, but are not required to, contribute to their own IRAs, up to a maximum of $12,500 per employee for calendar year 2017. The employer must contribute to each IRA each year, either by contributing a dollar-for-dollar match up to 3 percent of compensation for each employee or by contributing 2 percent of the employee's compensation up to a maximum of $270,000 for 2017. (Both the $12,500 and $270,000 limits are subject to cost-of-living adjustments after 2017.)

Simplified Employee Pension (SEP) Plans

Simplified employee pension (SEP) plans are available to businesses of any size. Under a SEP plan each participating employee sets up a

SEP-IRA with the financial institution designated by the employer. All employees who are at least 21 years old and who have worked for at least three of the past five years must be eligible to participate.

Only the employer may contribute to a SEP-IRA. The employer is not required to contribute each year; when the employer does contribute, the amount of the annual contribution is limited to the *lesser* of 25 percent of each employee's compensation for that year, or $53,000 (subject to future cost-of-living adjustments).

Payroll Deduction IRAs

A *payroll deduction IRA* is probably the easiest of all to establish and administer. Under this arrangement, each participating employee sets up his or her own IRA and authorizes the employer to deduct a specified amount from his or her compensation and remit it to the IRA—either a conventional IRA or a Roth IRA. Contributions are subject to the same limitations as individual IRAs. Employers do not contribute to payroll deduction IRAs.

ERISA

The Employee Retirement Income Security Act (ERISA) was passed in 1974 in response to abuses in the handling of pension funds. Before ERISA, it was not unusual for employers to make grossly unwise investments with pension funds, to underfund pension plans, to adopt a drawn-out vesting schedule, or to borrow from pension plans to cover operating expenses and then be unable to pay promised benefits when the time came. Employers also sometimes fired their senior workers just before those workers were to retire and become eligible for benefits. Top-heavy plans that favored owners or upper management were also common.

To cure these abuses, Congress enacted ERISA. ERISA has parallel labor law and tax law aspects. For example, ERISA has minimum participation and vesting requirements; it contains detailed reporting and disclosure requirements; it imposes fiduciary (trustee) standards on plan administrators; it requires defined benefit plans to be fully funded, meaning that the employer must contribute sufficient amounts on a current basis so that the promised benefits will be available at retirement time; and it even requires defined benefit plans to carry insurance against any shortfall in promised benefits should the plan terminate.

But ERISA goes far beyond pension plan abuses. Although it applies to employee benefit *pension* plans, it also applies to employee *welfare* benefit plans. Employee welfare benefit plans are defined by ERISA to include

> any plan, fund, or program ... established or maintained
> by an employer ... to the extent that such plan, fund, or
> program was established or is maintained for the purpose of
> providing for its participants or their beneficiaries, through
> the purchase of insurance or otherwise, ... medical, surgical,
> or hospital care or benefits, or benefits in the event of sick-
> ness, accident, disability, death or unemployment, or vaca-
> tion benefits, apprenticeship or other training programs, or
> day care centers, scholarship funds, or prepaid legal services.

In short, ERISA applies to almost every ongoing plan or program an employer has for providing group benefits to employees. The only exceptions are plans that are maintained solely to comply with workers' compensation or unemployment insurance laws, plans maintained by tax-exempt churches or associations of churches, and certain unfunded plans. In addition to those exceptions, the DOL has, by regulation, recognized that traditional payroll practices and unfunded vacation benefits are not ERISA welfare benefit plans.

CASE STUDY:
BENEFITS AS ERISA PLAN

A company with business interests in Latin America entered into an employment agreement with its vice president of Latin America operations. The agreement provided severance benefits, the amount of which varied depending on whether the vice president's employment terminated for cause, without cause, or by death or disability. Some seven years later the company fired the vice president without cause, but refused to pay any severance benefits. In response to the vice president's subsequent lawsuit, a federal court in Pennsylvania ruled that the severance provisions of the employment agreement constituted an ERISA plan because the agreement required the company to exercise discretion in deciding whether a termination was for cause or without cause, and because the benefits payable upon a termination without cause extended over a number of years.

In another case, a grocery store chain in the New Orleans area issued to its retired employees vouchers that they could use instead of cash to purchase goods at the chain's stores. When the chain decided to sell its business, it canceled the voucher arrangement, and retirees who had been receiving the vouchers sued. The 5th Circuit Court of Appeals (headquartered in New Orleans) ruled that the plan was subject to ERISA so that the retirees were entitled to money damages for loss of their vested pension benefit.

Preemption

What makes ERISA particularly powerful is its *preemption provision*. By its own terms, ERISA supersedes any and all state laws relating to employee benefit plans. One of Congress's purposes in enacting this preemption provision was to create a uniform body of *federal* law governing the administration of employee benefit plans.

In general, ERISA requires every employee benefit plan to meet the following requirements:

* be in writing
* place its assets in a trust (except when the assets of the plan consist of insurance contracts or policies)
* name one or more fiduciaries to administer the plan
* describe how the plan is to be funded
* describe the basis on which benefits are paid
* describe claim procedures

Employers must provide employees with a *summary plan description* (SPD) for every benefit plan covered by ERISA. SPDs describe plan eligibility requirements and procedures for claiming benefits and appealing benefits denials. SPDs must be provided within 90 days after an employee becomes a participant in the plan and after any significant modification of the plan. In addition, employers must provide SPDs every 5 years if there have been any amendments to the plan and every 10 years if there have not been any amendments. The actual plan documents must be made available to participants and beneficiaries on request.

Employers must file Form 5500 with the IRS each year for most types of benefit plans. The form is due on the last day of the seventh month after the end of each plan year. For plans that operate on a calendar year, the due date is July 31. The form calls for information as to the plan's financial condition, participation, and funding.

ERISA prohibits employers from interfering with employee rights under a plan or retaliating against employees for exercising plan rights. Employers are also prohibited from firing employees or taking other adverse action to avoid paying benefits. While an employer can, by amendment, reduce benefits under a plan (assuming the plan document permits such amendments) or even terminate a plan entirely, such actions cannot affect vested or accrued benefits.

⚠ ALERT!

Under the Patient Protection and Affordable Care Act (discussed in Chapter 10), employers with 50 or more full-time employees or full-time equivalent employees are required to offer health insurance to their full-time employees. Since *full-time* is defined generally as working at least 30 hours a week, some employers have reduced employee schedules to below 30 hours to avoid PPACA obligations. A federal district court in New York ruled that doing so violated ERISA because it interfered with the employees' ERISA rights.

Fiduciary Responsibilities

The fiduciary responsibilities imposed on persons who manage ERISA plans deserve mention. ERISA places managers in a special trust relationship with plan participants and beneficiaries. For example, plans must be managed in the best interests of participants and beneficiaries; they must segregate plan assets from the employer's operating funds, and plans (except ESOPs) are prohibited from engaging in transactions with the employer. Employers and individual managers can be held *personally liable* for a breach of these fiduciary duties.

When an employer communicates with employees about an ERISA benefit plan, the employer may be acting in a fiduciary (trustee) capacity. If so, the employer will be held to a much higher standard of truthfulness, accuracy, and completeness than if communicating just in an employer capacity. The dangers are especially great for ESOPs, in which company owners who also serve as fiduciaries routinely find themselves in conflict-of-interest situations. (See *Meeting Your Fiduciary Responsibilities*, available on the DOL's website.)

Employers can also get into trouble in the area of pension plan investments. Suppose a plan allows the participating employee to direct investments within his or her account, or it provides the participant with choices among a number of mutual funds, each of which has a different objective or investment strategy. In general, employers should not give investment *advice* to their employees, since giving investment advice may make them liable as fiduciaries. However, plan sponsors have an obligation to *educate* their employees about investment choices so that the employees themselves can make informed decisions.

The DOL has issued guidelines to help employers walk the fine line between advice and education. Under DOL guidelines, employers may provide the following in satisfaction of the affirmative obligation, without becoming a fiduciary:

• plan information, such as the benefits of plan participation, the benefits of increasing plan contributions, the impact of pre-retirement withdrawals, investment alternatives, and historical return information

- general financial and investment information, including investment concepts like diversification, risk and return, compounding, and investment time horizons
- asset allocation models that provide hypothetical results based on differing assumptions of age, age to retirement, life expectancy, inflation rates, time horizons, risk profiles, etc.
- interactive investment materials, such as worksheets and software, that enable the participant to estimate future retirement income needs and to assess the impact of different asset allocations.

When an employee becomes eligible for a pension plan distribution, plan administrators are also required to provide a written explanation of distribution options. An employee at a prominent chemical company, for example, successfully sued the company based on bad advice the company gave about the tax consequences of a rollover distribution from one of its pension plans.

SPOUSAL RIGHTS TO PENSION BENEFITS

ERISA intentionally makes it difficult for pension plan participants to divert benefits from their spouses. The law requires that when a plan participant retires and he or she has a spouse, benefits must be payable in the form of a *joint and survivor annuity*—an annuity that will be paid to the husband and wife jointly and that will continue to be paid (at a 50 percent rate) to the surviving spouse if the plan participant dies first. In order for benefits to be paid in some other fashion, such as to a different beneficiary or in a lump sum, the spouse must consent, and the consent must satisfy the following statutory requirements:

- be in writing
- designate another specific beneficiary, which may not be changed without the spouse's further consent (unless the spouse expressly agrees to further changes without consent)
- acknowledge the effect of the change
- be witnessed by a plan representative or notary public

Courts require strict compliance with these spousal consent requirements and will not enforce a consent unless requisite procedures have been followed.

Issues arise when parties who are about to be married enter into a prenuptial agreement in which each party waives any legal claim he or she might otherwise have in the other's property, including claims to the other's pension benefits. Several courts have ruled that only a *spouse* can execute a valid consent, so that in a prenuptial agreement, in which the parties are not yet married, a waiver of pension plan benefits is ineffective. Other courts have reached a contrary conclusion.

A similar issue arises in the case of a voluntary separation agreement in which a divorcing couple resolves property and support issues, including claims to each other's pension plans. At least one federal court of appeals has indicated that ERISA's statutory requirements are *not* applicable in a divorce context, so that a voluntary separation agreement in which one spouse gives up any claim against the other's pension is effective so long as the agreement specifically refers to the plan involved.

Until the Supreme Court definitively resolves these issues, pension plan administrators are in a quandary. Suppose a plan participant dies, and the participant's child claims benefits based on a separation agreement or prenuptial agreement that waives all spousal rights. However, the surviving spouse (who has since had a change of heart) also claims benefits, arguing that the waiver is invalid. If the plan administrator pays one of the claimants, the other might sue and force the administrator to pay again. So the safest course may be for the plan administrator to go to court and ask a federal judge to decide who is entitled—thereby incurring exactly the kind of expense and delay ERISA was designed to avoid.

Creditors' Claims and QDROs

ERISA requires plans to contain a provision exempting plan benefits from an employee's creditors. In other words, if an employee fails to pay a personal obligation and is sued, and a court judgment is entered against the employee, the party who holds the judgment cannot go after pension plan assets to satisfy the judgment. But again, spouses receive special protection. In a divorce proceeding, even if the parties have not reached agreement on how pension benefits should be allocated, the divorce court can issue a *qualified domestic relations order* (QDRO), awarding one spouse a portion (or all) of the other spouse's pension plan as alimony, child support, or as a division of marital property.

☞ **QUICK TIP**

One way to avoid the uncertainty surrounding the effect of a voluntary separation agreement (but not a prenuptial agreement) is to ask the divorce court to bless the agreement by entering a QDRO incorporating the provisions of the agreement that address pension plan rights.

To be recognized as a QDRO, an order must be made pursuant to state domestic relations law that relates to alimony, child support, or marital property rights for the benefit of someone who qualifies as an alternate payee—a spouse, former spouse, child, or other dependent. A separation or property settlement agreement between divorcing spouses will not qualify as a QDRO unless the agreement's provisions otherwise satisfy ERISA requirements *and* the agreement is approved by an order of the domestic relations court. (The term *court* here includes administrative agencies if they have the power under state law to issue support orders.)

The DOL takes the reasonable view that even before a QDRO is entered, the employer or plan administrator has an obligation to furnish a potential alternate payee (such as a spouse or dependent child) with information about the pension plan, the participating employee's benefit status, and interest in the plan. No such information should be furnished, however, without first obtaining satisfactory evidence that a domestic relations proceeding is in fact pending and that the potential alternate payee is attempting to obtain a QDRO in that proceeding. It also makes for good employee relations to notify the participating employee that plan information has been requested.

Another aspect of ERISA's preemption provision is illustrated by a Supreme Court case involving a Washington state statute. The statute said that a divorce decree had the effect of automatically revoking a beneficiary designation in favor of a former spouse. Presumably, the Washington legislature felt that after a plan participant gets divorced, he or she probably does not want an ex-spouse to receive plan benefits, even if he or she forgets to submit a beneficiary change. The Supreme Court invalidated the statute, saying that under ERISA the plan documents themselves govern the determination of who is the right beneficiary.

OTHER DEFERRED COMPENSATION ARRANGEMENTS

Top Hat and Excess Benefit Plans

Suppose that a company wants to hire away the star employee from one of its competitors and make that person its new CEO. The company is willing to pay whatever salary or bonus may be necessary to attract the star, but because of his or her tax status, the star does not really want or need more current taxable income. And making additional contributions to the company's qualified retirement plan for the star will not work because of the maximum contribution limits imposed by law. So the company promises to pay the new CEO deferred compensation on some future date. The amount promised may be a specified sum together with imputed earnings on that sum over the deferral period, or it may be tied to company performance or determined by some other formula.

⚠ ALERT!

Before making any final hiring commitments, the company should determine whether the star employee is bound by a noncompete agreement. (See Chapter 19 for a discussion of noncompete agreements.)

In terms of the tax consequence of this arrangement, all the new CEO is getting is a mere promise of compensation in the future (so long as the company does not *fund* the promise by setting aside amounts for the benefit of the CEO). Since no actual compensation is received by the CEO or subject to the CEO's control, he or she does not have to report the compensation as current income. At the same time, however, since all the employer has given is a mere promise, the employer receives no current deduction. Of course, when the CEO eventually receives the compensation (or once he or she is in *constructive receipt* of the compensation—defined as credited to the CEO's account or otherwise made available to him or her), he or she will have to report it as income, and the company may then claim it as a deductible expense.

⚠ ALERT!

If the arrangement is considered a nonqualified deferred compensation plan (discussed later in this chapter), and it does not meet the requirements for deferring tax on the compensation, the compensation may be immediately taxable to the employee.

In terms of ERISA, since the arrangement is not a plan and it is unfunded, it is not subject to any ERISA requirements. But suppose the company decides to establish more formal deferred compensation arrangements for the benefit of a number of high-level company executives. Will that trigger the tax and labor law provisions of ERISA? ERISA itself offers two techniques for avoiding, or at least reducing, the compliance burdens and limitations imposed by the statute.

A *top hat plan* is an *unfunded* plan the employer maintains *primarily* for the purpose of providing deferred compensation to a select group of management or highly compensated employees. Top hat plans are exempt from ERISA's vesting, participation, funding, and fiduciary rules, but they are subject to ERISA's enforcement provisions. This means that an employee who is a beneficiary of a top hat plan can sue the employer in federal court to collect promised benefits.

An *excess benefit plan* is an *unfunded* plan the employer maintains *solely* for the purpose of providing benefits for certain employees in excess of the limitations on contributions and benefits imposed by §415 of the Internal Revenue Code (I.R.C.). Excess benefit plans are not subject to either the substantive or the enforcement provisions of ERISA.

The italicized terms—*unfunded, primarily*, and *solely*—are critical. As used here, *unfunded* refers to whether the employer has actually set money aside, typically in a trust, to make good the promise of deferred compensation. If benefits are paid out of the employer's general assets and if employees have no greater rights to those assets than the employer's other creditors, the plan will be considered *unfunded*.

The purpose or purposes of the plan are also determinative. A top hat plan may have a number of purposes, including avoidance of various limitations imposed by the tax code. But to be an excess benefit plan, the plan must be limited to the single purpose of providing benefits in excess of I.R.C. §415 limitations.

Rabbi Trusts

Although top hat and excess benefit plans must be unfunded, the IRS has approved arrangements under which the employer can actually establish a trust as a *repository* for accumulating benefits, so long as trust assets remain subject to claims by the employer's creditors. The trust documents may establish broad investment policies, although specific investment authority must remain with the employer-designated trustee of the trust and cannot be given to the employee-beneficiaries. (If specific investment authority were given to the employee, the employee would be deemed to be in constructive receipt of the funds and they would be immediately taxable to him or her.) This type of trust is known as a *rabbi trust* because the first IRS ruling on such an arrangement involved a retirement plan adopted by a congregation for its rabbi.

To facilitate the adoption of rabbi trusts (and to reduce the IRS's burden of responding to ruling requests), the IRS in 1992 issued a

Revenue Procedure that sets out a model trust form that employers may use.

While a rabbi trust may give participating employees some level of assurance that the employer will eventually make good on its promise of deferred compensation, employees need to realize that trust assets still remain subject to claims by the company's creditors and that the employees may end up with nothing if the company fails.

Nonqualified Deferred Compensation

The American Jobs Creation Act of 2004 added §409A to the Internal Revenue Code for taxing compensation under *nonqualified deferred compensation plans.* The effect of the provision is to ignore artificial arrangements for spreading out compensation over multiple years, and instead tax compensation when it is actually earned.

For purposes of §409A, a *deferred compensation plan* is any arrangement under which an employee or independent contractor receives a legally binding right to compensation in one year but is not in actual or constructive receipt of that compensation until a later year. Short-term deferrals of up to 2 and one-half months after the end of a year are not considered deferrals, so that year-end bonuses that are not actually paid until February or early March are taxed to the employee in year 2, not year 1.

A *nonqualified* deferred compensation plan is any plan that provides for deferred compensation except a *qualified* employee plan (such as those discussed earlier in this chapter) and except a bona fide vacation, sick leave, compensatory time, disability pay, or death benefit plan. A *plan* is any arrangement or agreement with one or more persons. Compensation is *constructively received* when it is credited to an employee's or independent contractor's account or when it is otherwise made available to him or her.

Under §409A, deferred compensation pursuant to a nonqualified deferred compensation plan is subject to immediate taxation to the recipient, plus a 20 percent additional tax, unless the compensation is subject to a substantial risk of forfeiture, or unless the plan complies with detailed requirements relating to the timing of elections, funding, and distributions. Although the law does not define substantial risk of forfeiture, it does give the example of compensation that is conditioned on the future performance of substantial services.

In general, compensation distributed after an employee or independent contractor terminates, becomes disabled, or dies is subject to taxation when received, rather than to immediate taxation in the year the right to receipt arose. In the case of termination of service by a specified employee, however, distributions cannot be made until six months after the termination. A *specified employee* is any officer of a company with publicly traded stock whose annual compensation exceeds $130,000, an owner of a publicly traded company who owns more than 5 percent of the company, or an owner who owns more than 1 percent of the company and whose annual compensation exceeds $150,000. (The $130,000 and $150,000 compensation amounts are subject to future cost-of-living adjustments.)

Severance agreements offered to departing executives need to be drafted with the nonqualified deferred compensation rules in mind to avoid unanticipated tax consequences.

CHAPTER 10
Group Health and Other Benefit Plans

- Patient Protection and Affordable Care Act
- HSAs and Other Tax-Favored Plans
- COBRA
- Mandated Benefits
- Qualified Medical Child Support Orders
- Claims Administration
- Stock Options
- Employee Stock Ownership Plans
- Other Plans

Group health insurance competes with retirement plans as the most common type of employee benefit plan. Various funding arrangements are available. For example, the employer may pay the entire premium, in which case the plan is called *noncontributory*. Or the employer may adopt a *contributory* plan requiring the employees to contribute some of the premium. For qualified health insurance plans, whatever portion of the premium the employer pays is deductible to the employer. Even better, the employee does not pay income tax either on the portion of the premium paid by the employer or on the value of the medical services when received.

Various risk-sharing and administrative arrangements also are available. For smaller companies, probably the most common arrangement is for a health insurer both to administer the plan and to assume the full risk, subject only to deductible and co-pay requirements. As companies get larger, they may want to undertake some of the administrative burdens, and they may also want to self-insure some or most of the risk. Some companies self-insure as to routine claims and buy a *stop-loss policy* that kicks in when claims reach an agreed level.

Companies that self-insure may self-administer. Alternatively, they may hire their stop-loss carrier to administer the plan, or they may hire a third-party administrator (TPA) to handle claims and other administrative burdens. When the plan participants—the employee and any covered family members—choose their own health care providers and the insurance company reimburses the employee or pays the provider directly according to some policy formula, the plan is known as an *indemnity plan*.

The past 50 years have seen an explosive growth in *managed care plans*, driven largely by efforts to contain health care costs. Managed care plans are primarily subscription-based, such as *preferred provider organizations* (PPOs) and *health maintenance organizations* (HMOs) rather than indemnity plans. In a subscription-based plan, the subscriber (the participating employee or his or her employer) pays a fixed fee in exchange for whatever medical services he or she may need. The plan participant is required to stay within the provider network and pays nothing or only a nominal amount when medical care is received. If the participant goes out of plan, he or she may not be covered at all or may have a substantial co-pay obligation.

Managed care plans attempt to contain health care costs in other ways as well. For example, some plans use general practice physicians, internists, or family practitioners as gatekeepers who must approve referrals to specialists. Pre-certifications for hospitalizations and surgeries are also common in both managed care plans and indemnity plans.

Group health plans usually impose a participation requirement that allows for cancellation of the group contract unless at least a minimum number of employees (such as 75 percent) participate in the plan. This helps ensure that the group is broadly representative of the workforce. It avoids anti-selection in which only less healthy employees elect to participate. Also, participation is usually limited to employees who work at least a specified number of hours per year, such as 1,000.

☞ **QUICK TIP**
Provisions in group health plans that exclude or limit coverage for particular disabilities could violate the Americans with Disabilities Act. (See Chapter 17 for more on disability discrimination.)

PATIENT PROTECTION AND AFFORDABLE CARE ACT

The *Patient Protection and Affordable Care Act* (PPACA), signed in 2010 and gradually becoming effective over a period of years, is a massive effort to regulate the health insurance industry and, at the same time, extend coverage to (or force coverage on) millions of uninsured Americans. Among its insurance regulatory provisions are the following:

• a prohibition on lifetime or unreasonable annual limits of benefits
• a prohibition on rescinding coverage (except for fraud or misrepresentation)

- a requirement to cover preventive services and immunizations
- a requirement that plans offering dependent coverage allow unmarried children to remain covered under their parents' policies until age 26
- a prohibition on pre-existing condition exclusions
- guaranteed availability and renewability of coverage
- a limitation on waiting periods

The PPACA also prohibits exclusion of individuals from participation in or obtaining benefits from any health insurance program or activity on any of the grounds listed in various federal civil rights and nondiscrimination laws.

Unless exempt, individuals who fail to secure *minimum essential coverage*, either under their employer's group plan (if offered) or privately through individual policies, must pay a penalty for each month they are not covered. The penalty is reportable on and payable with their income tax returns. Health insurance marketplaces (called *exchanges*) are established, either by individual states, or by the U.S. government in states that fail to establish exchanges, to facilitate the purchase of insurance. Individuals below certain income levels may qualify to have their premiums subsidized.

☞ **QUICK TIP**

As of this writing, efforts by Congress to repeal the PPACA have been unsuccessful. Although President Trump directed federal agencies to minimize the economic burden imposed by the PPACA, the IRS has confirmed that it will continue to enforce the employer shared responsibility provisions of the law.

Employer Shared Responsibility

The PPACA imposes insurance obligations on *applicable large employers* (ALEs). An ALE is an employer with 50 or more full-time employees, including full-time equivalents. A full-time employee is someone who works on average at least 30 hours a week or 130 hours per month. The hours of part-time employees are aggregated so that, for example, two part-timers who each work 15 hours per week amount to one full-time equivalent.

An ALE is required to offer *minimum essential coverage* that is *affordable* and that provides *minimum value* to all its full-time employees and their dependents. Although part-time employee hours are aggregated to determine full-time equivalents in determining whether an employer is an ALE, part-timers are not required to be covered by the PPACA. For PPACA purposes, a *dependent* is a child of the employee (including an adopted child and a child placed with the employee for adoption) who is under 26 years of age. A spouse is not considered a dependent, nor is a stepchild or foster child.

🔔 ALERT!

Reducing an employee's hours below 30 per week to avoid having to offer him or her health insurance may constitute unlawful interference with the employee's rights in violation of the Employee Retirement Income Security Act (ERISA).

Employers with 200 or more employees must automatically enroll their employees in a plan providing minimum essential coverage. Enrolled employees must be given notice that they are enrolled and an opportunity to opt out.

🔔 ALERT!

Automatic enrollment in a contributory plan—a plan in which the employee pays a portion of the premium—could conflict with state wage and hour laws, which generally prohibit any payroll deductions unless required by law or authorized by the employee.

Minimum Essential Coverage and Minimum Value

Any job-based plan, including COBRA coverage, satisfies the *minimum essential coverage* requirement, presumably because it must comply with the insurance regulatory provisions listed above.

A plan offers *minimum value* if it is designed to pay at least 60 percent of the total cost of medical services for a standard population, and its benefits include substantial coverage of physician and inpatient hospital services. A plan at the 60 percent level is called a *bronze* plan, 70 percent coverage is *silver*, 80 percent coverage is *gold*, and 90 percent coverage is *platinum*.

Affordability

In general, affordability is measured on an employee-by-employee, month-by-month basis. A plan is *affordable* if the employee is required to pay no more than 9.69 percent of the employee's total household income for self-only coverage under the lowest-priced plan offered by the employer. *Total household income* means income from everybody in the employee's household who is required to file a tax return. Even though the plan must include dependent coverage, only the cost of self-only coverage is considered in determining affordability: the plan still qualifies as affordable if the employee's cost exceeds 9.69 percent of household income to cover dependents, to cover a spouse (if the employer offers that coverage), or to upgrade to a better, costlier plan that the employer may also offer. The plan will also qualify as affordable even if the total premium for self-only coverage is much more than 9.69 percent, so long as the employer pays the difference.

In an effort to simplify the affordability calculation, the U.S. Department of the Treasury permits ALEs to rely on one of three safe harbors explained in department regulations. To qualify for any of the safe harbors, an ALE must offer its full-time employees and their dependents the opportunity to enroll in minimum essential coverage. The plan will be considered affordable for a particular employee if it meets one of the following:

- *Form W-2 safe harbor.* The plan is offered for an entire calendar year, and the employee's cost for that year does not exceed 9.69 percent of the employee's W-2 wages for that year.
- *Rate of pay safe harbor.* For an hourly employee, the employee's cost for a particular calendar month does not exceed 9.69

percent of the employee's lowest hourly pay rate for the month multiplied by 130; and for a salaried employee, the employee's cost for a particular month does not exceed 9.69 percent of the employee's salary for that month.

• *Federal poverty line safe harbor.* The employee's cost for a particular calendar month does not exceed 9.69 percent of a monthly amount determined as the federal poverty line for a single individual for the current calendar year, divided by 12.

☞ **QUICK TIP**

Although affordability is measured on an employee-by-employee basis, one way to avoid numerous affordability calculations is to set the maximum amount any employee has to pay at 9.69 percent of the lowest-paid employee.

Shared Responsibility Payments

To avoid any *shared responsibility payment*, an ALE must offer minimum essential coverage, that has minimum value and that is affordable, to at least 95 percent of its full-time employees and dependents. The employer is required only to *offer* such coverage; it is up to each employee whether to participate.

The PPACA imposes two types of shared responsibility payments on employers that fail to offer affordable plans with at least minimum value. The first type of payment is triggered if at least one full-time employee purchases coverage through an exchange and receives a premium tax credit. The payment applies for each month the employer fails to offer coverage. On an annual basis, the payment is $2,000 (indexed for future years) for each full-time employee, with the first 30 employees excluded from the calculation. If an ALE with, say, 60 employees fails to offer coverage for a full 12 months, and at least one employee receives a premium tax credit on an exchange purchase of coverage, the payment would be $60,000 (30 x $2,000).

The second type of payment applies if an employer does offer minimum essential coverage to at least 95 percent of its full-time employees, but the coverage does not provide minimum value or is not affordable. This payment is also triggered if at least one full-time employee purchases coverage through an exchange and receives a premium tax credit. On an annual basis, the payment is equal to $3,000 (indexed for future years) for each full-time employee who receives a premium tax credit.

To establish compliance with the PPACA, ALEs must file IRS Form 1095-C for each of their employees (using transmittal Form 1094-C) by February 25 each year (March 31 if they are filing electronically). A copy of Form 1095-C goes to each employee as proof of availability of coverage or, if applicable, to establish eligibility for a premium subsidy when purchasing individual insurance through an exchange.

Small Employers

Small employers—employers with fewer than 50 employees—are, of course, encouraged to offer health insurance, but they are not subject to the PPACA's shared responsibility payments if they do not.

Small employers can purchase affordable group health coverage through the Small Business Health Options Program (SHOP). And employers with fewer than 25 employees and average annual wages of less than $52,000 (indexed for future years) are entitled to a sliding-scale credit against their income tax if they purchase insurance through the SHOP marketplace and pay at least half their employees' premiums.

Cadillac Plans

The PPACA added yet another provision to the tax code, imposing a 40 percent excise tax on the excess benefit provided by so-called *Cadillac plans*. The excess benefit is the monthly amount by which the plan cost exceeds the applicable dollar limit for the month. The applicable dollar limit is currently $10,200 (divided by 12) per employee for self-only coverage and $27,500 (divided by 12) for nonself-only coverage (coverage for the employee and a spouse or dependent). The dollar amounts are indexed for 2018 and thereafter and are subject to various other upward adjustments. The excise tax is now scheduled to take effect beginning in 2020.

HIPAA

The federal *Health Insurance Portability and Accountability Act* (HIPAA) imposed a number of requirements on group health plans to make health coverage more portable, so that when an employee changes jobs, he or she will more quickly qualify for full coverage from the new employer without regard to pre-existing conditions. The PPACA has made most of these requirements irrelevant.

⚠ ALERT!

U.S. Department of Health and Human Services regulations under HIPAA impose strict confidentiality requirements on the handling of protected health information (PHI) relating to employees. (Chapter 18 provides details on employee privacy rights.)

HSAs AND OTHER TAX-FAVORED PLANS

The Internal Revenue Code permits various tax-favored arrangements to help employees and other individuals offset health care expenses, including health savings accounts, health flexible spending arrangements, and health reimbursement arrangements. Dependent care flexible spending arrangements may also be used to cover dependent care expenses. A general feature of these plans is that they reimburse medical expenses with before-tax dollars, and the reimbursement benefit is not taxable income. This tax treatment is similar to the employee's taking a deduction on his or her tax return for uninsured medical expenses. However, medical expense deductions are limited to employees who itemize deductions and are further limited to expenses that are greater than 7.5 percent of the employee's adjusted gross income. Therefore, from the employee's viewpoint, the practical benefit of these plans is that it allows him or her to deduct *all* uninsured medical expenses, rather than just those that are above the 7.5 percent floor, whether or not he or she itemizes.

Health Savings Accounts

A *health savings account* (HSA) is a trust or custodial account an employee sets up with a bank, other financial institution, or a trustee approved by the IRS. An HSA may be established only if the employee is covered by a *high-deductible health plan* (HDHP)—a plan that meets the following requirements (figures are for 2018; they are indexed for future years):

* It has a minimum annual deductible of $1,350 for self-only coverage and $2,700 for family coverage.
* It has a maximum annual out-of-pocket expense limit (other than for premiums) of $6,550 for self-only coverage and $13,300 for family coverage.

Contributions to an HSA may be made by the employer, the employee, or both, subject to maximum contributions from all sources (for 2018) of $3,450 for self-only coverage and $6,900 for family coverage. The contribution limits for employees age 55 and older are increased by $1,000, but the limits go to zero for employees enrolled in Medicare.

The employee's contributions are excludible from taxable income (if made through a payroll deduction) and are deductible by the employee (if paid with after-tax dollars), even if the employee does not itemize deductions. The employer's contributions are deductible by the employer, yet not includable in the employee's taxable income. Income earned on the account is tax-exempt.

After an employee has paid medical expenses up to the annual amount of the HDHP deductible (which can be paid out of the HSA), he or she may be reimbursed tax free from the HSA for subsequent qualified medical expenses of the employee and his or her spouse and dependents. In general, a *qualified medical expense* is an expense that would qualify for deduction as a medical expense on the employee's individual tax return, including the following:

* prescription drugs
* over-the-counter drugs that are prescribed

- insulin
- long-term-care insurance premiums (subject to certain limits based on age)
- premiums for COBRA coverage
- premiums for Medicare and other health care coverage (but not premiums for a Medicare supplemental policy)

Amounts on deposit in an HSA can be carried over from year to year and applied to future medical expenses, even expenses incurred after the employee is no longer eligible to make contributions to the account.

☞ **QUICK TIP**
Archer medical savings accounts (MSAs) are similar to HSAs, in that they are tied to a high-deductible health plan, but they are limited to employees of small employers and to the self-employed. MSAs are also more restrictive than HSAs in terms of who can contribute and in what amounts. The MSA pilot program has since been discontinued, although contributions may continue to be made to existing plans.

Flexible Spending Arrangements
A *flexible spending arrangement* (FSA) is an employer-sponsored benefit program. It is typically part of a cafeteria plan, to which both the employee and the employer may contribute pretax funds that then reimburse the employee for qualified health care, dependent care, or adoption expenses. So long as the reimbursements are for qualified expenses, they are not taxable to the employee.

Health Flexible Spending Arrangements
A *health FSA* allows employees to put aside before-tax dollars to cover uninsured medical expenses. Once an employer has approved inclusion of an FSA in its cafeteria plan, each employee individually designates the amount of his or her income for the following plan year to be paid in the form of regular payroll deductions into a fund established by the employer. The amount designated is decided

by the employee, subject to any outside limit imposed by the plan and to the overall annual limit of $2,600. Employers may also contribute to the fund without limitation. Like HSAs, both employee and employer contributions are excluded from the employee's gross income for income tax purposes, but unlike HSAs, FSAs are not tied to high-deductible health plans.

During the year, if the employee incurs qualified medical expenses not covered by any health insurance, the employee submits receipted bills to the administrator of the fund and is reimbursed. The reimbursement is also not included in gross income, so the net effect is that the employee pays uninsured medical expenses with before-tax dollars rather than with after-tax dollars.

The downside of an FSA for employees is that, in general, any money left in their accounts at the end of a plan year is forfeited to the employer. For that reason, employees should be conservative in their estimates of uninsured medical expenses. The law does allow employers to include in their FSA plans either, but not both, of the following features to somewhat reduce the forfeiture aspect of health FSAs:

• The plan may grant employees a grace period of 2 and one-half months after the end of the plan year to incur qualified medical expenses reimbursable by the plan.

• The plan may allow employees to carry forward up to $500 in unused amounts to the following plan year.

The downside for employers is that if an employee has substantial reimbursable expenses early in the plan year, before enough funds are accumulated to cover the expenses, the employer must advance the reimbursement to the employee. If the employee then quits, there will be no more payroll deductions, and the employer will be left holding an FSA with a negative balance. To guard against this possibility, employers may limit the size of each employee's FSA to an amount even less than the overall $2,600 maximum allowed by law.

Qualified medical expenses under a health FSA are similar to those that qualify for HSA reimbursement, except that health insurance and long-term-care insurance premiums do not qualify.

Dependent Care Flexible Spending Arrangements

Although called a flexible spending arrangement, a *dependent care FSA* is in some respects different from a health FSA, discussed above. Both allow employees to contribute pretax money to an employer-established fund, and both allow tax-free reimbursement for qualified expenses, but as the name implies, a dependent care FSA is only for care of dependents to enable the participating employee, or the employee and spouse, to work or to enable the employee's spouse to go to school. Dependent care FSAs are not available to any employee whose stay-at-home spouse provides the care.

A *dependent* for these purposes is any of the following:

- a child under age 13
- a person of any age who is mentally or physically unable to care for himself or herself and who is claimed as a dependent on the employee's federal tax return
- an adult, if the employee provides more than half that person's maintenance costs

Eligible expenses include day care and preschool expenses, babysitters, and before- and after-school programs for dependents under age 13.

Annual pretax employee contributions to a dependent care FSA are limited to the smallest of the employee's income, the spouse's income, or $5,000 (if married filing jointly) or $2,500 (if married filing separately).

Unlike health FSAs, an employee participating in a dependent care FSA can seek reimbursement only up to the current balance in the employee's account; the employer has no obligation to advance reimbursements.

Health Reimbursement Arrangements

Health reimbursement arrangements (HRAs) are funded solely by the employer. While employees cannot contribute to their accounts, there is no limit on the amount the employer can contribute. Distributions from an HRA account reimburse the employee for his or her own qualified medical expenses and qualified medical expenses of a spouse and dependents. Any remaining balances are carried over to subsequent plan years. Qualified medical expenses for HRA purposes include prescription drugs, over-the-counter drugs that are prescribed, and insulin.

According to an IRS notice issued in 2013, arrangements that allow reimbursement for premiums on individual health policies fail to satisfy the PPACA's market reforms and subject employers to an excise tax of $100 per day per affected employee. Because of the popularity of HRAs with small employers, the 21st Century Cures Act, passed in late 2016, excludes *qualified small employer HRAs* (QSEHRAs) from the excise tax. For QSEHRA purposes, a small employer is any employer that is not an ALE under the PPACA, that is, an employer that has fewer than 50 full-time employees. The maximum funding allowed for QSEHRAs is $4,950 for self-only coverage and $10,000 for family coverage.

Cafeteria Plans

Sometimes referred to as §125 plans (because they are authorized under that section of the Internal Revenue Code), *cafeteria plans* are employer-sponsored benefits packages that give each employee a choice between taking cash or receiving qualified benefits such as HSA or FSA contributions, health insurance, group term life insurance, and disability insurance. If the employee elects cash, the cash must be reported as taxable income; if he or she elects a qualified benefit, the benefit is excludible to the extent allowed by law.

A *simple cafeteria plan* is available for employers with 100 or fewer employees, under which certain nondiscrimination requirements applicable to cafeteria plans are generally deemed satisfied.

Cafeteria plans are attractive in that they allow each employee to tailor benefits to his or her particular circumstances—as, for example, when an employee does not need health insurance due to coverage through his or her spouse's employer, but would like life insurance for which he or she cannot otherwise qualify.

COBRA

Employers with 20 or more full-time or full-time equivalent employees (except churches and certain church-related organizations) that provide group health coverage need to know about one of the strangest acronyms in the employment field—COBRA. It stands for the *Consolidated Omnibus Budget Reconciliation Act* of 1985. The act was really a catchall piece of legislation that just happened to include an amendment to ERISA. That amendment requires employers to make health coverage available to employees and their dependents who, for various reasons, would otherwise lose coverage.

Before COBRA, an employee who quit or was fired would automatically lose health coverage for himself or herself and for any participating family members. Similarly, a spouse's coverage would terminate on divorce, as would a child's coverage on completion of his or her education or reaching a specified age. Some group policies had conversion privileges, which entitled the departing employee to purchase an individual policy, but the individual policies were usually expensive and provided only limited coverage. Conversion privileges were usually not available to the divorced spouse or graduated child.

COBRA changed all that. Now, when a *qualifying event* occurs, the employer must offer continuing coverage at the participants' cost to those who would otherwise lose benefits. The following are qualifying events that trigger COBRA coverage:

- The employee voluntarily quits.
- The employee is fired (except in cases of gross misconduct).
- The employee becomes ineligible for coverage because of a reduction in hours of work.
- The employee dies leaving a covered spouse or dependent.

- A covered spouse is divorced or becomes separated.
- A covered dependent ceases to be a dependent—reaches age 26, according to the PPACA.

Under U.S. Department of Labor (DOL) regulations, employers that provide group health coverage and are subject to COBRA are required to notify all new employees and their spouses about COBRA continuation coverage within 90 days after they become covered. The notice must include the following:
- the name of the plan and the name, address, and telephone number of someone whom the employee and spouse can contact for more information on COBRA and the plan
- a general description of the continuation coverage provided under the plan
- an explanation of what qualified beneficiaries must do to notify the plan of qualifying events or disabilities
- an explanation of the importance of keeping the plan administrator informed of addresses of the participants and beneficiaries
- a statement that the general notice does not fully describe COBRA or the plan and that more complete information is available from the plan administrator and in the summary plan description

Once on notice of a qualifying event, the employer must, within 14 days, offer continuing COBRA coverage. The employee, spouse, or dependent who is otherwise losing coverage then has 60 days to elect COBRA benefits.

What if a participant's coverage ends in anticipation of a qualifying event? For example, an employee with family coverage is in the midst of a divorce but, before the divorce is final, instructs his employer to drop his wife from the plan. Assuming the employee's instructions are consistent with plan requirements, and the employer is not on notice of a court order prohibiting the employee from dropping his wife's coverage, the employer has no choice but to comply. But, under DOL regulations, once the divorce is final, the employer must then give the usual COBRA notice to the employee's ex-wife. It does not matter that the wife was not participating at the time of the divorce, since she was dropped in anticipation of that event.

⚠ **ALERT!**
Employers must continue health insurance coverage for an employee on leave under the *Family and Medical Leave Act* on the same basis as if the employee had continued to work. Health insurance continuation requirements also apply to some employees on military leave.

The cost of the continuing benefits must be paid 100 percent by the participant (the employee, spouse, or dependent), even if the employer was paying all or a portion of the premium before the qualifying event. The employer may also charge an additional 2 percent of the premium to cover administrative costs.

COBRA benefits do not continue indefinitely. For a terminated employee and his or her spouse and dependents, benefits last only 18 months. For a spouse or dependents who lose benefits due to divorce or separation from the employee or due to the employee's death, benefits last up to 36 months.

Detailed information about COBRA is available in the booklet *An Employer's Guide to Group Health Continuation Coverage under COBRA*, available at the DOL's website.

Some states have laws similar to COBRA applicable to employers that do not meet the 20-employee threshold under federal law.

MANDATED BENEFITS

In addition to provisions of the PPACA discussed above, the federal *Newborns' and Mothers' Health Protection Act* prohibits group health plans from cutting off hospitalization benefits for a mother and her newborn child for the first 48 hours of hospitalization after a normal vaginal delivery and for the first 96 hours of hospitalization after a Cesarean section.

The act also prohibits health plans and insurers from offering financial incentives to mothers or health care providers to encourage hospital stays shorter than these minimums. Of course, in consultation with her physician, a mother is free to leave sooner if it is medically appropriate. The act does not require that births take place in a hospital.

The insurance laws of most states specify certain coverages that must be included in group health plans. Mental health coverage is a typical mandated benefit. Additional examples include chiropractic treatment and other treatments that have not always been considered in the health care mainstream. For the most part, the courts have upheld these requirements, despite claims that they are preempted by ERISA.

In 1978, Congress passed the *Pregnancy Discrimination Act* (PDA) amending Title VII of the federal Civil Rights Act. The PDA expands the definition of sex discrimination to include discrimination on account of pregnancy, childbirth, or related medical conditions. Under the PDA, a group health plan must cover pregnancy, childbirth, and related medical conditions to the same extent the plan covers similar medical conditions. Abortions do not need to be covered except when the mother's life is endangered.

QUALIFIED MEDICAL CHILD SUPPORT ORDERS

ERISA requires that group health plans contain provisions to recognize *qualified medical child support orders* (QMCSOs). QMCSOs are somewhat similar to QDROs (qualified domestic relations orders, discussed in Chapter 8) in that they give alternate payees—persons other than the participating employee—rights with respect to an employer-sponsored benefit plan.

Under a QMCSO, an employee who has child support obligations may, as part of the obligation, be ordered to provide any available health insurance coverage for the dependent children. Assuming the employer's plan includes family coverage, delivery to the employer of such an order has the effect of requiring the employer to enroll the employee's dependent children. The employer may not disen-roll the children unless the employee quits or obtains replacement coverage or unless the employer eliminates family coverage from the plan. However, the employer is *not* required to provide any type or form of benefit or option not already provided under the plan. For example, if a plan limits participation just to employees and does not cover other family members, then a QMCSO cannot require the plan to begin providing family coverage.

The costs of enrolling a dependent child for coverage under a QMCSO are covered by deductions from the employee's pay.

CLAIMS ADMINISTRATION

The DOL has developed an elaborate set of regulations governing health plan claims procedures. Under these regulations, an insurer must process an initial claim according to the following:

- within 72 hours for urgent claim care
- within 15 days for pre-service claims (with one 15-day extension allowed)
- within 30 days for post-service claims (with one 15-day extension allowed)

Claimants have 180 days to appeal a claim denial, and the appeal itself must be decided within 72 hours for urgent claim care, within 30 days for pre-service claims, and within 60 days for post-service claims.

Plans are prohibited from imposing fees or costs as a condition of filing or appealing a claim. Appeals must also be decided by a person different from the decision-maker on the initial claim denial. When an appeal involves a medical judgment, such as the medical necessity of a particular procedure or drug, appropriate health-care professionals must also be consulted. Finally, plans must:

- provide participants with a full description of claim procedures
- provide specific reasons for claim denials, including identification of and access to guidelines or rules relied upon in denying the

claim, along with all other documents and records relevant to the denial
- disclose the names of any medical professionals consulted as part of the claim process

STOCK OPTIONS

More and more companies find it attractive to include, as part of their compensation package for key employees, some equity participation in the company. In a tight labor market, the opportunity to become a stockholder in the company may even be a necessary part of the recruitment and retention process. The idea is to provide an incentive to key employees by enabling them to share in the company's growth. The amount of stock involved is usually small enough that there is no significant effect on control of the company.

For start-ups with limited cash, an equity interest may be a major component of key employees' compensation.

The company could simply give company stock to an employee as additional compensation or sell stock to the employee at some price that is below actual market value. However, any difference between the actual value of the stock and the amount paid by the employee will be income to the employee that is immediately taxable at ordinary income (not capital gains) rates. The employee may have to sell some of the stock to raise cash to pay the tax, defeating the purpose of the arrangement. Worse, if there is no market for the stock or the stock declines in value, the employee may be stuck with a big tax bill and have no way to pay it.

A more typical approach is to use *stock options* in which the company grants the employee a right, exercisable during a specified time period, to acquire company stock (or stock in a parent or subsidiary company) at a stated price, called the *option price* or *strike price*. While the grant of the option is not immediately taxable, the exercise of the option may or may not have tax consequences, depending on whether the arrangement qualifies as a *statutory* stock option or a *nonstatutory* stock option. But regardless of the tax consequences at the time the option is exercised, the grant of the option itself gives the employee a tax-free opportunity to participate in the growth of the company.

Statutory Stock Options

A *statutory stock option* is an option that qualifies as either an *incentive stock option* (ISO) under §422 of the Internal Revenue Code or as an *employee stock purchase plan* under §423.

Under an ISO, when the employee exercises an option, pays the option price, and acquires company stock, no taxable income is incurred (but the company gets no tax deduction, either). Should the employee later sell the stock after satisfying applicable holding periods, he or she is taxed at capital gains rates on the difference between the option price and selling price.

To qualify for this favorable tax treatment, the option must meet the following requirements:
- The option must be granted pursuant to a written plan approved by the company's shareholders. The plan must specify the total number of shares that may be issued under the plan and must identify the employees or class of employees eligible to receive options. (The identity-of-the-employees requirement can be met if the plan simply says that the employees will be chosen by a specified person or committee.)
- The option must be in the form of a written agreement between the company and the employee.
- The option must be granted within 10 years after adoption of the plan.
- The option must state that the option can be exercised only within 10 years after being granted.
- The employee cannot be eligible to exercise more than $100,000 in options within any 12-month period.
- The option holder must be an employee when the option is granted and must continue to be an employee until three months before the option is exercised. (Special rules apply to employees who die or become disabled.)

- The option holder can own no more than 10 percent of the voting stock of the company. (This requirement does not apply if the option price is at least 110 percent of the fair market value of the stock, and if the option cannot be exercised for at least five years.)
- The option price must be at least equal to the fair market value of the stock at the time the option is granted.
- The option cannot be exercisable by anyone other than the employee personally, and the option must be nontransferable during the employee's lifetime. (Special rules apply to the exercise of options by a deceased employee's estate.)
- After the option is exercised, the shares themselves must be held for at least two years after the option was granted and for at least one year after the option is exercised.

One disadvantage of an ISO is that the company must determine the fair market value of the stock subject to the option to set the option price. If the company's stock is publicly traded, the trading value is used. But if the company is privately held, hiring an outside valuation expert may be necessary. (The company need only make a good-faith effort to value its stock. However, restrictions on transferability *cannot* be considered as reducing the value of the stock.) The ISO agreement can state that the company will issue a special class of stock, such as nonvoting stock, to satisfy the exercise of an option, but this further complicates the valuation process because of the need to value the special class of stock separately.

Backdating

A number of public corporations have come under scrutiny for secretly *backdating* options. Normally, when an option is granted, it is dated as of the date of the grant. That date determines the option's strike price, which is normally the price at which the company's stock was trading on that date. When an option is backdated, however, the option holder gets to pick the date of the option. By picking a date on which the company's stock was trading at a lower price, the option holder enjoys a lower strike price and maximizes his or her potential gain. This, of course, defeats the performance incentive aspect of the option grant. In addition, backdating exposes the company to shareholder suits for fraud, and it raises a host of tax and accounting problems.

☞ **QUICK TIP**

ISOs are not subject to ERISA because their purpose is to provide a current incentive, much like salary, and not to defer compensation or provide retirement benefits.

Employee Stock Purchase Plans

Under an *employee stock purchase plan* (not to be confused with an employee stock ownership plan discussed later in the chapter), an employer grants options to its general workforce in proportion to employees' compensation. The plan *must* exclude employees who own 5 percent or more of the company. It *may* exclude part-time and seasonal employees, employees who have worked less than two years, and highly compensated employees. The option price cannot be lower than 85 percent of the value of the stock at the time the option is granted (or, alternatively, at the time the option is exercised).

Other restrictions apply, including a $25,000 per year limitation on the amount of stock for which a single employee can hold options. As with ISOs, the exercise of the option does not result in taxable income. The sale of stock acquired through the option receives capital gain treatment so long as applicable holding periods are satisfied.

Nonstatutory Stock Options

In a *nonstatutory stock option* (NSO), the tax advantages shift to the employer. Specifically, when the employee exercises the option and acquires company stock with a value higher than the option price, the employer can take a deduction for the difference. However, the employee must report the difference as ordinary income. An option will be nonstatutory if the option does not meet the statutory requirements listed earlier, or the option expressly states that it is *not* an ISO.

Although NSOs are not required to satisfy the conditions applicable to ISOs, a company may choose to impose certain conditions, such as holding periods and restrictions on transfer.

🔔 ALERT!

Businesses that grant NSOs to their employees must separately identify on the employees' Forms W-2 any compensation received by the employees from the exercise of NSOs.

Once the employee exercises the option and acquires company stock, the employee can sell it immediately if the stock was acquired through an NSO. (This is subject, however, to any restrictions in the option agreement and to any securities law restrictions.) If it was acquired through an ISO, the employee can sell it after satisfying the ISO holding period requirements, any additional restrictions in the option agreement, and any securities law restrictions. But if the company is privately held, there is not likely to be any market for the stock. So in practical terms, the option plan must allow the employee to sell the stock back to the company. Such a repurchase obligation may entail yet another expensive valuation. If the employee sells back less than all the stock, he or she may be deemed to have received a taxable dividend.

Companies contemplating a stock option plan should consider the effect on employee incentive if the stock goes down instead of up. Employees whose primary compensation has been stock options may become discouraged and leave sooner than if their compensation had not included options. Companies should also consider their increased litigation exposure should a fired employee sue for wrongful discharge and claim not only the wages he or she would have received, but also the value of unvested stock options.

Publicly traded companies should also be mindful of SEC rules designed to protect against *dilution in the dark*. Under these rules, companies are required to provide detailed information about their equity compensation plans in their annual reports to the SEC. The information is also required to be included in proxy statements whenever the company is submitting an equity compensation plan for approval by shareholders.

EMPLOYEE STOCK OWNERSHIP PLANS

An *employee stock ownership plan* (ESOP) is a form of defined contribution plan in which the plan's primary investment is in stock of the employer company. (Under ERISA's self-dealing rules, most pension plans are prohibited from holding significant investments in the sponsoring company. ESOPs fall within an exception to these rules.) An ESOP is a way for employees to own the company or at least own a significant part of the company.

ESOPs have a number of advantages over other pension plans, particularly when the company is a closely held corporation whose stock is not publicly traded. Among those advantages are the following:

- Employees are more highly motivated, since they have an ownership interest in the company and their productivity increases the value of their stock.
- The added control and bargaining power employees have through stock ownership may make unionizing less attractive to employees.
- When an ESOP acquires its stock by purchase of newly issued company shares, the company can, in effect, use pension plan contributions as a source of capital for company operations or expansion.
- When an ESOP acquires its stock by purchase from existing shareholders, the ESOP provides a market for those shares and provides liquidity to existing shareholders. (If the ESOP is acquiring at least a 30 percent interest in the company from

existing shareholders, the selling shareholders may defer recognition of capital gains on those shares.)

- An ESOP can leverage its stock ownership by borrowing money from a bank or other lender to purchase stock, thereby providing additional capital to the company or liquidity to its selling shareholders. Future pension plan contributions by the company to the ESOP to service the loan are fully tax deductible; in effect, they enable the company to deduct otherwise nondeductible principal repayments.
- An ESOP provides continuity of ownership and management of the company. Without an ESOP, the death or retirement of a principal shareholder often means liquidation of the company or the involvement of new owners who are strangers to the company.
- Premiums for *key person* life insurance owned by an ESOP are fully tax deductible. (A key person is an employee whose death would cause substantial financial harm to the business.)

⚠ ALERT!
Employee ownership of company stock, whether obtained through the exercise of stock options or otherwise, requires attention to insider trading restrictions.

ESOPs have some disadvantages. When the company's stock is not publicly traded, the company must pay for expensive stock valuations to determine the fair market value of the stock being contributed or sold to the ESOP. These valuations are typically required on an annual basis.

Then there is the question of who will serve as trustees of the trust that holds the ESOP stock. Banks and other financial institutions are increasingly reluctant to assume the trustee role because of the fiduciary responsibilities and risks involved. (In March 2017 a federal district judge in Virginia awarded almost $30 million in damages against Wilmington Trust for investing in stock at inflated values, in violation of its duty as trustee. The decision is on appeal.) But if company officers or directors are appointed as trustees, they may find it difficult to subordinate their own self-interest to the interests of participating employees, for whose benefit the ESOP is supposed to be managed.

The conflict of interest is heightened when the company is considering out-of-the-ordinary corporate actions, such as implementing a nonqualified deferred compensation plan for senior executives or responding to a merger proposal. In these instances, it may be necessary for the company to obtain a *fairness opinion* from an outside advisor as to the fairness of a proposed transaction.

ESOPs may not be for everyone, but their unique advantages deserve consideration.

OTHER PLANS

Retirement and group health plans are probably the most significant employee benefits, both in terms of tax savings and in terms of popularity with employees. Other arrangements are available, however, and should not be overlooked. As with retirement and group health plans, these other arrangements generally must satisfy applicable tax and ERISA requirements.

Group Term Life Insurance

An employer may provide group term life insurance to employees either as part of a group health plan or as a separate plan. The first $50,000 in coverage is tax free to the employee. The premium for coverage in excess of $50,000 is taxable income to the employee.

Disability Insurance

Premiums on employer-sponsored group disability insurance if paid by the employer are deductible by the employer, but are not includable in the employee's income. However, if an employee becomes disabled and collects benefits under the policy, the benefits are taxable income to the employee. Disability benefits are also taxable to the employee if the employee paid the premiums with before-tax dollars. Alternatively, if the employee pays the premiums with after-tax dollars, then the benefits are not taxable to the employee.

Under one clever arrangement, the employer paid the disability insurance premiums but gave each employee an election between having the premium amounts included or excluded in the employee's gross income. The IRS concluded in a private letter ruling that if the employee becomes disabled in a plan year in which he or she has elected to *include* the premiums in gross income, then the benefits are not taxable. However, if the employee becomes disabled in a plan year in which he or she has elected to *exclude* the premiums, the benefits are taxable.

Long-Term-Care Insurance
Premiums on employer-sponsored group long-term-care insurance are deductible by the employer. If the coverage qualifies as medical care and the premiums are below certain limits specified in the Internal Revenue Code, the premiums are not includable in the employee's income. Benefits, when paid, are not taxable.

🔔 ALERT!
Although the IRS permits employers to enroll employees automatically in cafeteria plans (subject to the employee's opting out), state wage and hour laws may prohibit an employer from making payroll deductions without the employee's express consent.

Employee Assistance Plans
Employee assistance plans (EAPs) may provide counseling and related services to employees who have emotional or substance abuse problems and various other benefits, such as wellness care, financial consultation, and legal advice. Typically, the employer contracts with an outside agency to provide the services. EAP records relating to substance abuse services are subject to special confidentiality provisions of federal law. (Chapter 18 covers employee privacy in more detail.)

Qualified Transportation Fringe Benefits
The Internal Revenue Code allows employers a deduction for pro-

viding the following nontaxable commuting benefits between home and work either by providing the benefit directly or by reimbursing employees for the following expenses:
- a ride in a commuter highway vehicle (defined as a vehicle that seats at least six adults not including the driver)
- a transit pass
- parking at or near the worksite (or at or near the point from which the employee takes another form of transportation to get to work)

The above three benefits can be provided in any combination. The first two are subject to a combined monthly limit of $255 for 2017, and parking is subject to separate monthly limit of $255 for 2017 (both amounts indexed for future years).

The code also allows tax-free reimbursement of an employee's bicycle commuting expenses of up to $20 per month for each month during which the employee regularly uses the bicycle for a substantial portion of travel between home and work. Bicycle expenses include the bicycle's purchase price and improvements, repairs, and storage. Bicycle expense reimbursement is not available for any month in which the employee receives one or more of the other transportation benefits.

CHAPTER 11
Workers' Compensation

- Coverage
- Course and Scope of Employment
- Claim Procedure
- Benefits
- Second Injury Fund
- Rights against Third Parties

Before the adoption of workers' compensation laws, an employer could, at least in theory, be held liable in court for work-related injuries suffered by employees. The employer might have to pay damages if, for example, it failed to provide a safe place to work or failed to provide a sufficient number of suitable fellow employees to accomplish the job at hand.

As a practical matter, however, the defenses available to the employer often prevented the employee from receiving any compensation for injuries. Those defenses included the following:

- *fellow servant doctrine*, which insulated employers from liability when the injury was caused by the negligence of a fellow employee
- *contributory negligence*, which barred the employee from recovery if he or she contributed in any way to the cause of the injury
- *assumption of the risk*, under which the employee was held to have assumed the risk of injury normally associated with the particular job

In essence, workers' compensation acts are *no fault* laws under which the employer is automatically obligated to pay compensation and benefits for each employee who suffers a work-related illness or injury or who is killed in the course of employment. This obligation, which is usually funded by mandatory workers' compensation insurance, applies whether or not the employer was negligent and whether or not the employer could have raised defenses to liability.

The trade-off for the employer is that providing workers' compensation benefits is the employer's *exclusive liability* for work-related injuries or illnesses. Unless the employer deliberately intended to injure or kill the employee, the employee cannot sue the employer in court, the employee cannot demand a jury trial, and the employee cannot obtain open-ended damages for pain and suffering.

COVERAGE

Workers' compensation acts apply to virtually all employers and, with few exceptions, all their employees. For purposes of these acts, the term *employee* means someone whose method of work the employer has a right to control. The acts apply to minors, even if they are employed unlawfully, and in some states to domestic workers in private homes.

State law typically defines *covered employee* broadly as any individual while in the service of an employer under an express or implied contract of apprenticeship or hire. The statutes then go on to list a number of exceptions and special provisions. For example, sole proprietors, partners, and officers of closely held corporations may not be covered at all, or they may have a right to opt into or opt out of coverage.

The acts do not apply to independent contractors or to *casual employees*—employees who work irregularly, for a brief period only, doing work not normally performed by employees of the employer.

Workers' compensation acts require employers to secure compensation for their covered employees by maintaining insurance through authorized insurance companies or through self-insurance. Insurance premiums are calculated as a percentage of payroll. The actual percentage varies for each employer based on factors such as the employer's industry classification and claim history. Employers may self-insure if they can demonstrate their financial ability to pay compensation. Self-insurers usually must put up security or a bond to cover their compensation obligations.

☞ **QUICK TIP**

Workers' compensation programs are exempt from the Employee Retirement Income Security Act (ERISA).

State laws generally require employers to post a notice in the workplace as to the existence of workers' compensation coverage and the procedure to be followed after an injury or death. It is illegal for an employer to charge employees, such as by a wage deduction, for any part of the cost of providing workers' compensation. It is also illegal for an employer to retaliate against an employee for filing a compensation claim or for testifying in a compensation proceeding.

Personal Injury

Workers' compensation acts cover accidental *personal injury*, which is usually defined as including the following:

- an accidental injury that arises out of and in the course of employment
- an injury caused by the willful or negligent act of a third person in connection with a covered employee's employment
- a disease or infection that naturally results from an accidental injury, such as frostbite or sunstroke
- an occupational disease

The acts typically *do not* cover these types of injuries:

- that are intentionally self-inflicted
- that result from the injured employee's attempt to injure or kill another or other willful misconduct
- that occur solely from intoxication while on duty and, in some states, from illegal drug use

It is sometimes argued that the likelihood of injury in certain occupations is so great that when an injury does occur, it cannot fairly be called accidental. A professional football team, for example, sought to deny compensation to one of its offensive linemen who injured his ankle in a game. The team claimed that when injuries are customary, foreseeable, and expected—in other words, are simply part of the game—they are not accidental within the meaning of the workers' compensation statute. The Virginia Supreme Court rejected the team's argument, saying that just because an occupation is high-risk does not mean the compensation statute is inapplicable.

COURSE AND SCOPE OF EMPLOYMENT

Workers' compensation laws cover employees who suffer accidental injuries *arising out of and in the course of employment*. Sometimes it is difficult to tell whether or not an injury arose out of and in the course of employment.

Take, for example, an employee who is injured while commuting to or from work. The general rule (sometimes called the *going-and-coming rule*) is that employees are not covered while commuting. But there are exceptions. Despite the going-and-coming rule, coverage will be provided in situations like these:

- An employee is going from one of the employer's places of business to another during the workday.
- An employee is exposed to a special hazard, which the public at large is normally not exposed to, while gaining access to the employer's place of business.
- The means of transportation are provided by the employer, or the employee is being paid while commuting.
- The employer requires the employee to commute in a specified way or follow a specified route.

When an employee is on travel for the employer, he or she generally *is* covered, even if not specifically engaged in work at the time of the injury. Covered injuries include hotel bathroom falls, choking on a meal, suffering a criminal assault, or being injured in a hotel fire. Only if the employee is injured while on a distinct departure from work and on a personal errand will there be no coverage.

CASE STUDY:
NO COVERAGE FOR AFTER-HOURS ASSAULT

A professional hockey player with a National Hockey League team traveled to New York for a game with the New York Rangers. After the game he and some 20 other teammates went to dinner at a restaurant, paid for by their employer. While there, the player in question drank a substantial amount of beer and vodka. They then went to a club where they drank more beer and vodka. After the club closed and while the team members were out on a street near the club, the player in question tried to persuade a woman to accompany him in a limousine. The woman's companion then hit the player over the head with a bottle. The player was denied compensation for the resulting injury.

CLAIM PROCEDURE

If an employee suffers a work-related injury or illness, he or she must both notify the employer and file a claim for compensation with the state agency that administers the compensation act. Once the employer learns of a compensable injury, the employer, too, must file a report with the state agency.

The time limits applicable to notification and reporting requirements vary from jurisdiction to jurisdiction. Failure to meet these deadlines may bar the employee's right of recovery, although the government agency that administers the law usually has authority to excuse a late filing.

After a claim is filed, the employer or its insurance carrier must either begin paying benefits or *controvert* (contest) the claim. If the claim is controverted, the government agency investigates, conducts a hearing if necessary, and then issues an award or denies coverage. Further appeal may be made to the courts. The parties are entitled to be represented by attorneys in a contested matter, but the amount of attorneys' fees charged the employee is often subject to approval by the administering agency.

BENEFITS

Workers' compensation acts typically provide these types of benefits:
- disability benefits to the covered employee for lost wages or loss of earning capacity
- medical benefits
- death benefits to the employee's dependents
- funeral benefits
- vocational rehabilitation

The actual amount of disability benefits is calculated from statutory formulas based on the employee's average weekly wage. The following benefits formulas (subject to statutory maximums and minimums) are typical:

- for *temporary partial disability*—up to two-thirds of the employee's lost wage-earning capacity
- for *temporary total disability*—two-thirds of the employee's average weekly wage
- for *permanent partial disability*—up to two-thirds of the employee's average weekly wage (if the injury falls in one of the categories listed in the act, such as loss of a specific appendage, loss of a sensory organ, or loss of various combinations of appendages and sensory organs, the benefit continues only for the number of weeks specified in the law)
- for *permanent total disability*—two-thirds of the employee's average weekly wage

Workers' compensation premiums are deductible by the employer for federal income tax purposes. Benefits paid to an employee are exempt from federal income tax.

Terminating an employee for excessive absenteeism when the employee is out from a work-related, compensable injury is allowable in most states. However, doing so is risky for these reasons:

- The employee may claim that the termination was abusive or in retaliation for filing a workers' compensation claim.
- If the employer is subject to the Family and Medical Leave Act (FMLA), the employee may be entitled to FMLA leave.
- If the disabling condition is not merely temporary and if it substantially interferes with one or more major life activities, the employer's duty of reasonable accommodation under the Americans with Disabilities Act (ADA) may be triggered.

SECOND INJURY FUND

Suppose an applicant suffered an injury at another job but is nevertheless able to work. Some employers may be reluctant to hire the applicant, fearing that a subsequent injury on top of the earlier one, even if minor, could disable the employee and expose the employer to liability for permanent disability benefits. Recognizing that the workers' compensation system may inadvertently discourage the hiring of employees who have suffered previous injuries, many states have created a *second injury fund* that pays a portion of the compensation benefits due a reinjured employee.

Since the purpose of second injury funds is to discourage employers from discriminating against employment applicants who have suffered previous injuries, the question arises whether an employer that was *unaware* of a previous injury at time of hire can obtain reimbursement from the fund after paying benefits to a reinjured employee.

Some courts have adopted the rule that the employee's previous injury must be *manifest* for the employer to recover from the fund. As a practical matter, this means either that the employer must have actual knowledge of the earlier injury at hiring time or that the earlier injury must be obvious or documented in medical records available to the employer such that a reasonable person in the employer's shoes would have known about the previous injury. The requirement that a previous injury be manifest for the employer to have access to the second injury fund in the event of a subsequent injury is one reason why an employer may want to condition a job offer on completing a medical exam, including a medical history.

Asking about previous workers' compensation claims on a job application is not explicitly prohibited, but if the applicant reveals a previous history and he or she is then rejected, the applicant may claim that he or she was discriminated against for exercising a statutory right—seeking workers' comp benefits. The inquiry could also reveal a disability contrary to the ADA. The safer practice is to require a medical exam *after* an offer of employment has been made.

⚠ ALERT!

The ADA prohibits pre-employment physicals unless the employer has already made a conditional offer of employment to the employee. The ADA also prohibits inquiries that could lead to disclosure of a disability. (Chapter 17 discusses disability discrimination more fully.)

RIGHTS AGAINST THIRD PARTIES

Although workers' compensation acts prohibit an employee from suing his or her own employer for a work-related injury, the acts do not prohibit an employee from suing a third party who may have caused the injury.

EXAMPLE: An employee is a passenger in his employer's truck that is being driven by a fellow employee. If the truck is hit at an intersection because another vehicle ran a red light, the employee-passenger can sue the driver of the other vehicle. However, if the accident occurred because the employee-passenger's fellow employee ran the red light, the employee-passenger may or may not be able to sue his fellow employee, depending on state law.

In the above illustration, regardless of how the accident occurred, the employee-passenger can of course collect workers' compensation benefits. But the employee-passenger is not allowed to invoke the legal doctrine of *respondeat superior* and attempt to hold his own employer vicariously liable.

State laws differ as to whether the injured employee has to elect between accepting workers' compensation benefits or suing the negligent third party. In some states, by accepting benefits the employee, in effect, assigns to the employer the right to sue the third person up to the amount of benefits paid by the employer. In other states, the employee may accept compensation *and* sue the third person, but if the employee's suit is successful, the employee has to reimburse the employer up to the amount of the benefits paid by the employer.

If an injured employee enters into a settlement agreement with the third party and, in exchange for a cash payment, releases the third party from further liability, the employer may be able to raise the settlement as a defense to the employer's own workers' compensation obligation. The reason is that, by releasing the third party, the employee has also compromised the employer's *right of subrogation* to recover against the third party. So the employee should obtain the employer's consent (and the consent of the employer's workers' compensation insurance carrier) before suing, or settling with, a third party.

Independent Contractors

Suppose an employer engages an independent contractor to perform some function at the workplace and, as a result of the independent contractor's negligence, an employee suffers an injury on the job. Certainly the employee can recover workers' compensation benefits, but can the employee sue the independent contractor as well? In other words, is the independent contractor considered so connected with the employer as to enjoy the employer's immunity from suit? Or is the independent contractor a third party who is subject to suit?

The answer usually depends on whether the independent contractor is a stranger to the employer's business or whether the independent contractor was performing an essential part of the employer's business. The following examples illustrate this concept.

EXAMPLE 1: A retail company hires an architect to design a warehouse for storing out-of-season merchandise. The architect negligently designs an overhead door at the warehouse, which later falls and injures one of the company's regular employees. The architect will in most instances be considered a *stranger* to the employer's business who is not protected by workers' compensation immunity and who can be sued by the injured employee.

EXAMPLE 2: That same retail company hires a cleaning company to assist with store maintenance and to perform cleaning and janitorial functions, both during and after normal store hours. Here the cleaning company is performing an essential part of the employer's business and will not be subject to suit for negligence that results in injury to the retailer's regular employees.

🔔 ALERT!

Health and safety laws require employers to provide medical first aid supplies and, in the absence of nearby medical facilities, ensure the presence of a person trained in first aid. (See Chapter 13 on workplace safety.)

A related issue is the *dual capacity* doctrine. Take, for example, a hospital employee who is injured on the job and receives negligent medical treatment at the employer's hospital. Can the employee sue for the negligent medical treatment, or is the suit barred by the exclusivity provision of the workers' compensation statute?

A few states take the view that when an employee is acting in a capacity other than as the employer, the employer becomes a third party and is no longer immune from employee suits for negligence. Other states have ruled that when an employer negligently administers first aid to an employee who was injured on the job, the employer enjoys protection under the workers' compensation act not only for the initial injury, but also for the emergency medical treatment.

CHAPTER 12

Unemployment Insurance

- Employer Contributions
- Coverage and Eligibility
- Misconduct and Quitting for Cause
- Claim Procedure
- Benefits

Unemployment insurance benefits, together with workers' compensation, provide a safety net for employees. While workers' compensation protects employees who suffer loss of earning capacity through work-related injuries, unemployment benefits protect against involuntary job loss due to economic or other reasons not the fault of the employee.

The unemployment insurance system is a cooperative arrangement between the federal government and participating state governments. In essence, the federal government supervises the system, and state governments administer the system within federally established guidelines. The system is financed through mandatory taxes (called *contributions*) imposed on covered employers by state unemployment insurance laws and, at the federal level, by the *Federal Unemployment Tax Act* (FUTA).

Each new business that has one or more employees must register under the unemployment insurance laws. Tax-exempt organizations described in §501(c)(3) of the Internal Revenue Code are exempt from FUTA, but not from state laws. (See Chapter 23 for more on nonprofit and tax-exempt organizations.)

EMPLOYER CONTRIBUTIONS

At both the federal and state levels, an employer's unemployment insurance contribution is calculated as a percentage of wages paid in *covered employment* up to a cap. The amount of wages that are subject to tax is called the *wage base*. The federal wage base under FUTA is currently $7,000 per covered employee. Each state establishes its own wage base. In general, an employer is subject to the FUTA tax if it employs one or more individuals for at least 20 weeks, or pays wages of $1,500 or more per calendar quarter.

At the federal level, the tax rate applied to the wage base is normally 6 percent. However, the employer is entitled to credit its state unemployment tax against the federal tax (up to a maximum of 5.4 percent of taxable wages) if the state tax was paid in full and on time.

Therefore, the effective federal rate for most employers is 0.6 percent, or $42, per employee per year.

At the state level, the tax rate depends on whether the employer is a *new employer* or whether the employer is entitled to an *earned rate*—a rate based partly on actual claims experience. A new employer is typically defined as an employer that has reported taxable wages for less than some specified period, such as three years. State unemployment contributions are usually due quarterly.

While earned rates are computed differently from state to state, in general they include these two factors: the employer's actual claims experience, and an adjustment or pooling charge to cover shortfalls in the benefit fund. Because of the experience factor, hiring and firing practices can have a significant impact on the amount of future unemployment tax due.

To determine an employer's claims experience, the state agency that administers unemployment insurance maintains a separate account for each covered employer. Although specific accounting practices differ from state to state, in general the account is charged with benefits that are paid out. The employer's earned rate is then determined based on benefits charged against its account over some previous period such as three years.

Base Period

The process of determining which employer to charge for particular benefits gets complicated. One concept is *base period*. The base period is the most recent four of the employee's last five completed calendar quarters before the filing of the claim for unemployment benefits. If a claimant had only one employer during the base period, then 100 percent of the benefits are charged against that employer's account.

If a claimant had two or more employers during the base period, then, depending on the state, each base period employer is charged with a percentage of the benefits based on the ratio of the wages paid by that employer to the employee's total base period wages, or the employer for whom the claimant last worked for 30 days is charged with 100 percent of the benefit.

If an employee works in more than one state, the employer should typically report the wages for unemployment insurance purposes as follows:

- If substantial work (work that is not merely incidental, transitory, or occasional) is performed in several states, one of which is the employer's home office or a branch office, then that state is the state to which wages are reported.
- If no substantial work is performed in the state where the employer's home office or a branch office is located, then the employee's state of residence is the state to which wages are reported.

⚠ ALERT!

Employers are prohibited from deducting any part of their required contributions from employee wages. Agreements between employers and employees to waive unemployment insurance benefits are unenforceable.

COVERAGE AND ELIGIBILITY

By definition, independent contractors are not employees. Therefore, compensation paid to them is not subject to unemployment tax. (However, compensation paid to an employee who is *misclassified* as an independent contractor is subject to tax.) Under federal law, general partners in a partnership and students who perform services for their schools are also excluded from coverage. Household employees and agricultural workers are specially treated. Each state has its own list of additional jobs not covered by the unemployment insurance laws.

Employers do not have to pay state unemployment tax for employees who are not covered, and such employees are not entitled to claim benefits if they become unemployed.

To be eligible for benefits, a claimant must first have been employed in a type of job covered by the unemployment insurance law. In addition, the claimant must be *unemployed* (defined to mean not working at all for any wages) or be *underemployed* (working less than full time and earning wages that are less than the benefit amount that would be payable to the claimant). The claimant must also be actively seeking work and must be available for and able to perform work. Failure to meet these qualifications or failure to accept suitable work will temporarily disqualify the claimant from receiving benefits.

⚠ **ALERT!**

An employee who is out of work due to an injury or illness is ineligible for unemployment benefits since he or she is not able to work. However, he or she may be eligible for leave under the *Family and Medical Leave Act* and eligible for workers' compensation benefits. If the injury or illness is not work-related, benefits may also be available under any group disability insurance policy maintained by the employer.

If an individual receives a severance package or dismissal payments covering some period of time after employment ends, he or she may also be eligible for unemployment insurance depending on the form that the severance package takes. If an employer intends to offer a severance package, it makes sense to offer the package in the form of a specified number of weeks of continuing compensation and benefits. That should render the departing employee ineligible for unemployment insurance during the severance period. Even better, if the departing employee finds new work during the severance period, he or she may not make any claim at all.

MISCONDUCT AND QUITTING FOR CAUSE

At the heart of unemployment insurance is the requirement that the person claiming benefits be out of work involuntarily, through no fault of his or her own. Therefore, state law often disqualifies an individual from receiving benefits if he or she is fired for misconduct or leaves work voluntarily without good cause.

Some states have gradations of misconduct, such as *aggravated misconduct*, *gross misconduct*, and (ordinary or simple) *misconduct*.

In states with gradations of misconduct, the most serious level may disqualify the employee from benefits entirely, whereas lesser degrees of misconduct may result in only temporary disqualification.

Normally, if an employee voluntarily quits, he or she is not entitled to benefits. But unemployment insurance statutes usually specify that the disqualification applies only if the employee leaves work *without good cause*. Stated another way, if an employee voluntarily quits with good cause or good reason, he or she is not disqualified and may receive benefits.

In general, for there to be good cause, the cause must be connected in some way to the job the employee is leaving. A purely personal decision by the employee will not qualify. For example, leaving to take a better job, to become self-employed, to return to school, or to relocate with a spouse are not good causes. On the other hand, failing to pay the employee or maintaining discriminatory working conditions may amount to good cause depending on the circumstances.

☞ **QUICK TIP**

If a reasonable person would find the working conditions intolerable, involving, say, severe and persistent discrimination, quitting to escape those conditions may be considered a *constructive discharge*. (See Chapter 4 for more on constructive discharges.)

Employees on Strike

In general, benefits are denied to employees who are out of work because of a labor dispute at their worksite. However, a claimant will generally qualify for benefits despite the existence of a labor dispute at the worksite if the claimant is not personally involved in the labor dispute and does not belong to a grade or class or workers whose members are involved in the labor dispute.

An individual who is receiving benefits may turn down a job that has become vacant because of a strike and still continue to receive benefits. Unemployment laws do not force workers to become strikebreakers.

CLAIM PROCEDURE

An individual who loses his or her job or becomes underemployed must register for work and file a claim with the appropriate state agency. Since benefits are generally not paid retroactively, any delay in filing a claim results in loss of benefits.

When the state agency receives a claim, it notifies all the claimant's base period employers. All base period employers are asked to submit *separation information* to the state agency, giving the reason why the employment terminated, the last day of employment, the claimant's wage rate, and other information that might affect eligibility for or the amount of benefits.

⚠ ALERT!

Providing false separation information is criminal. In addition, if the termination itself involved discrimination, an employer's subsequent attempt to disqualify a claimant for unemployment benefits could expose the employer to an additional claim of illegal retaliation.

Once the state agency makes an initial determination that the employee is entitled to benefits, the employer may contest the determination by appealing to a hearing examiner. When the basis for the contest is employee misconduct, the employer normally must prove the following:

- The employer had a clear, well-established work rule.
- The employee knew about the work rule.
- The employee willfully violated the work rule.

The employee then has an opportunity to show that the employer frequently failed to enforce the work rule.

One obvious reason for an employer to contest benefits (assuming there are reasonable grounds to do so) is to protect the employer's earned rate. Recall that employers other than new employers are entitled to be rated based (in part) on the employer's actual claims experience. Each benefit payment pushes that rate higher and increases the employer's required contribution for future years.

☞ **QUICK TIP**

The employer will have an easier time proving the existence of a work rule and the former employee's awareness of the rule if the rule is contained in an employee handbook and if the employee signed an acknowledgment that he or she received and will read the handbook. (Chapter 3 discusses employee handbooks.)

A less obvious reason to contest a claim is to get a preview of any related claims the former employee may intend to bring against the employer. Suppose, for example, that the employee voluntarily quits but says in the claim for unemployment benefits that he or she had good cause to leave because of racial discrimination on the job. Or suppose the employee says he or she was fired for refusal to perform an illegal act such as lying to an inspector from the Occupational Safety and Health Administration. In those circumstances, the employer can reasonably expect to face not only an unemployment compensation claim, but also a charge of discrimination or a suit for abusive discharge.

If benefits are contested, the state unemployment agency must conduct a hearing at which the employee may testify, call other witnesses, and present documents. The employer, usually with the assistance of an attorney, can cross-examine the employee and his or her witnesses, examine documentary evidence, and call its own witnesses.

In some states, the results of a contested unemployment insurance hearing, at which both sides had an opportunity to present evidence and cross-examine witnesses, will be legally binding on the parties in subsequent, related litigation. If the hearing examiner, after considering all the evidence, concludes, for example, that the employee quit for good reason based on race discrimination, the employer may be prohibited from contesting that fact in a later discrimination suit. Even if the results of an unemployment insurance hearing are not binding as to subsequent, related litigation, statements made at the unemployment insurance hearing may be admissible in the litigation. Employers should therefore think carefully before appealing an adverse claim decision to a hearing examiner when there is a risk of related litigation. If an employer decides to appeal, it should be prepared to put on a strong defense on all the issues, just as if it were litigating in court.

BENEFITS

Assuming the claimant qualifies for benefits, the amount of the benefit is determined by statutory formulas based on the claimant's base period wages.

Benefits last up to 26 weeks, which may be extended in certain circumstances. After using up the maximum benefit, the claimant is ineligible for additional benefits until he or she has worked in covered employment.

CHAPTER 13
Workplace Safety

- Overview of OSH Act
- Safety and Health Standards
- Ergonomics
- Record-Keeping and Reporting
- Inspections and Citations
- The FDA's Food Code
- Retaliation and Refusal to Work
- State Requirements
- Smoking
- Violence in the Workplace
- Guns in the Workplace
- Disaster Planning

Workers' compensation laws largely eliminated employer liability for failing to provide a safe workplace. Occupational safety and health laws, such as the federal *Occupational Safety and Health Act* (OSH Act), restore that liability by imposing detailed safety and health standards on employers, by authorizing unannounced inspections, compliance orders, and injunctions, and by imposing civil fines and criminal penalties for violations. While safety and health laws impose obligations on both employees and employers, generally only the employer is subject to penalties.

OVERVIEW OF OSH ACT

The OSH Act, passed in 1970, imposes on every employer the general duty to furnish to each of its employees employment and a place of employment that are free from recognized hazards that are causing or are likely to cause death or serious physical harm—the so-called *General Duty Clause*. To ensure that obligation is met, the OSH Act requires every employer to comply with specific occupational safety and health standards promulgated by the secretary of labor. The OSH Act also imposes posting, record-keeping, and reporting requirements on employers.

The OSH Act requires the secretary of labor, through the Occupational Health and Safety Administration (OSHA) in the U.S. Department of Labor (DOL), to issue safety and health standards in three categories:

- *established federal standards*, meaning standards that were in effect when the act was passed, either as part of some other act of Congress, or contained in regulations of a federal agency
- *national consensus standards*, meaning broadly accepted standards adopted by nationally recognized organizations
- *additional standards*, meaning additional occupational safety and health standards that the secretary determines would serve the purposes of the OSH Act.

Employers are required to comply with all applicable standards issued by OSHA. Many standards are industry-specific, such as those dealing with longshoring and the fishing industry. Many others are broadly applicable.

SAFETY AND HEALTH STANDARDS

The standards adopted to date fill thousands of pages in the Code of Federal Regulations. A comprehensive analysis is not possible here. What follows is a brief discussion of a few standards of more general applicability or interest. Employers should contact their trade associations or obtain copies of OSHA publications for guidance as to specific standards or standards uniquely applicable to their industry or profession.

Generally Applicable Standards

As examples of generally applicable standards, employers are required to do the following:

- keep work areas clean, orderly, and sanitary, and keep floors clean and dry
- protect stairwells by guardrails and guard or cover other floor openings
- provide free and unobstructed exits from all parts of a building or other structure when occupied, mark exits by lighted signs, and maintain and test fire alarm and sprinkler systems
- provide readily accessible fire extinguishers
- provide medical first aid supplies and, in the absence of nearby medical facilities, ensure the presence of a person trained in first aid

Employers are also required to have an *emergency action plan* covering, at a minimum, the following:

- procedures for reporting a fire or other emergency
- procedures for emergency evacuation
- procedures to be followed by employees who remain to handle critical plant operations

- procedures to account for employees after evacuation
- procedures to be followed by employees performing rescue or medical duties
- the names or job titles of employee contacts who know about the plan

For employers with more than 10 employees, the plan must be in writing and kept available in the workplace for review. Employers with 10 or fewer employees may communicate the plan orally to employees.

AEDs

Although OSHA standards do not specifically require that employers install *automated external defibrillators* (AEDs) at the worksite, OSHA offers nonbinding advice that they do so and provide personnel trained in their use.

Hazardous Materials

Handling of hazardous materials is the subject of extensive regulation. OSHA has established detailed requirements for products such as flammable and combustible liquids, explosives, and liquefied petroleum gases. For highly hazardous chemicals (substances that are toxic, reactive, flammable, or explosive and are stored in sufficient quantities to cause a catastrophe if released), the employer must inform employees of the hazard involved and must consult with employees to develop safety management plans and training.

Closely associated with OSHA's hazardous materials standards are its hazard communication standards. Chemical manufacturers and importers are obligated to determine the hazards of each of their products. That information, along with protective measures for each product, is communicated downstream to distributors, who in turn distribute it to their customers. OSHA has developed a multipage form for communicating this information, known as a *safety data sheet* (SDS) (formerly known as a materials safety data sheet) that must contain the following information at a minimum:

- identification of the product; recommended use and restrictions on use; name, address, and telephone number of the chemical manufacturer, importer, or other responsible party; and emergency phone number
- identification of hazards
- chemical name, common name and synonyms
- impurities and stabilizing additives that are themselves classified and that contribute to the classification of the substance
- first-aid measures
- firefighting measures, including special protective equipment and precautions for firefighters
- accidental release measures, including personal precautions, protective equipment, emergency procedures, and methods and materials for containment and cleaning up
- handling and storage
- exposure controls/personal protection
- physical and chemical properties—appearance, color, odor, pH, melting point, freezing point, boiling point, flash point, evaporation rate, flammability, density, solubility, and viscosity
- stability and reactivity
- toxicological information

All employers along the way, from manufacturer to end user, are required to communicate the SDS information to their employees who come in contact with the product and to train their employees in handling the product. This communication and training program must be in writing; sample programs are available from OSHA. The hazardous products themselves must be appropriately tagged or marked.

Employers must have on hand, and make available to their employees, copies of the SDS for each hazardous chemical at the workplace.

Lockout/Tagout Standard

Another widely applicable standard is OSHA's *Lockout/Tagout Standard*, designed to prevent the accidental startup of machines and equipment while being serviced or the accidental release of hazardous energy. The standard requires that any machinery or equipment that is being serviced must be isolated from its energy source, and the isolation device must be locked. If the device cannot be locked, it must be tagged with a warning such as DO NOT START. The lock or tag may be removed only by the person who put it in place. Before removal, he or she must conduct an inspection. After removal but before startup, he or she must notify affected employees that the machine or equipment is about to be placed back in service. The standard also requires employers to train their employees in complying with lockout/tagout procedures.

Personal Protective Equipment

OSHA has adopted a number of standards dealing with use of *personal protective equipment* (PPE). PPE standards are designed to protect the eyes, face, head, extremities, respiratory system, and the body generally. For example, when exposure to noise in the workplace exceeds specified levels or extends beyond specified durations, protective devices must be worn to reduce effective exposure below permitted levels. Respirators are required in dusty or smoky environments. Hard hats are a common sight at construction jobs.

Who pays for PPE—the employer or the employee? In the past, OSHA regulations required only that PPE must be *provided*. Some employers read these regulations as allowing them to charge their employees for hard hats, wire-mesh gloves, ear plugs, and other equipment. In response, OSHA issued final regulations requiring employers to pick up the cost of all PPE *except* the following:
- nonspecialty safety footwear and nonspecialty prescription safety eyewear, provided the employer permits such items to be worn off the jobsite
- boots with built-in metatarsal guards

- ordinary clothing, such as long-sleeve shirts, long pants, street shoes, and normal work boots
- items used solely for protection from weather, such as winter coats, jackets, gloves, parkas, rubber boots, hats, raincoats, ordinary sunglasses, and sunscreen
- replacement PPE, when the replacement is necessary because the employee has lost or intentionally damaged the PPE
- PPE voluntarily provided by the employee

Bloodborne Pathogens

The health care and medical research community may be particularly interested in OSHA's *bloodborne pathogen* standards. Bloodborne pathogens are infectious microorganisms in human blood that can cause disease in humans, such as hepatitis B (HBV), hepatitis C (HCV) and human immunodeficiency virus (HIV). Needlesticks and other sharps-related injuries may expose workers to bloodborne pathogens. Workers in many occupations, including first responders, hospital laundry employees, and nurses and other health care personnel, may be at risk for exposure to bloodborne pathogens.

To reduce or eliminate occupational exposure to bloodborne pathogens, an employer must implement an *exposure control plan* for the worksite with details on employee protection measures. The plan must also describe how an employer will use engineering and work practice controls, personal protective clothing and equipment, employee training, medical surveillance, and other provisions as required by OSHA's Bloodborne Pathogens Standard. HBV vaccinations must also be made available free of charge to all employees who face an exposure risk; in addition, the employer must pay the employee's travel expenses to receive HBV vaccinations and treat his or her travel time as work time.

The employer must also follow *universal precautions*, which require that all blood and certain bodily fluids be treated as if known to be infectious for HIV, HBV, and other bloodborne pathogens. Universal precautions include proper labeling, decontamination and disposal procedures, and use of PPE such as gloves and eye protectors.

⚠ ALERT!

Safety considerations may justify placing limits on soliciting and distributing literature at the workplace. However, unless the rules are consistently enforced, the employer may be subject to unfair labor practice charges for prohibiting pro-union solicitations and literature. (See Chapter 24 for information on unions.)

ERGONOMICS

OSHA tells us that *musculoskeletal disorders* (MSDs) affect the muscles, nerves, blood vessels, ligaments, and tendons. Workers in many different industries and occupations can be exposed to risk factors at work, such as lifting heavy items, bending, reaching overhead, pushing and pulling heavy loads, working in awkward body postures, and performing the same or similar tasks repetitively. Exposure to these known risk factors for MSDs increases a worker's risk of injury.

OSHA pushed for mandatory ergonomic standards, but its efforts have so far been delayed or overturned by Congress. Despite congressional resistance, OSHA never abandoned the field and has been studying ergonomics ever since. As part of that process, it announced in 2002 a protocol for developing industry- and task-specific guidelines. As of this writing it has issued voluntary guidelines for nursing homes, retail grocery stores, poultry processing, beverage distribution, foundries, and shipyards. OSHA also identifies certain industries at high risk for MSDs, including the following:

- nurses, nursing assistants, and psychiatric aides
- firefighters and law enforcement officers
- laborers and freight, stock, and materials movers
- janitors
- truck and bus drivers
- maids and house cleaners
- plumbers and heating, ventilation, and air conditioning (HVAC) mechanics and installers

Although OSHA's ergonomics guidelines are nonbinding, in the sense that OSHA will not rely on them for enforcement purposes, employers still have a duty under the General Duty Clause of the OSH Act to provide a safe workplace. Despite their nonbinding status, the guidelines could conceivably be used to show that an employer has violated the General Duty Clause.

Employers should anticipate that ergonomics litigation will increase and that federal or state safety standards in some form will eventually be adopted.

RECORD-KEEPING AND REPORTING

All employers, regardless of size, must report any work-related fatality to OSHA within eight hours and any work-related, in-patient hospitalization, amputation, or loss of eye within 24 hours.

Employers that employ more than 10 employees must maintain an annual log and summary of all recordable injuries and illnesses. A *recordable* injury or illness is one that is work-related and that results in any of the following:

- a fatality
- a lost workday
- restricted work activity or job transfer
- medical treatment beyond mere first aid
- loss of consciousness
- a significant illness or injury diagnosed by a health care professional, including cancer, tuberculosis, chronic irreversible disease, a fractured or cracked bone, or a punctured eardrum
- a needlestick injury or cut from a contaminated object
- an injury or illness requiring the employee to be medically removed
- significant hearing loss

The records are kept on an annual basis, and each year's records must be retained for five years. OSHA provides a set of forms, instructions, and worksheets for satisfying record-keeping requirements, including Form 300 (Log of Work-Related Injuries and Illnesses),

Form 300A (Summary of Work-Related Injuries and Illnesses), and Form 301 (Injury and Illness Incident Report), all available on OSHA's website. Employees have a right to review these records, and the annual summary must be posted in a location accessible to employees.

Employers must also establish reasonable procedures for employees to report injuries and illnesses to the employer.

INSPECTIONS AND CITATIONS

OSHA inspectors (called *Compliance Safety and Health Officers*) are authorized to enter and inspect any workplace at all reasonable times to ensure compliance with OSHA standards. The inspections are unannounced—it is illegal for anyone to forewarn an employer that an inspection will take place—and may include interviewing employees in private, taking photographs and environmental samples, and reviewing records. A representative of the employer and an employee representative may accompany the inspector during the inspection.

An inspection may be initiated by OSHA itself, or it may be conducted at the request of an employee who believes that a safety violation exists. It is illegal for an employer to retaliate against an employee for complaining about an OSH Act violation or for giving testimony or otherwise cooperating in an OSHA matter.

Inspections and other proceedings under the OSH Act present the risk that an employer's trade secrets will be disclosed. The act, as well as DOL regulations, contain special provisions to protect the confidentiality of trade secrets. Inspectors also need appropriate security clearances to inspect areas containing classified information, and they must comply with the employer's health and safety rules, such as wearing PPE.

Employers may refuse to admit an OSHA inspector and insist that he or she obtain a search warrant. Putting an inspector to this added burden obviously does not create a cooperative atmosphere, and it may in fact encourage the inspector to perform a more detailed, intrusive procedure. Nevertheless, there are times when the employer should insist on a warrant. For example, if the employer suspects that a violation exists, a brief delay may provide just the opportunity needed to fix the problem. A delay might also be needed if a particular company official who should be present during the inspection is away. The company might also want advice from its attorney before permitting the inspection. If an inspector anticipates that the company will insist on a warrant, the inspector may obtain one beforehand, thus defeating any advantage the employer had hoped to gain from delay.

At the conclusion of the inspection, the inspector must inform the employer of any apparent health and safety violations. The employer also has an opportunity to point out conditions or procedures related to the apparent violations. After the inspection, the inspector submits a report to OSHA's local area director. If the report indicates a violation, the area director issues either a *citation* or a *notice of de minimis violation* (a violation that has no direct or immediate relationship to health or safety). OSHA must issue citations and notices within six months of the inspection.

Citations must describe with particularity the nature of the alleged violation, including a reference to the safety or health standard allegedly violated. The citation must also fix a reasonable time within which to abate the violation. Employers are required to post a copy of the citation at or near the site of the violation for at least three days or until the violation is abated, even if the citation is being contested.

In addition to the citation, OSHA's area director notifies the employer of a proposed penalty. (No penalty is proposed for *de minimis* violations.) Penalties can be as high as $12,675 per violation, depending on the seriousness of the violation. A failure-to-abate violation can be up to $12,675 per day. And willful or repeated violations can cost an employer $126,749 per violation. The secretary of labor may also go to federal court for an injunction to stop any practices or procedures that pose an imminent threat of death or serious physical harm.

The OSH Act provides for criminal penalties in case of a willful violation resulting in the death of an employee.

The employer has 15 working days after receipt of a citation to contest the alleged violation, the proposed penalty, or the time allowed for abatement of the violation. Contests are initially handled through administrative proceedings, followed by a right of appeal to the courts.

THE FDA'S FOOD CODE

The federal Food and Drug Administration (FDA) issues the Food Code: a set of model regulations offered by the FDA for adoption by state and local government agencies that have public health responsibilities. The regulations in turn govern food service industry procedures. Unless adopted by other government agencies, the Food Code itself is not a binding regulation. The Food Code is published every four years with interim supplements. It is available on the FDA's website.

RETALIATION AND REFUSAL TO WORK

The OSH Act prohibits retaliation against an employee because the employee filed an OSH Act complaint, testified in a OSH Act proceeding, or exercised any other rights afforded him or her by the act. But the act generally does not protect an employee who walks off the job out of safety concerns. In that situation, the employee's remedy is to notify his employer of the danger and, if the employer fails to take appropriate action, to request an OSHA inspection. The statute does not authorize *unilateral self-help*.

There may be situations, however, in which the employee faces an impossible choice of either immediately complying with a supervisor's instructions and risking serious injury or death, or not complying and being fired. In other words, the right to complain may simply not be a viable remedy. For those situations, OSHA has adopted regulations that say if the employee, with no reasonable alternative, refuses in good faith to expose himself or herself to the dangerous condition, the employee will be protected against subsequent retaliation.

The condition causing the employee's apprehension of death or injury must be of such a nature that a reasonable person, under the circumstances then confronting the employee, would conclude that there is a real danger of death or serious injury and that there is insufficient time, due to the urgency of the situation, to eliminate the danger by resorting to regular statutory enforcement channels. In addition, in such circumstances, the employee, when possible, must also have sought from his employer, and been unable to obtain, a correction of the dangerous condition.

In a 1980 decision, the Supreme Court upheld this regulation in a case in which an employee refused to work on a steel mesh that other workers had fallen through and suffered injury or death. Later court decisions have emphasized that the specific requirements of the regulation must be met: the employee must be acting reasonably and in good faith, the danger must be both real and serious, and the employee must have no opportunity to address the danger through regular channels.

The *National Labor Relations Act* (NLRA) protects workers who voice safety concerns or who engage in a job action to protest safety conditions. Under the NLRA, an employer may not take adverse action against employees who engage in concerted activity to complain about safety issues or other job-related conditions. The NLRA also provides that employees who quit work in the good-faith belief that their workplace is abnormally dangerous are not deemed to be on strike. That provision has been interpreted to mean that, like workers who are on strike to protest an unfair labor practice, workers who are absent for safety reasons may not be permanently replaced. (In contrast, workers who are on strike for purely economic reasons may be permanently replaced. See Chapter 24 for more on unions.) Fear of exposure to asbestos in an apartment complex and fear of exposure to radioactive depleted uranium dust have also justified employee refusals to work.

CASE STUDY:
PROTECTED JOB ACTION

In a 1962 Supreme Court decision involving a factory in Baltimore, seven employees walked off the job on a bitter cold January day because their work area was unheated. The area was often uncomfortably cold anyway (a matter of repeated complaint) and, on the day in question, the furnace that usually supplied some heat had broken down. The Supreme Court ruled that the job action was protected under federal labor law, so the employer had no right to fire the workers.

STATE REQUIREMENTS

The OSH Act provides that individual states may assume responsibility for occupational safety and health matters by developing a plan that is *at least as effective* as the OSH Act itself. State plans are subject to review and approval by the U.S. secretary of labor.

At this writing, the following states, along with Puerto Rico and the Virgin Islands, have approved state plans:

- Alaska
- Arizona
- California
- Connecticut
- Hawaii
- Illinois
- Indiana
- Iowa
- Kentucky
- Maine
- Maryland
- Michigan
- Minnesota
- Nevada
- New Jersey
- New Mexico
- New York
- North Carolina
- Oregon
- South Carolina
- Tennessee
- Utah
- Vermont
- Virginia
- Washington
- Wyoming

Once a state plan has received final approval, enforcement of workplace safety and health matters shifts to the state, and OSHA's enforcement authority no longer applies with respect to any issue covered by the state plan.

SMOKING

Most of the issues relating to smoking involve the rights of nonsmokers to be free from secondhand smoke. Many states and local jurisdictions have laws requiring employers to restrict smoking in the workplace. Some employers have responded by prohibiting smoking altogether. Others have designated a specific area for smoking that is sealed from the remainder of the workplace or that is under negative pressure so that smoke-filled air does not escape.

Aside from state and local law obligations, employers could conceivably face liability to nonsmokers under the following conditions:

- based on a violation of the OSH Act's General Duty Clause
- under workers' compensation laws if an allergic employee suffers a temporary disability from cigarette smoke
- under the Americans with Disabilities Act, on the theory that an employee who is allergic to cigarette smoke is disabled and is entitled to reasonable accommodation
- for unemployment insurance benefits, if the nonsmoker claims he or she quit for good reason to avoid a smoke-filled, unsafe workplace

A prudent employer will adopt and enforce a smoking policy designed to protect the health of nonsmokers.

Do employees have a right to take smoke breaks? With few exceptions, most state laws do not entitle employees to any breaks at all, so that a break policy (including cigarette breaks) is a matter within the employer's discretion. An employer that does permit short breaks (up to 20 minutes in the view of the U.S. DOL) cannot exclude that time for purposes of computing hourly wages.

Even though employers do not have to permit smoke breaks, they are prohibited by laws in some jurisdictions from discriminating against smokers, provided the smokers limit their smoking to off-duty hours.

☞ **QUICK TIP**
For unionized shops, smoking policy is a subject of mandatory bargaining.

VIOLENCE IN THE WORKPLACE

According to OSHA, homicide is one of the leading causes of fatal occupational injury in the United States. OSHA also reports that nonfatal violence is a widespread and growing phenomenon, particularly in jobs involving the exchange of money with the public (for example, retail, home delivery), working alone, working late at night, guarding valuable property, and working in a community setting (for example, taxicab drivers, health care workers).

OSHA does not have any specific standards for workplace violence. OSHA points out, however, that the General Duty Clause—that every employer furnish employment free from recognized hazards—may itself impose duties on employers whose workers are at risk.

Whether or not employers owe a specific legal duty to prevent workplace violence, it makes good business sense to offer at least a minimum level of protection. Employers should consider these steps:

- Be alert to any history of violence in applicants for employment.
- Adopt, disseminate, and enforce a policy that any violence or threats of violence by employees will be met with dismissal.
- Prohibit employees from bringing weapons of any kind to the employer's place of business or from carrying weapons during working hours (unless state law provides otherwise; see the following discussion).
- Prohibit employee use or possession of alcohol and illegal drugs, or being under the influence of alcohol or drugs, while on the job.
- For larger employers, require photo ID badges for all employees.
- Secure nonpublic work areas and limit access to those with keys/ passcards.
- Secure all areas after normal working hours.
- Provide adequate lighting for storage and garage areas.
- Provide cellphones to employees who work off premises.
- As necessary, contract with a security firm to provide security personnel, remote monitoring, emergency phones, alarms, etc.

- Restrict distribution of employee directories, particularly if they contain home addresses, home telephone numbers, names of spouses or children, or other personal information.
- Establish an employee assistance program (EAP) and encourage its use.
- Alert employees to any special risks the job may present and invite employees to express their concerns.
- Develop policies for responding to emergencies and train employees in recognizing and responding to emergencies.

GUNS IN THE WORKPLACE

The Second Amendment to the U.S. Constitution says: "A well regulated Militia, being necessary to the security of a free State, the right of the people to keep and bear Arms, shall not be infringed." Before the Supreme Court's 2008 decision in *District of Columbia v. Heller*, there was debate whether the Second Amendment recognized an individual right to bear arms or whether it applied only to members of the militia (read "National Guard"). In *Heller* the Court ruled that the right applies to individuals (with certain exceptions, such as for felons and people with mental illness).

Under the Second Amendment, neither the federal government, nor by extension, the states, may infringe on this individual right to bear arms. But the Second Amendment says nothing about nongovernmental organizations and persons infringing on the right. So at least as far as the Constitution is concerned, a homeowner may forbid guests from bringing weapons into his or her home, a retail store or place of worship may ban weapons on premises, and a manufacturer may prohibit guns in its factory.

With homicide being the second leading cause of death in the workplace (according to OSHA), banning guns in the workplace might seem like good sense. It might be argued, for example, that such a rule is consistent with, even required by, the OSH Act's General Duty Clause. Or that reducing the risk of serious injury or death to employees will likely reduce workers' compensation claims. Or that an employer that knows about an employee's violent propensities but that fails to restrict weaponry in the workplace may be liable for any injury or death the employee causes.

A number of states see the issue differently. As of this writing close to half the states have passed laws allowing employees to bring their guns to work, despite an employer policy to the contrary. So-called *parking lot laws* are typical: they permit employees to have weapons in their locked vehicle while at work. Some laws also prohibit employers from searching vehicles parked on the employer's lot, inquiring about possession of fire arms, or discriminating against gun owners.

We may never know what effect these state laws have on violence in the workplace. For more than 20 years, the Centers for Disease Control and Prevention (CDC) has avoided studying gun deaths following threats by Congress to defund the agency. After the Sandy Hook school shootings, then-President Obama directed to CDC to research the causes and prevention of gun violence, but to date nothing has come of that directive.

DISASTER PLANNING

Recent events have focused attention on responding to disasters of both the terrorist and the natural kind. While complete protection is impossible, advance planning can minimize injury and death.

Building Owners

An employer that owns the building in which the workplace is located must, of course, maintain the building in compliance with local and state safety codes. This compliance may include, for example, fire alarm and sprinkler systems, fire extinguishers, and exit lights. Emergency exits must be accessible and unlocked.

Building owners can take additional steps which, though not required, may go a long way to protecting employees. The National Institute for Occupational Safety and Health (NIOSH), which is part of the federal CDC, has issued its *Guidance for Protecting*

Building Environments from Airborne Chemical, Biological, or Radiological Attacks.

NIOSH's recommendations regarding chemical, biological, or radiological (CBR) attacks include the following:

- preventing access to outdoor air intakes, such as by relocating them on secure building roofs
- securing roofs and other areas where mechanical equipment is located
- isolating lobbies, mailrooms, loading docks, and storage areas
- securing return air grilles
- restricting access to information about building operations and systems
- installing high-efficiency filters in the HVAC system
- developing a response plan for a CBR emergency, such as shutting down the HVAC system entirely

Other Employers

Employers that are not directly responsible for building maintenance and operation can also prepare for disasters, by means such as the following:

- maintaining duplicate employee information (such as names, addresses, payroll data, and emergency contacts) offsite
- establishing a phone tree or blast email or text system to alert employees about whether to report to work
- determining in advance (in consultation with local disaster planning agencies) which emergencies require evacuation of the workplace and which require sheltering in place
- conducting practice drills for various types of emergencies
- if evacuation is appropriate, such as in response to a fire emergency, establishing a gathering point for all employees so that an accurate count can be obtained and emergency personnel can be informed whether all persons are accounted for
- identifying persons with disabilities or who may have special needs in an emergency and assigning appropriate personnel to assist them

☞ **QUICK TIP**

The Equal Employment Opportunity Commission (EEOC) has ruled that an employer may inquire about a worker's disability so that the employer can assist the worker in a disaster. However, it is up to the worker to decide whether assistance is necessary. Any information obtained about the worker's disability or need for assistance is subject to special confidentiality requirements.

Pandemics

Outbreaks of highly contagious, even deadly, infections seem to be more common, including Legionnaires' disease, severe acute respiratory syndrome (SARS), Middle East respiratory syndrome (MERS), Ebola, and Zika. It makes good business sense for employers to take whatever steps they can to protect their workforce from these infections. They may even have a legal obligation to do so under federal and state occupational safety and health laws. This means limiting the spread by enforcing good sanitation practices and social distancing. For example, employers should do the following:

- educate employees as to means of transmission, symptoms, treatment, and prevention
- encourage frequent hand washing
- suspend social customs like handshaking
- encourage employees to clean work areas frequently with alcohol wipes
- provide and encourage use of hand sanitizers
- provide and encourage use of face masks or respirators
- spread employees out over work areas and stagger their shifts
- substitute videoconferencing for face-to-face meetings
- require symptomatic or exposed employees to stay away from the workplace
- implement a teleworking policy for as many employees as possible (see Chapter 20 for more on teleworking)
- limit nonessential travel, especially to regions where disease is prevalent
- isolate employees who are returning from disease-prevalent regions

Despite these efforts, a local outbreak is still likely to cause substantial reductions in the workforce. To prepare for that event, employers need to identify critical functions that must be performed; provide backup for those critical functions, such as cross-training of employees; and postpone or eliminate noncritical functions. If the business is one that can switch to a related product or service, employees will need to be trained in providing that product or service. A restaurant, for example, might add home-delivery services, which will affect staffing—fewer waiters, but more delivery personnel. Delivery employees will need to learn safe food-handling practices and how to process credit card payments offsite.

Businesses will also need to develop alternatives to face-to-face communications. Experience with recent disasters shows that landline and mobile telephone systems may either be down or unreliable due to overload. Alternatives might include email, text messaging, a company intranet, and a virtual private network. Each of these systems needs to be put in place and tested before the pandemic hits.

CHAPTER 14

Discrimination in General

- Title VII of the Civil Rights Act
- Covered Employers and Employees
- Religious Discrimination under Title VII
- Genetics
- Retaliation
- Anatomy of a Title VII Case
- Other Nondiscrimination Laws
- State and Local Prohibitions
- Professional Codes of Ethics
- Record-Keeping
- Employment Practices Liability Insurance

The Civil War made clear that slavery would no longer be tolerated in the United States, but it did little to remedy rampant discrimination. It was not until 1964, through the efforts of Presidents Kennedy and Johnson and after bitter congressional debate, that the first significant nondiscrimination laws were passed. Since then, numerous protections have been added, not only at the federal level, but also at state and local levels.

This chapter addresses employment discrimination in general, including religious and genetic discrimination. Subsequent chapters deal with discrimination on account of gender, age, and disability.

TITLE VII OF THE CIVIL RIGHTS ACT

The *Civil Rights Act of 1964* is the first modern piece of federal legislation to address discrimination generally. The act deals not only with discrimination in employment but also with discrimination in public accommodations. The act was amended in 1991 to clarify and strengthen certain provisions and to expand the range of available remedies to include compensatory and punitive damages in cases of intentional discrimination.

Title VII of the act addresses employment discrimination. It applies to all employers that have 15 or more employees and to employment agencies and labor unions. The *Equal Employment Opportunity Commission* (EEOC), created by Title VII, together with cooperating state and local agencies, enforces Title VII at the administrative level by investigating charges, recommending remedies, and conciliating disputes between employers and employees. The EEOC can also bring suit in its own name against employers in federal court. EEOC guidelines interpreting Title VII are a useful resource.

At the heart of Title VII is the following provision:

It shall be an unlawful employment practice for an employer:

(1) to fail or refuse to hire or to discharge any individual, or otherwise to discriminate against any individual

with respect to his compensation, terms, conditions, or privileges of employment, because of such individual's race, color, religion, sex, or national origin; or

(2) to limit, segregate, or classify his employees or applicants for employment in any way which would deprive or tend to deprive any individual of employment opportunities or otherwise adversely affect his status as an employee, because of such individual's race, color, religion, sex, or national origin.

Those two paragraphs have generated whole libraries of commentary and many thousands of court decisions. Many of the Supreme Court's landmark cases during the last 50 years have involved Title VII. It would be impossible to digest that body of material here. What follows is a brief overview of Title VII principles and a discussion of some of the more important issues employers are likely to face.

Title VII is not limited to traditional minorities. Everyone—whites as well as blacks, males as well as females, Christians as well as Jews—is protected. In other words, Title VII does not protect special groups from adverse employment decisions. Rather, it prohibits an employer from using *certain criteria* when making decisions. So, for example, a more qualified white male who is passed over for promotion in favor of a less qualified black female has a good Title VII claim if the employer was motivated by race or gender.

Reverse Discrimination

The discrimination that a nonminority member suffers when an employer discriminates in favor of a minority member is sometimes called *reverse discrimination*. Although the Supreme Court has made clear that such favoritism is plain and simple discrimination, the court's current views on this topic are not entirely clear. In a pair of widely publicized decisions involving the University of Michigan, the court ruled that the university's law school may consider race as a plus factor in evaluating individual applicants to the law school. According to the court, the law school had a legitimate educational interest in assembling a diverse student body.

In 2016, the Supreme Court considered a case involving the admissions policy of the University of Texas at Austin. Under the policy, the school admitted all applicants who graduated from a Texas high school in the top 10 percent of his or her class (a requirement of state law), and it filled the remainder of its incoming freshman class by combining an applicant's "academic index" (SAT scores and high school academic performance) with the applicant's "personal achievement index," which the court described as a holistic review containing numerous factors, *including race*. The court upheld UT's admissions policy despite the inclusion of race as a consideration.

Since employers, too, have a legitimate interest in a diverse workforce, the court's reasoning would seem to apply to employment as well as higher education. It remains to be seen, however, just how these decisions might transfer to the workplace.

Disparate Treatment and Disparate Impact

Discrimination under Title VII is sometimes classified as either *disparate treatment* discrimination or *disparate impact* discrimination. The first category includes what immediately comes to mind—intentionally making a personnel decision, such as refusing to hire or promote a particular individual because of race, color, gender, or other characteristic. That type of discrimination is prohibited by Title VII. So too is an employer practice of grouping employees by race, color, gender, or other prohibited factors and treating the groups differently. Employment ads that indicate a preference for or against a particular race, color, or sex are also illegal, whether or not any actual discrimination is shown.

Disparate impact discrimination is more subtle. Suppose an employer adopts a policy that on its face seems neutral but that turns out to have an adverse impact on a particular ethnic group or gender. Take, for example, a private security company that has a minimum height and weight requirement for its patrol officers, the net effect of which is to exclude most females, but almost no males.

Other practices that could give rise to disparate impact claims include minimum education or experience requirements that do not serve a legitimate business purpose, use of tests scores in hiring or promoting if the test is culturally biased or is not related to job performance, or blanket exclusion of applicants with criminal records or whose wages have been garnished.

Terms, Conditions, and Privileges of Employment

Title VII prohibits discrimination in hiring, firing, compensation, and other *terms, conditions, and privileges* of employment. Ready examples of what is meant by terms, conditions, and privileges of employment include shift assignments; fringe benefits such as vacation, sick leave, or insurance programs; and access to facilities such as the cafeteria and fitness center. Courts have ruled that the *intangible work environment* is covered by Title VII as well. Under those rulings, an employer that promotes or tolerates a workplace environment filled with demeaning racial or sexual slurs can be sued by the target of those slurs and by others who find the environment offensive if the slurs are *severe and pervasive* and a *reasonable person* would find the environment offensive.

Trivial or inconsequential workplace actions by the employer will not support a Title VII discrimination action. The Supreme Court has said that a job action must amount to a *significant change in employment status.* The action must also be *objectively detrimental*, not just something a particular employee dislikes. As one court put it, not everything that makes an employee unhappy is an actionable adverse action, nor are changes that make a job less appealing but that do not affect a term, condition, or benefit of employment.

☞ **QUICK TIP**

A less-than-favorable evaluation, minor change in duties, or a change in title, with no effect on pay or status, even for allegedly discriminatory reasons, is not illegal. But if the evaluation leads to a loss of bonus or a demotion and the employee can show discriminatory motive, a good Title VII claim will result.

Bona Fide Occupational Qualification

An employer charged with discrimination on the grounds of sex, religion, or national origin (but not discrimination on the grounds of race) may, in theory, raise a defense of *bona fide occupational qualification* (BFOQ). However, the defense is narrowly interpreted and as a practical matter is rarely available. In the airline industry, for example, a carrier that fails to hire male applicants as flight attendants under the belief that passengers expect females in that role does not have a good BFOQ defense. On the other hand, an employer may rely on the BFOQ exception in hiring actors for male roles and actresses for female roles.

Testers

Private organizations and even the EEOC sometimes use *testers* to obtain evidence of discrimination in the workplace.

EXAMPLE: Suppose an employer that is suspected of having racially discriminatory hiring practices advertises a job opening. Two testers—one white, one black—apply for the job and give fake credentials that are substantially the same. The employer interviews the black candidate first but says he needs to check references before making any offer. He then interviews the white candidate and makes an offer on the spot. If this pattern is repeated several times, the employer will have a difficult time explaining its actions in the discrimination suit that is sure to follow.

Claims of discrimination by testers, and by the organizations that employ them, do not always fare well in court, since the testers are not really candidates and they cannot really claim to have been denied a job.

☞ **QUICK TIP**

The term *employee* as used in Title VII includes former employees. Therefore, it is illegal, for example, for a company to give a bad reference to a former employee in retaliation for the former employee's filing a charge of race discrimination after he or she was fired.

Training

It is not enough for a company to include nondiscrimination provisions in its employee handbook. To have an *effective* nondiscrimination policy, companies must periodically train their employees as to what constitutes discrimination and how to complain about discrimination. As part of the training, employees must be assured that their complaints will not result in retaliation.

Training, as part of an effective nondiscrimination policy, is particularly important with regard to sexual and other types of harassment. Absent an effective policy, the employer will be unable to defend a claim that a supervisor harassed a subordinate employee. (See Chapter 15 for more on harassment.)

COVERED EMPLOYERS AND EMPLOYEES

Title VII defines *employer* as a person or organization engaged in an industry affecting commerce that has 15 or more employees for each working day in each of 20 or more calendar weeks in the current or preceding calendar year.

The term *industry affecting commerce* means any activity, business, or industry in commerce in which a labor dispute would hinder or obstruct commerce or the free flow of commerce—in other words, just about any activity in which an employer might engage. (Title VII is tied to the Commerce Clause of the U.S. Constitution because all federal legislation must be based on one or another of the powers granted the federal government by the Constitution.)

Although failure to meet the 15-employee threshold does not affect a court's power to hear a Title VII case (that is, it does not deprive the court of jurisdiction), an employee bringing a Title VII case must prove that the 15-employee threshold is satisfied as part of his or her case. Failure to do so could result in the case being dismissed. Determining who are employees is therefore critical to a Title VII claim. And, of course, the person making the claim must be an employee (or an applicant for employment or a former employee) to invoke federal nondiscrimination laws in the first place.

The discrimination laws themselves are not at all helpful in answering the question of who are employees. They typically define *employee* as an individual employed by an employer. In the Supreme Court's words, that is a mere nominal definition that is completely circular and explains nothing.

One issue is how to deal with individuals who are carried on the employer's books as employees, but who are not physically at work for a full 20 weeks. In a 1997 Supreme Court case, the employer had between 15 and 17 employees on its payroll for at least 20 weeks, but during 11 of those weeks, it was not actually compensating 15 or more employees. The difference resulted from the fact that two of its employees were part time who worked fewer than five days per week.

The court ruled that the employer was subject to Title VII, adopting what has become known as the *payroll method* for counting employees. Under that method, if an employee appears on the employer's payroll records, he or she is counted whether or not he or she is actually being compensated on a particular day. In short, part-time employees, full-time employees, and presumably persons on leave all count.

☞ **QUICK TIP**

The employee-counting question is broadly applicable to a wide range of federal employment-related laws, even though they may have different numerical thresholds.

Professional Corporations

Yet another issue involves shareholder-directors of professional corporations, such as doctors and lawyers. While they may be classified as employees for federal tax and pension plan purposes, they also manage the professional corporation. (Professional corporations and other types of business entities are discussed in Chapter 1.)

CASE STUDY:
SHAREHOLDER-DIRECTORS AS EMPLOYEES

In a Supreme Court case called Clackamas Gastroenterology Associates, P.C. v. Wells, *an Oregon medical clinic was sued for discrimination by the clinic's bookkeeper. The bookkeeper argued that the clinic met the 15-employee threshold so long as four of its physician-shareholders were counted. The bookkeeper pointed out, for example, that the physician-shareholders had employment contracts, they were salaried, and they were treated as employees for tax purposes. The clinic claimed otherwise—that the physician-shareholders were really more like partners in a partnership and should therefore not be counted. Citing EEOC regulations, the Court in* Clackamas *listed the following six factors to be considered in determining whether a shareholder-director of a professional corporation is an employee for discrimination purposes:*

- *whether the organization can hire or fire the individual or set the rules and regulations of the individual's work*
- *whether, and if so, to what extent, the organization supervises the individual's work*
- *whether the individual reports to someone higher in the organization*
- *whether, and if so, to what extent, the individual is able to influence the organization*
- *whether the parties intended that the individual be an employee, as expressed in written contracts*
- *whether the individual shares in the profits, losses, and liabilities of the organization.*

Whatever the merits of the *Clackamas* decision, the six factors the Supreme Court listed are highly fact-specific. Having to deal with these additional factors adds further uncertainty to discrimination claims and increases associated costs and delays.

Contingent Workers

In general, independent contractors are not covered by the employment provisions of the nondiscrimination laws because they are not employees. However, the *misclassification* of a true employee as an independent contractor is as disastrous for non-discrimination law purposes as it is for tax and benefits entitlement purposes. (Independent contractors are discussed in more detail in Chapters 1 and 7.)

All other categories of contingent workers—such as part-timers, job-sharers, teleworkers, and day laborers—are fully protected by the nondiscrimination laws. For example, a company whose staff includes temporary workers (temps) furnished by an agency cannot direct the agency to furnish (or not furnish) temps of a particular race or gender. Nor can the company accept temps from an agency when the company knows that the agency itself discriminates in selecting persons to be temps.

For certain categories of contingent workers, such as leased or joint employees, it is not always clear who the actual employer is—the staffing firm, the company that controls the actual worksite, or both. The EEOC has developed elaborate guidelines to determine the identity of the employer for purposes of applying the federal nondiscrimination laws. The guidelines turn on such factors as who does the hiring and firing, who handles payroll, and who controls the employee's day-to-day work environment. While it may be possible in any particular circumstance for either the staffing firm or the worksite owner to avoid being tagged as the employer, any company that tolerates or commits discrimination against a member of its workforce is exposed to substantial risk.

Extraterritorial Application

Activities by employers outside the U.S. could certainly affect commerce within the U.S. But the Supreme Court has held that Title VII does not have *extraterritorial application*, so that U.S. citizens employed abroad, even U.S. citizens employed by U.S. employers, have no Title VII protection. Title VII itself exempts aliens employed outside the U.S., and it permits employers operating in a foreign country to comply with that country's law even if compliance amounts to a violation of Title VII.

RELIGIOUS DISCRIMINATION UNDER TITLE VII

Title VII makes it illegal for an employer to discriminate against an employee on the basis of his or her religion. *Religion* includes all aspects of religious observance, practice, and belief. This means, for example, that an employer cannot refuse to hire an applicant because the applicant is a member of a particular religious sect any more than the employer can refuse to hire an applicant on the basis of the applicant's race or gender. Harassment based on religious beliefs or practices also violates Title VII.

But special rules apply to religious discrimination. The First Amendment to the U.S. Constitution says that "Congress shall make no law respecting the establishment of religion, or prohibiting the free exercise thereof." Based on the First Amendment, the courts have developed the so-called *ministerial exception* to Title VII, under which religious organizations may discriminate in connection with the selection and employment of their own clergy.

The term *clergy* has been broadly defined by the courts to include lay employees whose primary duties consist of teaching, spreading the faith, church governance, supervision of religious orders, or participating in religious ritual and worship. So, for example, a nun who was an assistant professor of canon law at Catholic University could not sue for sex discrimination when she was denied tenure. And a lay music teacher at a Catholic elementary school who directed a church choir also could not complain of sex discrimination because, as the court recognized, music is important in the spiritual and pastoral mission of the church and plays in integral role in religious tradition. Even for nonclergy, religious organizations may discriminate against employees on religious grounds. (See Chapter 23 for more on religious organizations.)

Title VII also requires employers to *reasonably accommodate* their employees' religious observances and practices. In this respect it is similar to the Americans with Disabilities Act (ADA) (discussed in Chapter 17), which requires reasonable accommodation of employees with disabilities. As with the ADA, the burden is on the employee to ask for a reasonable religious accommodation.

One difference between disability accommodation under the ADA and religious accommodation under Title VII is that under the ADA the employer must, in effect, conduct an interactive dialogue with a disabled employee to arrive at what is reasonable. Under Title VII, the employer can offer any reasonable accommodation in satisfaction of its obligation.

The employer is excused from accommodating a religious practice if the accommodation would impose an undue hardship. While anything more than a minimal cost to the employer will qualify as an undue hardship, the hardship must be real and not merely speculative or hypothetical.

Following are cases in which employees or applicants claimed that the employer failed to accommodate their religious observances or practices.

Sabbath Day

A number of cases have involved work on a Sunday or other Sabbath day. The courts have ruled that an employer must attempt to accommodate a good-faith belief prohibiting work on Sabbath, such as by allowing the employee to switch with another employee or by having a flexible leave policy that allows the employee to choose the Sabbath as a leave day. However, the employer does not have an absolute duty to accommodate such religious beliefs. If, due to the employer's workload, weekend work is necessary, and if excusing some employees completely from all weekend work would create disruption within the workplace, or would violate established seniority rules or a union contract, the employer may insist that employees participate in weekend work schedules despite their religious scruples to the contrary.

Religious Garb

If there is a good business reason, such as interference with job performance or safety concerns, an employer may prohibit employees from wearing religious garb, such as crucifixes, yarmulkes, or chadors. Otherwise, the employer is likely obligated to accommodate the practice. One way to accommodate might be to transfer the employee to a position that does not involve safety issues. (Dress codes are discussed in Chapters 2 and 15.)

In a case involving Abercrombie & Fitch, a practicing Muslim applicant wore a head scarf at her initial job interview. The scarf would have violated the store's dress code, and she was not hired. The Supreme Court ruled that the applicant stated a good claim of failure to accommodate her religious practice, even though the applicant's religion was never discussed during the interview and the applicant never requested an accommodation.

Abortion and Birth Control

Cases in this area provide a good illustration of what is, and what is not, required of an employer. In one case an anti-abortion activist took a religious vow always to wear a particular button depicting a fetus and containing anti-abortion slogans. The button was disturbing to many of her co-workers for reasons unrelated to religious beliefs. Her employer offered her the option of covering the button while at work, wearing a different button that contained the slogans but not the fetus, or removing the button when she left her immediate work area. She refused all of these options and was fired. In her Title VII suit for religious discrimination, the court held that the employer had offered a reasonable accommodation and was justified in firing her when she rejected the accommodation.

In another case, an orthodox Jewish pharmacist, who was unwilling to sell condoms on religious grounds, applied for a job at a drugstore. The drugstore refused to consider his application and was sued for discrimination. The court agreed with the pharmacist, noting that the drugstore made no effort whatever at accommodation and that the drugstore's claim of undue hardship, had it tried to accommodate, was merely speculative.

The Patient Protection and Affordable Care Act (PPACA), discussed in Chapter 10, requires employer group health plans to provide preventive care and screenings to women without any additional cost to the female patients. Regulations adopted under the PPACA identify some 20 contraceptive methods (including four that prevent a fertilized egg from attaching to the uterus) that are included within the PPACA's preventive care requirement. However, consistent with another federal law—the Religious Freedom Restoration Act—the regulations exempt churches and religious nonprofit organizations from the contraceptive mandate. The question before the Supreme Court in *Burwell v. Hobby Lobby Stores, Inc.* was whether for-profit companies, whose owners held the religious belief that life begins at conception, had to comply with the contraceptive mandate. The court ruled that the companies did not have to comply.

Praying and Preaching

To what extent may an employee actively promote his or her religious beliefs to fellow employees? In one case a management-level employee, who had become an evangelical Christian, wrote a letter to her supervisor stating that because of certain unidentified actions the supervisor had taken, he needed to "get right with God." The supervisor's wife saw the letter and took it to mean that her husband was having an affair. The same employee wrote a second letter to a subordinate of hers, suggesting that the subordinate's illness was punishment for premarital sex. The employee's firing over the letter-writing was justified, said the court, because the employer had no obligation to accommodate such inappropriate behavior by an employee with management responsibilities, even if the behavior was religiously motivated.

In another case, a born-again Christian occasionally prayed in his office with other employees, and he made isolated references to his Christian beliefs. The court ruled that tolerating these trifling incidents imposed no hardship on the employer and could not justify termination.

Refusal to Comply with Tax Laws

When an applicant for employment refused, on religious grounds, to provide his Social Security number, the prospective employer was justified in rejecting his application. The court held that the employer was not required to accommodate the applicant by violating Internal Revenue Service (IRS) regulations or by seeking a waiver from the IRS.

Mandatory Flu Vaccinations

May a hospital or other health care provider require its employees to be vaccinated against seasonal flu? Although the EEOC has no formal rule on the subject, in a 2009 technical assistance document and in a 2012 informal discussion of the matter, the EEOC basically said yes, provided the employer allow exemptions for persons who have sincerely held religious beliefs against the practice, or who cannot be vaccinated for medical reasons.

GENETICS

By use of genetic testing, it is possible to calculate the probability that a person who is now symptom-free will develop a disabling or fatal disorder. Biomedical research continues to increase the number of conditions known to be genetically linked. While some genetic markers increase only slightly the statistical risk that an associated disease will become manifest, other genetic markers are virtual guaranties of eventual sickness or death.

Title II of the *Genetic Information Nondiscrimination Act* (GINA) generally prohibits the use of genetic information in employment, including discrimination on the basis of genetics and the requiring, requesting, or purchasing of genetic information about employees and applicants. The law defines genetic information as the following:

- genetic tests of an individual or his or her family member
- the manifestation of a disease or disorder in family members of such individual
- genetic services provided to an individual or any family member, or the individual's or family member's participation in clinical research that includes genetic services

A *genetic test* means analysis of human DNA, RNA, chromosomes, proteins, or metabolites that detects genotypes, mutations, or chromosomal changes. A *family member* is an individual's dependent or anyone within the fourth degree of relationship.

The problem is, employers routinely acquire medical information about employees that might just include genetic information. For example, an employee applies for leave under the Family and Medical Leave Act (FMLA), and the supporting report from his physician discloses that the employee suffers from a genetic disorder. Does receipt of that report amount to a violation of GINA?

Under regulations adopted by the EEOC, the general prohibition against acquiring genetic information does not apply when an employee is asking for leave under the FMLA (or other leave policies established by the employer) to care for an ill family member and is required to provide medical certification in support of the leave request. There is also no GINA violation when an employer inadvertently acquires the information. Inadvertent acquisition may occur, for example, when an employee just happens to mention his or her own genetic condition or that of a fellow employee—the so-called water-cooler problem.

Acquisition of genetic information will also be considered inadvertent if the employer uses language such as shown in Figure 14.1 in any request for medical information.

FIGURE 14.1: GINA DISCLAIMER

The Genetic Information Nondiscrimination Act of 2008 (GINA) prohibits employers and other entities covered by GINA Title II from requesting or requiring genetic information of an individual or family member of the individual, except as specifically allowed by this law. To comply with this law, we are asking that you not provide any genetic information when responding to this request for medical information. "Genetic information," as defined by GINA, includes an individual's family medical history, the results of an individual's or family member's genetic tests, the fact that an individual or an individual's family member sought or received genetic services, and genetic information of a fetus carried by an individual or an individual's family member or an embryo lawfully held by an individual or family member receiving assistive reproductive services.

RETALIATION

Title VII also prohibits *retaliation* against an employee who has complained about discrimination or who has assisted another complainant, such as by testifying on his or her behalf.

Whenever a discrimination charge is pending—even an informal one that is still at the internal investigation stage—employers should exercise extraordinary caution in making personnel decisions that affect the complaining employee or others involved in the matter. Any adverse action taken after the initial charge has been made is likely to generate a further charge of retaliation. A weak discrimination claim that would likely fail if pursued before the EEOC or in the courts is all too frequently converted into a successful retaliation claim after the complaining employee suffers an adverse action at the employer's hands. (According to the EEOC's *Performance and Accountability Report: Fiscal Year 2016*, retaliation led the list of charges filed with the EEOC that year.)

The Supreme Court has made clear that to constitute retaliation, the retaliatory acts must be *material and adverse*. However, unlike discrimination itself, the retaliation need not affect the terms or conditions of employment. Under this ruling, an act can qualify as retaliatory even if it is unrelated to the job, so long as it would dissuade a reasonable employee from filing a discrimination charge.

In a 2017 federal court case from New York, the trial court dismissed a claim of disability discrimination, but it allowed a retaliation claim to go forward to trial. The employee's evidence in support of retaliation was that, after the employee made a claim of disability discrimination, his supervisors stopped saying good morning to him, they spoke to him without a warm welcome and as if he were a criminal, they closely monitored his work, and they asked about two instances of unapproved overtime. While this evidence would seem to fall short of the material-and-adverse standard, it illustrates the care an employer must take in the face of a discrimination claim.

ANATOMY OF A TITLE VII CASE

Employers are well-advised to develop in advance procedures for handling a claim of discrimination, whether the claim is simply an internal complaint or a formal charge filed with the EEOC. Missteps at this critical juncture can convert an otherwise straightforward, easily handled matter into costly and disruptive litigation. Competent legal guidance in developing the plan and responding to the claim is essential.

Investigation

Internal complaints must be investigated promptly, thoroughly, and objectively, and appropriate discipline must be imposed when warranted. If the complaint involves, say, only a single inappropriate comment of a sexual nature, perhaps it would be sufficient to have a trained manager or an HR representative conduct the investigation. In most cases, however, an outside, independent investigator is needed. Hiring an independent investigator excludes the lawyers who regularly represent the company, both because they will not be perceived as independent and objective and because the company risks losing the protection of the attorney-client privilege as to other matters on which the lawyers advised the company.

While investigations should be conducted as confidentially as reasonably possible (since unnecessary dissemination of information about the matter could be seen as retaliatory), investigators should not promise confidentiality to the parties or witnesses involved. Further, employers should not impose a blanket prohibition on participants' discussing the matter, because (according to the National Labor Relations Board), doing so could amount to interference with employees' right to engage in concerted activity. Figure 14.2 is a suggested handbook provision addressing investigations.

FIGURE 14.2: COMPANY INVESTIGATIONS

Following receipt of a complaint of discrimination or receipt of other evidence of suspected misconduct, the company will normally conduct an investigation, either by company personnel or by outside professionals. When requested to do so, employees must cooperate with the company and its agents in any such investigation by providing accurate and complete information.

The company has a compelling interest in protecting the integrity of its investigations. In every investigation, the company has a strong desire to protect witnesses from harassment, intimidation, and retaliation; to keep evidence from being destroyed; to ensure that testimony is not fabricated; and to prevent a cover-up. The company may decide in some circumstances that in order to achieve these objectives, the investigation must be conducted in strict confidence. If the company reasonably imposes such a confidentiality requirement and an employee does not maintain confidentiality, the employee may be subject to disciplinary action up to and including termination.

Notice of Charge

Often the first time an employer learns of a discrimination complaint is when it receives notice from the EEOC (or a state or local *fair employment practice agency,* or FEPA) that a formal charge has been filed. Sometimes the EEOC notice advises the employer that no action is currently needed. More likely, the notice includes a lengthy request for company information and records and gives the company a deadline for filing a position statement in response to the charge. The notice will also be accompanied by information regarding the EEOC's voluntary *mediation process* that, if agreed to by the employee and the company, eliminates the need to provide information, records, and a position statement.

If the parties do not agree to mediation, or if mediation is unsuccessful, then the company must comply with the EEOC's information requests and provide a position statement. The EEOC may also ask to interview company personnel who have knowledge pertinent to the discrimination charge.

☞ **QUICK TIP**

Under EEOC rules announced in 2017, an employer's position statement will be shared with the complaining party, but the complaining party's response to the position statement will not be shared with the employer. It is not clear why the EEOC has unleveled the playing field this way.

Probable Cause

When the EEOC completes its investigation, it usually issues a written finding either that there is *probable cause* to believe discrimination occurred or that there is no probable cause. Or it may just dismiss the charge without any finding. In the event of a probable cause finding, the EEOC then invites the parties to *conciliate*—a step the EEOC is legally required to take. Conciliation is different from mediation, because at the mediation stage the parties can generally resolve the charge on any terms they deem appropriate. At the conciliation stage, however, the EEOC is effectively a party to the negotiations and will insist that remedial measures be included in any final agreement, such as that the company agree to monitor its employment practices and that it post a notice in the workplace concerning the discrimination.

If conciliation is unsuccessful, or if the EEOC finds no probable cause or dismisses the case without any finding, then the EEOC issues a *right-to-sue letter* authorizing the complaining party to file suit in court within 90 days. Receipt of such a letter is a prerequisite for going to court on any discrimination or retaliation claim over which the EEOC has jurisdiction.

If the parties reach agreement, either during mediation or after conciliation, the agreement will be binding on them just like any other contract. But absent agreement, the EEOC has no authority to decide discrimination charges or impose enforceable remedies on employers in the private sector. So an employer may be tempted simply to ignore the EEOC charge. This is usually a mistake.

Ignoring the EEOC means missing the opportunity to convince the EEOC that the charge is groundless. If the EEOC finds no probable cause, the complaining employee may well be discouraged from pursuing the matter in court or may have difficulty finding a lawyer to take his or her case. Even if the charge is not groundless, ignoring the EEOC means missing the opportunity to mediate or conciliate the charge and avoid costly litigation. Finally, the EEOC itself can file suit and may decide to do so when faced with a recalcitrant employer.

Remedies

A successful plaintiff in a Title VII discrimination case can be awarded a variety of remedies by the court. In a failure-to-hire or wrongful termination case, for example, the remedies might include the following:

- back pay—pay and benefits the plaintiff would have received from the time of the discrimination to the time of the court judgment
- reinstatement—an order that the employer hire or reinstate the plaintiff
- front pay—if hiring or reinstatement is not feasible, pay and benefits the plaintiff would have received from the date of the court judgment until he or she can reasonably be expected to obtain comparable employment
- compensatory damages—money damages for humiliation and embarrassment the plaintiff suffered in connection with the dis-

crimination, capped as follows: for employers with between 15 and 100 employees, $50,000; for employers with between 101 and 200 employees, $100,000; for employers with between 201 and 500 employees, $200,000; and for employers with more than 500 employees, $300,000

- punitive damages—damages to punish the employer acting with malice or reckless indifference to the employee's federally protected rights
- attorney's fees and costs—fees of the plaintiff's attorney and court costs incurred in the litigation (in addition, of course, to the fees and costs the company has to pay its own attorney to defend the case)

After-Acquired Evidence

When faced with a formal, EEOC charge of discrimination, the employer, usually through its attorneys, undertakes its own investigation to determine whether the charge has merit and whether any defenses are available. Sometimes an investigation turns up evidence about the complaining employee, such as false resume statements, that would have justified firing the employee or not hiring him or her in the first place. Such *after-acquired evidence* is not a complete defense to a discrimination claim, but it does limit the remedies available to the aggrieved employee. As the Supreme Court said in such a case, it makes no sense to compel an employer that fired an employee for discriminatory reasons to rehire the employee, and then turn around and fire the employee again based on resume fraud. But it does make sense to allow a back-pay award for the period before the resume fraud was discovered.

OTHER NONDISCRIMINATION LAWS

Although Title VII is by far the broadest and most significant federal nondiscrimination law, it is not the only one. Other federal laws apply in more limited circumstances.

Section 1981

A Reconstruction-era statute guarantees to all persons within the United States "the same right ... to make and enforce contracts ... as is enjoyed by white citizens." (Lawsuits brought under this statute are known as *§1981 actions* because the statute is codified at Title 42 §1981 of the United States Code.) Congress has amended the statute to cover not only the formation and enforcement of contracts but also the making, performance, modification, and termination of contracts, and the enjoyment of all benefits, privileges, terms, and conditions of the contractual relationship. And the courts have interpreted the statute to cover ethnicity as well as race.

Section 1981 is an important statute. Even though Title VII also prohibits racial and ethnic discrimination, Title VII is limited to employers with 15 or more employers. Section 1981 has no such limitation, and it protects independent contractors as well as employees. In addition, claims under §1981 are not subject to the abbreviated time limits set by Title VII, they can be filed in court without first going through the administrative procedures applicable to Title VII claims, and they are not subject to the compensatory damage caps applicable to Title VII.

Immigration

When Congress passed the *Immigration Reform and Control Act* in 1986 making it illegal for employers knowingly to hire persons who are not eligible to work in the U.S., Congress included a provision prohibiting discrimination on the basis of citizenship or national origin. The prohibition applies to employers with four or more employees. Title VII, in contrast, prohibits national origin discrimination by employers with 15 or more employees, and it does not address citizenship status at all.

Military Service

Federal law prohibits any employer from discriminating against employees and applicants for employment on account of their military service. Persons who are members of the uniformed services, who have applied to become members, or who have obligations to one of the uniformed services are protected against discrimination in hiring, retention, re-employment, promotion, or the granting of any employment benefit.

☞ **QUICK TIP**

Nondiscrimination clauses are frequently contained in construction and other contracts with government agencies. (See Chapter 22 for specifics.)

Financial Discrimination

Federal law prohibits an employer from discharging an employee whose earnings have been subject to garnishment for any one debt, regardless of the number of levies made or proceedings brought to collect it. Discrimination against a person who has filed for bankruptcy is also prohibited.

STATE AND LOCAL PROHIBITIONS

Most states and many local governments have their own laws prohibiting discrimination on grounds of race, color, and so on. These laws are not just duplications of federal law, since they often prohibit additional forms of discrimination not specifically covered by federal law, such as ancestry, marital status, sexual orientation, and transgender individuals. These laws also reach smaller employers not covered by Title VII, and they typically do not cap compensatory damage awards. (Gender discrimination, including sexual orientation and gender identity, is covered in Chapter 15.)

When a FEPA provides procedures similar to those available under federal law, the EEOC may enter into a *work-sharing* agreement with the agency. When such a work-sharing agreement is in place, a charge of discrimination filed with either the EEOC or the FEPA is considered dual-filed with both agencies. Work-sharing agreements normally provide that the FEPA will initially handle the charge, subject to final review by the EEOC.

PROFESSIONAL CODES OF ETHICS

The *codes of ethics* of some professional groups contain nondiscrimination clauses. A professional who discriminates in employment may become subjected to disciplinary proceedings before his or her state licensing board and may suffer suspension or revocation of his or her license to practice.

RECORD-KEEPING

Under EEOC regulations, private employers with 100 or more employees and U.S. government contractors with 50 or more employees are required to file an Employer Information Report EEO-1 (also called Standard Form 100) each year. The EEO-1 report calls for data about employees' ethnicity, race and sex by job category. A proposal to add a summary of pay and hours worked was scrapped by the Office of Management and Budget under President Trump.

EEO-1 reports are due by March 31 of each year based on data from any pay period during the last quarter of the previous year. The EEOC does not prescribe any particular records that must be kept to support the information contained in an EEO-1 report, but whatever records are prepared must be kept for a least a year. Records relating to a pending charge of discrimination must be kept until the charge is finally resolved.

EEOC regulations permit employers to collect information on race and national origin for affirmative action compliance and EEO-1 reporting purposes (unless prohibited by state law), but the EEOC recommends that any such records be kept separate from other personnel data, such as evaluations.

The *statutes of limitations*—the time period within which an employee or enforcement agency can bring a claim—should also be considered in establishing record retention policies. Those statutes differ from state to state, and they may even vary for different types of claims. Although charges of Title VII discrimination must be initiated within a relatively brief time period (180 days or 300 days, depending on the particular federal, state, or local agency that has jurisdiction), other types of claims may be filed as late as three or more years after the events take place. A five-year retention policy— that is, a policy of retaining all employment-related documents and information for five years after an employee terminates or an applicant is rejected—may seem a bit excessive, but can prove helpful.

The retention policy should apply not only to documents and information that relate to individual applicants and employees but also to items such as employee handbooks and policy directives that have become out-of-date or superseded. That way, the employer can show what the rules were at a particular time, even if the rules have since changed.

EMPLOYMENT PRACTICES LIABILITY INSURANCE

Most standard premises liability insurance policies and comprehensive general liability (CGL) insurance policies exclude claims arising out of employment matters. This means that if you are sued for abusive discharge, for race or sex discrimination, or for employment-related defamation, your insurance carrier will not provide a defense attorney, and it will not pay any judgment against you. Unless, that is, you have *employment practices liability insurance* (EPLI).

A number of companies offer coverage that picks up where the usual exclusion leaves off. While the coverage may be expensive, it is probably a good idea at least to discuss EPLI with your insurance broker and find out whether it is available and at what cost. Some carriers offer loss control services as part of their coverage, such as reviewing employment application forms and handbooks and counseling on compliance issues.

CHAPTER 15
Gender Discrimination

- Equal Pay Act
- Pregnancy
- Harassment in General
- Employer Liability for Harassment
- Sexual Orientation and Gender Identity
- Other Issues

Sex discrimination in employment, along with discrimination based on race, color, religion, or national origin, is covered by Title VII of the Civil Rights Act. It is just as illegal for an employer to reject an applicant on gender grounds as it is to reject the applicant on racial or religious grounds. Establishment of a glass ceiling, which limits promotion opportunities for women but not for men, is also illegal under Title VII. In other words, all the Title VII principles that apply to discrimination based on race, color, religion, and national origin generally also apply to gender-based discrimination.

But sex discrimination has some unique features. For one thing, sex discrimination is covered by two additional federal laws—the Equal Pay Act and the Pregnancy Discrimination Act—which do not apply to other forms of discrimination. For another, while the inherent differences between persons of varying races, religions, or national origins are superficial at best, there are real biological differences between men and women. Finally, while the term *sex* as used in Title VII was probably intended to mean *gender*, the term can also refer to activity that has nothing to do with discrimination.

The special aspects of sex discrimination are discussed in the following sections of this chapter.

EQUAL PAY ACT

In addition to its minimum wage and overtime pay provisions, the federal Fair Labor Standards Act (FLSA) as amended by the *Equal Pay Act* prohibits employers from paying males and females at different rates for the same work, unless the differential is based on a factor other than sex. And while executives, administrators, and professionals, among others, are exempt from the overtime pay requirements of the FLSA, they are *not* exempt from its equal pay requirements. So an employer that pays males more than females for equal work violates the Equal Pay Act and, if the discrimination is intentional, also violates Title VII.

As noted in Chapter 2, some local jurisdictions, such as New York City, have enacted laws prohibiting employers from asking candidates about their compensation history, on the theory that using such information to set salaries just perpetuates gender discrimination. In the absences of such a law, may an employer base its salary offer on the candidate's compensation history? The Equal Employment Opportunity Commission (EEOC) says no; the few courts that have considered the question are split.

PREGNANCY

In 1978, Congress enacted an amendment to Title VII known as the *Pregnancy Discrimination Act* (PDA). As a result of the PDA, Title VII now defines *because of sex* as including "because of or on account of pregnancy, childbirth, or related medical conditions; women affected by pregnancy, childbirth, or related medical conditions shall be treated the same for all employment-related purposes, including receipt of benefits under fringe benefit programs, as other persons not so affected but similar in their ability or inability to work."

In other words, discrimination because of pregnancy, childbirth, or a related medical condition is sex discrimination, so that an employer cannot refuse to hire a pregnant woman or a woman of childbearing age because of her pregnancy or because of the possibility she may become pregnant.

Nor may an employer have special rules for pregnant women. For example, sick leave must be available to pregnant women on the same basis as it is to others. Similarly, employers that have health or disability insurance plans must cover pregnancy-related expenses and disabilities the same as other medical expenses or disabilities.

Title VII does not require an employer to cover abortions in its group health insurance policies, except when the mother's life would be endangered if the fetus were carried to term and except when medical complications have arisen from an abortion. However, Title VII *permits* a plan to cover abortions.

☞ **QUICK TIP**

The federal *Newborns' and Mothers' Health Protection Act* prohibits group health plans from cutting off benefits for a mother or her newborn child after less than 48 hours of hospitalization following a normal vaginal delivery or after less than 96 hours of hospitalization following a Cesarean section. (See Chapter 10 for more on group health insurance.)

⚠ **ALERT!**

For employers with 50 or more employees, extended leave without pay for complications of pregnancy and childbirth, and to care for newborn children, may be required by the *Family and Medical Leave Act* (FMLA). (Chapter 8 discusses the FMLA.)

Forced Leave

Generally an employer may not require pregnant women to take leave at a specified point in their pregnancies unless the employer can demonstrate a business necessity or bona fide occupational qualification (BFOQ) for the rule. Compulsory leave policies for school teachers have routinely been held to violate Title VII. On the other hand, several cases involving the airline industry have held that mandatory maternity leave for flight attendants was justified by passenger safety considerations.

Job Reassignment

An important Supreme Court case involved the use of lead in battery manufacturing. Lead poses substantial health risks, including risks to the fetus of a pregnant woman who is exposed to the substance. When a manufacturing company discovered high lead levels in the blood of its pregnant employees, the company adopted a policy barring all women of childbearing age from jobs involving exposure to lead unless they could document that they were incapable of having children.

The Supreme Court held that the policy amounted to sex discrimination despite the company's benign motives. The court said that the policy could not be justified as a BFOQ, since there was no evidence that pregnant women were less able than others to manufacture batteries. The court concluded that the question of fetal safety should be for the mother, not the company, to decide, and it dismissed as only a remote possibility the company's fear of suit by children with birth defects attributed to fetal lead exposure.

Maternity Leave and Reinstatement

The EEOC takes the position that since pregnancy and childbirth are conditions unique to women, refusal to grant special leave to a pregnant employee may amount to sex discrimination. In other words, according to the EEOC, the employer had better grant leave (assuming it is medically justified) and hold the job open when the mother is ready to return, unless the employer can show that the job cannot remain vacant and it cannot be filled by a temporary replacement. It remains to be seen whether the EEOC's position will be upheld in the courts.

Paternity Leave

Unless the FMLA or a state or local mandatory leave law applies, employers are not legally required to grant paternity leave. However, if the employer offers maternity leave *unrelated* to the mother's medical needs, failure to offer equivalent paternity leave would be discriminatory.

HARASSMENT IN GENERAL

When the authors of Title VII added the word *sex* to the list of characteristics that an employer could not consider in making personnel decisions, they probably intended the term to be synonymous with *gender*. In other words, employers cannot consider gender when establishing pay rates or deciding whether to hire, promote, or fire, just as they cannot consider other characteristics, such as race or color, deemed irrelevant to job performance.

But the courts and the EEOC have ruled that *sexual harassment* is also a form of discrimination prohibited by Title VII. According to the EEOC, unwelcome sexual advances, requests for sexual favors, and other verbal or physical conduct of a sexual nature constitute sexual harassment when any of the following occurs:

- Submission to such conduct is made either expressly or implicitly a term or condition of employment.
- Submission to or rejection of such conduct by an individual is used as the basis for employment decisions affecting the individual.
- Such conduct has the purpose or effect of unreasonably interfering with an individual's work performance or creating an *intimidating, hostile, or offensive working environment.*

The illegality of some forms of sexual harassment can probably be explained by traditional Title VII analysis. Take, for example, a male company supervisor who requests a female subordinate to sleep with him, promising her a promotion if she does and threatening to fire her if she does not. This type of sexual blackmail is discriminatory because the supervisor does not make the same request of any male subordinate. In other words, the supervisor has imposed on a female employee, because of her sex, a term or condition of employment that he has not imposed on a similarly situated male. Sex discrimination of this type has sometimes been called *quid pro quo harassment.*

Hostile Environment

The courts and the EEOC have gone beyond quid pro quo harassment, ruling that Title VII is violated by a *hostile environment* as well. To illustrate, suppose the branch manager of a bank requests sex from a teller who works for him, he touches her sexually, and he makes sexual jokes and comments directed to her or in her presence, but he never promises any tangible job benefit, nor threatens to take any away. The courts have held that the mere creation of an intimidating, hostile, or offensive work environment is a form of sex discrimination because, in effect, the employee must tolerate the hostile environment to keep her job. (If the employee finds the environment so hostile that she actually quits, she may have been constructively discharged and have a claim of quid pro quo harassment as well. See Chapter 4.)

The above example involves a male seeking sex from a female. But make no mistake—a male who is threatened with dismissal or harassed by a female supervisor has just as good a claim. The EEOC even takes the position (not well supported in the case law) that when an employee of either sex is promoted because he or she sleeps with the boss, *other employees* who do not get the promotion suffer sex discrimination.

CASE STUDY:
TOO HOT TO WORK

An Iowa dentist hired a dental assistant just after the assistant received her community college degree. The dentist acknowledged that she was a good assistant during her 10-plus years in his employ, and the assistant herself said that the dentist treated her with respect and was a person of high integrity. The problem was that the dentist developed a strong attraction to his assistant that troubled and distracted him. The two started texting each other on both work and personal matters, although the texts were apparently innocuous and not sexual in nature. At one point, the assistant made a statement about the infrequency of her sex life, and the dentist responded, "That's like having a Lamborghini in the garage and never driving it." So far as the court case discloses, however, the dentist never took the Lamborghini for a ride himself.

When the dentist's wife (who also worked in the dental office) found out about the texting, she demanded that the assistant be fired. After consulting with his pastor, the dentist did exactly that. The assistant then sued, claiming sex discrimination. The Iowa Supreme Court rejected her claim, saying that the civil rights laws are not general fairness statutes. In response to the assistant's argument that but for her gender she would not have been fired, the court recognized a distinction between an employment decision based on a personal relationship (as this one was) and a decision based on gender itself.

It should be noted that other courts have held a termination under these circumstances to be sex discrimination.

☞ **QUICK TIP**
Although harassment is most often associated with sex discrimination, harassment based on any discriminatory factor—race, color, religion, national origin, age, or disability—is also illegal if it is sufficiently severe to create a hostile work environment.

Same-sex harassment is also illegal under Title VII. In a case involving a male roustabout on an oil rig who was repeatedly subjected to sex-related, humiliating actions against him by other male members of the crew—including physical assaults and threats of rape—the Supreme Court ruled that sexual harassment *of any kind* is prohibited.

An offensive environment must be *severe* and *pervasive*, but it need not be so intolerable as to force the employee to quit or to cause the employee to suffer psychological injury. It is an environment that the complaining employee finds offensive and that a reasonable person would find objectionable as well. (In other words, the environment must be both subjectively and objectively offensive to support a Title VII claim.)

A super-sensitive employee, for example, who takes offense at the retelling of an off-color TV episode, does not have a good claim. But note that the offended employee need not be the specific target of the harassment in order for the environment to be considered hostile. The routine exchange of pornographic email among a willing group of employees may create a hostile work environment for another employee who is not involved in the exchange but who is simply exposed to the material.

Workplace Civility Code
A number of courts have ruled that Title VII is not intended as a code of workplace civility. For example, there should be no Title VII violation when the work environment is equally offensive to

both male and female employees. This occurred in a strange case involving a supervisor who sought sexual favors from two subordinates who happened to be husband and wife. The court found no violation of Title VII because Title VII is premised on eliminating discrimination; inappropriate conduct that is inflicted on both sexes or is inflicted regardless of sex is outside the statute's ambit.

⚠ ALERT!

When workplace incivility becomes extreme, the employee-victim may have a claim for intentional infliction of emotional distress (discussed in Chapter 4) whether or not the incivility amounts to discriminatory conduct.

CASE STUDY:
DETERMINING DISCRIMINATORY SEXUAL HARASSMENT

A security guard supervisor working under contract at the Environmental Protection Agency disciplined two other guards at the worksite. The two guards, apparently infuriated by the discipline, launched a retaliatory campaign against the supervisor that began by repeated slashing of his tires. Later they taunted him in a sexual manner that included lewd gestures and comments.

In response to the supervisor's Title VII claim, the court ruled that the harassment he complained about, although tinged with offensive sexual connotations, was not based on his sex. The supervisor did not claim, for example, that the two guards were homosexual or that they were seriously proposing to have sex with him. Nor did the supervisor show that the guards were motivated by general hostility to males in the workplace. Instead, according to the court, the guards were motivated by a workplace grudge having nothing to do with sex.

On the other hand, the U.S. Court of Appeals for the 9th Circuit ruled in effect that even equal opportunity harassment could result in employer liability. In that case, a senior official with an office of the National Education Association was rude, overbearing, obnoxious, loud, vulgar, and generally unpleasant. Significantly, none of the official's conduct was of a sexual nature.

The 9th Circuit said that even if male and female employees were being treated the same, a reasonable woman may well have a more negative reaction than her male counterpart to the official's conduct. In other words, according to the court, because women by nature may feel more intimidated or threatened than men by a supervisor's obnoxious behavior, even when that behavior is directed equally at all employees, women enjoy less desirable working conditions, and they therefore suffer sex discrimination. (Some would argue that this decision promotes the very gender stereotypes that Title VII was intended to abolish.)

How can an employer possibly distinguish between sexual harassment that *is* discriminatory and sexual harassment that *is not?* The short answer is there is no safe way to make the distinction. And despite pronouncements that Title VII was not intended as a workplace civility code, that is exactly what it may have become. At the risk of incurring substantial liability, employers have little choice but to prohibit all teasing, horseplay, banter, and other conduct with sexual overtones for fear that a court may view the conduct as discriminatory harassment.

EMPLOYER LIABILITY FOR HARASSMENT

Employer liability for sexual harassment has been a controversial issue in the courts. The controversy was heightened by the 1991 amendment to Title VII, which added compensatory and punitive damages as available remedies in cases of intentional discrimination.

The Supreme Court has ruled that an employer is always liable for a hostile work environment created by a supervisor when the discrimination takes the form of a *tangible employment action*—defined as a significant change in employment status. Usually, but not always, a tangible employment action results in economic injury because it relates to matters such as hiring, firing, failing to promote, reassignment with significantly different responsibilities, or a significant change in benefits. The theory is that when a supervisor takes a tangible employment action with respect to a subordinate, he or she is exercising authority delegated by the employer company, and the company is automatically responsible for how that authority is exercised.

In a hostile environment case involving no tangible job action, the employer is only presumed liable for a supervisor's harassment. The employer may have an affirmative defense against such a claim, and avoid liability, if the employer can show that it had and enforced a policy against sexual harassment and that the complaining employee unreasonably failed to take advantage of preventive or corrective opportunities provided by the employer.

To evoke this affirmative defense, the employer must *have and enforce* a policy against sexual harassment. It is not enough simply to adopt a written policy. Many courts have recognized that employers must educate their workforce about the policy, such as by conducting periodic training for both managers and rank-and-file employees. And employers must promptly and objectively investigate complaints of harassment and take appropriate action if the complaint is found to be justified.

Nonsupervisor Conduct
Workplace sexual misconduct is not limited to a supervisor's mistreatment of subordinates. The employer can also be liable for tolerating a hostile work environment created by an employee's fellow employees and even nonemployees, such as customers, if the employer knows (or should know) about the offensive work environment but fails to take appropriate remedial action. In effect, the law requires employers to make reasonable efforts to provide a working environment free from hostile or offensive harassment; the law does not necessarily care who is doing the harassing.

298 The SHRM Essential Guide to Employment Law

Protective Policies

Employers have tried different techniques to protect themselves from claims. Some employers require that employees who are involved in an office romance, particularly if the romance is between a higher-level supervisor and a lower-level employee, sign a *love contract* setting out the ground rules for the relationship. The contract might have the parties acknowledge, for example, that the relationship is consensual and that it can be terminated by either party at any time. Love contracts seem extreme, however, and may expose the employer to liability for invasion of privacy (discussed in Chapter 18).

While no list of do's and don'ts can completely protect employers from sexual harassment claims, the following suggestions should go a long way:

- Establish a written nondiscrimination policy, including a specific policy against sexual (and all other forms of) harassment. The policy should define sexual harassment. It should be published in the employee handbook and posted conspicuously at the workplace. In the absence of a written policy, an employer has no chance at all of defending against a claim of hostile-environment sexual harassment by a supervisor against a subordinate.

- Include in the policy various means by which an employee can complain about sexual harassment. The complaint route should not be limited to the employee's immediate supervisor, since he or she may be the harasser.

- Consider installing an anonymous hotline or an interactive website for employees to report harassment and other types of workplace problems.

- Conduct regular training seminars on sexual harassment, attendance at which should be mandatory.

- Keep careful records of who attended each training session and what material was presented.

- Plan in advance who will be in charge of investigating complaints of sexual harassment and how the investigation will be conducted. (Making those determinations after a complaint is received will cause delay and could result in the harassment policy being ruled unreasonable or ineffective.)
- On receipt of a complaint of sexual harassment, review your employment practices liability insurance policy and give notice of the complaint to your insurance carrier.
- If the complaint involves sexual assaults or other criminal conduct, suggest that the complaining party make a police report.
- Investigate *all* complaints of sexual harassment promptly, thoroughly, and objectively. Consider hiring experienced employment counsel to conduct the investigation or a company that specializes in such investigations.
- Include an interview with the complaining party in the investigation. Gather as much detail from him or her as possible about what happened, when and where it happened, and who else saw or knows about the harassment. Also, ask the complainant how he or she would like the matter to be resolved (without making any promises about what action will be taken).
- Treat as confidential all information developed during the investigation. However, do not promise confidentiality, since complete confidentiality is probably not possible. Be careful about prohibiting your workforce from discussing the matter, since that may constitute an unfair labor practice.
- Make a contemporaneous, detailed written record of the investigation.
- If the investigation shows that the complaint is justified, take immediate and appropriate corrective action against the harasser. Inform the complaining party about the action taken and ask whether there is anything further he or she wishes to bring to the employer's attention.
- For serious, ongoing incidents, consider temporarily reassigning the alleged harasser or complaining party, or placing one

or both of them on temporary leave with pay, to prevent additional incidents pending your investigation. (This step involves some risk, since the reassignment or leave could be construed as retaliation against the complainant or defamation of the alleged harasser.)

- If the investigation shows the complaint to be unfounded, inform the complaining party and the accused harasser and close the investigation.
- Do not take disciplinary action against the complainant unless it is clear that he or she intentionally lied about the matter. (Retaliation against an employee for exercising rights protected by law, such as the right to complain about harassment, itself constitutes illegal discrimination.)

Sometimes an employee may complain about harassment but then ask management not to take any action, perhaps out of fear that the workplace environment will be further poisoned by an investigation. While it may be tempting to honor this no-action request, once management is on notice of harassment, it has no choice but to address it appropriately.

☞ **QUICK TIP**

The complainant's own conduct is relevant when investigating a claim of sexual harassment, such as whether the complainant willingly participated in the activity that he or she now claims was offensive. However, an investigation that focuses primarily on the complainant's own conduct may be viewed as retaliatory and may subject the employer to additional claims of discrimination.

SEXUAL ORIENTATION AND GENDER IDENTITY

Title VII does not explicitly outlaw discrimination because of sexual orientation so, historically, the courts rejected sexual orientation as covered by Title VII. In effect, the courts said that *sex* (meaning gender) and *sexual orientation* are two distinct concepts.

An early case involved a homosexual male nurse who worked for a hospital in Indianapolis. The nurse complained that one of his physician supervisors made fun of his homosexuality, yelled at him during telephone conversations, and otherwise treated him poorly, all of which were based on his sexual orientation. The court ruled that Congress used the term sex in Title VII to mean a biological male or biological female and not one's sexuality or sexual orientation. Therefore, according to the court, harassment based solely on a person's sexual preference or orientation (and not on one's sex) is not an unlawful employment practice under Title VII.

Since then, however, both the judicial meaning of the term sex and the country's attitude toward acceptable sexual conduct have undergone dramatic changes. Consider, for example, the following line of Supreme Court cases:

- Sexual harassment is a form of sex discrimination (*Meritor Savings Bank v. Vinson*, 1986).
- Discrimination against a female because she does not conform to stereotypical female behavior violates Title VII *(Price Waterhouse v. Hopkins*, 1989).
- Male-on-male sexual harassment is sex discrimination (*Oncale v. Sundowner Offshore Services*, 1998).
- A Texas statute outlawing consensual sex between two adults of the same sex is unconstitutional (*Lawrence v. Texas*, 2003).
- The Defense of Marriage Act's definition of *spouse* as excluding same-sex partners is unconstitutional *(U.S. v. Windsor*, 2013).
- Gays have a constitutional right to marry (*Obergefell v. Hodges*, 2015).

In 2015 the EEOC announced its position that Title VII's prohibition on sex discrimination encompasses discrimination on the basis of sexual orientation. The EEOC has since filed several lawsuits against employers accused of discriminating against gay and lesbian employees.

The weight of current authority at the federal appeals court level still excludes sexual orientation as discriminatory under Title VII. However, a federal trial court in Pennsylvania recently concluded that Title VII flatly prohibits discrimination on the basis of sexual orientation. The court said: "There can be no more obvious form of sex stereotyping than making a determination that a person should conform to heterosexuality."

Even more recently, in *Hively v. Ivy Tech Community College*, the U.S. Court of Appeals for the 7th Circuit (headquartered in Chicago), upheld a claim of sexual orientation discrimination under Title VII, saying that "it is actually impossible to discriminate on the basis of sexual orientation without discriminating on the basis of sex." The case is particularly important because it was an *en banc* decision, meaning that the entire court, not just a three-judge panel of the court, participated. (Eight judges were in favor of the decision, and three dissented.)

Although the EEOC's position is that Title VII covers sexual orientation discrimination, the U.S. Department of Justice (DOJ) under the Trump administration takes the opposite view. In July 2017, DOJ filed a friend of the court brief in *Zarda v. Altitude Express, Inc.*, pending before the U.S. Court of Appeals for the 2nd Circuit, arguing that sexual orientation is excluded from Title VII protection. Recognizing that the EEOC also filed a brief in *Zarda*, DOJ said, "the EEOC is not speaking for the United States and its position about the scope of Title VII is entitled to no deference beyond its power to persuade."

Transgender discrimination has been the subject of fewer cases, although the EEOC's current position is that transgender discrimination is covered by Title VII. The EEOC has filed lawsuits to promote that view as well.

Ultimately, the Supreme Court will need to determine whether Title VII protects gays, lesbians, and other members of the LGBTQ community. Given the court's 2015 ruling in *Obergefell v. Hodges* that gay marriage is a constitutional right, it would not be surprising for the Court to side with those lower court decisions that read Title VII as broadly protective of LGBTQ individuals. And regardless of whether Title VII applies, many states and local jurisdictions do explicitly protect LGBTQ individuals from discrimination.

☞ QUICK TIP

A Guide to Restroom Access for Transgender Workers from the Occupational Safety and Health Administration (OSHA) offers as a "core principle" and "best practice" that all employees, including transgender employees, should have access to restrooms that correspond to their gender identity. OSHA's suggested alternative options include providing single-occupancy, gender-neutral (unisex) facilities or multiple-occupant, gender-neutral facilities with lockable single-occupant stalls.

OTHER ISSUES

Title VII's prohibition of sex discrimination gives rise to additional workplace issues from time to time, discussed below.

Dress Codes

A few federal court cases have ruled that employers have a certain amount of latitude in adopting dress and grooming standards that are not entirely gender neutral and that minor differences in personal appearance regulations do not constitute sex discrimination under Title VII. As a caveat, however, the dress codes must be enforced evenhandedly between men and women.

Many of the dress code cases have involved hair length. A few have involved earrings. The issue typically arises when a male employee is disciplined for violating policies that prohibit long hair for men but not for women or that prohibit earrings on males but not females. The courts have said that while long hair and earrings on men may be fashionable in some circles, an employer may legitimately wish to present a more conservative image and need not tolerate the outer bounds of current fashion. But if the business justification for a gender-specific dress code is to present a more conservative image, application of the dress code to employees who do not interact with the public would be difficult to justify.

⚠ **ALERT!**
A dress code policy that prohibits clothing or accessories associated with particular religious beliefs or practices may constitute religious discrimination under Title VII. (See Chapter 14 for more on religious discrimination.)

Retirement Plans
An employer cannot provide smaller monthly retirement payments to women just because women, on average, live longer than men and collect benefits for a longer time.

Physique
A number of cases have involved size and strength differences between men and women. If an employer sets minimum height and weight standards that tend to exclude most female applicants but few male applicants, the standards will be deemed discriminatory unless the employer can show a business necessity for the standards.

Age Discrimination

The purpose of the federal *Age Discrimination in Employment Act* (ADEA) is to promote employment of older persons based on their ability rather than age by prohibiting age-based discrimination against employees and job applicants. Consistent with that purpose, the ADEA applies only to persons 40 years of age or older, so that an age-based decision affecting only persons under 40 does not violate the ADEA.

🔔 ALERT!

Many states and local jurisdictions have their own age discrimination laws that apply to all employees, not just those 40 years of age or older.

Hiring or promoting a 35-year-old employee instead of a 45-year-old for reasons other than age is perfectly legal. However, the employer should identify the objective, job-related, nondiscriminatory criteria used in making the decision. In making personnel decisions, employers should avoid using terms such as *dead wood*, *fresh faces*, *new blood*, or *more energy*. These terms are often viewed as evidence of discriminatory intent and will hurt the employer in defending an age discrimination claim.

Harassment with respect to age can constitute age discrimination, just as harassment with respect to race or sex can violate Title VII. Employers should not tolerate workplace jokes or teasing aimed at older employees, their medical conditions, or other factors common to age.

There has been some doubt just how the ADEA works in certain circumstances. For example, is favoring a 45-year-old over a 60-year-old illegal, even though both workers are within the protected, over-40 class? Alternatively, may an employer favor a 60-year-old over a worker age 45?

In 1996 the Supreme Court answered the first question, ruling that when an older worker is replaced by someone younger because of age, it does not matter that the younger worker is also in the 40-and-older protected class. A case of age discrimination can be based just on a significant age difference even though both workers are over 40, said the court.

The Supreme Court later answered the second question as well. The court ruled that an employer practice that favors older workers is permitted under the ADEA, even though it discriminates against younger workers who are in the 40-and-over protected class. In the court's words, the ADEA does not look both ways.

COVERED EMPLOYERS

The ADEA covers most employers with 20 or more employees. Specifically, it covers employers engaged in an industry affecting commerce that have 20 or more employees for each working day in each of 20 or more calendar weeks in the current or preceding calendar year. The coverage provisions track Title VII, except that the employee threshold for Title VII is 15 employees instead of the 20-employee threshold of the ADEA. (See Chapter 14 for the meaning of *industry affecting commerce* and the methodology for counting employees.)

EXCEPTIONS

As with Title VII, there is an exception in the ADEA for a bona fide occupational qualification (BFOQ); however, the exception has been narrowly applied by the courts. For example, an airline had a rule that its flight engineers must retire at age 60 on the theory that many persons over that age have limitations that preclude safe operation of aircraft. The airline argued that it would be impractical, if not impossible, to examine all flight engineers and identify those with limitations. A jury found the rule illegal under the ADEA and awarded damages. The Supreme Court let the jury verdict stand, saying that it was not enough for the airline to have a rational basis for its policy. Instead, the airline had to prove that its policy was reasonably necessary to the normal operation or essence of the particular business. (Ironically, the Federal Aviation Administration long had a rule that *pilots* must retire at age 60; Congress has raised that age to 65.)

The ADEA also permits an employer to have a bona fide seniority system provided it is not intended to evade the purposes of the ADEA. A seniority system cannot be used to justify involuntary retirements.

The ADEA has other exceptions that make the act unique among federal nondiscrimination laws. For one, the ADEA does not apply to persons under age 40, so age discrimination against persons younger than 40 is not illegal under the ADEA. (As pointed out above, it may be illegal under state or local laws.)

Although the act generally prohibits compulsory retirements based on age, *bona fide executives* or *high policymakers* may be forced to retire. A bona fide executive is a person who exercises substantial managerial authority over a significant number of employees and a large volume of business. A high policymaker is an employee other than a bona fide executive who plays a significant role in developing and implementing corporate policy. The act allows forced retirement of a bona fide executive or high policymaker if the person held the position for two years preceding retirement, is at least 65 years old, and is entitled to annual retirement benefits of at least $44,000 based solely on employer contributions.

☞ **QUICK TIP**

The definition of a bona fide executive for ADEA purposes is different from the Fair Labor Standards Act's definition in connection with exemption from overtime requirements. (Chapter 5 addresses overtime requirements.)

State and local governments are also permitted to establish mandatory retirement ages for firefighters and law enforcement officers.

BENEFIT PLANS

Almost all retirement plans make age-based distinctions. Plans stating that employees who have attained a specified age (such as 65) may retire and begin receiving benefits are lawful. However, employers must take caution when changing the terms of plans to ensure that benefits are not being taken from a class of persons protected by the ADEA.

For example, when an employer converts from a defined benefit plan to a cash balance plan (discussed in Chapter 9), employees lose the back-loaded boost they had anticipated from their defined benefit plan. Since this loss is borne most heavily by older workers who are near retirement, some have argued that such conversions amount to age discrimination.

PROVING AGE DISCRIMINATION

Although an older worker may be the victim of age discrimination, the worker still has to *prove* that the adverse employment decision was age-based. It is often difficult to find such direct evidence of discriminatory motive. In the more usual case, the boss's motive is unclear (or at least unexpressed), and circumstantial evidence is all that is available.

One type of circumstantial evidence is a significant age differential between the fired person and his or her replacement. Courts have come up with a variety of answers as to what is significant, ranging from 3 years to 10 years. Five to seven years seems to be emerging as a standard, so that an age differential of less than that should not provide circumstantial evidence of age discrimination. But even when the age difference is less than five years, an employee could still prevail in court if he or she has other evidence of age discrimination.

Employers should be alert to code words that often stand for age, such as describing an employee as *tired* or *inflexible*, or seeking to hire *new blood* or a *digital native*.

Salary may also be seen as a proxy for age, since older, more senior workers are generally paid more than younger, more junior workers. Is it alright to discriminate on the basis of salary, such as by choosing more highly paid employees for termination during a reduction in force? The courts have generally said yes.

RELEASE OF ADEA CLAIMS

A *release* is a type of contract by which one party gives up a legal right or claim in exchange for valuable consideration—usually money. In general, no special form of contract is required to release most types of claims, including discrimination claims.

ADEA cases are different. Unlike other employment-related disputes, the release of an ADEA claim will be ineffective unless the employer follows very specific procedures spelled out in the law. For example, the employee must be advised in writing to consult with an attorney before signing the release. Then, the employee must be given at least 21 days to consider the release before signing it. Also, the employer must give the employee an additional seven-day rescission period after the signing date to change his or her mind.

The law does not require the employee to actually wait 21 days before signing the release. The employee can sign earlier, so long as his or her right to take a full 21 days is not restricted. However, the seven-day rescission period after signing cannot be shortened.

The Supreme Court has ruled that when a release did not comply with ADEA requirements, an employee who received severance pay in exchange for a release of her ADEA claim was entitled to keep the severance pay and still sue her employer for age discrimination. Therefore, an employer that has required a release of all claims in exchange for a severance package should not begin making severance payments to its age 40-plus former employee until the seven-day rescission period has expired.

If a release of ADEA claims is requested in connection with an exit incentive or other employment termination program offered to a group or class of employees, the 21-day period increases to 45 days. In addition, the employer must provide all persons in the class or group with a description of the class or group. The employer must also inform them of the job titles and ages of all employees eligible or selected for the program. The ages of all employees in the same job classification or organizational unit who are not eligible or selected for the program must also be disclosed.

REMEDIES UNDER THE ADEA

The remedies available to an individual who has suffered age discrimination in employment are similar to those under the Fair Labor Standards Act (discussed in Chapter 5) and unlike those available under Title VII (discussed in Chapter 14).

Persons with Disabilities

The *Americans with Disabilities Act* (ADA) is intended to be a clear and comprehensive national mandate for the elimination of discrimination against individuals with disabilities.

In the employment context, the ADA applies to employers that have 15 or more employees. It prohibits discrimination against a qualified individual with a disability with respect to application procedures, hiring, promotion, discharge, compensation, training, and other terms, conditions, and privileges of employment. A *qualified individual* is a person who, with or without reasonable accommodation, can perform the essential functions of the job he or she holds or is applying for.

⚠ ALERT!

An employee who applies for or receives benefits under the Social Security Disability Insurance (SSDI) program may still be a qualified individual entitled to reasonable accommodation under the ADA.

DEFINITION OF DISABILITY

As used in the ADA, *disability* means a physical or mental impairment that substantially limits one or more major life activities. *Major life activities* include caring for oneself, performing manual tasks, seeing, hearing, eating, sleeping, walking, standing, lifting, bending, speaking, breathing, learning, reading, concentrating, thinking, communicating, and working. They also include major bodily functions, such as functions of the immune system, normal cell growth, digestive, bowel, bladder, neurological, brain, respiratory, circulatory, endocrine, and reproductive functions. An impairment that is episodic or in remission is a disability if it would substantially limit a major life activity when active.

The physical and mental impairments that can give rise to a disability would fill a medical encyclopedia. Generally speaking, any condition that can be diagnosed by a health care provider is an impairment within the meaning of the ADA. If the impairment does not substantially limit one or more major life activities, however, it is not a disability for ADA purposes.

By statute, the following are not considered impairments for ADA purposes:

- homosexuality and bisexuality
- transvestism and transsexualism
- pedophilia, exhibitionism, and voyeurism
- gender identity disorders not resulting from physical impairment
- other sexual behavior disorders
- compulsive gambling
- kleptomania
- pyromania
- psychoactive substance abuse disorders resulting from current illegal use of drugs

Diagnoses that are generally unaccepted in the medical community will not trigger ADA obligations. For example, several courts have held that multiple chemical sensitivity syndrome falls in this category.

The existence of even a significant impairment does not necessarily render a person disabled. There is no such thing as a *disability per se* under the ADA since each impairment, no matter how serious, must still be shown as substantially limiting a major life activity. An individualized, case-by-case inquiry is required to determine whether, as a result of the impairment, a particular employee is in fact substantially limited in one or more major life activities.

⚠ **ALERT!**

Employees who suffer temporary illnesses and injuries, even though they are not disabled under the ADA, may be entitled to workers' compensation benefits (covered in Chapter 11) and leave under the Family and Medical Leave Act (discussed in Chapter 8).

Special rules apply to substance abuse. Addiction to drugs or alcohol is an impairment that may trigger ADA coverage, depending on the particular individual's circumstances. However, employers *may* discriminate against current, illegal drug users and persons who traffic in drugs at the workplace, whether or not they are addicted. Employers may also prohibit intoxication or use of alcohol at the workplace and may impose discipline for poor performance or absenteeism related to alcohol use, even if the employee is an alcoholic.

In general, determining whether an impairment substantially limits a major life activity must be made without regard to the ameliorative effects of mitigating measures, such as medication, medical equipment or appliances, prosthetics, and hearing aids. In other words, a person will be considered as having a disability even though, through use of mitigating measures, he or she is not substantially limited in any major life activity. Ordinary eyeglasses and contact lenses, however, may be considered in determining whether there is a substantial limitation in the major life activity of seeing.

Obesity

When the Equal Employment Opportunity Commission (EEOC) amended its regulations after 2008 statutory changes to the ADA, it removed a regulatory provision saying obesity was not an impairment. The EEOC currently takes the view that severe obesity, without more, is an impairment that can support a claim of disability.

Although a few courts have agreed with the EEOC, most courts—including, significantly, three federal appellate courts as of this writing—have concluded that weight is simply a physical characteristic, like hair color or left-handedness. As one appellate court said, weight "qualifies as a physical impairment only if it falls outside the normal range *and* it occurs as a result of a physiological disorder. [Emphasis in original.] Both requirements must be met. In other words, even weight outside the normal range—no matter how far outside that range—must be the result of an underlying physiological disorder to qualify as a physical impairment under the ADA."

DUTY OF REASONABLE ACCOMMODATION

Included within the ADA's definition of employment discrimination is failing to make *reasonable accommodations* to the known physical or mental disability of an otherwise-qualified applicant or employee. *Otherwise qualified* means a person with a disability who, with or without reasonable accommodation, can perform the essential functions of the particular position he or she holds or is applying for.

The key concept here is *essential*. The employee has to be able to perform at least the essential functions of the job for ADA protections to apply. In determining what is essential and what is merely marginal, the employer's judgment is given substantial weight.

CASE STUDY:
ESSENTIAL JOB FUNCTIONS

Rite Aid, like other large pharmacy chains, requires its pharmacists to perform immunizations. Rite Aid's job description for pharmacists lists immunizations as an essential job function, and Rite Aid requires its pharmacists to hold a valid immunization certificate. When Rite Aid first began imposing this requirement, a pharmacist (who had been with Rite Aid and its predecessor pharmacies for 34 years) asked for an accommodation because he suffers from trypanophobia—a fear of needles. According to the pharmacist, his condition causes him to become lightheaded, pale, and feeling like he is going to faint. The U.S. Court of Appeals for the 2nd Circuit agreed that giving immunizations was an essential job function, and it upheld the pharmacist's termination.

☞ QUICK TIP

An employer should determine the essential functions of a particular position and include them in a written job description before advertising or interviewing for the position. A determination of essential functions after a disabled applicant has been rejected carries less weight.

To discriminate means to fail to make reasonable accommodations for the known physical or mental limitations of an otherwise-qualified applicant or employee. Under this definition, the employee has the burden of identifying his or her disability and requesting the accommodation, unless the need is obvious. The employer does not have an obligation to inquire about a nonobvious disability and, in fact, is prohibited from doing so. The employer may, however, make general inquiries as to the ability of an applicant or employee to perform job-related functions.

⚠ ALERT!

When an employer suspects a psychological impairment that manifests as, for example, moodiness, rudeness, or a short temper, the employer should address only the unacceptable behavior and leave it to the employee to raise the matter of any underlying disability.

Reasonableness of Requested Accommodation

If an employee informs the employer of a disability and requests the employer to accommodate, the employer must do so unless the accommodation would impose an *undue hardship*—that is, if the accommodation would be significantly burdensome or expensive.

It is often difficult to know whether a requested accommodation is reasonable or is an undue hardship. The ADA gives some examples of what is reasonable. For one, the employer's facilities must be readily accessible and usable. Wheelchair ramps may have to be installed, and doorways and restroom facilities may need to be enlarged. Other examples include the following:

- restructuring jobs
- modifying work schedules
- relaxing workplace rules
- making reassignments to vacant positions
- modifying or replacing existing equipment
- providing qualified readers or interpreters

The list of what is reasonable goes on, but it is not limitless. The courts have ruled, for example, that an employer has no duty to grant indefinite leave, since the ADA protects people who can perform the essential functions of their job presently or in the immediate future. Nor is an employer required to create a new position tailored to an employee's abilities.

What employers need to remember is that when a disabled employee or applicant for employment requests an accommodation, the employer must engage in a good-faith interactive process with the employee to identify accommodations that might enable him or her to perform the essential functions of the job. It could be that no accommodation will actually work, or that while a particular accommodation might work, it is unreasonable or imposes an undue hardship on the employer. Should that be the case, the employer is free to terminate the employee or reject the applicant. However, if the employer fails to engage in an interactive process or delays doing so, the employer will almost certainly lose any ADA claim that follows.

CASE STUDY:
PROVIDING AN INTERPRETER

A nurse applied for clinical position with Johns Hopkins Hospital for which she was otherwise well qualified, except that she was deaf. Although she could read lips, she communicated more effectively using American Sign Language (ASL). As part of her application, she requested the hospital to provide her with an ASL interpreter at an estimated annual cost of $120,000 (against an annual hospital budget of $1.7 billion). The hospital declined to hire her, claiming that the cost was an undue hardship. A federal district court in Maryland ruled that the hospital violated the ADA by failing to provide the requested interpreter, because the cost was not an undue hardship.

Teleworking
The courts have ruled that, generally, an employer is not required to accommodate a disability by allowing a disabled employee to telework. The reason is that most jobs require the kind of teamwork, personal interaction, and supervision that simply cannot be per-

formed at home without compromising the quality of the employee's performance. But in situations in which an employee with a disability could in fact perform all essential job functions from home, teleworking might well be a reasonable accommodation. (Teleworking is discussed in Chapter 20.)

Assignment to Vacant Position

One form of reasonable accommodation involves assignment of an employee with a disability from a job he or she cannot perform to a vacant position he or she *can* perform. However, seniority systems normally prevail over a disabled employee's interest in being assigned to a particular position. It is unreasonable, said the Supreme Court, to require an employer to violate a seniority system to accommodate a disability. Seniority systems, whether imposed under a collective bargaining agreement or unilaterally imposed by management, provide important employee benefits by creating and fulfilling employee expectations of fair and uniform treatment, job security, and predictable advancement based on objective standards, said the court. However, in *special circumstances* the ADA rights of the person with a disability trump a seniority system. If an employee could show, for example, that the employer made frequent exceptions to its seniority system, then one more departure to accommodate a disabled employee might well be reasonable.

A related question is whether an employer may refuse to accommodate a disabled employee who is qualified for a vacant position by selecting a more qualified person for the position. In other words, does the ADA require an employer to *assign* a disabled but otherwise qualified employee to a vacant position, or does it merely require the employer to allow the disabled employee to *compete* for the position? The EEOC takes the view that the employee should simply receive the job without having to complete, but the courts have generally disagreed with the EEOC and ruled that in most circumstances the disabled employee is only allowed to compete for the position.

☞ **QUICK TIP**

The seniority problem is further complicated when a union asks for copies of the disabled employee's medical records to determine whether a company's decision to override normal seniority rules is justified. Both the EEOC and the National Labor Relations Board take the position that disclosure of the records is a matter for good-faith collective bargaining.

Service Animals

The U.S. Department of Justice defines *service animals* for purposes of the public accommodation provisions of the ADA as dogs that are individually trained to do work or perform tasks for people with disabilities, such as guiding people who are blind, alerting people who are deaf, pulling a wheelchair, alerting and protecting a person who is having a seizure, reminding a person with mental illness to take prescribed medications, and calming a person with post-traumatic stress disorder (PTSD) during an anxiety attack. Although EEOC regulations do not specifically address service animals as an accommodation in the employment context, the EEOC has filed suit against a trucking company that refused to allow one of its drivers, who had PTSD, to travel with an emotional support dog prescribed by the driver's treating psychiatrist.

One further point about accommodation: the accommodation must *relate to* the disability such that, if granted, it would enable the applicant or employee to perform essential job functions that he or she would otherwise be unable to perform. Employers have no obligation under the ADA to offer an accommodation that might make some nonwork-related aspect of a disabled worker's life more convenient.

MEDICAL EXAMINATIONS AND INQUIRIES

The ADA has special rules for medical examinations. Before actually offering employment, an employer may *never* require an applicant to undergo a medical exam. While testing for illegal drugs is not considered a medical exam and is permitted before making a job offer, just about every other form of pre-offer medical test is illegal.

When the employer actually *offers* employment, the offer may be conditioned on the results of a medical exam if the following apply:

- All entering employees in the job category are subject to examination.
- The exam requirement can be shown to be job-related and consistent with business necessity.
- The resulting medical information is separately maintained and treated as confidential.
- The results are not used to discriminate against persons with disabilities.

If the results of the exam show that the candidate would be unable to perform the essential functions of the job with or without reasonable accommodation, or that the candidate would pose a direct threat (discussed below), then the offer may be withdrawn.

⚠ **ALERT!**

The pre-employment medical exam may be conducted when passing the exam is the *only* condition to an otherwise firm offer of employment. If any other conditions remain, such as checking references, the exam will be illegal.

The EEOC defines *medical examination* as a procedure or test that seeks information about an individual's physical or mental impairments or health. In determining whether a test is medical or nonmedical, the EEOC looks to the following factors:

- Is it administered by a health care professional or someone trained by a health care professional?
- Are the results interpreted by a health care professional or someone trained by a health care professional?
- Is it designed to reveal an impairment or physical or mental health?

- Is the employer trying to determine the candidate's physical or mental health or impairments?
- Is it invasive (for example, does it require the drawing of blood or testing urine or breath)?
- Does it measure a candidate's performance of a task (permitted), or does it measure the candidate's physiological responses to performing the task? (not permitted).
- Is it normally given in a medical setting (for example, a health care professional's office)?
- Is medical equipment used?

According to the EEOC, a psychological test that is designed to identify a mental disorder or impairment is medical, whereas a psychological test that measures only personality traits such as honesty, preferences, and habits is not.

Once an employee is on the job, the employer may require a medical exam but only if it is job-related and consistent with business necessity. Specifically, if an employer has a reasonable belief, based on objective evidence, that the employee's ability to perform essential job functions will be impaired by a medical condition, or that a medical condition may pose a direct threat to the employee or others, the employer may require a medical exam.

Closely related to medical examinations are disability-related inquiries. In general, an employer may not ask an applicant or employee about a disability and may not ask questions designed to elicit information about a disability. An employer may, however, ask whether an applicant or employee can perform job functions, ask about current illegal drug use, and ask whether an employee has been drinking.

CASE STUDY:
SICK LEAVE POLICY VIOLATED ADA

The prohibition against disability-related inquiries invalidated one employer's sick leave policy. The policy required employees who

*were absent on sick leave to furnish a medical certification that
included a general diagnosis of the condition that gave rise to the
absence. The court ruled that since some diagnoses are bound to
reveal underlying disabilities, the policy violated the ADA.*

Of course, once an applicant or employee discloses information
about a disability and requests an accommodation, the employer
not only *may* make disability-related inquiries; the employer is
required to do so.

☞ **QUICK TIP**

The EEOC has ruled that an employer may inquire about a worker's disability in
connection with disaster planning, so that the employee's need for special assistance can be identified in advance. However, it is up to the worker to decide whether
assistance is necessary.

OTHER PROHIBITED CONDUCT

The ADA also prohibits employment discrimination against individuals who have a record of having a disability (whether or not
they are currently disabled) or who are regarded as having a disability (even if they are not in fact disabled). But even if an individual has a record of, or is regarded as, being disabled, if he or
she is not actually disabled, then the duty of reasonable accommodation cannot, as a logical matter, apply.

Another form of discrimination prohibited by the ADA arises
when an applicant or employee is known to be in a relationship or
be associated with someone else who has a disability. Suppose an
employer knows that a job applicant's spouse or child has a chronic
condition that, the employer fears, may distract the applicant or
require extra time off. A refusal to hire for that reason violates the
ADA. As noted above, however, excessive absenteeism does not
need to be tolerated. Nor is an employee entitled to reasonable
accommodation under the ADA when it is not the employee, but
someone with whom he or she is associated, who is disabled.

⚠ **ALERT!**

Other laws may, of course, apply in the so-called associational disability situations, such as the Family and Medical Leave Act or state or local mandatory leave laws. (The FMLA is covered in Chapter 8.)

Many states and local governments have their own disability discrimination laws that may be similar (but not identical) to the ADA. California, for example, defines *disability* as an impairment that *limits* one or more major life activities as contrasted with the ADA's *substantially limits*. State and local laws often have thresholds lower than the ADA's 15-employee requirement.

WELLNESS PROGRAMS

A *wellness program* is an employer-sponsored plan to improve employee health. Wellness programs might encourage employees to exercise, lose weight, or quit smoking. Biometric and health screenings might be included in the program. Some programs offer financial incentives to employees to participate, such as reduced health insurance premiums, gift cards, or cash. Employers see wellness programs as a way to reduce absenteeism, lower health care costs, and generally improve workplace morale and productivity.

A potential problem with wellness programs is that they often involve disability-related inquiries and medical exams prohibited by the ADA, or they involve requests for genetic information in violation of the Genetic Information Nondiscrimination Act (GINA). Under regulations issued by the EEOC in 2016, wellness programs are permitted as an exception to the ADA and GINA, but they must meet the following strict criteria:

- The program must be reasonably designed to promote health or prevent disease.
- Employee participation must be voluntary.
- Employer-offered financial and in-kind incentives to encourage participation are generally limited to 30 percent of self-only health insurance coverage. (The AARP has challenged in court

the allowance of incentives up to 30 percent, claiming that such a large incentive effectively makes the program involuntary.)

- Employees with disabilities who cannot participate in the program must be reasonably accommodated by being offered alternative means of participating and earning any financial incentives.

- Employees from whom medical information will be obtained must be provided with a notice describing the medical information to be obtained, the purposes for which it will be used, and restrictions on disclosure of the information. (The EEOC has developed a sample form of notice, available on the EEOC's website.)

Other laws potentially affecting wellness programs are the Employee Retirement Income Security Act (ERISA), discussed in Chapter 9, and the Patient Protection and Affordable Care Act (PPACA), discussed in Chapter 10.

Employers are well advised to consult appropriate professionals for help in designing an effective and lawful wellness program.

DIRECT-THREAT DEFENSE

The ADA allows employers to exclude persons who pose a *direct threat* to the health or safety of the disabled person or to others in the workplace when the threat cannot be eliminated by reasonable accommodation.

The food industry, for example, may exclude persons from food handling who have infectious or communicable diseases that are transmitted to others through the handling of food if those persons cannot otherwise be reasonably accommodated. The ADA also permits enforcement of state and local laws dealing with food handling by persons with infectious or communicable diseases. The secretary of the U.S. Department of Health and Human Services is required to publish a list of such diseases and the manner in which they are transmitted.

Other situations in which the direct-threat defense applies include a worker with diabetes and hypertension who is at risk for coma and stroke and who seeks employment as a bus driver or a restaurant employee with epilepsy who is at risk for seizures and seeks a promotion to cook, a position in which he or she would be working with dangerous appliances and equipment. In both these situations, the employer may rely on the ADA's direct-threat defense and refuse to place the worker in the position sought.

☞ **QUICK TIP**

The direct-threat defense is unique to the ADA and does not spill over to other areas of discrimination law.

The conclusion that a direct threat exists cannot be based on ignorance or irrational fear. When AIDS first came to public attention, but before the means of transmission were well understood, some employers simply fired or refused to hire infected individuals. The courts held that practice to be illegal under the ADA.

CHAPTER 18

Employee Privacy

- Private Places
- Sensitive Records
- Surveillance
- Electronic Monitoring
- Lie Detectors
- Drug and Alcohol Testing
- Marijuana
- Employee Mail
- Social Media Policies
- Criminal Records
- Driving Records
- Identity Theft

Privacy is the right to be left alone. When someone's privacy has been wrongfully invaded, he or she may have a claim for damages. The types of invasions that can give rise to a claim for damages include the following:

- unreasonable intrusion upon the seclusion of another person
- appropriation of another's name or likeness
- unreasonable publicity given to another's private life
- publicity that places another in a false light.

Invasions of privacy do not usually arise in the employment context. After all, the workplace and the equipment in it belong to the employer. Those assets are there to promote the employer's business, not the employee's. When an employee is at the workplace using the employer's equipment, he or she is supposed to be acting for the employer's exclusive benefit. His or her performance is constantly being evaluated, and normally there is no expectation that his or her activities are personal and private. But there are exceptions.

PRIVATE PLACES

Most employees would expect their bodies, pockets, purses, wallets, and briefcases to be private and not open to inspection by their employer. If an employer intends to inspect those private places, a compelling business reason must exist, and a clear written statement of this intention should be established and disseminated to all employees. In the diamond mining industry, for example, body cavity searches might be justified. Technicians working with lethal viruses might reasonably be put through decontamination at day's end. Perhaps retail store workers should expect to have their packages inspected as they leave the store premises.

Less clear are places such as an employee's desk. An employer's right to go through an employee's desk without the employee's permission depends on the circumstances. If the employer has an announced policy of doing so, or if the employee shares the desk with others and could have no reasonable expectation of privacy, then the employer probably has the right. But if there is no announced policy, if the employer does not make it a practice of inspecting desk drawers, and if employees routinely lock their desks without objection from the employer, then the employer probably does not have the right.

Fourth Amendment

Among the rights granted by the Constitution's Bill of Rights is the "right of the people to be secure in their persons, houses, papers, and effects, against unreasonable searches and seizures." As pointed out in Chapter 4, these rights protect individuals from *government* abuses, not from employer or other private actions. But the line between government and private action can become blurred, as the following case study shows.

CASE STUDY:
EMPLOYER MAY CONSENT TO POLICE SEARCH OF OFFICE

The Internet service provider for a Montana company notified the Federal Bureau of Investigations (FBI) that one of the company's employees had accessed child pornography websites from a company computer. The FBI investigated and, in the process, obtained a copy of the suspect employee's hard drive. Doing so involved obtaining a key to the employee's private office, entering the office, and opening the computer's outer casing to gain access to the hard drive. When later prosecuted for child pornography, the employee tried to exclude the contents of the hard drive as evidence against him. The U.S. Court of Appeals for the 9th Circuit treated the employer as agent of the government, triggering a Fourth Amendment search and seizure issue. The court ruled, however, that the seized hard drive could be admitted in evidence because the employer retained control over the employee's office and computer and could therefore consent to the search and seizure.

SENSITIVE RECORDS

Employers frequently acquire highly sensitive, personal information about their employees, such as the following:

- drug test reports
- results of medical exams
- information about physical or mental disabilities that need to be accommodated under the Americans with Disabilities Act (ADA)
- medical information about the employee or employee's family in support of leave requests under the Family and Medical Leave Act
- workers' compensation records
- health insurance utilization records
- substance abuse treatment records in connection with employee assistance programs
- tax and financial information
- information about family problems, divorces, and separations.

The confidentiality of some of this information is guaranteed by law. Even if no specific law applies, employees expect such information to be kept confidential and to be used strictly for its intended purpose. Employers should live up to those expectations. Sensitive records should be kept in a secure area, and access should be limited to those with a legitimate need to know. When employers store sensitive information electronically, they should install appropriate computer security systems to prevent unauthorized access.

ADA

The *ADA* generally prohibits pre-employment medical examinations (except drug tests) and prohibits inquiries as to disabilities. The ADA permits an employer to conduct post-hiring medical exams so long as certain requirements are met, including the requirement that information obtained regarding medical condition or history be treated as a confidential medical record. (See Chapter 17 for a more detailed discussion of medical examinations under the ADA.)

Drug and Alcohol Abuse Treatment
Substance abuse records may be disclosed only with the patient's consent, in cases of medical emergency, or when authorized by court order based on a showing of good cause for disclosure. This means that, in the absence of consent by the employee, even a subpoena issued to an employer is insufficient to justify disclosure. Instead, the party desiring the records must obtain a specific court order for disclosure.

HIPAA
Extensive regulations implement the privacy requirements of the *Health Insurance Portability and Accountability Act.* The regulations are expressly applicable only to health plans (except for plans with fewer than 50 participants that are self-administered solely by the sponsoring employer), health care clearing houses, and health care providers that electronically transmit health information. However, employers are affected by the regulations in important ways.

Health insurers and health maintenance organizations (HMOs) are prohibited from disclosing *protected health information* (PHI) to employers that sponsor health plans, except to enable plan sponsors to carry out plan administration functions that the plan sponsor performs, and then only upon certification that the plan documents have been amended as required by the regulations.

Employers in turn must do the following:
- amend their plan documents to set out the permitted and required use of PHI
- require others who gain access, such as agents and subcontractors, to comply with use and disclosure restrictions
- provide for return or destruction of information that is no longer needed
- provide for separation between the group plan itself and the plan sponsor
- describe those employees or classes of employees who have access to the information

🔔 **ALERT!**

Employers are specifically prohibited from using PHI for any employment-related action or decision.

SURVEILLANCE

An employer may install surveillance cameras around the workplace, as long as the cameras are located in places where there is no reasonable expectation of privacy. Having a stated legitimate business reason for installing cameras—safety in garage areas or to stop employee theft—is a good idea. Cameras installed in private areas, such as restrooms, would be difficult to justify.

🔔 **ALERT!**

In a unionized shop, the installation of surveillance cameras is a matter for mandatory bargaining. Surveillance to determine who is supporting a union organizing effort is an unfair labor practice. (See Chapter 24 for more on collective bargaining and unfair labor practices.)

Surveillance outside the workplace is slightly different. Take, for example, an injured employee who is on leave and collecting workers' compensation benefits. If the employer has a reasonable suspicion that the employee is malingering and hires an investigator to videotape the employee surreptitiously outside the workplace, there is no invasion; the employer has a legitimate business purpose in conducting the surveillance and does so in an unobtrusive manner. However, if the employer instructs the investigator to interview all the employee's neighbors, golfing buddies, and bowling team, as well as take the video, the employer may have invaded the employee's privacy.

Some companies take surveillance to a whole new level by inquiring into or investigating an applicant's or employee's after-hours, leisure activities, and lifestyle in making employment decisions. Claiming a desire to hold down health insurance costs, absenteeism, or negligent employment suits, companies have been known to inquire about tobacco and alcohol use, participation in dangerous sports like motorcycle racing or sky diving, and even sexual activities. Balancing the invasive nature of these inquiries against the questionable value of the information obtained suggests that such practices are ill conceived. Some states prohibit an employer's using information about lawful after-hours activities to make employment decisions.

GPS Tracking

Smartphones and GPS devices installed on vehicles afford employers yet another way to monitor their employees. The Supreme Court has ruled that use of such devices by government authorities requires a search warrant. But no similar requirement applies to private employers. Instead the issue is privacy.

Companies that are considering using such tracking devices should establish a clear, written policy before doing so, which might include the following:

- identify and articulate a legitimate business reason for doing so, such as improving delivery routes or tracking work hours
- identify those positions, and only those positions, that will be subject to tracking
- limit monitoring to work hours (unless, for example, the purpose is to investigate violations of company policy regarding personal use of company vehicles)
- inform employees of the policy, so that they have no expectation of privacy while being monitored
- inform employees of the disciplinary consequences of violating any vehicle use policies
- explain to employees how the resultant data will be used
- maintain resultant data securely, especially if the data inadvertently contain any personal information, and use the data only for the intended business purpose
- in unionized shops, consider whether monitoring needs to be the subject of collective bargaining

ELECTRONIC MONITORING

Under the federal *Electronic Communications Privacy Act* (ECPA), it is illegal to intentionally intercept a wire, oral, or electronic communication. *Intercept* means the aural or other acquisition of the contents of any wire, electronic, or oral communication through the use of any electronic, mechanical, or other device. Telephone conversations, voice mail messages, face-to-face conversations, and email (while being transmitted) are all protected by the ECPA. Employers are subject to the ECPA just like other interceptors.

The ECPA prohibition does not apply when one of the parties to the conversation has consented to an intercept. So at least under federal law, if two persons are engaged in a telephone or face-to-face conversation, one of them may record the conversation without the consent or even the knowledge of the other.

A provision of the ECPA exempts telephone equipment so long as the equipment is being used in the ordinary course of business. Extension telephones and speaker phones, for example, normally qualify under this exemption, even though they can be used to intercept electronic communication.

Many states have enacted laws similar to the ECPA. Be warned, however, that unlike the ECPA, which is a *one-party consent* statute, some states have *two-party consent* statutes. In a two-party consent state, both parties to the conversation (or all parties if there are more than two) must consent to the intercept. State two-party consent statutes are not preempted by the ECPA and are fully enforceable.

Some companies find it helpful to record telephone conversations between employees and customers for quality control or verification purposes. If the company is doing business in a two-party consent state, it must obtain the consent of both the *employee* and the *customer*. The employee's consent will be presumed if the employer notifies the employee of its intentions to record the communication beforehand. (It is a good idea to give the notice in writing and have the employee sign a receipt. A monitoring policy should also be stated in the employee handbook.) As for the customer, the employer should have a recorded announcement at the beginning of each telephone conversation that the conversation may be monitored. If the customer proceeds with the conversation, his or her consent is also presumed. Even in one-party states, it is a good idea to let both the employee and the customer know in advance that conversations may be monitored.

Stored Communication

The ECPA also prohibits unauthorized access to stored communications (as distinguished from real-time, ongoing communications), but it has an exception for the provider of the communications service. This exception probably allows an employer to access employee emails that are backed up on the employer's own email server, as well as logs showing an employee's Internet surfing habits.

△ ALERT!

Posting employee photographs or other personal information about employees on a company website, if done without their permission, may not only be a privacy violation, but it may also increase the risk that employees will become victims of identity theft or violence.

Word-processing and other data files stored on the employer's network server or on the employee's workstation hard drive are not covered by the ECPA since they are not communications. However, even as to materials that are exempt from or not covered by the ECPA or comparable state statutes, employers need to be concerned about common-law privacy rights. As with searches of private places, the test is whether the employee had a reasonable expectation of privacy. To dispel any possible expectations of privacy, the employer should make clear in its employee handbook that the entire computer network, including individual workstations, belongs to the employer and that the employer may, at any time and without notice, inspect any files stored, processed, or transmitted on company computers. Figure 18.1 is a suggested handbook provision on privacy.

FIGURE 18.1: HANDBOOK PROVISION ON PRIVACY

All communications sent or received via the company's communications facilities, including communications using a personal email account, or created by or stored in the company's communications facilities or computer equipment, belong to the company and are subject to interception, monitoring, and inspection. Employees should have no expectation of privacy while at any company facility, while on company business, while using or accessing the company's computer equipment or communications facilities, or while using a company vehicle.

Personal Use of Equipment

Some companies go so far as to prohibit any personal use of communications equipment, such as telephones and email. While such a policy may be perfectly legal, it is difficult to enforce. Failure to enforce a policy consistently can give rise to employee expectations that the policy is one in name only. It makes more sense to recognize that some personal use will inevitably take place and to adopt a policy limiting personal use to no more than a few minutes a day. The policy should also prohibit any improper or illegal use.

⚠ ALERT!

Prohibiting employees from using the company email system for concerted activity relating to union organizing or conditions of employment could constitute an unfair labor practice. (See Chapter 24 for more on union activity.)

If an employer discovers a computer file on the company's server that appears to be personal and in violation of company policy, the employer should normally not study its contents except to determine that the file is in fact personal. Studying the file's contents beyond that point serves no legitimate business purpose, since the employer's interests are normally sufficiently served by instructing the employee to remove the file and imposing appropriate discipline. If the employer reasonably suspects that the employee is using office computers to engage in illegal activity, such as gambling, theft of trade secrets, or distribution of pornography, further inspection of the file's contents may be justified.

BYOD

Should employees be allowed to use their own devices—such as smartphones, tablet, laptops—for company business? Employees like the opportunity because they are comfortable with their devices and because the company may subsidize a portion of the cost. But it raises a number of legal concerns that employers need to consider when adopting a bring your own device (BYOD) policy. For example:

- Who owns the device if its cost is subsidized by the employer?
- Will security features be installed on the device, such as passwords, to protect confidential company data?
- How will confidential data be protected if the device is lost or when employment terminates?
- If the employee receives emails or other company communications during nonworking hours, should those hours be counted for wage and hour purposes?
- Will company access to the device amount to an invasion of the employee's privacy with respect to personal data stored on the device?
- What restrictions will be imposed on downloads of personal apps to prevent corruption or infection of company data or copyright violations?

BYOD policies are particularly troublesome when it comes to texting. If employees are texting each other or with customers or vendors using company equipment, then the company at least has the means of capturing and preserving the messages. But if employees are using their own devices for business texts, message capture and preservation may be difficult or impossible.

LIE DETECTORS

With very limited exceptions, a federal law known as the *Employee Polygraph Protection Act* (EPPA) prohibits use of lie detectors in employment situations. The term *lie detector* as used in the federal statute includes not only polygraph equipment (which measures pulse, respiration, and perspiration) but also any other device, such as a voice stress analyzer. The EPPA goes so far as to prohibit an employer's even requesting or suggesting that an employee submit to a lie detector test. Discharging an employee for refusing to submit to a test is abusive and subjects the employer to civil damages.

Exceptions

Exceptions to the EPPA include tests administered by federal, state, and local government employers and tests administered by the federal government to employees of government contractors in connection with security, counterintelligence, and law enforcement functions.

Exceptions for private employers include the following:

- *Ongoing investigation.* An employer may request its employees to submit to a polygraph test in connection with an ongoing investigation involving economic loss or injury to the employer's business such as theft, embezzlement, misappropriation, or an act of unlawful industrial espionage or sabotage. The employees must have had access to the property or information that is the subject of the investigation, and the employer must have a reasonable suspicion that the employee was involved in the incident or activity under investigation.
- *Security personnel.* Prospective employees may be required to undergo polygraph tests in connection with employment as armored car personnel; personnel engaged in the design, installation, and maintenance of security alarm systems; and security personnel whose functions include protection of facilities that have a significant impact on public health or safety (for example, nuclear power plants and public water supply).
- *Controlled substances.* Prospective employees who will be involved in the manufacture or distribution of controlled substances may be required to undergo polygraph tests. In addition, an existing employee may be required to undergo a polygraph test in connec-

tion with an ongoing investigation involving loss of a controlled substance if the employee had access to the substance.

The EPPA goes on to specify requirements and procedures that must be complied with for the exemptions to apply.

Some states also prohibit or restrict the use of lie detectors. Maryland, for example, requires all written employment applications to contain a notice, in bold-faced, uppercase type, to the effect that employers may not require or demand polygraph examinations as a condition of employment.

As a practical matter, most private employers simply rule out lie detectors as a workplace tool.

DRUG AND ALCOHOL TESTING

Employers and employees have sharply competing interests over drug and alcohol testing. On the one hand, an employer has a strong, sometimes compelling interest in maintaining a drug- and alcohol-free workplace: The employer is legitimately concerned with the safety of employees, customers, and the public generally, and with the effect of drug and alcohol abuse on job performance, accident rates, and absenteeism. Some employers, such as those regulated by the U.S. Department of Transportation (DOT), discussed below, are even *required* to test for drugs and alcohol under certain circumstances.

In contrast, employees have privacy rights. They object to employer scrutiny of their off-hours conduct. They question the accuracy of testing procedures. And they worry about the confidentiality of unrelated medical information obtained in the testing process.

The ADA generally prohibits discrimination against, and requires reasonable accommodation of, people with disabilities—including addictions. While people with drug and alcohol addictions fall within these general ADA provisions, an employer, consistent with the ADA may do the following:

- test for illegal drugs, such tests being excluded from the definition of a medical exam
- discriminate against current users of illegal drugs
- discipline employees for use or possession of drugs or alcohol at the workplace in violation of company policy, even if the use or possession is the result of addiction

Employers need not tolerate poor work performance or behavioral issues, even if they are the result of addiction.

🔔 **ALERT!**

While testing for illegal drugs is excluded from the definition of a medical exam, testing for *alcohol* is a medical exam and is subject to ADA restrictions regarding medical exams.

Department of Transportation

Employers in the various transportation industries regulated by the DOT (aviation, mass transit, interstate pipelines, railroads, shipping, and trucking) are required to establish drug and alcohol policies for employees performing safety-sensitive jobs. Under these requirements, covered employees are prohibited from using, possessing, being under the influence of, or being impaired by alcohol or controlled substances while performing their jobs.

Covered employees are subject to drug and alcohol tests in the following situations:

- as part of their employment application process (drug testing required; alcohol testing permitted)
- when there is a reasonable basis to suspect drug or alcohol abuse
- on a random basis
- following an accident, if (a) the accident involved loss of life, or (b) the driver received a citation and the accident involved bodily injury requiring medical treatment, or the accident disabled a motor vehicle

DOT regulations have come under constitutional attack as a violation of the employees' Fourth Amendment right to be free from unreasonable searches and seizures. The Supreme Court has ruled, however, that while the Fourth Amendment applies to drug and alcohol testing conducted pursuant to government regulation, such testing is not unreasonable, even in the absence of a search warrant and even absent any basis to suspect the individual being tested.

In contrast to DOT's mandatory post-accident drug- and alcohol-testing requirement for transportation employees, the Occupational Safety and Health Administration (OSHA) recommends a more limited use of post-accident testing. OSHA says that

> drug testing policies should limit post-incident testing to situations in which employee drug use is likely to have contributed to the incident, and for which the drug test can accurately identify impairment caused by drug use.... Employers need not specifically suspect drug use before testing, but there should be a reasonable possibility that drug use by the reporting employee was a contributing factor to the reported injury or illness in order for an employer to require drug testing. In addition, drug testing that is designed in a way that may be perceived as punitive or embarrassing to the employee is likely to deter injury reporting.

Employers that decide to have a drug-testing program should engage an outside consultant to set up the program and perhaps even administer it on an ongoing basis. This will help ensure that the program is run professionally and in accordance with any applicable law, that drug screens are accurate and reliable, and that medical information obtained in the process is handled appropriately. Using an outside consultant may also help insulate the employer from liability should a breach of confidentiality occur or should an employee be falsely reported as an illegal drug user.

MARIJUANA

Marijuana remains a Schedule I controlled substance (that is, a drug having no medical use and a high potential for abuse), and its manufacture, possession, use, or distribution remains illegal under federal law. Yet more than half the states have decriminalized possession and use at the state level for medical purposes, and a handful of states—Alaska, California, Colorado, Massachusetts, Maine, Nevada, Oregon, and Washington state at this writing—have gone further and legalized possession of limited quantities for recreational purposes.

Faced with these liberalizing state laws, the Obama administration's Department of Justice (DOJ) sent a memorandum to the U.S. Attorneys in states with medical marijuana laws, encouraging them not to focus federal resources on individuals who are in clear and unambiguous compliance with existing state laws providing for the medical use of marijuana. In other words, do not bother prosecuting under *federal law* if the possession or use is consistent with *state law*.

In addition, in 2016, Congress enacted the following rider to an omnibus appropriations bill:

> None of the funds made available in this Act to the Department of Justice may be used, with respect to the states of Alabama, Alaska, Arizona, California, Colorado, Connecticut, Delaware, District of Columbia, Florida, Hawaii, Illinois, Iowa, Kentucky, Maine, Maryland, Massachusetts, Michigan, Minnesota, Mississippi, Missouri, Montana, Nevada, New Hampshire, New Jersey, New Mexico, Oregon, Rhode Island, South Carolina, Tennessee, Utah, Vermont, Washington, and Wisconsin, to prevent such states from implementing their own state laws that authorize the use, distribution, possession, or cultivation of medical marijuana.

That rider has been included in subsequent appropriations acts and continuing resolutions. A 2016 decision by the U.S. Court of

Appeals for the 9th Circuit ruled that the rider even prohibits the DOJ from prosecuting violations of federal marijuana laws in the listed states so long as the conduct involved is permitted under state law. (According to news reports, the Trump Justice Department has asked Congressional leaders to eliminate the rider in future appropriations legislation.)

So how should employers respond when an employee uses marijuana for medical or recreational purposes in violation of federal law but in compliance with state law?

It seems clear that an employer may still prohibit manufacture, possession, use, or distribution of marijuana in the workplace. Similarly, being under the influence of marijuana at work may be prohibited, but determining whether an employee is in fact under the influence is problematic. Behavior may suggest recent marijuana use, but it is far from definitive. And while chemical testing will disclose the presence of marijuana or its metabolites, there is no generally accepted quantitative benchmark (as there is with alcohol) to determine impairment. Further, a positive urine test does not establish current impairment, since it may take a month or more from last use before a chronic user will have a negative urine test.

How about a blanket policy of testing for marijuana and other illegal drugs and rejecting any candidate or firing any employee who turns up positive, regardless of whether the use was at work or off duty? Such a policy would generally be consistent with *federal* law. Remember that illegal drug use is not protected under the ADA, and testing for such drugs is not a prohibited medical exam under the ADA. In addition, most U.S. government contractors and federal grant recipients are required to have a drug-free workplace policy, and employees in safety-sensitive jobs regulated by the DOT are subject to drug and alcohol testing.

A case from Washington state, decided when only medical marijuana use was legal there, ruled that an employer may have a zero-tolerance policy and reject a candidate who tests positive for marijuana. But it is far from clear that other courts would agree. At least one state—Maine—prohibits employers from discriminating against applicants and employees solely because they use marijuana recreationally during nonwork hours. (As of this writing the Maine legislature has delayed implementation of the nondiscrimination provision until February 2018.)

Rhode Island prohibits employers from denying a job to someone "solely for his or her status as a [medical marijuana] cardholder." And a 2017 decision from Massachusetts's highest court ruled that an employer had a duty under that state's disability discrimination law to accommodate an employee who used medically-prescribed marijuana to alleviate symptoms of a disabling bowel condition. The Massachusetts court rejected the employer's claim that any accommodation would be per se unreasonable because of marijuana's status as a Schedule I drug under federal law. A federal district court in Connecticut also reached a similar decision under that state's medical marijuana law. Other states do not explicitly address marijuana use, but they prohibit adverse employment actions based on off-duty conduct generally. Finally, a number of states permit, but regulate, drug and alcohol testing.

So, despite marijuana's illegality under federal law, employers need to carefully consider the law of the state or states in which they operate to determine just what their policy regarding marijuana should be.

EMPLOYEE MAIL

Federal law prohibits obstruction of mail correspondence. If a letter arrives addressed to a former employee that is obviously personal—the envelope is the size and shape of a greeting card; the address is handwritten; it is addressed to the former employee in care of the company; it has a handwritten, nonbusiness return address; and it was hand-stamped rather than metered—then the employer's clear duty is to return it unopened to the U.S. Postal Service for forwarding.

In contrast, if the envelope has all the earmarks of a business correspondence, including a preprinted return address of one of the company's customers, most employers would not hesitate to open the letter, but their right to do so is not clear. A federal criminal statute prohibits the taking of mail out of any post office or authorized depository "with design to obstruct the correspondence, or to pry into the business or secrets of another," or opening or destroying the same. An 1877 federal court case says it is no defense to prosecution under the statute that the letter in question related in part to the defendant's business.

Figure 18.2 is a suggested employee handbook provision that may help address the matter.

FIGURE 18.2: EMPLOYEE MAIL

Mail arriving at the company's place of business that reasonably appears to be business mail intended for the company may be opened by any authorized company employee, even if it is addressed to another specific employee or former employee. By accepting employment, an employee grants permission to the company to open mail in accordance with the foregoing and that the permission continues throughout the employment and after it ends.

SOCIAL MEDIA POLICIES

Faced with concerns about the accuracy of resumes, the reliability of reference information, and the risk of negligent employment claims, employers are more and more turning to the Internet to investigate prospective employees. There they can often find a wealth of information. For example, a job candidate may have a Facebook page or other social media accounts (some two billion individuals regularly use Facebook, according to press reports), may be listed on the website of a club or organization in which he or she is a member, or may maintain a blog on a topic of personal interest. Some candidates, perhaps out of youthful exuberance (and indiscretion), may even brag electronically about alcohol consumption, drug use, or sexual exploits, providing photos or videos of the conduct being described.

An employer's collection and use of online information raises a number of legal questions. Postings can reveal information, such as ancestry, family status, religious affiliation, political belief, or sexual orientation that is otherwise unavailable to the employer and that should not be considered in the hiring process. Once an employer has obtained such information, it is open to a charge of using the information in its decision-making.

Some states prohibit employers from considering after-hours activities in making employment decisions, so long as the activity is otherwise lawful and does not interfere with job performance. A handful of states specifically prohibit employers from requesting usernames and passwords to online accounts. Even in the absence of such laws, obtaining personal information from social media may amount to a common-law invasion of privacy. And if the employer obtained the information by circumventing a security device, such as by guessing a password or by misrepresenting the employer's identity, the employer may have violated federal law, such as the ECPA.

Employers that decide to include Internet searches as part of the application process might consider using a nondecision-maker to screen purely personal or otherwise irrelevant information, so that the ultimate decision-maker has only job-related data on which to base his or her decision.

CASE STUDY:
IMPROPER ACCESS TO SOCIAL MEDIA ACCOUNT

A server at a New Jersey restaurant created a private, password-protected account at Myspace to vent about work, and he invited other present and former restaurant employees to participate. Postings on the account came to include vulgar, critical comments about the restaurant and its policies, about its managers and customers (many of whom were identified by name), mentions of drug use, and suggestions of possible violence against the restaurant and its managers. When a supervisor learned of the existence of the account, he pressured a participant-employee to provide her password, and he then shared the password with upper management. Management accessed the account a number of times, read the postings, and then fired the employee who created the account and an employee who had posted there. The two fired employees sued the restaurant on a variety of claims, including violation of the federal Stored Communications Act and invasion of privacy. A jury agreed and awarded them money damages.

🔔 **ALERT!**
As explained in Chapter 2, the federal Fair Credit Reporting Act (FCRA) regulates an employer's obtaining consumer reports from consumer reporting agencies such as Equifax and Experian. A recent Supreme Court case called *Spokeo, Inc. v. Robins* seems to imply that an online people search engine could also qualify as a consumer reporting agency (CRA), triggering an employer's FCRA duties.

CRIMINAL RECORDS

The EEOC and some courts have taken the view that using criminal convictions as a basis for employment decisions has a disparate impact on certain minorities. (Disparate impact discrimination is discussed in Chapter 14.) Nevertheless, employers are generally free to inquire about and base decisions on conviction records and pending charges so long as they can show a reasonable business purpose for doing so.

🔔 **ALERT!**
A number of states and local jurisdictions have enacted *ban-the-box* laws that either restrict when an employer may inquire about a candidate's criminal record or (with limited exceptions) prohibit the inquiry entirely. States that allow old convictions to be expunged often prohibit inquiry about expunged records.

To establish a reasonable business purpose and reduce the risk of a successful disparate impact claim, employers should adopt a policy that includes the following:
• Only relatively recent convictions are considered.
• The policy is crime-specific, in only excluding applicants for crimes that, if committed during employment, would have a significant

negative impact on the employer's business (for example, a financial institution asking about convictions for dishonesty, or a retail establishment asking about theft and shoplifting convictions).

- The policy is position-specific (in the financial institution example, only applicants who will be dealing with customers' or the employer's funds are excluded).
- The employer has a factual basis for the policy, such as statistics showing that the rejected applicants, as a class, are significantly more likely than the general population to commit the crimes the employer is concerned about.

Asking about arrests that did not result in a conviction is much more likely to result in a successful disparate impact claim. In general, employers should not ask about or consider arrest records.

DRIVING RECORDS

The federal *Driver's Privacy Protection Act of 1994* prohibits state motor vehicle departments from disclosing a driver's personal information without the consent of the person involved. Personal information is defined as information that identifies an individual, including an individual's photograph, Social Security number, driver identification number, name, address, telephone number, and medical or disability information. Excluded from the definition is information on vehicular accidents, driving violations, and driver's status.

When an employer needs to check a candidate's or employee's driving records, the simplest procedure is to require the candidate or employee to obtain the record himself or herself. As always, the decision should be supported by a reasonable business purpose and should be invoked on a nondiscriminatory basis.

IDENTITY THEFT

Identity theft is a serious and growing national problem. According to some reports, the top cause of identity fraud is theft of records from employers or other businesses that maintain personal information on individuals. The information that employers necessarily obtain as part of the employment relationship—name, birthdate, address, and Social Security number—is the very information that enables an identity thief to commit crimes. Employers need to safeguard that information, and failure to do so could result in legal liability. Employers should consider the following steps to protect employee personal information:

- Keep records containing employee information in a secure room or file area and separate from other company records.
- If employee information is maintained electronically, be sure the files are protected by a password. Change passwords frequently, particularly when an employee with password access leaves the company.
- Consider encrypting any employee information that is electronically stored; also, consider isolating the information from the office computer network and from the Internet.
- Perform thorough background checks on all employees who have access to personal employee information.
- Do not allow access by unauthorized employees, particularly temporary employees who sometimes take jobs for the sole purpose of obtaining identity theft data.
- Do not use Social Security numbers for identification purposes or on employee badges; in addition, do not print Social Security numbers on paychecks or other documents that could be available to the general public. (In some states, it is illegal for an employer to print Social Security numbers on checks or use Social Security numbers for employee identification purposes.)
- Limit distribution of company directories and allow employees to exclude personal information—such as home addresses, phone numbers, and spouse's and children's names.
- Develop a records retention policy that requires destruction of all obsolete records; in addition, shred obsolete records, rather than merely discarding them.

- Ask vendors that have access to personal information about your employees—your payroll service, third-party benefit plan administrators, etc.—what steps they have taken to safeguard the information.
- Consider requiring contractual provisions with vendors, obligating them to maintain appropriate safeguards, to notify you immediately about unauthorized access or other problems and to indemnify you if one of their employees compromises your information.

CHAPTER 19
Employee Loyalty

- Competing with an Employer
- Trade Secrets and the Defend Trade Secrets Act
- Computer Fraud
- Loyalty by Contract
- Remedies for Breach of Contract
- Employee Dishonesty

Every employee owes a common-law duty of loyalty to his or her employer. The duty is an implicit part of the employment relationship unless the employer and employee agree otherwise. Under this duty, an employee is bound to serve his or her employer diligently and faithfully, to refrain from knowingly or willfully injuring the employer's business, and to avoid any conflict between the employer's interest and the employee's own self-interest.

Corporate officers and directors have heightened duties of loyalty to their employers. Officers and directors are generally considered fiduciaries, meaning that they must act for the benefit of their employer and stockholders. They may not use corporate facilities or assets for personal gain. An even higher standard of loyalty and fiduciary duty is sometimes applied to trustees of charitable, nonprofit organizations. (See Chapter 23 on nonprofit organizations.)

COMPETING WITH AN EMPLOYER

In the absence of a contract that restricts an employee's right to compete with his or her former employer, the duty of loyalty ends when the employment relationship ends. So an employee is perfectly free to quit and go with a competitor or start a competing business.

As a general rule, an employee may *make plans* to compete while still employed. This includes gathering information, consulting with advisors, developing a business plan, creating a business entity, arranging for financing, negotiating to purchase a rival business, and even letting existing customers and fellow employees know about his or her intentions.

But when the employee goes beyond the planning stages or engages in unfair, fraudulent, or wrongful conduct, he or she has crossed the legal line. Examples of improper conduct by an employee include the following:

- actually beginning business in competition with a current employer
- misappropriating the employer's trade secrets
- pirating confidential customer lists

- soliciting current customers or fellow employees for the new business
- conspiring to bring about a mass resignation of key employees
- usurping business opportunities, such as by diverting new business or asking a customer to delay a purchase until the employee's new company is operating
- corrupting the employer's records or computer files

TRADE SECRETS AND THE DEFEND TRADE SECRETS ACT

As a supplement to common-law duties of loyalty, most states have adopted the *Uniform Trade Secrets Act* (UTSA), which prohibits the misappropriation of trade secrets by improper means. A *trade secret* is defined as information that has economic value because it is not generally known to others and that the employer makes reasonable efforts to keep secret. Examples include a closely guarded process like the formula for a soft drink or a computer operating system's source code. *Improper means* includes theft, bribery, misrepresentation, breach of duty to maintain secrecy, and espionage. So if an employee steals information or documents while still employed, in anticipation of leaving that job and going with a competitor, the company will have a claim under the UTSA.

Theft of a trade secret is also criminal under the federal Economic Espionage Act.

The UTSA authorizes the courts to issue an injunction prohibiting an employee from misappropriating trade secrets. However, under the statute, there must be an actual or threatened misappropriation. Normally, to base an injunction on threatened disclosure, the courts at a minimum require evidence of intent to disclose.

Courts in a few states—most notably, Illinois, North Carolina, and Ohio at this writing—have adopted a legal doctrine known as *inevitable disclosure*. Under that doctrine, even when no actual or threatened disclosure exists, the court may issue an injunction against a former employee who had access to highly confidential, specifically identified trade secrets, if the employee's old and new companies are in direct competition and if the employee's old and new jobs are so similar as to make disclosure of the secrets inevitable. Other courts have rejected the inevitable disclosure doctrine.

Defend Trade Secrets Act

A relatively new federal law, the *Defend Trade Secrets Act* (DTSA), gives federal district courts jurisdiction to hear claims of trade secret misappropriation. The courts are empowered to award the usual remedies of injunctions and money damages. In addition, they can award exemplary (punitive) damages in cases of willful and malicious misappropriation, and they can order the misappropriator to pay the attorneys' fees of the party that suffered the misappropriation. The federal courts can even order the seizure of property necessary to prevent the propagation or dissemination of the trade secret that is the subject of the suit without advance notice to the misappropriator.

For an employer to obtain exemplary damages and an award of attorneys' fees against an employee or former employee, the employer must have given prior notice to the employee that he or she is immune from criminal or civil liability for certain trade secret disclosures, including a disclosure to law enforcement or an attorney and including a court filing if made under seal. Figure 19.1 is a suggested form of notice for inclusion in an employee handbook and any employment contracts.

FIGURE 19.1: DTSA NOTICE

Pursuant to the federal Defend Trade Secrets Act of 2016 (DTSA), no employee will be held criminally or civilly liable under any federal, state, or local trade secret law for the disclosure of a trade secret that is made in confidence to a government official or to an attorney solely for the purpose of reporting or investigating a suspected violation of law. No employee will be held criminally or civilly liable under any federal state or local trade secret law for the disclosure of a trade secret that is made in a complaint or other document filed in a lawsuit or other proceeding, if such filing is made under seal. An employee who files a lawsuit for retaliation by an employer for reporting a suspected violation of law may disclose the trade secret to the attorney of the employee and use the trade secret information in the court proceeding, if the individual files any document containing the trade secret under seal and does not disclose the trade secret except pursuant to court order.

COMPUTER FRAUD

The *Computer Fraud and Abuse Act* (CFAA) is a potentially powerful weapon in an employer's hands. The CFAA covers virtually any computer that is connected to the Internet.

Under the CFAA, it is criminal for anyone to access a protected computer without authority or to exceed authorized access. Trafficking in passwords or similar information is also a crime if done with intent to defraud. Persons or companies injured by violations of the CFAA can sue in civil court for money damages.

What makes the CFAA so powerful is that when, for example, a data entry clerk takes a peek at his or her boss's personnel file using someone else's password, the CFAA is violated. Even high-level employees who have access to the entire computer system can be charged with a CFAA violation if they access information for an improper purpose, such as to sell it to a competitor.

Intentionally causing damage to a company's computer system by transmitting a program, information, code, or command is a violation of federal criminal law. Denial-of-service attacks or deletion of valuable data are good examples.

LOYALTY BY CONTRACT

An employer can gain protection beyond that provided by the common-law duty of loyalty, the UTSA, the DTSA, and the CFAA. So long as the employer acts reasonably and for legitimate business reasons, an employer may require employees to sign binding contracts that go well beyond the limited protections provided by law. A typical contract might contain some or all of the following clauses:

- a noncompetition clause (sometimes called a noncompete clause, a restrictive covenant, or a covenant not to compete)
- a nonsolicitation clause
- a confidentiality clause
- a work-for-hire clause

These clauses are discussed in the sections that follow.

Noncompetition

A contract that imposes restrictions on an employee's ability to compete with a former employer is enforceable in most (but not all) states if the restrictions are reasonable. The general rule is that an employee's agreement not to compete with an employer upon leaving employment will be upheld if the following conditions are met:

- The restraint is supported by adequate consideration.
- The restraint is confined within limits that are no wider as to geographic area and duration than are reasonably necessary for the protection of the employer's business.
- The restraint does not impose an undue hardship on the employee.
- The restraint is not contrary to the interests of the public.

Noncompete agreements may be used to prevent unfair competition. They cannot, however, be used to gain an unfair advantage. For example, it would not be appropriate to ask lower-level or clerical employees, whose employment skills are fairly fungible, to sign a noncompete. The general public also has an interest in free competition. If your employee really can provide a product or service that is better, cheaper, and more reliable than yours, the public would certainly want him or her free to do so.

Here are some circumstances in which a noncompete agreement might be used:

- C-level positions (such as CEO and COO)
- sales positions, when the business is heavily dependent on the relationship between the salesperson and the customers and when the customers would likely follow the salesperson to a new employer
- professional practices, when the clients or patients tend to identify with particular professionals in the firm and not with the firm as a whole
- jobs for which the employer must make a substantial initial investment in the employee's education or training or when the employee is unproductive while awaiting a security clearance or a special license or certification

- jobs requiring unique skill sets
- jobs involving access to highly confidential trade secrets
- high-tech positions in which the employee is likely to generate or have access to intellectual property such as computer programs or patentable devices

A noncompete agreement that restricts an employee for six months from working for companies that compete directly with the employer within a radius of 10 miles of the employer's place of business is likely to be held reasonable. A restriction of as much as two or even three years may be upheld as reasonable depending on the circumstances. But an agreement that prohibits an employee from working in any similar line of business, anywhere in the United States, for five years is likely to be held an unreasonable restraint of trade. Unfortunately, drawing the line between reasonable and unreasonable is a case-by-case process, and it is difficult to predict in advance whether the courts will uphold a particular restriction.

The geographic restriction factor may be disappearing. As information technology assumes a greater role in the economy, and as the speed and ease of communications increase, it makes little difference whether a computer programmer works in the employer's office, in the employee's own mountain retreat, or in Bangalore, India. So merely prohibiting the programmer from competing within a 10-mile radius of the office will not be very effective.

⚠ ALERT!

The code of ethics governing lawyers in most states prohibits lawyers from being parties to a noncompete agreement except an agreement concerning benefits upon retirement.

Nonsolicitation

When an employee leaves with the intention of competing with a former employer, he or she will likely plan to contact former

customers and invite them to become customers of the new busi
ness. Similarly, he or she will likely try to induce fellow employ
ees to come work for the new business. A standard provision in
noncompete and confidentiality agreements is a prohibition on
soliciting customers and fellow employees.

A nonsolicitation provision may prohibit the departing employ
ee from servicing the customers of the employer with whom the
employee had contact or with whom he or she worked while
employed. A nonsolicitation provision may even be applied to
customers that the employee brought to the employer, since rela
tionships with those customers become part of the employer's
goodwill. Thus, in defending a claim for breach of a nonsolic
itation clause, it is no excuse that the customers for whom the
employee did work after leaving the employer were also custom
ers for whom he or she had done work before starting with the
employer.

However, a nonsolicitation provision that restricts the depart
ing employee from contacting all the employer's customers
including those with whom the employee had no contact, may
be deemed overbroad and unenforceable.

⚠ ALERT!

Some states view nonsolicitation agreements as little more than thinly veiled non
compete covenants and limit their enforcement to the same extent as noncompete
agreements.

One other aspect of nonsolicitation clauses deserves mention
Companies that provide contract services to other businesses
know only too well the risk of having their business customers
cherry-pick their best employees by hiring them away and bring
ing the contract work in-house. While nonsolicitation and non
compete clauses should help prevent that practice, the company
is in an even stronger position if its *business-to-business contract*
prohibit nonsolicitation.

Confidentiality

In a typical confidentiality clause, an employee acknowledges that all company information, trade secrets, customer lists, business plans, procedures, cost structures, profit margins, and so on belong to the company. The employee promises to maintain the confidentiality of that information throughout his or her employment and after the employment ends.

Confidentiality agreements supplement the UTSA in important ways. Such agreements demonstrate that the employer is making reasonable efforts to keep information confidential, thus bringing the information within the definition of trade secret. Such agreements also impose a duty to maintain secrecy, so that breach of a confidentiality agreement may in certain circumstances be a violation of the UTSA as well.

Unlike noncompete agreements, confidentiality agreements may last for an indefinite period, or at least until the confidential information becomes known to the public generally.

Confidentiality provisions do run some risks, however. They cannot do the following:

- bar employees from filing discrimination charges or participating in proceedings before the EEOC or state or local nondiscrimination agencies
- interfere with an employee's right to engage in concerted activities under federal labor laws
- prevent employees of U.S. government contractors from reporting waste, fraud, or abuse
- prevent employees of public companies from reporting securities law violations to the Securities and Exchange Commission (SEC).

Figure 19.2 is a suggested disclaimer to be included in employee handbooks and noncompete agreements.

FIGURE 19.2: CONFIDENTIALITY DISCLAIMER

Nothing in this handbook/agreement is intended to do the following:

- interfere with or restrain any employee's rights under the federal labor laws, including the right to engage in concerted activities for the purpose of collective bargaining or other mutual aid and protection, and including the right to discuss with others the terms and conditions of employment
- prohibit an employee from complying with a lawfully issued summons or subpoena; answering questions truthfully while under oath in a judicial or administrative proceeding; or assisting or participating in an investigation, proceeding, or hearing before the U.S. Equal Employment Opportunity Commission or any other agency or commission in connection with a claim under any nondiscrimination law
- [for U.S. government contractors] prohibit an employee from reporting waste, fraud, or abuse to a government agency or official
- [for public companies] impede an employee from communicating directly with Securities and Exchange Commission staff about a possible securities law violation, including enforcing or threatening to enforce a confidentiality agreement with respect to such communications

Intellectual Property

In general, the right to patent an invention belongs to the inventor personally, and ownership of the copyright of a work belongs to the author personally. When a patentable invention or a copyrightable work is produced by an employee, the law grants only limited rights to the employer.

As to a patentable invention created by an employee on the employer's time and using the employer's money, property, and labor, the *shop rights doctrine* grants the employer a nonexclusive right to use the invention. However, the employee owns the patent rights and can use the invention himself or herself, license it for use by others, or assign the patent to third parties, all without the employer's consent.

While federal copyright law does provide that an employer is considered the author of a *work made for hire*—defined as a work prepared by an employee within the scope of his or her employment—a question can arise whether a particular work was prepared within or outside the scope of employment.

EXAMPLE: A salesperson's job is to sell complex medical equipment to hospitals and to train hospital personnel on the

equipment. If the salesperson writes a lengthy manual on the maintenance and use of the equipment, who owns the rights to the manual—the salesperson or the employer? The salesperson's employer certainly cares about ownership of the manual because it likely contains valuable information not generally available to the public. The employer could also profit from the manual, either by selling it to customers or by giving it to them as part of a service package. Alternatively, the employer may want to keep the manual secret and out of the hands of competitors. The employer gains no benefit and actually stands to be harmed if the manual is not a work made for hire. If the salesperson was instructed to write the manual and did so on the company's time and money, using a company word processor, then the manual is probably a work made for hire, and therefore owned by the employer. But if the employee wrote the manual on his or her own time, at home, using a home computer, then probably the employee owns the manual, even though the employee acquired most of the information in the manual during the course of his or her work.

In short, when an employer hires someone to work on a potentially patentable invention or a copyrightable work, the employer needs greater protection than federal law provides. The solution is to have the employee sign an agreement that all inventions and works created during employment and for some reasonable period after the employment ends are considered made for hire and belong to the employer. Such agreements usually contain an express assignment of all rights to the employer.

Consideration

As a matter of basic contract law, for a contractual promise to be enforceable it must be supported by *consideration*. In the case of a newly hired employee, the consideration for a noncompete agreement is the offer of employment itself. Even an offer of employment at will is sufficient consideration in most states to support a non-compete agreement.

In the case of existing employees, continuing employment may provide the consideration. Employers should be aware, however, that not all states reach that conclusion. Some states require *fresh consideration* to support an existing employee's promise not to compete, in the form of a raise, a bonus payment, or some other benefit or item of value.

Departing employees are often asked to sign noncompete, nonsolicitation, and confidentiality agreements. In that case, the employer must definitely offer fresh consideration, such as a severance payment or salary continuation. The departing employee is also unlikely to sign the agreement in the first place without some new consideration. For these reasons, it makes sense to have noncompete agreements signed at initial hire or at least at a time when employment is likely to continue for some substantial period.

⚠ ALERT!

Threatening to withhold a departing employee's final paycheck until he or she signs a noncompete agreement does not solve the consideration problem, since the employer has no right to withhold pay that is clearly due.

REMEDIES FOR BREACH OF CONTRACT

The typical remedy sought by an employer when a former employee breaches a noncompete, nonsolicitation, confidentiality, or work-for-hire agreement is an *injunction*. An injunction is a court order prohibiting specified conduct, violation of which could result in fines or jail time. The alternative remedy would be a suit against the employee for money damages, but the employer may have difficulty proving the dollar value of the injury suffered or proving that a decline in sales was caused by this particular employee's disloyalty and not by market conditions or some other event.

☞ **QUICK TIP**

A liquidated damages clause, specifying the amount of damages recoverable in case of breach, could overcome the problem of proving damages, so long as the amount specified is a reasonable estimate of actual damages and not merely punitive.

When an employer learns that a former employee is now working for the competition in violation of a noncompete agreement, the first step should be to write a *cease and desist letter* to the former employee. Whether the employer should also write to the new employer depends on how confident the employer is that the noncompete agreement is valid and enforceable.

A letter to the new employer, informing it about the agreement and insisting it not participate in the employee's breach of the agreement, can often be the simplest and cheapest means of enforcing the agreement. This works because the new employer, once on notice of the agreement, can be sued for *tortious interference with contract* if it ignores the agreement and continues to enjoy the benefits of the former employee's misconduct.

On the other hand, if the noncompete agreement has been poorly drafted so as not to apply in this particular circumstance or if it is unreasonably broad or otherwise unenforceable, the employer may have liability for interfering with the new employment relationship.

☞ **QUICK TIP**

Arbitration agreements that require employment disputes to be resolved by binding arbitration instead of by lawsuits should contain an exception permitting the employer to go to court for an injunction against violations of restrictive covenants. (Arbitration agreements are discussed in Chapter 1.)

EMPLOYEE DISHONESTY

Employee theft is a recurring and, some say, growing problem. It covers a wide range of activities—from personal long-distance phone calls, to the misappropriation of goods held for sale, to embezzlement of hundreds of thousands of dollars—all of which are costly to the employer. Listed below are some safeguards that can deter employee dishonesty:

- Obtain background checks on prospective employees, particularly those who will have access to company finances or merchandise.
- Consider instituting a drug-testing program.
- Be sure company financial records are secure. Electronic records should be protected by passwords, passwords should be changed frequently, and an electronic log should be maintained showing who accessed the records and when he or she did so.
- Separate financial functions. The employee who draws company checks should not be the same person who signs them. Bank and other financial institution statements should be reconciled by yet a third person.
- Assign someone not involved in company finances to open all mail and maintain a log of all payments received. The log should be reconciled periodically against bank deposits.
- Insist on seeing original vendor invoices before signing checks. Once a check is signed, the invoice should be marked paid, and the date and check number should be written on the invoice.
- Compare invoices against a current list of vendors to guard against fictitious bills. Invoices should also be checked against contractual arrangements to prevent an overbilling or kickback scheme.
- Except in emergencies, limit check-signing responsibility to one person whose familiarity with billing cycles will help spot unusual invoices.
- Require a second signature for checks over a specified limit.
- Review payroll records periodically to weed out phantom employees.
- Cancel a departing employee's password and signature authority over bank accounts.
- Distribute company credit cards sparingly and have a supervisor who is familiar with specific employee assignments review each employee's monthly account statement.
- When a company event is being charged on a credit card, require that the card of the highest-ranking employee present be used, so

that the charge record is reviewed by someone above him or her who did not participate in the event.

- Require employees with financial responsibilities to take periodic vacations so they are not able to continue a cover-up of improper activities.
- Adopt, publicize, and enforce a company code of ethics for all employees.
- Buy employee dishonesty insurance coverage.

If employee dishonesty is discovered, the employee involved will likely be terminated or at least be removed from the duties that enabled him or her to commit the dishonesty. If termination is appropriate, standard termination procedures (listed in Chapter 4) should be followed. The employer will also want to give prompt notice of any loss to its insurance carrier.

The decision whether to report employee theft to law enforcement is a delicate one. Some companies are reluctant to go public with internal problems for fear their clients or customers will lose confidence in them. On the other hand, the company's insurance carrier may require a police report as a condition to covering the loss. One thing the company cannot do is threaten the employee with criminal charges unless he or she repays the loss; doing so constitutes *blackmail*.

If the terminated employee applies for unemployment insurance benefits, the company's decision about going public may have to be made quite quickly. Misconduct usually disqualifies an employee from benefits, either permanently or for a specified period depending on the degree of misconduct. Gross misconduct also disqualifies a fired employee from COBRA benefits.

Faithless Servant Doctrine

New York and a handful of other states have developed a legal rule known as the *faithless servant doctrine* (*servant* being an outdated term for employee). Under the doctrine, an employee who is disloyal—who, for example, competes with the employer, steals from the employer, or takes kickbacks from vendors—must disgorge (repay) all compensation paid during the period of disloyalty and forfeits any contractual right to future compensation. In those states that have adopted the doctrine, courts require disgorgement even though the employer suffered no actual damages from the disloyalty and even though the employee's services were otherwise of value to the employer.

The doctrine is based on the notion that an employee is a fiduciary who owes duties to his or her employer much like a trustee's duties owed to the beneficiaries of a trust. It is a powerful weapon in the hands of the employer because the disgorgement and forfeiture remedies go far beyond what the employer might otherwise recover in a breach of contract suit against the disloyal employee.

CHAPTER 20
Alternative Work Arrangements

- Teleworking
- Flextime
- Contingent Workers

Employees, especially those in two-wage-earner households, are becoming less interested in money and more interested in lifestyle issues, such as time with their families and opportunities for leisure activities. In a tight labor market, employers have to recognize these trends to compete for quality employees.

Employers that are willing to be creative and to consider alternative working arrangements can reap huge rewards in terms of worker satisfaction, leading to greater productivity and less turnover. A number of options are suggested below.

TELEWORKING

Teleworking (also known as telecommuting) means working at a remote location that is connected with the office by high-tech communications equipment. Many jobs are susceptible of being performed at the employee's home or elsewhere than at the employer's place of business. There is no technical reason why a computer programmer, for example, or a customer service representative, cannot work just as effectively in the suburbs as in a cubicle in the central business district. And establishing a virtual office for selected employees may well be in the employer's best interests. Consider the following:

- Many quality employees find the idea of teleworking attractive. Implementing a teleworking program should therefore help attract and retain just such employees.
- So long as care is taken in selecting participants for a teleworking program, productivity should not suffer. With fewer distractions, productivity may even increase.
- Teleworking encourages employees to work independently and to problem-solve on their own (again, careful selection is critical).
- Office space (and rent) can be reduced.

Employers that are considering a teleworking program often worry about trust. They are concerned whether an employee who spends most of his or her time out of the employer's presence will work as diligently as in the office. This concern is probably overstated, given that good candidates for teleworking are the very employees who should be encouraged to work independently and whose productivity is not measured by hours logged. The programmer, for example, is evaluated less on the time put in, or even on the sheer volume of code produced, and more on the quality and timeliness of the product. If his or her programs work as required and are delivered by deadline, it makes little difference that he or she may have attended to personal matters during normal working hours.

Teleworking is not risk-free. The employer has less direct control over participating employees, office supplies and equipment, and confidential business information. Perhaps for these reasons, some large companies have recently been curtailing their teleworking programs.

If you decide to try teleworking, consider these suggestions:

- Start the program on an experimental basis. For example, limit the program to a particular department, start it on a one- or two-day-per-week basis, and set a trial period of no more than six months.
- Establish eligibility requirements for participation: limit the program to particular job categories and to persons who have been with the company for a minimum time period.
- Choose no more than half of those eligible as participants. That way a control group is retained to compare such things as productivity, turnover, and job satisfaction.
- Select participants carefully. Those who require close supervision and constant feedback, who do not enjoy working alone, or who do not have appropriate work space at home are not good candidates.
- Select only those who want to try teleworking. And allow them to opt out if they find their work quality or job satisfaction deteriorating.

- Insist that teleworkers designate an appropriate space at home that is dedicated to work. (Some employers actually inspect the work area before allowing an employee to begin teleworking.)
- Consider whether a local coffee shop, with associated confidentiality and security concerns, qualifies as an approved location for telecommuting.
- Stress that teleworking is not intended to resolve day care problems, nor is it a fringe benefit or perk. It is simply a different job assignment. (Some employers require evidence that the employee has made appropriate day care arrangements, although inquiring about day care arrangements may seem unnecessarily intrusive.)
- Be sure that teleworkers understand they must be willing to come to the office for face-to-face meetings as needed.
- Remind participating employees that they, not the employer, are responsible for any tax consequences of maintaining a home office and for complying with zoning laws.
- Require nonexempt employees (those subject to minimum wage and overtime requirements) to maintain an accurate log of hours worked for Fair Labor Standards Act (FLSA) purposes. An employee who was nonexempt *before* he or she began teleworking continues to be nonexempt *while* teleworking.
- Do not consider a switch to teleworking as an opportunity to reclassify your employees as independent contractors.
- Do not consider a switch to teleworking as an opportunity to reduce employee pay. This may give rise to equal pay violations, and it will certainly hurt morale.

Teleworking also raises some legal issues.

FLSA

Under the FLSA, nonexempt employees must be paid time-and-a-half for overtime. As with other nonexempt employees, a nonexempt teleworker must keep accurate time records so that wage and hour laws can be complied with. It may be more difficult to track hours and ensure compliance for teleworkers.

OSHA

The Occupational Safety and Health Administration (OSHA) initially took the position that the federal safety and health law applies to all worksites, including home worksites. OSHA withdrew its ruling in the face of widespread opposition. OSHA continues to take the position that the federal act does apply to hazardous or dangerous work assigned to teleworkers.

Workers' Compensation

An accidental personal injury that arises out of and in the course of employment is covered by workers' compensation. For traditional employees who work nine to five at the employer's regular worksite, an injury that occurs offsite and after normal working hours would generally not be covered. But with an injury to a teleworker, chances are there were no witnesses, so neither the employer nor the workers' compensation carrier can verify the employee's version of how the injury occurred. In other words, in the teleworking situation, the employer is at the mercy of the employee in terms of coverage for injuries.

ADA

The Americans with Disabilities Act (ADA) requires employers to make reasonable accommodations for persons with physical or mental disabilities. If a disabled worker requests teleworking as an accommodation, the employer should at least consider such an arrangement. On the other hand, at least for some jobs, being physically present is an essential job function, so in those situations teleworking is not a reasonable accommodation.

Title VII

Discrimination laws apply to all employment policies and practices, including teleworking. The opportunity to telework must be made available, without discrimination, to both genders and without regard to race or other prohibited criteria.

Intellectual Property

Unless you have a contract with your employees as to ownership of intellectual property (see Chapter 19), employees may have a claim to any copyrightable works or patentable devices they create. Their claims may be particularly difficult to defeat if they are teleworkers and spend most of their time at home.

Business Tax Liability

Most companies have obligations to file business reports and pay income, payroll, and other taxes to the state in which they do business. Generally, however, companies do not have any such obligations to states where they do not maintain a business presence. But what if an employee teleworks in a state where the company otherwise has no business presence—will that trigger reporting and tax obligations to the employee's home state? At least one court has said yes.

CASE STUDY:
TAXATION BASED ON TELEWORKER'S RESIDENCE

A Delaware corporation that did business in Maryland allowed one of its employees to work from home in New Jersey. A New Jersey appellate court ruled that, due to the teleworker's presence in that state, the company was subject to New Jersey's annual corporate franchise tax "for the privilege of doing business, employing or owning capital or property, or maintaining an office, in this state."

FLEXTIME

Flextime is an arrangement by which an employee works a normal 40-hour week, but does not work the normal five 8-hour days. Instead, the employee and employer agree on some alternative that yields 40 hours. If, for example, an employee's long-term, trusted babysitter is available only Mondays through Thursdays, the employee could work four 10-hour days and take Fridays off. Another employee might have a much easier commute working 10 a.m. to 6 p.m. rather than 9 a.m. to 5 p.m. If you can accommodate these needs without significant disruption or loss of productivity, then it may be to your benefit to do so. Listed below are some suggestions that could make a flextime policy workable in your business environment:

- Flextime means only that the employer is flexible in setting an alternative schedule. It does not mean that the employee can constantly reshuffle his or her workweek to suit the employee's day-by-day whim or convenience.
- As with all other employment decisions, the decision to permit or deny flextime must be made on a nondiscriminatory basis.
- Flextime may not work for all positions. Identify in advance which positions are likely candidates and which positions are not.
- Granting flextime may be a reasonable (and therefore a required) accommodation under the ADA in situations in which, for example, a disabled employee needs regularly scheduled medical treatment.
- Remember that whatever arrangements are made, the total number of hours a nonexempt employee can work in any given workweek without triggering overtime pay obligations is 40.

CONTINGENT WORKERS

The term *contingent worker* is loosely defined as any worker who is outside the employer's core workforce of full-time, long-term employees. As used here, the term refers to independent contractors, part-time employees, job-sharing employees, temporary employees, leased employees, and employees of joint employers.

Independent Contractors

Classifying workers as independent contractors is fraught with peril. Nevertheless, in a few, carefully designed situations, an independent contractor arrangement can be both safe and effective.

Suppose a key employee, with years of experience and a wealth of institutional knowledge, is approaching retirement age. With the employee's stock options, retirement plan, and independent savings, the employee no longer needs to work and is looking forward to the free time retirement offers. Yet the employee is not quite ready for a clean break from the company.

A possible solution? A consultant agreement for a fixed time period, say two years, renewable year-by-year thereafter if both parties agree. The employee retires and then signs on to be available whenever needed to advise on strategic planning, special projects, and the like. In consideration for agreeing to hold himself or herself available, he or she is paid a monthly retainer by the company, perhaps in the neighborhood of one-half or two-thirds of the employee's former salary. However, the employee is not expected to work any particular hours, no longer has his or her own office or support staff at the company, receives none of the fringe benefits provided regular employees, and is free to consult with other companies. The employee therefore will likely qualify as an independent contractor.

An independent contractor relationship also arises when a company contracts out certain functions without retaining control over who specifically performs those functions or how they are performed. Examples might include operating a company cafeteria and processing payroll. Legal and accounting services are examples of functions that could be performed by in-house employees or by outside independent contractors.

Part-Time Employees

Say a valued employee or well-qualified candidate for employment is available only on a part-time basis. In the past, the company took an all-or-nothing approach—an employee worked either full time or not at all. By abandoning this rigid approach, the company can benefit from the services of a valued worker, and the worker can remain productive without being tied to the daily 9 a.m. to 5 p.m grind. Many companies report that their part-timers are so appreciative of the opportunity that their briefcases are always filled with homework, and they end up working close to full time. If you are uncertain whether a part-time arrangement will work, try it on an experimental basis.

If you decide to try a part-time arrangement, be sure that you and the employee are clear about what benefits the employee will and will not qualify for. While it is theoretically permissible to provide the same benefits to part-timers as to full-timers—medical expense insurance or retirement, for example—your plan documents may limit eligibility to employees who work a minimum number of hours, such as 1,000 hours per year. Other benefits, such as vacation and sick leave, need to be considered as well.

Finally, keep in mind that discrimination laws apply to part-time as well as full-time employees. For example, the opportunity to go part time should be made available without regard to sex, race, etc. Allowing a disabled employee or candidate to work part time may also be a required reasonable accommodation under the ADA, so long as the employee can still perform the essential functions of his or her job.

Job-Sharing

A variation on part-time employment is an arrangement by which two part-time employees share the same job, either long term or for a temporary period. The difference is that, from an organizational viewpoint, the job is still considered a single position.

Frequently, although not always, a proposal to job-share will be initiated by the employee whose changed circumstances limit him or her to part-time work. Before making the proposal, the employee should first choose a compatible partner.

The employer and employees also need to think through issues such as the following:
• How will the time be shared? Will the employees work half days? Alternate days? Half weeks? Alternate weeks?

- How will the work be allocated? Will each employee perform all functions or only certain tasks?
- How will the employees communicate with each other to keep current?
- Will they overlap on a scheduled or as-needed basis?
- When travel is necessary, will they both go?
- Will the nonworking employee be available, if necessary, to provide continuity in resolving an ongoing problem or working on a long-term project?
- What impact will job-sharing have on the cost of employer-provided benefits?
- Will the employees be evaluated individually or as a team?
- What will the effect be on the remaining employee if one of the job-sharers quits or is fired?

Job-sharing can reduce an employer's overtime pay obligations. Even though the job is considered a single position for organizational purposes, if two part-time, nonexempt employees together work more than 40 hours per week, but neither employee individually works more than 40 hours, the employer will not have to pay time-and-a-half for the excess hours.

Temporary Employees

The term *temporary employee* is used here to mean a full-time or part-time employee whose salary or wages are paid by the employer in the usual way, but whose job is expected to last for only a limited period of time. It does not refer here to a *temp* who is provided by an agency and who remains on the agency's payroll. When an employer hires a temporary employee, say to perform a specific, nonrecurring job, the employer usually indicates that the employment is expected to terminate by a certain date. In doing so, the employer should also make clear that, despite the stated duration of the employment, the employee is still at will and can be terminated at any time. The employer should also make clear what benefits will or will not be provided.

△ **ALERT!**

If the temporary employee is kept on past the expected termination date, the employer should consider the need to enroll him or her in the same benefit plans it provides to regular employees. Failure to enroll a so-called perma-temp in plans for which he or she is eligible could violate plan documents and cause loss of favorable tax treatment for the plan.

Leased Employees

Leasing arrangements may take several forms. In the familiar temp situation, a temp agency provides a worker for a short period of time, typically to fill in for an employee on leave or to help finish a major project. The employer describes the position to be filled but does not identify any particular employee to fill it. Although the temp is subject to the employer's control while actually at the employer's worksite, the agency hires, compensates, and fires the employee.

Another leasing arrangement involves shifting a company's existing employees from the company's payroll to a leasing agency's payroll, although the company, not the agency, continues to make all hiring and firing decisions. The purpose is simply to free the employer from payroll and related duties while retaining operational control over the employee.

In a leasing arrangement a question may arise as to who the actual employer is for discrimination law purposes. The Equal Employment Opportunity Commission has issued guidelines addressing the question under various scenarios. For example, the true temp is generally considered the employee of the temp agency only, whereas the leased employee is generally considered an employee of both the leasing agency and the company that has retained operational control. In the final analysis, these distinctions may not really matter. The company that operates the worksite will be guilty of illegal discrimination if it discriminates against temps or leased employees at its worksite, if it encourages a temp agency to discriminate with regard to the selection and treatment of temps, or even if it simply knows that the temp agency discriminates.

Professional Employer Organizations

When a worksite employer enters into arrangements with a *professional employer organization* (PEO), its employees are considered to be jointly employed by both the worksite employer and the PEO. While the arrangement is similar to leasing, a PEO typically provides a wider range of employment-related services than just payroll. For example, a PEO might provide workers' compensation and unemployment insurance, and it might assist in hiring, evaluations, discipline, and firing (with the worksite company retaining ultimate control over those decisions). It might also provide qualified benefits (for example, health insurance, disability insurance, pension plan), and it could handle discrimination and other employment-related claims. PEOs advertise themselves as being in the business of employment, enabling the PEO's client to focus on the business of business. Through economies of scale, PEOs may well be more cost-effective and efficient in providing employment-related services.

The relationship between a PEO and the worksite company is based on a lengthy written contract that spells out in detail the parties' responsibilities and their respective liabilities. Any employer considering the PEO option will want to review the contract with great care and arrive at a thorough understanding of just how the relationship works. The PEO should also be able to provide a comparative cost analysis showing whether the arrangement will, in fact, be a financial benefit. Finally, the employer should be satisfied as to the PEO's integrity, experience, and financial standing before signing on. The employer should also inquire whether the PEO is a member in good standing of any PEO trade associations or certification agencies and whether it is registered or licensed under applicable state laws.

CHAPTER 21

Foreign Workers

- Form I-9 Requirements
- E-Verify
- Work Visas Generally
- High-Tech H-1B Visas
- H-2B Visas
- TN Visas under NAFTA
- Workplace Protections
- Remedies Available to Undocumented Workers

Foreign workers have long played a significant role in our workforce. Some claim that foreigners take positions from U.S. citizens. Others argue that they fill jobs U.S. workers either do not want or are not trained to do. Both perceptions are reflected in current law. On the one hand, employers face criminal penalties for knowingly hiring an undocumented alien. On the other hand, visa policies make it easier for high-tech employees such as computer programmers to work in the U.S.

With terrorism now firmly planted in our collective consciousness, rules and restrictions affecting foreign workers are bound to play an increasing role in the workplace.

FORM I-9 REQUIREMENTS

It is illegal to knowingly hire, recruit, refer for a fee, or continue to employee persons who are not eligible to work in the United States. The *knowingly* qualification is not satisfied by staying ignorant. For these purposes, a don't-ask-don't-tell policy will not work.

Employers must check documents to establish the eligibility of *every* new employee (including U.S. citizens) to work in the U.S. It does not matter whether the employer knows to a moral certainty that the new employee is a U.S. citizen—the Form I-9 requirements must still be satisfied.

Form I-9 and accompanying instructions are available online from the U.S. Citizenship and Immigration Services (USCIS) of the U.S. Department of Homeland Security (DHS). USCIS also publishes a helpful guide, *Handbook for Employers*, Publication M-274 for completing the form and complying with Form I-9 requirements.

Among other things, Form I-9 requires the employer to attest that it has reviewed documentation—original documentation, not photocopies—provided by the employee to establish his or her eligibility and that the documentation appears genuine. The employee must also attest to his or her eligibility to work here.

A variety of documents can establish eligibility to work. However, in most cases it is up to the *employee* to choose which documents (among those listed on Form I-9) to show the employer; the employer cannot specify the documents it wishes to see. If the exhibited document or documents appear to be genuine, eligibility to work is established. Form I-9 should then be completed and kept on file for at least one year after the employee leaves, but not less than three years after the employment began.

☞ **QUICK TIP**

It is good practice, though not required, to make a photocopy of any documents exhibited by the employee to establish his or her eligibility to work. Note, however, that attaching a photocopy of an exhibited document is *not* a substitute for filling out Form I-9 completely.

The verification process must be completed within three working days after the employee begins work. (For employees who are hired for three days or less, the entire verification process must be completed on the first day of employment.) For employees whose initial eligibility to work here is only temporary, the employer must either reverify eligibility or terminate the employee upon expiration of the initial eligibility period.

In addition to criminal exposure, employers that fail to comply with Form I-9 requirements face civil liability. Several courts have ruled that an employer that uses undocumented workers can be sued by competitors under the federal Racketeer Influenced and Corrupt Organizations Act (RICO). U.S. government contractors are also subject to debarment.

The U.S. Department of Justice's Civil Rights Division has ruled that Forms I-9 can be used for employment eligibility verification only. The ruling was in response to an inquiry whether an employer could furnish copies of its Forms I-9 to an outside payroll service for payroll processing.

⚠ **ALERT!**

Firing the employee or taking other adverse action against him or her solely on the basis of a name or Social Security number (SSN) mismatch could be discriminatory.

☞ **QUICK TIP**

The Social Security Administration (SSA) has several procedures available electronically for employers to verify SSNs. Employers must register with the SSA to use the procedures.

E-VERIFY

Congress created *E-Verify* as part of the Illegal Immigration Reform and Immigrant Responsibility Act. Operated by the DHS and the SSA, E-Verify is an Internet-based system for electronically verifying eligibility to work in the U.S. According to the DHS, E-Verify is fast, free, and easy to use, and it is the best way employers can ensure a legal workforce. (Some have questioned the accuracy of the databases that the system uses to check eligibility.) E-Verify is not a substitute for any other procedures required by law, such as completing and maintaining Forms I-9 for every employee.

Employers wishing to use E-Verify must first register at the DHS's website. The registration process includes agreeing to a lengthy memorandum of understanding (MOU) that, among other things, requires the employer to use E-Verify for all employees. The MOU contains procedures employers must follow when they receive a tentative nonconfirmation—the equivalent of a no-match letter (discussed below).

A number of states have passed laws requiring private employers in their states to use E-Verify. Arizona was among the first. In 2011 the U.S. Supreme Court upheld Arizona's law, ruling that it is not preempted by or otherwise inconsistent with federal law.

⚠ **ALERT!**

Most U.S. government contractors are required to use E-Verify and to require their subcontractors to use the system as well. (See Chapter 22 for details.)

No-Match Letters

The employee's name and SSN shown on the Form W-2 (discussed in Chapter 7) must match the SSA's records. When they do not, the

SSA issues a no-match letter. Receipt of a no-match letter does not necessarily mean that the employee is in the country illegally or that he or she has falsified Internal Revenue Service (IRS) Form W-4 when hired. The mismatch could be the result of an employer error in recording the employee's SSN on the W-2, an employee name change through marriage or divorce, or an error on the employee's W-4. Of course, it could also be the result of the employee's using someone else's number or just making one up.

In 2007, U.S. Immigration and Customs Enforcement (ICE) issued regulations on how to respond to an SSA no-match letter and promised a safe harbor for employers that followed the regulations. In the face of litigation over their validity, ICE rescinded the regulations. The SSA also halted sending no-match letters. The SSA later resumed the practice, but now, when it sends a no-match letter, it also sends the employer an accompanying letter (available on the SSA's website) advising employers how to deal with the situation.

WORK VISAS GENERALLY

The immigration laws authorize a number of categories of *nonimmigrant* (temporary) work visas, including the following:

- B-1, for foreigners here on business for the benefit of, and on the payroll of, their foreign employers
- H-1B, for foreign professionals
- H-2B, for foreign skilled and unskilled workers
- L, for intracompany transferees
- O, for foreign nationals with extraordinary ability in the sciences, arts, education, business, or athletics
- TN, for professionals who are citizens of Canada or Mexico

In addition to the above, there are a few other specialized categories, such as for students and trainees, persons participating in exchange programs, nurses, and seasonal workers in short supply. The H-1B, H-2B, and TN categories, discussed below, are the most significant for U.S. employers.

Immediate family members of persons here on work visas qualify for derivative visas. However, a family member may not perform any work while here on a derivative visa.

HIGH-TECH H-1B VISAS

An H-1B visa allows a foreign *specialty worker* (a person whose profession requires at least a bachelor's degree or equivalent) to be employed in the U.S. for an initial three years, renewable for an additional three years. If the particular field of work also requires a license, then the worker must hold such a license as well. At the end of the renewal period, the worker must cease work and spend at least one year outside the U.S. before he or she is eligible for a new H-1B visa. H-1B visas are sometimes called high-tech visas because they have enabled many computer programmers and other high-tech workers to come here.

Obtaining an H-1B visa involves several steps, but they can usually be accomplished within a few months. The downside is that, while Congress has raised the number of H-1B visas that can be granted each fiscal year, the quota is still reached long before the end of the year.

The employer, not the foreigner seeking to come here, is responsible for initiating the process and paying associated costs and fees. Employers can be fined for requiring reimbursement from the foreign worker. To initiate the process, the employer must obtain from its local employment office a prevailing wage determination for the position to be filled. The employer then electronically files a Labor Condition Application (LCA), Form 9035E, with the U.S. Department of Labor (DOL) using the department's iCERT electronic system.

When the LCA has been approved, the employer then files a petition with the U.S. Citizenship and Immigration Services (USCIS) requesting issuance of an H-1B visa. If the petition is approved, the visa itself is issued to the alien by the appropriate U.S. consulate.

In addition to paying at least the prevailing wage to the foreign worker under an H-1B visa, the employer must also offer the same range of benefits as is available to its comparable U.S. employees. Even if the worker becomes unproductive ("benched") for some reason, he or she must still be paid. The employer must also pay for the worker's return trip home after the visa has expired.

H-1B visas are issued for employment in a specific position. If a foreign worker wants to change positions or employers once here, a new H-1B visa must be applied for. The foreign worker is not eligible for employment in the new position or by the new employer until the visa is issued.

Additional requirements apply to employers that are *H-1B dependent*, that is, employers whose workforce include H-1B individuals in amounts larger than specified numerical or percentage thresholds.

H-2B VISAS

H-2B visas are somewhat similar to H-1B visas, except that they apply to a far larger pool of prospective workers: the unskilled and those whose skills fall below the professional level covered in the H-1B category. For that reason, the employer must satisfy the secretary of labor that it has been unable to find a sufficient number of U.S. workers who are able, willing, and qualified to fill the positions for which it seeks to import foreign workers.

H-2B visas are generally issued for one year and are renewable in one-year increments for a total of three years.

TN VISAS UNDER NAFTA

In addition to opening our northern and southern borders to trade, the North American Free Trade Agreement (NAFTA) made it easier for Canadians and Mexicans to come to the U.S. to engage in business at a professional level. A *professional* for NAFTA purposes is similar to an H-1B specialty worker—basically a person whose job requires at least a bachelor's degree. Depending on the particular profession, experience may substitute for a degree. And in a few cases, both a degree and experience are required. More information about TN visas and the professionals who quality is available on the website of the U.S. Department of State (DOS).

The procedure for Canadian nationals is simple. An employer desiring to hire a Canadian national writes a letter to the Canadian citizen, describing the job, agreeing to employ the worker, setting out the terms of the arrangement (for example, salary), and the dates the employment is to begin and end. The worker then appears at a U.S. port of entry and presents the letter, along with evidence of the foreign worker's professional qualifications, proof of Canadian citizenship, and a $50 fee. Although Canadian citizens do not need Canadian passports, they must be able to prove that they are Canadian citizens. The worker is usually admitted to the U.S. on the spot.

Mexican nationals must obtain a TN visa to enter the U.S. According to the DOS, an interview at an embassy consular section is required for most visa applicants as part of the visa application process. Interviews are generally by appointment only. As part of the visa interview, an ink-free, digital fingerprint scan can generally be expected. The waiting time for an interview appointment for most applicants is a few weeks or less, but for some embassy consular sections, it can be considerably longer. Mexicans must also submit specific documentation in support of their TN visa application.

Entry under a TN visa may be denied when the secretary of labor certifies that entry may adversely affect the settlement of any labor dispute or the employment of any person who is involved in such dispute. In other words, an employer cannot import Canadian or Mexican professionals as strike breakers.

Persons in the U.S. under TN status may stay no longer than three years. While the USCIS can grant repeated three-year extensions, TN status is not for permanent residence.

WORKPLACE PROTECTIONS

With passage of the law prohibiting employment of undocumented workers, Congress had concern that employers would discriminate against persons who are in fact eligible to work but who look or sound foreign. So at the same time, Congress made it illegal for employers having four or more employees to discriminate based on citizenship status or national origin. (Remember that although Title VII addresses national origin, it only applies to employers having 15 or more employees; Title VII does not address citizenship status at all.) Under that law, it is generally illegal for an employer to adopt a U.S.-citizens-only policy.

Employers do not have an affirmative duty to sponsor foreign workers, and they may refuse to sponsor a foreigner seeking employment here, whatever the reason for the refusal. And while it is not illegal in theory for an employer to prefer a U.S. citizen over an eligible alien if the two are equally qualified, there may be a practical risk in rejecting a candidate based solely on his or her citizenship.

In addition to protecting foreign workers from discrimination on the basis of citizenship, U.S. laws generally cover foreign workers and workers employed in the U.S. by foreign employers to the same extent as U.S. citizens working here for U.S. companies. For example, Title VII, the Americans with Disabilities Act (ADA), the Age Discrimination in Employment Act (ADEA), wage and hour laws, and union nondiscrimination laws generally apply with full force to all persons working within the U.S., without regard to the worker's citizenship or the employer's foreign or domestic status.

There are several exceptions, however, discussed below.

FCN Treaties

One exception is based on treaties the U.S. has with many foreign countries. *Friendship, commerce, and navigation* (FCN) treaties permit foreign companies doing business in the U.S. to engage, at their choice, high-level personnel essential to the functioning of the enterprise. These treaty provisions have been held to permit foreign companies to discriminate in favor of their own nationals, even though doing so would otherwise constitute race or national origin discrimination.

Foreign Sovereign Immunities Act

Another exception is based on the *Foreign Sovereign Immunities Act* (FSIA). Under the FSIA, foreign states are immune from the jurisdiction of courts in the U.S. so long as they are engaged in governmental-type activities (as opposed to commercial activities).

CASE STUDY:
EMPLOYER PROTECTED UNDER FSIA

Saudi Arabia hired a Virginia security firm to work with the Saudi military in providing protection for the Saudi royal family at a family residence in California. A female employee of the security firm quit after the security firm refused to assign her to a command post position for which she was fully qualified. The security firm based its refusal on instructions of the Saudi military that such an assignment would be unacceptable under Islamic law, since the female officer would have to spend long periods working with her Saudi male counterparts.

The female officer filed suit against her former employer claiming sex discrimination. The 4th Circuit Court of Appeals ruled that providing security for members of the royal family is quintessentially an act peculiar to sovereigns and was therefore the type of government activity that fell within the FSIA's immunity protection. The court went on to hold that the security firm, even though it was a U.S. company, was entitled to derivative immunity when following the instructions of the foreign sovereign not to assign its female officer to the command post.

English Language Ability

Many employers require their employees—particularly those who must deal with the public—to be able to speak English. Even though such a policy might inadvertently exclude certain immigrant groups, it is usually a justifiable requirement. Employers cannot discriminate against those with accented English so long as the employee can communicate effectively.

Some employers go further and prohibit their bilingual employees from even using a language other than English while at work. It is difficult to see how that policy could be justified.

REMEDIES AVAILABLE TO UNDOCUMENTED WORKERS

Suppose an employer discriminates against an undocumented worker by refusing to promote him or her solely on the basis of nationality, or suppose an employer violates the Fair Labor Standards Act (FLSA) by refusing to pay overtime, or the employer violates federal labor law by firing him or her for protected union activity. May the undocumented worker go to court? And if so, what remedies does he or she have?

A pair of Supreme Court cases provides some guidance.

In 1984, in a case called *Sure-Tan, Inc. v. NLRB*, the court ruled that an employer committed an unfair labor practice by reporting his illegal aliens to the immigration authorities in retaliation for the employees' pro-union votes. The court said if undocumented alien employees were excluded from participation in union activities and from protections against employer intimidation, a subclass of workers would be created without a comparable stake in the collective goals of their legally resident co-workers, thereby eroding the unity of all employees and impeding effective collective bargaining.

In 2002, the Supreme Court decided *Hoffman Plastic Compounds, Inc. v. NLRB*, which involved the question whether an illegal alien who was fired for union activity could be awarded back pay as a remedy for the employer's unfair labor practice. (Remember that back pay is pay the employee would have earned between the date he or she was fired and the date the court rules.) By a slim, 5-4 majority, the court pointed out that Congress made combating the employment of illegal aliens central to the immigration laws. Under those laws it is impossible for an undocumented alien to obtain employment in the United States without some party directly contravening explicit congressional policies. Awarding back pay in a case such as this, said the court, not only trivializes the immigration laws, but it also condones and encourages future violations.

The employer in *Hoffman*, although avoiding liability for a back-pay award, was still subject to a cease and desist order and an order to post a notice setting forth employee rights under the federal labor law. Such orders are enforceable by contempt proceedings should the employer fail to comply.

Sure-Tan and *Hoffman* dealt with unfair labor practices in violation of the National Labor Relations Act (NLRA). Do the same rules apply for employment discrimination against illegal aliens? Although the Supreme Court has not had occasion to answer the question as of this writing, there is every reason to think that the holdings in *Sure-Tan* and *Hoffman Plastics* will apply here as well. In other words, while discrimination against undocumented workers is illegal, the remedies available to them for illegal discrimination probably do not include reinstatement and back pay, since those remedies would contravene federal immigration policy.

Recognizing the likely impact of *Hoffman* on employment discrimination, the Equal Employment Opportunity Commission (EEOC) rescinded provisions in its Enforcement Guidance regarding seeking back pay for undocumented workers.

🔔 **ALERT!**

Sure-Tan and *Hoffman* resolved possible inconsistencies between two *federal* laws—the NLRA and the Immigration Reform and Control Act. Some courts have ruled, however, that back pay is available when an employee is fired in violation of *state* nondiscrimination laws.

Yet another question involves violations of wage and hour laws. Suppose, for example, that, contrary to the FLSA, an employer fails to pay an undocumented worker the minimum wage or overtime for work already performed. Most courts considering the question have concluded that payment should be ordered. They have reasoned that the *Hoffman* rule against back pay does not apply, since back pay involves compensation the employee failed to earn because he or she was improperly fired, not compensation that he or she actually earned but was not paid.

CHAPTER 22

Government Contractors and Grantees

- Statutory Framework
- Executive Orders
- Rehabilitation Act
- Veterans
- Drug-Free Workplace
- Affirmative Action
- Reporting Waste, Fraud, and Abuse
- State and Local Government Contractors

Organizations that choose to do business with the federal government must comply with the same employment laws that apply to purely private-sector employers. In addition, a number of requirements are uniquely applicable to government contractors. This chapter highlights some of the more important requirements.

STATUTORY FRAMEWORK

The four basic statutes governing employer-employee relations of U.S. government contractors are the Walsh-Healey Public Contracts Act, the Davis-Bacon Act, the McNamara-O'Hara Service Contract Act, and the Contract Work Hours and Safety Standards Act.

Walsh-Healey Public Contracts Act

The *Walsh-Healey Public Contracts Act* requires contractors engaged in the manufacturing or furnishing of materials, supplies, articles, or equipment to the U.S. government or Washington, D.C., to pay employees who produce, assemble, handle, or ship goods under contracts exceeding $10,000 the federal minimum wage for all hours worked and time-and-a-half their regular rate of pay for all hours worked over 40 in a workweek.

Davis-Bacon Act

The *Davis-Bacon Act* requires all contractors and subcontractors performing on federal contracts in excess of $2,000 for the construction, alteration, or repair of public buildings or public works to pay their laborers and mechanics not less than the prevailing wage rates and fringe benefits, as determined by the secretary of labor for corresponding classes of laborers and mechanics employed on similar projects in the area.

McNamara-O'Hara Service Contract Act

The *McNamara-O'Hara Service Contract Act* (SCA) applies to contracts entered into by the U.S. government, the principal purpose of which is to furnish services to the government. The SCA requires contractors and subcontractors performing services on covered federal contracts in excess of $2,500 to pay service employees in various classes no less than prevailing wage rates found in the locality or the rates (including prospective increases) contained in a predecessor contractor's collective bargaining agreement. The SCA also requires that employees receive fringe benefits and paid vacations and holidays. Safety and health standards also apply to such contracts.

Contract Work Hours and Safety Standards Act

The *Contract Work Hours and Safety Standards Act* (CWHSSA) requires contractors and subcontractors on prime contracts in excess of $100,000 to pay their laborers and mechanics one and one-half times their basic rates of pay for all hours over 40 worked on covered contract work in a workweek.

While the CWHSSA's overtime requirement is similar to the Fair Labor Standards Act (FLSA), discussed in Chapter 5, the exemptions are not identical. For example, the FLSA exempts drivers, drivers' helpers, loaders, and mechanics for motor carriers whose duties affect safe operation of commercial motor vehicles in interstate commerce and who are subject to regulation by the U.S. Department of Transportation; the CWHSSA does not.

EXECUTIVE ORDERS

In addition to statutory provisions, *executive orders* issued by the president, as head of the executive branch, impose a variety of requirements that must be included in procurement contracts between government contractors and executive branch departments. These requirements, along with any other legal requirements, are generally set out in the *Federal Acquisition Regulation*. The more significant executive orders (EOs) are described below.

Executive Order 11246

In 1965, President Lyndon Johnson issued EO 11246. As subsequently amended, EO 11246 requires all nonexempt government contracts to contain provisions pursuant to which the contractor agrees to the following:

- not to discriminate against any employee or applicant for employment because of race, color, religion, sex, or national origin
- to take affirmative action to ensure that applicants are employed and that employees are treated during employment without regard to their race, color, religion, sex, or national origin (discussed later in this chapter)
- to post notices of its obligations under EO 11246 in the workplace and to furnish notices to labor unions with which it has a collective bargaining agreement
- to include an equal opportunity provision in all employment ads and postings
- to furnish certain information and reports to the secretary of labor
- that the contract may be canceled for noncompliance
- to include all these same contract provisions in contracts with nonexempt subcontractors and vendors

Within the U.S. Department of Labor (DOL), administration of EO 11246 is handled by the Office of Federal Contract Compliance Programs (OFCCP). Under authority of EO 11246, the OFCCP has exempted the following:

- from all EO 11246 requirements: contracts and subcontracts of $10,000 or less
- from EO 11246 reporting requirements: prime contractors and first-tier subcontractors that have fewer than 50 employees or whose contracts are for less than $50,000, and all second-tier and lower subcontracts
- from EO affirmative action requirements: contractors that have fewer than 50 employees or whose contracts are for less than $50,000

⚠ ALERT!
An exemption from EO 11246 requirements does not excuse an employer from complying with other, generally applicable nondiscrimination, record-keeping, and reporting laws.

Nonexempt government contractors are required to file an Employer Information Report, (EEO-1 report) within 30 days after the award of a contract and annually thereafter. (EEO-1 report requirements are covered in Chapter 14.)

Executive Order 12989
EO 12989, signed by President Clinton in 1996, provides for *debarment of government contractors* that fail to comply with the employment provisions of the Immigration and Nationality Act. Under the order, whenever the attorney general determines that a contractor is not in compliance, he or she is required to transmit that determination to the contracting agency. The agency is then required to consider possible debarment of the contractor.

Executive Orders 13201 and 13496
In 2001 President George W. Bush issued EO 13201 requiring contractors to post a notice—the so-called *Beck notice*—in the workplace informing nonunion employees of their right to opt out of paying union dues. Shortly after President Obama took office, he issued EO 13496 revoking President Bush's order and requiring contractors to post a notice informing employees of their rights under the National Labor Relations Act to bargain collectively and engage in other protected, concerted activities. What the current administration may do about the notice requirement remains to be seen.

Executive Order 13495
EO 13495 and associated regulations require that workers on a federal service contract who would otherwise lose their jobs as a result of the completion or expiration of a contract be given the *right of*

first refusal for employment with the successor contractor. The regulations apply to all service contracts (prime and subcontracts) above the $150,000 threshold that succeed contracts for the same or similar services at the same location. Managers and supervisors are exempt from the right-of-first-refusal requirement.

Executive Order 13658

Most federal contractors and their subcontractors are required by EO 13658 to pay a *minimum wage*, set at $10.35 per hour beginning January 1, 2018 and indexed thereafter based on the Consumer Price Index.

Executive Order 13672

EO 13672 prohibits contractors and subcontractors with contracts in excess of $10,000 from discriminating on the basis of sexual orientation and gender identity and requires them to include these additional protected categories in their equal employment opportunity (EEO) policies and notices.

Executive Order 13673

Known as the *Fair Pay and Safe Workplaces* rule, and dubbed the *Blacklisting* rule, EO 13673 (the provisions of which were later included in the Federal Acquisition Regulation), required most federal contractors to self-report a range of labor law violations and to provide detailed wage statements to employees. Contractors with contracts of at least $1 million were also prohibited from requiring employees to agree to mandatory arbitration of Title VII discrimination claims. A federal judge in Texas issued an injunction against portions of the rule. In early 2017, Congress adopted a resolution under the Congressional Review Act, that was later approved by the president, permanently revoking the rule.

Executive Order 13706

Joining a trend set by a number of state and local jurisdictions

President Obama issued EO 13706 in September 2015 directing the secretary of labor to develop regulations mandating *paid sick leave* for most U.S. government contractors. DOL issued regulations in September 2016, applicable to contracts entered into or renewed beginning January 1, 2017. Under the rule, employees accrue one hour of paid leave for every 30 hours working on or in connection with the government contract. (Exempt employees are presumed to work 40 hours per week, even if they actually clock more time.) Contractors may limit the amount of leave accrued to 56 hours per year, but accrued leave may be carried forward from year to year. Accrued leave on termination does not need to be cashed out, but if the employee is rehired within 12 months, any forfeited leave must be reinstated.

Leave under the rule may be used (in increments as small as one hour) for (a) the physical or mental illness, injury, or medical condition of the employee; (b) obtaining diagnosis, care, or preventive care from a health care provider by the employee; (c) caring for the employee's child, parent, spouse, domestic partner, or any other individual related by blood or affinity whose close association with the employee is the equivalent of a family relationship who has any of the conditions or need for diagnosis, care, or preventive care described in (a) or (b); or (d) victims of domestic violence, sexual assault, or stalking, if the time absent from work is for the purposes described in (a) or (b) or to obtain additional counseling, seek relocation, seek assistance from a victim services organization, take related legal action, or assist an individual related to the employee as described in (c) in engaging in any of these activities.

Under the rule, if the employer provides paid time off (PTO) accruing at a rate of one hour for every 30 hours worked and allows employees to use PTO for any purpose, the employer is in compliance with the rule, even if the employee uses all accrued PTO for vacation and has none left for the purposes specified in the regulations.

⚠ ALERT!

Most U.S. government contractors are required to use E-Verify for verifying the employment eligibility of all employees assigned to the contract and all other employees working in the U.S. (See Chapter 21 for more on E-Verify.)

REHABILITATION ACT

The *Rehabilitation Act of 1973* served as a model for the 1990 Americans with Disabilities Act (ADA), covered in Chapter 17. Both laws address, in similar terms, employment discrimination against persons with disabilities. While the ADA applies to all employers with 15 or more employees, the Rehabilitation Act is limited to federal contractors and subcontractors whose contracts exceed $10,000.

In addition to prohibiting disability discrimination and requiring reasonable accommodation, the Rehabilitation Act requires inclusion of an equal opportunity clause in the contract itself. The Rehabilitation Act also requires contractors with 50 or more employees and contracts of $50,000 or more to have written affirmative action plans for employing persons with disabilities.

The OFCCP administers and enforces the Rehabilitation Act's federal contractor requirements.

VETERANS

The *Vietnam Era Veterans' Readjustment Assistance Act of 1974* (VEVRAA) applies to federal contractors and subcontractors whose contracts exceed $10,000. VEVRAA prohibits discrimination against "special disabled veterans" and "veterans of the Vietnam era." A *special disabled veteran* is defined generally as a veteran who has a 30 percent or greater disability rating or who was released from active duty because of a service-related disability. A *Vietnam-era veteran* is defined generally as a veteran (other than a veteran with a dishonorable discharge) who served in Vietnam or who served between August 1964 and May 1975 regardless of location.

In addition to prohibiting discrimination against disabled and Vietnam-era veterans, VEVRAA requires inclusion of an equal opportunity clause in the contract itself. VEVRAA also requires contractors with 50 or more employees and contracts of $50,000 or more to have written affirmative action plans for employment of disabled and Vietnam-era veterans. The OFCCP administers and enforces VEVRAA's federal contractor requirements.

DRUG-FREE WORKPLACE

The *Drug-Free Workplace Act* (DFWA) requires most federal contractors and federal grant recipients to take the following actions:

- adopt and publish a policy prohibiting the unlawful manufacture, distribution, dispensation, possession, or use of a controlled substance in the workplace and specifying the disciplinary action that will be taken for violations
- establish a drug-free awareness program to inform employees about the dangers of drug abuse and the availability of any drug counseling, rehabilitation, and employee assistance programs
- require employees to notify the employer within five days of any criminal convictions relating to drug violations in the workplace
- notify the federal granting or contracting agency within 10 days after receiving notice of the conviction
- either discharge the convicted employee or require him or her to participate satisfactorily in a drug abuse assistance or rehabilitation program

AFFIRMATIVE ACTION

Federal contractors and subcontractors covered by the affirmative action requirements of EO 11246, the Rehabilitation Act, and VEVRAA must take affirmative actions to recruit and advance qualified minorities, women, persons with disabilities, and covered veterans. Affirmative actions include training programs, outreach efforts, and other positive steps. These procedures, known as *affirmative action plans* (AAPs), should be incorporated into the company's written personnel policies. Employers with written AAPs must implement them, keep them on file, and update them annually.

Although the OFCCP has posted sample AAPs on its website, this is probably a topic on which outside expert advice is warranted.

REPORTING WASTE, FRAUD, AND ABUSE

Federal *whistle-blower* laws and regulations protect employees of U.S. government contractors, subcontractors, and grantees from discharge, demotion, or any other form of adverse employment action as a reprisal for reporting information that the employee reasonably believes is evidence of gross mismanagement of a federal contract or grant, gross waste of federal funds, abuse of authority, a danger to the public health or safety, or a violation of a law, rule, or regulation relating to the contract or grant. Reports are protected if made to the following:

- a member of Congress or representative of a congressional committee
- an inspector general
- the Government Accountability Office
- a federal employee responsible for oversight of the contract or grant
- an official of the U.S. Department of Justice or other law enforcement agency
- a court or grand jury
- a management official or other employee of the contractor, subcontractor, or grantee who has responsibility to address misconduct

Thus, *internal reports* are now fully protected, as well as reports to government officials. Further, the Federal Acquisition Regulation prohibits confidentiality agreements that restrict an employee's right to report waste, fraud, or abuse. (See the suggested confidentiality disclaimer in Figure 19.2.)

STATE AND LOCAL GOVERNMENT CONTRACTORS

State and local procurement regulations often have their own requirements. Typical are provisions requiring public works con tracts to contain nondiscrimination clauses, requiring contractors to place similar clauses in all subcontracts, and requiring contractors to post notices informing employees of the nondiscrimination clauses.

Companies doing business with a state or local government may also be required to pay a prevailing wage or a specified living wage to employees doing work on the contract.

Nonprofit Organizations

A typical business corporation is formed by shareholders who invest their capital in the business with the expectation of earning a profit in the form of dividends or on the later sale of their stock. Shareholders hold ultimate power over the corporation by electing directors and by deciding issues that are fundamental to the corporation's existence, such as whether to change the company's capital structure or to merge with another company. The directors, in turn, manage the company by setting broad policies and appointing and overseeing corporate officers.

A nonprofit organization, on the other hand, is not formed to make a profit. Typically, it is a corporation organized under special provisions of state law that prohibit issuance of shares and the payment of dividends. Nonprofit organizations therefore have no shareholders, and they do not distribute earnings to owners. (Nonprofit organizations may have members who elect directors or trustees, but the members do not own the organization. In fact, nobody *owns* a nonprofit.)

Although not organized to make a profit, nonprofit organizations are not required to operate at a loss. The point here is that any surplus of revenues over expenses must be retained or applied to nonprofit purposes and cannot be distributed to individual members.

TAX-EXEMPT STATUS

The term *nonprofit* is often used synonymously with *tax-exempt*. The two concepts, though related, are distinct. Nonprofit refers to the organization's purposes as expressed in its articles of incorporation and as governed by state law. Tax-exempt, on the other hand, means that the organization's net earnings are not subject to income tax. All tax-exempt organizations must be nonprofit but just because an organization is nonprofit does not necessarily mean it qualifies for a tax exemption. Of course, the reason why an entity organizes as a nonprofit is usually to obtain tax-exempt status.

Section 501(c) of the Internal Revenue Code contains a long list of organizations that qualify for tax-exempt status, including the following:

- corporations organized and operated exclusively for religious, charitable, scientific, testing-for-public-safety, literary, or educational purposes, or for the prevention of cruelty to children or animals, no part of the net earnings of which inures to the benefit of any private shareholder or individual—so-called 501(c)(3) organizations
- civic leagues organized and operated exclusively for the promotion of social welfare
- labor, agricultural, or horticultural organizations
- business leagues, chambers of commerce, real estate boards, and boards of trade
- recreational clubs

To achieve tax-exempt status, a nonprofit organization must submit an application to the Internal Revenue Service (IRS). If the IRS is satisfied that the organization is organized and is being operated for one of the exempt purposes listed in the Internal Revenue Code, it issues a determination letter to that effect. Exemption from state income taxes can usually be obtained on the basis of the IRS determination letter.

Another distinction that is often blurred has to do with the deductibility of contributions. While a tax-exempt organization pays no income tax, it does not necessarily follow that contributions to that organization qualify for a charitable deduction. Deductibility of contributions to §501(c)(3) organizations are governed by §170 of the Internal Revenue Code. Payments to other types of nonprofit organizations, such as business leagues, may qualify as trade or business expenses under §162 of the Internal Revenue Code.

Although tax-exempt nonprofits receive special treatment for some purposes, with few exceptions federal and state employment laws apply to nonprofits to the same extent as they apply to for-profit businesses. For example, nonprofits must withhold taxes from employee salaries, they must provide workers' compensation, they cannot discriminate (except in limited circumstances involving religious organizations), and they must provide safe workplaces.

This chapter discusses the exceptions applicable to nonprofit organizations.

POLITICAL ACTIVITY AND LOBBYING

Section 501(c)(3) organizations are absolutely prohibited from directly or indirectly participating in, or intervening in, any *political campaign* on behalf of (or in opposition to) any candidate for elective public office. Contributions to political campaign funds or public statements of position (oral or written) made on behalf of the organization in favor of or in opposition to any candidate for public office clearly violate the prohibition against political campaign activity. A violation of this prohibition may result in denial or revocation of tax-exempt status and the imposition of excise taxes.

Under the so-called Johnson Amendment to the Internal Revenue Code, 501(c)(3) organizations are prohibited from endorsing or opposing candidates for public office. In May 2017, President Trump issued Executive Order 13798 directing the secretary of the U.S. Department of the Treasury to "ensure, to the extent permitted by law, that the Department of the Treasury does not take any adverse action against any individual, house of worship, or other religious organization on the basis that such individual or organization speaks or has spoken about moral or political issues from a religious perspective." It is not clear what effect this order will have on the IRS's enforcement policies.

Similarly, no substantial part of the activities of a 501(c)(3) organization may be attempting to influence legislation (commonly known as *lobbying*). Legislation includes action by Congress, any state legislature, any local council, or similar governing body, with respect to acts, bills, resolutions, or similar items (such as legislative confirmation of appointive office), or by the public in referendum, ballot initiative, constitutional amendment, or similar procedures. It does not include attempting to influence executive, judicial, or administrative bodies.

Employees of 501(c)(3) organizations need to be familiar with the rules against involvement in political campaigns and lobbying on behalf of their organizations.

EMPLOYEE COMPENSATION AND WITHHOLDING

The Internal Revenue Code allows for-profit corporations to deduct from gross income a reasonable allowance for salaries or other compensation for personal services actually rendered. As a result of this provision, every dollar a for-profit business corporation pays out in salaries or employee benefits, so long as the amounts are reasonable, reduces the corporation's federal and state tax liability by almost 50 cents, depending on the state. In effect, the government may pay almost half of a business corporation's employment-related costs.

Because of its tax-exempt status, the same is not true for a nonprofit organization. Salaries and benefits are borne 100 percent by the organization itself and reduce the amounts available for its nonprofit purposes on a dollar-for-dollar basis. The employees themselves pay tax on their incomes just like employees of for-profit companies, although special rules apply to clergy.

Ministers and members of religious orders are considered self-employed for Social Security purposes with respect to their ministerial duties. This means that the church or other ecclesiastical organization they work for does not withhold FICA from their compensation or make matching FICA contributions. (FICA is discussed in Chapter 7.) In addition, ministers and members of religious orders who have taken a vow of poverty are automatically exempt from FICA tax on self-employment income. Even if they have not taken a vow of poverty, they may obtain an exemption if they are opposed to Social Security on conscientious or religious grounds.

Ministers who are provided a parsonage or a payment specifically designated as a rental allowance do not need to include those items in gross income for income tax purposes.

EXECUTIVE COMPENSATION

Organizations such as charitable, religious, or educational organizations that are exempt under §501(c)(3) of the Internal Revenue Code must be *operated exclusively* for the charitable, religious, or educational purposes for which they were organized. If they abuse their exempt status by engaging in nonexempt activities, the IRS has the power to revoke their tax exemption.

Revocation is a drastic remedy. It would often mean the end of the organization. So historically, minor abuses either went unpunished, or they got punished in a disproportionately severe way. Now the IRS has a less deadly weapon—an excise tax to punish abusers.

A 1996 amendment to the tax code, coupled with more recent IRS regulations, prohibit *disqualified persons* from receiving *excess benefits* from a tax-exempt organization. A disqualified person includes any person who is in a position to exercise substantial influence over the affairs of the organization. This would cover high-level employees, board members, and officers. Family members of those persons are also covered. An excess benefit is any economic benefit provided to a disqualified person in excess of the consideration received by the organization. For example, the board of a charitable organization cannot vote itself exorbitant directors' fees, nor can senior managers pull down salaries far above the norm for comparable positions.

A disqualified person who receives an excess benefit is subject to an initial 25 percent excise tax on the amount of the excess. The management of the organization is also subject to a 10 percent tax. If the excess benefit transaction is not promptly corrected, then the disqualified person is subject to an additional *20 percent* excise tax.

BENEFIT PLANS

With limited exceptions, the same array of benefit plans that are available to for-profit companies are also available to tax-exempt organizations. (Deferred compensation plans and other types of employee benefit plans are discussed in Chapters 8 and 9.) Tax-exempt organizations may even have a profit-sharing plan, although they do not have profits in the normal sense.

403(b) Plans

Organizations that are exempt under §501(c)(3) of the Internal Revenue Code—such as educational organizations, churches, public and private schools—may adopt a special type of pension plan available only to them, called a *tax-sheltered annuity* or *403(b) annuity*. Although called annuity plans, the funding vehicle for these plans is not limited to annuity contracts issued by insurance companies. Other vehicles, such as bank custodial accounts, are also available.

Before 1958, employees of tax-exempt organizations could divert any or all of their compensation to an annuity on a tax-sheltered basis. In 1958, Congress imposed a ceiling on the amounts that could be diverted. Subsequent amendments to the Internal Revenue Code have made tax-sheltered annuities conform in many respects to other types of pension plans. Nevertheless, tax-sheltered annuities retain some attractive features. One feature is their portability. When the funding vehicle is an individual annuity contract owned by the employee, the employee can leave one tax-exempt organization, go to work for another, and simply have his or her new employer make contributions to his existing plan.

Church Plans

A *church plan* is a plan established and maintained for employees of a tax-exempt church or a convention or association of churches. Unless a church plan voluntarily elects to be subject to the Employee Retirement Income Security Act (ERISA), it is exempt from most of ERISA's requirements, including requirements relating to coverage, vesting, benefit accrual, and funding. (ERISA is discussed in Chapter 9.)

☞ **QUICK TIP**
While being exempt from ERISA is generally considered beneficial from the employer's viewpoint, one downside is that ERISA's preemption provision does not apply. This makes nonelecting church plans subject to state laws, rather than uniform federal law. As a result, church plans and their sponsors can be sued in state court, can be subjected to jury trials, and can have compensatory and punitive damages awarded against them if permitted under state law.

In a 2017 decision, the U.S. Supreme Court ruled that a plan maintained by a "principal-purpose organization," that is, by a church-associated organization whose chief purpose or function is to fund or administer a benefit plan for the employees of either a church or a church-affiliated nonprofit, qualifies as a "church plan," and thus is exempt from the requirements of ERISA, regardless of whether a church originally established the plan.

Since nonelecting church plans are generally exempt from ERISA, they do not have to provide health insurance continuation benefits under the amendment to ERISA known as COBRA. (COBRA is covered in Chapter 10.)

UNEMPLOYMENT INSURANCE

Some states allow tax-exempt organizations described in §501(c)(3) of the Internal Revenue Code the option of either contributing state unemployment tax just like other employers or reimbursing the state dollar for dollar for actual claims charged to their accounts. Electing to reimburse may improve a charity's current cash flow, but it could prove expensive if several employees are terminated at the same time.

VOLUNTEERS

The Fair Labor Standards Act (FLSA) allows individuals to volunteer their services, without pay, to state or local government agencies and to nonprofit food banks for humanitarian purposes. U.S. Department of Labor guidance goes further, recognizing that individuals may volunteer their time, freely and without anticipation of compensation, for religious, charitable, civic, or humanitarian purposes to nonprofit organizations. (See Chapter 5 for a more detailed discussion of volunteers and unpaid interns.)

RELIGIOUS ORGANIZATIONS

The First Amendment to the Constitution provides that Congress "shall make no law respecting an establishment of religion, or prohibiting the free exercise thereof." Countless federal statutes have the potential for interfering with religious practices, but either they contain express exemptions, or they have been held inapplicable or unconstitutional when applied to religious organizations.

Ministerial Exception

One such federal statute is Title VII of the federal Civil Rights Act, which prohibits discrimination in employment based on race, color, religion, sex, or national origin. (Title VII is discussed in Chapter 14.) Under a literal reading of Title VII, a Catholic church, for example, could be forced to ordain female priests, contrary to Catholic doctrine. But most federal courts that have considered the question recognize a *ministerial exception* that prevents such a controversial result.

A case in the D.C. Circuit Court of Appeals, for example, involved a nun who held a doctorate in canon law from Catholic University and was an associate professor in that school's canon law department. When the nun's application for tenure was rejected, she sued claiming sex discrimination. The court characterized the case as "a collision between two interests of the highest order: the Government's interest in eradicating discrimination and the constitutional right of a church to manage its own affairs free from governmental interference." The court resolved these colliding interests by dismissing the suit under the ministerial exception, saying that religious

institutions are exempt from civil suits in connection with the selec
tion and employment of clergy.

The ministerial exception is not limited just to members of the
clergy. It also covers lay employees of religious institutions whose
primary duties consist of teaching, spreading the faith, church gov
ernance, supervision of a religious order, or participation in reli
gious ritual and worship.

Discrimination Based on Religion

Even for employees who are not covered by the ministerial exception
religious organizations may discriminate on *religious* grounds. Title
VII, by its express terms, does not apply to religious organization
with respect to the employment of individuals of a particular religion
to perform work connected with the organization's activities.

Federal labor law offers another good example of potential
interference with First Amendment rights to religious freedom. By
statute, an employee in a union shop who is a member of a bona
fide religion that forbids union membership or union financial
support may pay his or her dues to charity instead of to the union
And a 1979 Supreme Court decision in *NLRB v. Catholic Bishop
of Chicago* held that teachers in parochial schools are exempt from
National Labor Relations Board (NLRB) jurisdiction. (In an April
2017 decision involving Xavier University, the NLRB did asser
jurisdiction over nonteaching employees of religious institutions—
in that case, housekeepers—who were not involved in fulfilling the
university's religious mission.)

TENURE

From the Latin *tenere* (to hold), the word *tenure* is usually asso
ciated with job security for faculty members at academic institu
tions. Basically, by granting tenure to a member of its faculty, the
employer institution agrees that the faculty member is no longer
an employee at will and can be discharged only for specified rea
sons and after following specified procedures. In simple terms, a

tenure arrangement is a contract of employment. (Employment at will and employment contracts are discussed in Chapter 1.)

🔔 ALERT!

Faculty members at *public* institutions are government employees and therefore enjoy certain due process rights not applicable in the private sector. (See the due process discussion in Chapter 4.)

Tenure is sometimes a controversial subject. Those in support argue that it is essential to protect teachers from arbitrary decisions, to promote institutional self-governance, and to preserve academic freedom. Critics contend that tenure encourages neglect of teaching responsibilities, removes any checks on the growth of irresponsible opinions, and generally fosters laziness and lack of productivity: tenure lets professors "think (or idle) in ill-paid peace, accountable to nobody," claimed one pundit. Regardless, in adopting a tenure policy, the employing institution retains ultimate control over how and when tenure is granted and how and when a tenured teacher can be removed.

Nearly all colleges and universities have a tenure system, according to the U.S. Department of Education. The specifics of the system are usually contained in the institution's bylaws or other governing documents or in a faculty handbook. Typically, the system provides for tenure-track professors to be considered for tenure after a probationary period lasting a specified number of years. (Nontenure tracks exist for part-timers, temporary appointees, and in some cases even regular, full-time teachers.) The system identifies the criteria to be considered in granting tenure, which normally includes an evaluation by faculty colleagues.

☞ QUICK TIP

Except for religious schools, academic institutions are no different from other employers when it comes to discrimination. The granting or withholding of tenure based on race, gender, age, or other prohibited grounds violates federal and local equal employment laws.

Once a professor is granted tenure, the employing institution is restricted in its ability to terminate him or her. Termination usually requires cause, based on such factors as neglect of duty, incompetence, or professional or personal misconduct. (See Chapter 4 for a discussion of for-cause terminations.) Termination is also typically permitted if the institution abolishes the professor's program or department, or if the institution faces serious financial problems.

Since tenure policies amount to employment contracts, an institution that fails to follow its policies can be sued for breach of contract. Courts are generally reluctant to inject themselves directly in the academic process by requiring, for example, that an institution grant tenure or rehire a professor who was wrongfully terminated. But courts will award money damages when tenure policies have not been followed.

CASE STUDY:
DAMAGES AWARDED FOR VIOLATION OF TENURE POLICY
George Washington University in Washington, D.C., had a tenure policy that required it to give a year's advance notice to any tenure-track professor who would not be receiving tenure at the expiration of his or her probationary period. The policy went on to say that any faculty member who is not so notified will acquire tenure at the end of the term.

When the university violated its own policy by terminating a particular professor without giving him the requisite notice, the professor sued, asking the court to order that he be granted tenure. The court refused to order tenure, reasoning that it would not serve the university's academic interests to have a body of professors whose tenure resulted from administrative neglect or oversight. The court did, however, require payment of money damages equal to one year's salary.

CHAPTER 24

Unions and Labor Relations

- NLRA Coverage
- Concerted Activities
- Representation Elections and Card Check
- Duty to Bargain
- Other Unfair Labor Practices
- Union Security and the Right to Work
- Strikes and Lockouts

An in-depth exposition on labor relations law would go well beyond the scope of this book. Employers need experienced labor law counsel when faced with union organizing activity, when engaged in collective bargaining, or when responding to a strike threat. What follows is a discussion of the basic principles arising under the *National Labor Relations Act* (NLRA).

According to the NLRA, inequality of bargaining power between employees and employers prevents the stabilization of competitive wage rates and working conditions. To remedy this inequality, the NLRA does the following:

- protects concerted activities by employees
- provides a mechanism for union representation elections
- promotes collective bargaining between employers and unions
- prohibits unfair labor practices by employers and unions

The principal enforcer of the NLRA is the *National Labor Relations Board* (NLRB). The board has primary jurisdiction over labor disputes and union elections. And when it is not clear whether an activity is governed by the NLRA, the board itself—not state or federal courts—gets to decide in the first instance whether the NLRA applies.

Despite having primary jurisdiction, however, the board often defers to arbitration procedures in a collective bargaining agreement (CBA) for resolving grievances, even when the grievance involves an unfair labor practice.

NLRA COVERAGE

The NLRA, and hence the NLRB's enforcement power, extends to any employer whose activities affect interstate commerce—virtually any employer. However, the board has chosen not to exercise its jurisdiction over employers in a variety of industries that fall below specified revenue levels.

In general, the NLRB does not exercise jurisdiction over nonretail establishments whose gross cash flow across state lines is less than

$50,000. As to retail establishments, at least $500,000 in revenue is required for the board to exercise its jurisdiction. Separate revenue tests also apply to office buildings, hotels and motels, private colleges and universities, symphony orchestras, and certain health care institutions, among others.

The NLRB does not have jurisdiction over federal, state, and local governments; wholly-owned government corporations; employers that employ agricultural laborers or that are engaged in farming operations; and employers subject to the federal Railway Labor Act, such as interstate railroads and airlines.

The NLRA protects employee rights. But typical of federal labor laws, the term *employee* is defined in an unhelpful, circular way. (See Chapter 14, discussing the term for federal nondiscrimination law purposes.) The NLRA does, however, exclude from the definition various specific groups, including independent contractors and supervisors.

Independent Contractors

Historically, the NLRB drew the employee/independent contractor distinction based on whether the employer exercised, or had the right to exercise, control over the means and manner by which the worker did his or her job—the common-law test. More recently, the board adopted a new test for independent contractors, which the D.C. Circuit Court of Appeals has approved.

The case involved Corporate Express Delivery Systems of Oklahoma City. Corporate Express engaged two types of drivers to deliver its packages—those who drove company vehicles and those who operated their own vehicles. The employer considered the first type as employees, but it treated owner-operators as independent contractors. When several of the owner-operators began holding meetings to discuss forming a union, the company spied on them, threatened to close its Oklahoma City branch, and fired three of the union organizers. The company's actions would clearly be illegal under federal labor law if the owner-operators were employees for labor law purposes, but if they were only independent contractors, there would be no violation.

In concluding that the owner-operators should be classified as employees, the NLRB and the Court of Appeals considered whether the workers had a significant entrepreneurial opportunity for gain or loss. Stated another way: who takes the economic risk connected with the worker's job—the company or the worker? If the risk is with the company, then the worker should be classified as an employee, but if the worker bears the risk, then he or she is an independent contractor. Applying this new test to Corporate Express's owner-operators, the court observed that the company prohibited them from employing others to do the company's work and that it also prohibited them from using their vehicles to deliver packages for other companies. This, said the court, made them employees, not entrepreneurs.

Supervisors

The NLRA defines *supervisor* generally "as any individual having authority ... to hire, transfer, suspend, lay off, recall, promote, discharge, assign, reward, or discipline other employees, or responsibly to direct them, or to adjust their grievances, or effectively to recommend such action." By statute, supervisors have no right to organize or to require employers to bargain with them, although employers may, if they wish, agree to treat supervisors as employees for bargaining purposes. Absent employer consent, however, the inclusion of supervisors in a bargaining unit is not permitted, and employers cannot be forced to bargain with such a unit.

Professionals

In contrast to the exclusion of supervisors from NLRA protection, professional employees are entitled to unionize. However, professionals cannot be forced into a bargaining unit with nonprofessionals unless a majority of the professionals approve the arrangement. While professionals necessarily exercise independent judgment in the course of supervising others, they still do not qualify as supervisors if their supervisory duties are merely routine or clerical and not independent.

Employees of Religious Institutions

Teachers, including lay teachers, at religious institutions are exempt from the NLRB's jurisdiction, according to the 1979 Supreme Court case *NLRB v. Catholic Bishop of Chicago*. In an April 2017 decision, however, the board gave a narrow reading to *Catholic Bishop*, holding that *nonteaching* employees at religious institutions are subject to the board's jurisdiction "unless their actual duties and responsibilities require them to perform a specific role in fulfilling the religious mission of the institution." The board's decision involved housekeepers who worked for Xavier University, a private Catholic university in Illinois.

CONCERTED ACTIVITIES

Employers are prohibited from interfering with employees' *concerted activities*—efforts to better wages, hours, and working conditions. This includes, among other things, the employees' right to self-organize by forming or joining a union.

Soliciting

Union organizing efforts have engendered bitter disputes and a multitude of reported cases. One recurring issue is the extent to which employees and outside organizers may solicit at the workplace and may distribute pro-union literature. As the Supreme Court has said, the right to unionize necessarily encompasses the right to communicate effectively with one another regarding self-organization at the jobsite. Employee rights at the jobsite are not unlimited, however, since those rights can conflict with the employer's own property rights and managerial interests. In short, some balance must be struck between the competing interests of employers and employees.

In general, an employer may ban solicitation by employees of other employees during working time, and it may ban distribution by employees during working hours and in working areas. Conversely, an employer generally may not restrict employee solicitation during nonworking time, and it may not ban employee distribution during nonworking time and in nonworking areas, such as employee lounges and parking lots. The only exception is if the employer can show special circumstances that would make a ban necessary to maintain production or discipline.

Outside Organizers

When it comes to outside organizers, the employer has greater rights. So long as the employer acts in a nondiscriminatory fashion, it may impose a blanket ban on solicitation and distribution by non-employees on employer property, unless the union can demonstrate that employees are not otherwise accessible to union organizers.

☞ QUICK TIP

Restrictions on soliciting and distribution—even those that are consistent with the rules stated here—should have a reasonable business justification other than anti-union animus. Employers that base restrictions on *safety concerns* can usually expect to have them upheld.

Selective (discriminatory) enforcement of nonsolicitation and nondistribution rules can be an unfair labor practice. By way of example, a company completely bans employee use of the company's bulletin board—a lawful rule under the NLRA if the employer is not unionized or if the rule is the result of good-faith bargaining. But then the company allows employees to post personal notices, such as items for sale, church raffle notices, and cartoons. Under these circumstances, the company's attempt to enforce its ban against pro union material will amount to an unfair labor practice.

In another example, a nurse at a Florida hospital programmed her computer to display a screen saver saying, "Look for the U," mean ing "Look for the Union." When she was disciplined for doing so, she filed an unfair labor practice charge. Finding that a wide variety of other personal screen saver messages were allowed, such as "Go Buccaneers" and "Have a nice day," the NLRB upheld the nurse's charge.

As a final example, the NLRB ruled in December 2014 that if a company grants its employees access to the company's email system, it generally must allow them to use the system for union organizing purposes during nonworking hours. The case, *Purple Communications, Inc.*, overruled an earlier board decision on the subject of email access.

Nonunion Shops

Although the right to engage in concerted activities covers self-organization, it also protects employees who are not unionized, and it protects activities that have little to do with the formation of a union. Examples of protected concerted activity, whether in a union or nonunion context, include the following:

- *Discussing wages and working conditions.* Since the right of employees to self-organize and bargain collectively necessarily encompasses the right to communicate with one another, an employer cannot adopt a rule prohibiting employees from discussing wages or other working conditions among themselves.
- *Discussing employee sexual harassment complaints.* The NLRB has ruled that a blanket company confidentiality requirement prohibiting discussion of a pending sexual harassment investigation is an unfair labor practice.
- *Inquiring about benefits.* Employees can be persistent in pursuing benefits claims as long as their conduct is not so flagrant or egregious as to interfere with company business practices.
- *Complaining about working conditions.* An employee cannot be disciplined for complaining to management about matters of common concern to all employees. Although the employee may initially be acting alone, his or her actions will be consid-

ered *concerted* so long as they are intended to initiate or induce group action. The intent to initiate or induce group action will be assumed if, for example, the complaint is voiced at a group meeting called to discuss working conditions.

- *Wearing pro-union buttons and insignia.* Wearing buttons and insignia is protected activity unless there are special considerations relating to employee efficiency and plant discipline.

△ ALERT!

In addition to NLRA protections, state law may also bar certain work rules, such as a prohibition on employees discussing their wages with each other.

Handbook Provisions

Certain employee handbook rules, though seemingly lawful and reasonable on their face, have been attacked by the NLRB as tending to inhibit employees from engaging in protected activity. Rules that the NLRB finds overly broad, in nonunion as well as union shops, include the following:

- at-will employment provisions that state the at-will relationship cannot be changed
- confidentiality rules that prohibit employees from discussing company and employment matters outside the workplace or discussing internal company investigations
- conduct rules that require employees to act respectfully toward the company, its management, and fellow employees and avoid insulting or abusive comments
- rules prohibiting media contact
- rules against any use of company logos, copyrights, or trademarks
- rules against taking photographs or making videos or recordings on company property
- rules against walking off the job
- a rule against disclosure of employee handbooks to third parties
- conflict-of-interest provisions, such as "employees may not engage in any action that is not in the company's best interest"

According to the NLRB, employees would reasonably construe these rules as prohibiting concerted activity, which is protected by the NLRA. How the board will fare in attempting to enforce its views in court remains to be seen. In any event, employers might find it helpful to include a disclaimer in their handbooks like that in Figure 24.1. (See also the disclaimer in Figure 19.2.)

FIGURE 24.1: DISCLAIMER

Nothing in this handbook is intended to interfere with or restrain any employee's rights under the federal labor laws, including the right to engage in concerted activities for the purpose of collective bargaining or other mutual aid and protection and the right to discuss with others the terms and conditions of employment.

☞ **QUICK TIP**

Concerted activity by union members or groups of employees to better wages and working conditions is exempt from anti-trust laws, even though the activity may amount to a restraint of trade.

REPRESENTATION ELECTIONS AND CARD CHECK

The NLRB has adopted detailed rules for initiating and conducting representation elections. The process usually starts with a union organizer obtaining signatures on union cards authorizing a particular labor organization to represent the employees. When a substantial number of employees (at least 30 percent) have signed such cards, the labor organization then files a petition with the board requesting recognition as the exclusive bargaining representative. The cards themselves also get filed with the board to demonstrate that there is in fact substantial union support. The board, through one of its field offices, then conducts an investigation to determine the following:

- whether the employer's operations affect commerce within the meaning of the NLRA
- the appropriateness of the bargaining unit

- whether the election would further the policies of the NLRA and reflect the free choice of employees in the bargaining unit
- whether there is a sufficient probability, based on the evidence of representation, that the employees have selected the union to represent them

If the NLRB is satisfied on these points, it orders a representation election to take place by secret ballot and supervises the actual conduct of the election. If a majority of employees in the bargaining unit vote in favor of the union, the union is then certified as the bargaining representative of all employees in the unit.

Ordinarily, the NLRB uses a simple formula to determine who is eligible to vote in a representation election: workers are eligible if they are employed on the date of the election itself and if they also were employed during the payroll period preceding the board's order that the election take place. However, in determining who has sufficient continuity and regularity of employment to be included in the bargaining unit, the NLRB sometimes has to tailor its usual formula to fit varying employment situations.

The NLRB also determines the appropriateness of the bargaining unit. As an example, the board has included temporary employees along with the employer's permanent employees in a unit for bargaining purposes. There are limits, however, on how far the board can go. As noted above, supervisors cannot be included without the employer's consent. Nor can the board fashion a multiemployer unit without the consent of the affected employers. The board is also prohibited from designating a unit that includes both professionals and nonprofessionals unless a majority of the professionals vote for inclusion.

☞ **QUICK TIP**

A rule adopted by the NLRB in late 2014, dubbed the *quickie election rule*, expedites the representation election process and, according to some, makes it difficult for management to mount an opposition to an organizing campaign.

An employer is free, if it wishes, to recognize the union without an election if more than 50 percent of the employees in the bargaining unit have signed cards indicating they want to be represented by the union. Alternatively, the employer can insist on an NLRB-supervised election. An employer is prohibited by law from recognizing a union without an election when fewer than 50 percent of the employees have signed authorization cards.

Laboratory Conditions

The elections themselves must be conducted in *laboratory conditions*, free from threats, coercion, promises, or other misconduct that might reasonably tend to interfere with the voters' free choice. An election can be set aside even if the misconduct does not arise to the level of an unfair labor practice.

Management need not, of course, muzzle itself during an organizing campaign. Management is free, for example, to express the company's views, arguments, and opinions about unionization. But management cannot threaten employees with retaliation for voting pro-union, make promises conditioned on rejection of the union, interrogate employees about their organizing activity, or conduct surveillance to determine who is supporting the union.

Union conduct, too, can destroy laboratory conditions and warrant setting aside an election. When union organizers at a clay mine in North Carolina made threats that employees could be "squeezed out of" their jobs if they did not support the union and told anti-union employees, "You won't be able to work here when the union comes in," the 4th Circuit Court of Appeals ruled that the resultant pro-union vote was invalid.

CASE STUDIES:
ABUSIVE LANGUAGE

A company that refurbishes rail cars for the Bay Area Rapid Transit System in California had an employee handbook rule that classified use of abusive or threatening language on company premises as serious misconduct warranting suspension for a first offense and possible termination for subsequent offenses. Since the company was not unionized, the International Association of Machinists and Aerospace Workers (part of the AFL-CIO) began organizing efforts in 1998. In December of that year an election was held, which the union lost. The union then filed unfair labor practice charges citing, among other things, the company's abusive and threatening language rule. The union argued that vulgar expletives and racial epithets are part and parcel of a vigorous exchange that often accompanies labor relations. The NLRB agreed and voided the election.

The D.C. Circuit Court of Appeals reversed, strongly criticizing the NLRB in the process. The court ruled that unions were perfectly capable of acting civilly while conducting organizing campaigns. The court also pointed out that an employer may be exposed to claims if it fails to maintain a minimal level of civility in the workplace and allows racial, gender, or similar forms of harassment.

More recently, however, the U.S. Court of Appeals for the 2nd Circuit (headquartered in New York City) ruled that the employer, a catering service known as Pier Sixty, committed an unfair labor practice by discharging an employee for a vulgar Facebook post. The post, directed at the employee's supervisor, said, "Bob is such a NASTY M***** F***** don't know how to talk to people!!!!!! F*** his mother and his entire f***ing family!!!! What a LOSER!!!! Vote YES for the UNION!!!!!!"

Card Check Representation

Legislation generally known as the Employee Free Choice Act (EFCA) is introduced from time to time in Congress to allow *card check* representation, skipping the election process entirely and requiring a union to be recognized based just on cards signed by more than 50 percent of employees. Proponents of such legislation claim it would reduce an employer's opportunity to mount drawn-out legal challenges or otherwise interfere in the organizing process. Opponents say it would eliminate the secret ballot aspect of union elections and allow organizers to coerce and intimidate employees into signing authorization cards.

The most recent legislation was H.R. 5000, introduced in April 2016. In September 2016 the bill was referred to the Subcommittee on Health, Employment, Labor, and Pensions of the House Committee on Education and the Workforce. As of this writing, no further action has been take.

DUTY TO BARGAIN

Federal labor law makes it an unfair labor practice for a unionized employer to refuse to bargain collectively with its unions. The term *bargain collectively* is defined by the NLRA as "the performance of the mutual obligation of the employer and the representative of the employees to meet at reasonable times and confer in good faith with respect to wages, hours, and other terms and conditions of employment."

Closely connected with an employer's duty to bargain is its duty to provide the union with all requested information relevant to the union's duties as representative of union members. The courts apply a broad definition of *relevant* in this context, so that there need only be a probability that the information will be useful to the union.

Normally, an employer's duty to bargain with a union does not arise until after the NLRB has conducted a union representation election, the union has been successful, and the board has certified the election results. This has been called the preferred and most satisfactory method for a union to obtain representative status. But the duty to bargain can apply to a union that has *lost* a representation election. Suppose an employer, motivated by anti-union animus, so poisons the atmosphere with unfair labor practices that a would-be union loses the election. Traditionally, the board orders a new election. But if the employer's actions make it impossible to conduct a fair and reliable new election, the board may simply treat the union as the employees' legitimate representative.

Project Labor Agreements

Special provisions of the NLRA apply to employers in the building and construction industry. An employer in that industry is allowed to enter into a *project labor agreement* (PLA) with a union, even though the union has not yet been established as the representative of a majority of the employees to be covered by the PLA. Typically, a PLA requires all contractors and subcontractors who will work on a project to agree in advance to a master CBA under which wages, hours, and other conditions of employment are standardized for all employees at the project. The PLA requirement is incorporated into bid specifications, so any company that is awarded a contract is bound to join in the PLA.

Mandatory vs. Permissive Bargaining

Bargaining over some subjects is *mandatory*, because those subjects involve wages, hours, and other terms and conditions of employment. Other subjects are *permissive*, in that employers and unions are free to bargain over them if they wish, but neither side can insist, to the point of impasse, on inclusion of a mere permissive subject in a CBA.

What are the mandatory subjects over which employers must bargain if requested to do so by their unions? According to the Supreme Court, they are subjects that are directly germane to the working environment. However, a company has a right to run its business without interference. So a company need not bargain over managerial decisions that lie at the core of entrepreneurial control such as decisions concerning the commitment of investment capital and the basic scope and direction of the enterprise.

In addition to wages, hours, and benefits, examples of mandatory bargaining subjects include the following:

- company decisions that directly affect job security, such as a decision to contract out work previously done by union employee (but decisions that only indirectly affect job security, such as a decision to discontinue a particular product line, are not subject to mandatory bargaining)

- changes in working conditions
- union security clauses, when such clauses are not forbidden under state right-to-work laws (discussed later in this chapter)
- seniority rights
- management rights clauses reserving, for example, the company's right to sell its business free of liabilities under the CBA, to discontinue operations, to determine the number of hours per day and per week that operations should be carried on, and to suspend, discharge, or otherwise discipline employees
- prices and availability of services at in-plant cafeterias and vending machines
- hiring practices
- tardiness policies
- use of a company bulletin board
- drug and alcohol testing
- installation of security cameras to deter employee theft

This last item is drawn from a case before the D.C. Circuit Court of Appeals affirming a decision by the NLRB. The case involved a company's practice over many years of installing hidden surveillance cameras to investigate specific cases of employee theft or other wrongdoing. Faced with unauthorized use of a manager's telephone for long-distance calls, the company placed a camera in the manager's file cabinet. The camera caught an employee (who happened to be a union member) using the phone, and the company promptly fired him.

The union filed a grievance over the firing and, at a subsequent hearing, discovered for the first time the company's practice of using hidden surveillance cameras. The union then asked the company for detailed information about the cameras, indicating that it wanted to bargain with the company over the practice. The company refused to provide the information, and it refused to bargain.

The board ruled that the company was wrong on both counts. It said use of surveillance cameras is a subject of mandatory bargaining, just like physical examinations, drug and alcohol testing, and other investigatory tools and methods used by employers to discover employee misconduct. Further, the company was required to provide pertinent information to the union—or at least bargain over what information would be provided. While the company may have a legitimate concern over keeping confidential such information as the location of the cameras, the company still had a duty to seek an accommodation that would meet the needs of both the union and the company.

Conflicts with Other Laws

Sometimes an employer's duty to bargain conflicts with, or appears to conflict with, other legal duties imposed on the employer. Take, for example, an employee with a disability who requests reassignment to a vacant position as an accommodation for his or her disability. (The duty of reasonable accommodation under the Americans with Disabilities Act, or ADA, is discussed in Chapter 17.) While ADA principles might well require the reassignment, doing so may at the same time violate established seniority practices. In that circumstance, the Supreme Court has ruled that in the run of cases seniority trumps ADA requirements. Of course, if the employer's seniority practice is one in name only, then the employer will have a difficult time defending its refusal to accommodate based on seniority.

In another Supreme Court case, a truck driver for a mining company twice tested positive for marijuana. The mining company attempted to terminate the employee, but the union filed a grievance and insisted on arbitration. The arbitrator ruled that, in light of certain mitigating circumstances, there was no just cause for termination (*just cause* being the standard prescribed by the CBA) and ordered the employee reinstated. The mining company then went to court, arguing that, notwithstanding its CBA and the arbitrator's order, public policy justified refusal to reinstate the employee. This was especially so, said the mining company, because the employee was engaged in safety-sensitive tasks requiring random drug testing under U.S. Department of Transportation regulations. The Supreme Court rejected the company's argument and upheld the reinstatement order, finding no overriding public policy that would justify refusal to comply with the order.

Or take the case of a union employee who was accused of sexual harassment. The employee in the case had a long history of offensive, sexually charged conduct directed at female co-workers. Finally, the employer's equal employment opportunity officer recommended that the employee be fired, but that recommendation had to be approved by the employer's labor relations manager, who was on vacation. By the time the labor relations manager returned, more than 30 days had expired. Since the employer's CBA required that discipline be imposed within 30 days of the misconduct, no further action was then taken. Eventually, after additional incidents, the employee was fired. In the meantime, however, the victims of his conduct filed sex discrimination charges.

The employer defended against the discrimination charges by claiming that under its CBA it could not fire the employee without following the procedures specified in the agreement. The 7th Circuit Court of Appeals ruled, however, that a collective bargaining agreement is not *imposed* on an employer. Rather, it is an agreement every provision of which has been consented to by the employer. In this case, for example, the employer could have negotiated for special rules applicable to harassment, but it did not. Since the employer cannot by agreement limit its obligations under federal nondiscrimination laws, the employer alone must bear the consequences of its labor-relations decisions.

This decision illustrates an important point. Just because a subject of negotiation falls in the mandatory category, employers should still remember that their only duty is to bargain on the subject in good faith. The duty to bargain does not mean that the employer is obligated to *agree* with the union's position.

The employer's duty to bargain ends if a majority of employees in the bargaining unit no longer support the union. For the first three years while a CBA is in place, a conclusive presumption exists that the union enjoys majority support. However, after three years or when a CBA expires, the presumption of majority support is no longer conclusive. The employer may then attempt to rebut the presumption by showing that, in fact, the union no longer represents a majority of workers.

OTHER UNFAIR LABOR PRACTICES

Unfair labor practices come in many varieties. A number of them have been discussed above, such as refusal to bargain, selective enforcement of nonsolicitation rules, and adoption of workplace policies that interfere with concerted activities. The NLRA itself lists the following as employer unfair labor practices:

- interfering with, restraining, or coercing employees in the exercise of the rights guaranteed by the NLRA
- dominating or interfering with the formation or administration of a labor organization or contributing financial or other support to it
- discriminating in regard to hiring or tenure of employment or any term or condition of employment to encourage or discourage membership in any labor organization
- discharging or otherwise discriminating against an employee because he or she has filed charges or given testimony under the NLRA
- refusing to bargain collectively with the employees' representative

A few of these ULPs merit further discussion.

Company-dominated employee committee. Historically, a favorite way for employers to keep out, or at least keep control of, unions was to form an organization for its employees that appeared to but in reality did not, give employees a voice in their conditions of employment. By making it illegal for an employer to dominate or interfere with a *labor organization* (defined as any organization of employees that exists to deal with the employer concerning grievances, wages, hours, or working conditions), the law effectively stops this practice.

Not all employee committees are illegal, however, as an NLRB decision shows. A nonunion manufacturer in Texas uses a management system under which it delegates substantial operational authority to its employees. It accomplishes this through numerous committees in which employees and management participate. These committees make decisions by consensus on a wide variety of workplace issues such as production, quality, training, attendance, safety, maintenance, and even discipline short of suspension or discharge. Although senior management retains ultimate authority, it routinely approves all committee recommendations.

The board ruled that these committees are not labor organizations because they do not exist to deal with management. Instead, the committees themselves perform management functions, exercising authority that, in the traditional plant setting, would be considered supervisory. So when a committee interacts with company officials, the interaction is really between two management bodies. In effect, these committees do not deal with management—they *are* management.

Discrimination against salts. In an attempt to unionize a nonunion shop, a union may *salt* the shop by sending union organizers as applicants for job openings. When an employer refuses to hire, or even consider, such applicants and the employer is motivated, at least in part, by anti-union animus, the employer commits an unfair labor practice. (Some say that the purpose of salting is not in fact to organize a union but to precipitate an unfair labor practice.) The 7th Circuit Court of Appeals has even held that a salt can lie on his or her job application, so long as the lie concerns his or her status as a salt and not his or her qualifications for the job. In the 7th Circuit case, for example, the salt said he was "laid off" from his previous job, at $11 an hour, when applying for an $8.50 an hour job. Had he told the truth—that he in fact took a voluntary leave of absence—the new employer might well have guessed his status as a salt.

Collusion with union. In a case before the 4th Circuit Court of Appeals, an employee of a Rochester, N.Y., freight company ran for union office against an incumbent Teamsters official. Despite a hard-fought campaign, the employee failed to defeat the incumbent. During later renegotiations of the labor contract between the Teamsters and the freight company, the union offered to concede on a point important to the company if the company would fire the employee. The company eventually did so. The court ordered reinstatement, saying that the NLRA prohibits the discharge of an employee for engaging in protected activity such as running for a union election. The court went on to say that unions themselves cannot cause an employee to be fired for engaging in protected activity, nor can unions act in a manner contrary to the interests of their members, as the Teamsters did here by putting the personal gain of incumbent union officers ahead of the interests of union members.

UNION SECURITY AND THE RIGHT TO WORK

Union security clauses are designed to protect union membership, or at least union revenue. A union security clause in a collective bargaining agreement might require that the employer be a *closed shop*—one in which the employer must hire only current union members, typically from a union hiring hall. Under a *union shop* arrangement, all eligible employees must join the union on being hired and must maintain membership as a condition of continued employment. And in an *agency shop*, employees do not need to be union members, but they must pay the same union dues that members pay.

Federal labor law permits union security clauses in collective bargaining agreements. However, since 1947 when the NLRA was amended by the Taft-Hartley Act, federal labor law has also permitted individual states to enact *right-to-work laws* making union security clauses illegal in those states. At this writing, 28 states have done exactly that:

- Alabama
- Arizona
- Arkansas
- Florida
- Georgia
- Idaho
- Indiana
- Iowa
- Kansas
- Kentucky
- Louisiana
- Michigan
- Mississippi
- Missouri
- Nebraska
- Nevada
- North Carolina
- North Dakota
- Oklahoma
- South Carolina
- South Dakota
- Tennessee
- Texas
- Utah
- Virginia
- West Virginia
- Wisconsin
- Wyoming

Suppose an employee in a union or agency shop holds religious or moral convictions against union participation. Federal law provides a limited escape clause. It says that any employee who is a member of a bona fide religion that has historically held conscientious objections to joining or financially supporting labor organizations may, instead of paying union dues, pay an equal amount to a designated charity.

STRIKES AND LOCKOUTS

The NLRA says that except as otherwise expressly stated in the act, nothing in the act may be construed so as either to interfere with or impede or diminish in any way the right to strike. The courts have characterized the right to strike as a legitimate economic tool that implements and supports the principles of the collective bargaining system and that labor unions may use as they see fit.

The right to strike includes the right to picket. In general, picketing must relate to a primary dispute (a labor dispute between the picketing workers and the employer being picketed). Secondary pickets, like secondary strikes, are not protected by the NLRA. The right to strike also includes the right to refuse to cross a picket line in connection with a primary dispute. The right to strike *does not* include slowdowns, unannounced walkouts, sit-down strikes, violence or threats of violence, or defamation of the employer's goods.

While the NLRA preserves the right to strike, it does not guaranty unions the right to choose the timing of a strike. Once the employer has exhausted its duty to bargain in good faith and reached an impasse, it is free to use the economic weapons at its disposal, just as the workers are free to strike. As the Supreme Court said in 1965, an employer's use of a lockout in support of a legitimate bargaining position is not in any way inconsistent with the right to bargain collectively or with the right to strike.

When workers are out on strike, they remain employees, since the NLRA's definition of *employee* includes "any individual whose work has ceased as a consequence of, or in connection with, any current labor dispute or because of any unfair labor practice, and who has not obtained any other regular and substantially equivalent employment." This means that an employer cannot retaliate against strikers for their union activity.

An employer's right to hire permanent replacements for striking workers depends on the nature of the strike. If the strike is economically motivated (to improve wages, hours, or other terms and conditions of employment), the employer may hire permanent replacements. However, if the strike is to protest an unfair labor practice, the strikers are entitled to reinstatement with back pay upon making an unconditional offer to return to work.

⚠ ALERT!

An employer cannot hire foreign workers on H-1B visas as replacements for economic strikers, since the employer must certify in its H-1B application that there is no strike in progress involving the job to be filled. Similarly, a TN visa may be denied if the secretary of labor certifies that issuance of the visa may adversely affect settlement of a labor dispute. (See Chapter 21 for more on work-related visas.)

Even for economic strikes, the employer faces certain limitations. For example, it cannot pick and choose who will be replaced based on the extent of involvement in union activities. The employer also cannot offer *super seniority* to replacements. In one case the employer did just that, arguing that it needed to offer super seniority as an inducement to the replacement workers. The Supreme Court held that doing so was an unfair labor practice because it discriminated between strikers and nonstrikers.

☞ **QUICK TIP**

A worker who is out on strike is generally ineligible for unemployment insurance benefits. However, a nonstriking, unemployed worker will not become ineligible for benefits by turning down a job offer that would involve replacing a striking worker.

An employee's good-faith refusal to work under abnormally dangerous conditions is not a strike under the NLRA. So unlike workers who are on strike for economic reasons, employees who are absent for safety reasons cannot be permanently replaced.

Limitations on the Right to Strike

Although the NLRA preserves workers' right to strike, the right is subject to a number of limitations, discussed below.

Duty to bargain. Perhaps the most import exception to the right to strike arises from the union's duty to bargain in good faith over mandatory subjects of bargaining. Until the employer and the union have bargained to impasse, the union may not strike, and the employer may not lock out.

No-strike clause. Employees can bargain away their right to strike by agreeing to a no-strike clause in their collective bargaining agreement.

Secondary strikes. The NLRA expressly prohibits labor unions from engaging in strikes or boycotts for the purpose of forcing a different employer to recognize or bargain with a labor union.

Taft-Hartley injunctions. When a strike or lockout affects an entire industry (or a substantial part of an entire industry) and, if permitted to occur or continue, would imperil the national health or safety, the president of the United States may appoint a board of inquiry to investigate the issues in dispute and make a report to the president. With the board of inquiry's report in hand, the president may direct the attorney general to go to court and request an 80-day injunction against the strike or lockout.

Health care institutions. The NLRA requires labor organizations whose employees work at health care institutions to give at least 10 days' previous notice, both to the institution itself and to the Federal Mediation and Conciliation Service, of its intent to strike, picket, or engage in some other concerted refusal to work. If the service believes a strike would substantially interrupt the delivery of health care in the locality concerned, the service may appoint a board of inquiry. Pending the board's report and for 15 days thereafter, the pre-impasse status quo must be maintained.

Conclusion

This book has accomplished much if it has provided you with a broad understanding of the employment relationship and alerted you to the hazards you face as an employer. The next time you hear a racial epithet on the factory floor or see a sexist cartoon on the company bulletin board, you will know that trouble lurks. And when rumors start flying that a handful of employees have been talking about a union, you will consult competent labor counsel instead of firing the troublemakers.

Equipped with this new knowledge, and no longer bewildered by the complexities of the employment relationship, you are now free to devote your energies where they belong—making your business or organization a success!

Acknowledgments

This is the first book I've had published by the Society for Human Resource Management (SHRM), and I am excited to be part of the SHRM family. SHRM's staff have been a delight to work with. Their editorial and design skills go well beyond anything I'm capable of, and I thank them for their encouragement and professionalism.

Thanks also to my two peer reviewers, Lilliam Machado and Mitchell Batt. Reading and commenting on a book-length, nonfiction manuscript is a true act of friendship. Lilliam and Mitch, both fine employment law practitioners in Montgomery County, Md., were extraordinarily helpful in reviewing the book, pointing out my mistakes, and generally improving the end product. Any remaining mistakes are, of course, mine alone.

I must also thank my law partners for allowing me to spend many hours on this project instead of practicing law.

Charlie Fleischer
December 2017

About the Author

Charles H. Fleischer has an undergraduate degree in political science from the University of Rochester in Rochester, N.Y., and a law degree (with honors) from the George Washington University in Washington, D.C. He is admitted to practice law in Maryland and the District of Columbia and before the U.S. Supreme Court. He is a member of the law firm of Oppenheimer, Fleischer & Quiggle, P.C., of Bethesda, Md. The firm's website is www.OFQLaw.com.

Fleischer was a principal author of the employer's briefs in *Meritor Savings Bank v. Vinson*, the first Supreme Court case dealing with sexual harassment. Fleischer's practice includes representing employers before the Equal Employment Opportunity Commission, state and local fair employment practice agencies, and the courts. He has advised numerous businesses and organizations on employment law issues, and he writes extensively on the topic.

Glossary

0-9

360-degree evaluation. An evaluation system under which employees are rated not only by supervisors but also by peers, direct reports, and sometimes clients and customers.

401(k) plan. A type of qualified retirement plan authorized by §401(k) of the Internal Revenue Code.

403(b) plan. A type of qualified retirement plan authorized by §403(b) of the Internal Revenue Code, available to tax-exempt organizations such as schools and charities.

A

abusive discharge. Sometimes called *wrongful discharge*, the termination of an at-will employee contrary to some important public policy.

affirmative action plan (AAP). Action required of most government contractors, subcontractors, and federal grant recipients to ensure equal employment of minorities, women, persons with disabilities, and certain veterans.

Age Discrimination in Employment Act (ADEA). A federal law that prohibits discrimination because of age against persons age 40 and older.

agent. A person who acts on behalf of another (called the *principal*) and has the power to bind the other person in contract. Employees and independent contractors can each be, but are not necessarily, agents of their employers.

agency shop. A type of union security arrangement in which union membership is optional. However, as a condition of continued employment, nonunion members pay to the union amounts equal to initiation fees and periodic dues paid by union members.

alternative dispute resolution (ADR). A procedure for resolving disputes other than by a lawsuit. Arbitration and mediation are forms of ADR.

alternate payee. An employee's spouse, child, or other dependent who, pursuant to a *qualified domestic relations order* (QDRO), is awarded an interest in the employee's pension plan. Also, an employee's child who, pursuant to a *qualified medical child support order* (QMCSO), becomes entitled to health insurance coverage under the plan in which the employee participates.

Americans with Disabilities Act (ADA). A federal law that prohibits discrimination against a qualified person with a disability, requires reasonable accommodation of disabled applicants and employees, and restricts medical examinations and disability-related inquiries.

anti-selection. The process of applying for insurance by those who face an increased risk of suffering an insured loss.

applicable large employer (ALE). For purposes of the *Patient Protection and Affordable Care Act*, an employer with 50 or more full-time (or full-time equivalent) employees. *arbitration.* One of several forms of dispute resolution that are alternatives to litigation in court.

at-will employment. Employment that is not for a fixed or definite term. In an at-will employment relationship, the employee can quit at any time, and the employer can fire the employee at any time with or without cause.

B

back pay. Pay awarded to an employee or applicant for employment that, but for discrimination, an unfair labor practice, or other wrongful conduct by the employer, would have been earned between the time of the wrongful conduct and the time the award is made.

ban-the-box laws. State and local laws that prohibit or restrict employers from inquiring about a candidate's criminal history.

base period. For unemployment insurance purposes, four out of the five completed

calendar quarters preceding the filing of a benefit claim.

base period employer. Any employer for which an unemployment insurance claimant worked during his or her base period.

Belo plan. An exception to the general overtime rules of the *Fair Labor Standards Act* that allows an employer to pay a fixed salary to nonexempt employees, such as emergency workers, who work an irregular number of hours from week to week because of the nature of the job.

blacklisting. The practice of circulating the names of former employees who should not be hired because of their history of union organizing efforts or other protected activity.

bona fide occupational qualification (BFOQ). Exceptions to certain forms of discrimination.

borrowed servant. An employee who is transferred from his or her regular employer to another employer on a temporary basis.

bring your own device (BYOD). A policy that allows employees to use their smartphones, tablets, or other electronic devices to conduct the employer's business.

C

Cadillac plan. A health insurance plan with particularly rich benefits. Under the *Patient Protection and Affordable Care Act*, the excess cost of a Cadillac plan is subject to a 40 percent excise tax.

cafeteria plan. See *Section 125 plan.*

cash balance plan. A pension plan that has characteristics of both a defined contribution plan and a defined benefit plan. In a cash balance plan, the ultimate benefit is the amount resulting from periodic contributions to a separate hypothetical account for each employee and an assumed interest rate earned on those contributions.

cash or deferral arrangement (CODA). A feature of some deferred compensation plans under which the employee can elect to take taxable cash or a nontaxable contribution to the plan.

casual employee. An employee who is not covered by workers' compensation because he or she works irregularly, for a brief period only, and does work not normally performed by employees of the employer.

cause. A reason that is legally sufficient to discharge an employee who is not an at-will employee.

Chapter 13. A provision of the U.S. Bankruptcy Code that allows an individual with a regular income to spread out repayment of his or her debts up to three years.

child labor. Labor by a person under 18 years of age. See also *oppressive child labor.*

Circular E. An Internal Revenue Service publication for employers, also known as Publication 15, containing instructions and tables for federal income tax withholding and payroll tax obligations.

Civil Rights Act of 1866. A Reconstruction-era federal statute that extends to all citizens the same right to make and enforce contracts as was previously enjoyed by white citizens.

Civil Rights Act of 1964. The principal federal statute prohibiting discrimination in employment and public accommodations. The act was substantially amended in 1991.

class action. A lawsuit brought by one or several named plaintiffs for themselves and as representatives of a class of other similarly situated individuals. Once a court certifies the class, the similarly situated individuals must opt out of the class to avoid being bound by the results of the lawsuit.

closed shop. A type of union security agreement under which employees must be union members to be hired.

collective action. A lawsuit brought under the *Fair Labor Standards Act* by one or several named plaintiffs for themselves and as representative of a class of similarly situated individuals. A collective action is similar to a *class action*, except that the similarly situated individuals must opt in to participate in and be bound by the results of the lawsuit.

collective bargaining agreement (CBA). An agreement between an employer and a union dealing with employee pay, benefits, discipline, grievance procedures, and other terms and conditions of employment.

commerce clause. A clause in Article I of the U.S. Constitution empowering Congress to regulate commerce with foreign nations, among the several states, and with American Indian tribes.

common law. The body of legal principles developed by court decisions in England and this country that are not based on legislative enactments.

comp time (compensatory time). Leave taken in lieu of overtime pay. Use of comp time to compensate a nonexempt employee who works more than 40 hours in one workweek generally violates the *Fair Labor Standards Act.*

concerted activity. Union organizing activity or other activity by employees for the purpose of bettering wages, hours, or working conditions. Concerted activity is protected by the *National Labor Relations Act.*

consideration. In contract law, the inducements, rights, or things of value that the parties to a contract agree to exchange.

Consolidated Omnibus Budget Reconciliation Act (COBRA). A federal law requiring continuation of group health insurance coverage under certain circumstances when coverage would otherwise end.

constructive discharge. A termination in which the employee is effectively forced to quit as a result of intolerable working conditions.

constructive receipt. In tax law, the doctrine that treats compensation as having been received by an employee when the compensation is credited to the employee's account or is otherwise made available to the employee.

consumer report. A credit report and/or an investigative report about a person. The obtaining and use of consumer reports by employers are regulated by the *Fair Credit Reporting Act* and by some state laws.

consumer reporting agency (CRA). A person or entity that, for a fee, regularly assembles or evaluates credit information or other information on consumers for the purpose of furnishing consumer reports to third parties. The obtaining and use of consumer reports by employers from a CRA is regulated by the *Fair Credit Reporting Act* and by some state laws.

contributory plan. A plan such as a group health insurance plan in which the employee pays a portion of the premium.

contingent worker. A worker who is outside an employer's core workforce of full-time, long-term employees. Contingent workers include independent contractors, part-time employees, job-sharers, temporary employees, and leased employees.

D

defamation. A false statement that injures a person's reputation. False written statements may be libelous, and false spoken statements may be slanderous.

deferral agency. See *fair employment practice agency.*

deferred compensation. Compensation set aside for an employee, but not currently taxable to the employee because the employee's receipt and enjoyment of the compensation is deferred.

defined benefit plan. A type of retirement plan in which the benefit amount is fixed by a predetermined formula including such factors as years of service and pre-retirement compensation. Employer contributions to the plan are calculated so that the plan will have sufficient funds to pay the promised benefit.

defined contribution plan. A type of retirement plan in which the amount contributed to the plan is fixed by a predetermined formula and the benefit amount depends on the value of each participant's separate account within the plan.

dilution. Reduction in the value of a company's outstanding stock caused by issuance of additional stock for less than the value or market price of the stock.

direct liability. Liability for an employer's own negligence in hiring, retaining, or failing to supervise an employee who presents an unreasonable risk of injury or damage to the public.

directors and officers (D&O) insurance. Coverage that protects company officials from personal liability for good faith actions taken in the course of their employment.

direct threat defense. A provision of the *Americans with Disabilities Act* that allows employers to exclude an employee with a disability from certain jobs in which the disabled person would pose a direct threat to his or her own health or safety or to the health or safety of others in the workplace.

disability. For *Americans with Disabilities Act* purposes, a physical or mental impairment that substantially limits one or more major life activities.

discovery. The formal pretrial process by which parties to court proceedings obtain information and documents from opposing parties and question opposing parties and nonparty witnesses under oath.

discrimination. Adversity suffered by an applicant, an employee, or a group of applicants or employees for a reason that is prohibited by law, such as race, religion, or gender.

disparate impact. In discrimination law, the effect of workplace rules or requirements that appear neutral on their face but that have an adverse impact on a particular race, religion, gender, or other protected category.

disregarded entity. A limited liability company with a single member (owner) who elects to be taxed as a sole proprietorship.

disparate treatment. In discrimination law, intentional adverse treatment of an applicant or employee because of his or her race, religion, gender, or other factor.

Dodd-Frank Act. Dodd-Frank Wall Street Reform and Consumer Protection Act. The act imposes wide-ranging regulations on the financial industry and on publicly traded companies.

due process clause. A clause in the Fifth Amendment to the U.S. Constitution that provides that no person may be deprived of life, liberty, or property without due process of law. The 14th Amendment also prohibits states from depriving any person of life, liberty, or property without due process of law.

E

earned income tax credit (EITC). A federal tax credit available to qualified low- and moderate-income employees.

earned rate. For unemployment insurance purposes, the rate used to compute an employer's contribution obligation based on the employer's actual claims experience.

Electronic Communications Privacy Act (ECPA). The federal law that regulates the interception of wire, electronic, and oral communications.

Electronic Federal Tax Payment System (EFTPS). The system for paying employment taxes and other federal taxes electronically.

emergency action plan. A plan required by the *Occupational Safety and Health Administration* for responding to workplace emergencies that affect employee safety or health.

employee. A person whose manner of work the employer has a right to control.

employee assistance plan (EAP). A fringe benefit some employers offer that may include short-term counseling, alcohol or drug abuse treatment, and similar services.

employee handbook. A handbook of rules, policies, and procedures issued by an employer for the guidance and information of its employees.

Employee Polygraph Protection Act (EPPA). A law prohibiting employers from using lie detectors except in extremely limited circumstances.

Employee Retirement Income Security Act (ERISA). The principal federal law regulating retirement plans and other employee benefit plans.

employee stock ownership plan (ESOP). A form of benefit plan in which the retirement fund holds stock of the employer company.

employee stock purchase plan. A plan for granting stock options to an employer's general workforce in proportion to the employees' compensation.

employer identification number (EIN). The number employers obtain from the Internal Revenue Service (IRS) for use in filing tax returns and reports.

Employer Information Report (EEO-1). The report filed annually with the *Equal Employment Opportunity Commission* (EEOC) by employers that have 100 or more employees, and by certain government contractors and federal grant recipients, to provide the EEOC with a breakdown of the workforce by sex, race, and national origin.

employment contract. An agreement that employment will last for a specific term and/or that the employment will be terminated only for cause or in accordance with specified procedures.

employment practices liability (EPL) insurance. A form of coverage that protects employers from employment-related claims.

Equal Employment Opportunity Commission (EEOC). The principal enforcer of *Title VII* of the federal *Civil Rights Act of 1964*, the *Age Discrimination in Employment Act*, the employment provisions of the *Americans with Disabilities Act*, and the *Genetic Information Nondiscrimination Act*.

Equal Pay Act. An amendment to the *Fair Labor Standards Act* that requires employ-ers to pay males and females equally when doing the same work.

ergonomics. The science that studies the relationship between workers and their work environment.

E-Verify. An Internet-based system operated by the U.S. Department of Homeland Security and the Social Security Administration for electronically verifying eligibility to work in the U.S.

excess benefit plan. An unfunded plan maintained by an employer solely to avoid the contribution and benefit limitations imposed on qualified plans by §415 of the Internal Revenue Code. Excess benefit plans are exempt from most provisions of the *Employee Retirement Income Security Act.*

exempt employee. An employee who is not covered by minimum wage and overtime requirements of the federal *Fair Labor Standards Act* (and the similar provisions of state law) because he or she is employed in an executive, administrative, or professional capacity or falls within some other statutory exemption.

Executive Order (EO). An order issued by the president to an executive branch of the government.

exit interview. A meeting between an employee and management in connection with the employee's voluntary termination.

F

Fair and Accurate Credit Transactions Act (FACT Act). Federal law that, together with Federal Trade Commission regulations, governs the disposal of consumer information.

Fair Credit Reporting Act (FCRA). Federal law regulating the obtaining and use of *consumer reports.*

fair employment practice agency (FEPA). State or local agencies that enforce nondiscrimination laws comparable to federal law. Also known as *deferral agencies.*

Fair Labor Standards Act (FLSA). Federal law establishing minimum wages and overtime requirements and prohibiting *oppressive child labor.* As amended by the *Equal Pay Act,* the FLSA also prohibits employers from paying different wages to males and females who do the same work. A more recent amendment requires certain employers to provide breaks and facilities for nursing mothers to express milk.

False Claims Act. A federal law that permits a *whistle-blower* to file suit in the name of the U.S. government against companies that have allegedly committed fraud against the government.

Family and Medical Leave Act (FMLA). A federal law requiring employers that have 50 or more employees to grant extended leave to employees with serious medical conditions, for the birth or adoption of a child, when a family member has a serious medical condition, and in exigent circumstances involving a service member.

Federal Arbitration Act (FAA). A federal law that provides for enforcement of arbitration agreements.

Federal Insurance Contribution Act (FICA). A federal law that imposes a tax on employers and an identical tax on employees to fund the Social Security system.

federal per diem rates method. A method for reimbursing employees for business travel based on daily rates established by the federal government. The rates are divided into two groups, known as CONUS (continental U.S.) and OCONUS (outside continental U.S.).

Federal Unemployment Tax Act (FUTA). A federal law that imposes a tax on employers to help finance the unemployment insurance program.

fiduciary. A person who holds a special position of trust with respect to other persons, such as the trustee of a pension plan. Fiduciaries are required to act solely in the best interests of the persons for whom they hold the special trust position and not in their own self-interest.

flexible spending arrangement or *flexible spending account (FSA).* An employer-sponsored arrangement under which an employee can contribute pretax dollars to a special trust account and obtain reimbursement out of the account for uninsured medical expenses and/or dependent care expenses.

flextime. An arrangement under which employees may choose a work schedule different from the employer's normal work schedule, so long as the total hours worked per week meet the employer's minimum requirement.

Foreign Sovereign Immunities Act (FSIA). A federal law, under which foreign states are immune from the jurisdiction of courts in the U.S. so long as they are engaged in governmental activities.

fresh consideration. Something of value, such as a bonus or pay raise, offered to an existing or departing employee in exchange for the employee's signing a *noncompete agreement.*

friendship, commerce, and navigation (FCN) treaties. Treaties permitting foreign companies doing business in the U.S. to engage, at their choice, high-level personnel essential to the functioning of the enterprise, effectively permitting them to discriminate in favor of their own nationals.

front pay. Pay awarded to an employee or applicant for employment who, but for discrimination, an unfair labor practice, or other wrongful conduct by the employer, would have been earned after the time the award is made. Front pay is awarded when it would be impractical to require the employer to offer continuing or future employment.

full faith and credit clause. A provision in Article IV of the U.S. Constitution that requires each state to recognize the laws of every other state.

full-time equivalent (FTE). An aggregation of part-time employees whose hours, considered together, equate to the hours of one full-time employee.

G

garden leave. Paid leave granted an employee following notice that the employment will be terminated but before the effective date of termination.

garnishment. A wage attachment. A court order requiring the employer to pay a percentage of the wages of an employee to someone (the garnisher) who has obtained a money judgment against the employee.

General Duty Clause. The *Occupational Safety and Health Act* requirement that every employer furnish its employees with employment and a place of employment free from recognized hazards that cause or are likely to cause death or serious physical harm.

general employer. An employer that transfers an employee to another employer (called the *special employer*) for a limited period of time. While the transfer is in effect, the special employer has temporary responsibility and control over the employee's work.

glass ceiling. The invisible barrier to advancement sometimes faced by women and minorities.

golden parachute. Payments promised to key personnel in the event of a change in ownership or control of a company. See *say-on-pay rule.*

H

half-time plan. Sometimes called a fluctuating workweek plan, an exception to the *Fair Labor Standards Act's* general overtime rules that allows an employer to pay only half-time, instead of time-and-a-half, for overtime worked by nonexempt employees.

harassment. A form of discrimination involving conduct that has the purpose or effect of unreasonably interfering with a person's work performance or that creates an intimidating, hostile, or offensive work environment.

Health Insurance Portability and Accountability Act (HIPAA). A federal law that imposes confidentiality requirements on employers, health care providers, and others with respect to an individual's medical information. HIPAA's requirements regarding portability of group health plans have largely been superseded by the *Patient Protection and Affordable Care Act.*

health reimbursement arrangemen (HRA). An employer-funded health insurance plan, often paired with a high-deductible group health insurance policy, to reimburse employees for uninsured medical expenses.

health savings account (HSA). An account established by an individual employee in conjunction with a *high-deductible health plan* and funded by the employer, employee, or both, to pay the employee's current and future medical expenses.

high-deductible health plan (HDHP). A health insurance plan that satisfies statutory limits on deductible and out-of-pocket expense amounts.

hostile environment. A work environment made offensive by sexual or other *harassment.*

I

I-9. The form employers must complete and maintain for each employee as a record that the employee is eligible to work in the U.S.

Immigration and Customs Enforcement (ICE). A part of the U.S. Department of Homeland Security that enforces U.S. immigration and customs laws.

Immigration Reform and Control Act of 1986 (IRCA). An amendment to the Immigration and Nationality Act. IRCA prohibits employers from hiring aliens who are ineligible to work in the U.S. IRCA also prohibits discrimination against noncitizens.

impasse. The point to which company and union representatives must bargain before imposing a lockout or strike. An impasse occurs when good-faith bargaining has not resolved a key issue and when there are no definite plans for further efforts to break the deadlock.

indemnity plan. A type of health insurance plan in which the plan participant chooses his or her own health care provider, and the insurer pays the provider directly or reimburses the participant according to a formula or schedule specified in the plan.

independent contractor. A person whose work methods the employer does not have a right to control.

indexed. Subject to cost-of-living adjustments. The Internal Revenue Service publishes Revenue Procedures each year listing the adjustments for amounts subject to indexing under the Internal Revenue Code.

inevitable disclosure. A legal doctrine, adopted in a few states, permitting a court to enjoin a former employee from working for a competitor when the former employee has confidential information and when the old and new jobs are so similar that disclosure of the confidential information is considered inevitable.

inside buildup. The accumulation of tax-exempt income within a deferred compensation plan.

insider trading. Buying or selling publicly traded securities using information that is generally not available to the public. Insider trading is illegal under federal and state laws.

International Labour Organization (ILO). An agency of the United Nations that promotes rights at work, encourages decent employment opportunities, enhances social protection, and strengthens dialogue in handling work-related issues.

involuntary servitude. Slavery or other forms of compulsory work, prohibited by the 13th Amendment to the Constitution and federal law.

IV-D agency. A state agency that is responsible for administering Child Support Enforcement programs under Part D of Title IV of the Social Security Act.

L

last chance contract. An agreement between an employer and an employee that gives the employee a final opportunity to conform to company requirements or else be fired.

LGBTQ. Lesbian, gay, bisexual, transgender, and queer.

libel. See *defamation.*

liquidated damages. In contract law, an amount specified by the parties in advance that a party would be entitled to receive if the other party breaches the contract. Also, damages awarded for minimum wage and overtime violations of the *Fair Labor Standards Act* in addition to the wages due.

living wage. A wage rate higher than the federal minimum wage that some local jurisdictions require government contractors to pay their employees. *litigation hold.* An employer policy of preserving documents and data that may be relevant to a pending or threatened claim.

lock-in letter. A letter from the Internal Revenue Service (IRS) directing an employer to disregard an employee's Form W-4 and withhold in accordance with IRS instructions.

love contract. A contract required by some employers that sets certain ground rules for an office romance.

M

major life activity. For *Americans with Disabilities Act* purposes, activities such as caring for oneself, performing manual tasks, seeing, hearing, eating, sleeping, walking, standing, lifting, bending, speaking, breathing, learning, reading, concentrating, thinking, communicating, and working.

managed care plan. A type of subscription-based health insurance plan in which the participant is limited in his or her choice of health insurance providers but pays either nothing or only a small amount for services.

management rights clause. A provision in a *collective bargaining agreement* reserving certain decisions to management that are not subject to good-faith bargaining.

managers-only manual. A manual of workplace policies and procedures distributed only to management-level employees.

mass layoff. Under the *Worker Adjustment and Retraining Notification Act,* a layoff of at least 50 employees at a single site that amounts to at least 33 percent of the workforce at that site.

master-servant relationship. An outdated reference to an employer-employee relationship.

material safety data sheet (MSDS). The former name for *safety data sheet (SDS).*

minimum wage. The minimum hourly amount that employers must pay employees pursuant to the *Fair Labor Standards Act* and similar provisions of state and local law.

ministerial exception. An exception, available to religious organizations, to discrimination laws. Under the ministerial exception, religious organizations may discriminate in the selection of their clergy.

N

negligent employment. See *direct liability.*

nepotism. The practice of hiring relatives or favoring them in workplace decisions.

no-match letter. A letter issued by the Social Security Administration to an employer stating that an employee's name and Social Security number as reported on a Form W-2 do not match the administration's records.

noncompete agreement. An agreement that an employee will not compete with his or her former employer for a specified period after the employment terminates.

noncontributory plan. A plan such as a group health insurance plan in which the employer pays the entire premium.

nonexempt employee. An employee who is covered by minimum wage and overtime requirements of the *Fair Labor Standards Act* and similar provisions of state law.

nonqualified deferred compensation plan. Any arrangement other than a *qualified plan* under which a worker receives a legally binding right to compensation in one year but is not in actual or constructive receipt of that compensation until a later year. Unless such plans satisfy detailed Internal Revenue Code requirements, the compensation may be immediately taxable to the worker.

no-poaching agreement. An agreement among employers in a particular industry not to raid each other's employees. Such agreements violate the anti-trust laws.

O

Occupational Safety and Health (OSH) Act. A federal law that requires employers to comply with a variety of safety and health standards for the protection of their employees.

Occupational Safety and Health Administration (OSHA). An agency within the U.S. Department of Labor that administers and enforces the *Occupational Safety and Health (OSH) Act.*

Office of Federal Contract Compliance Programs (OFCCP). An office within the U.S. Department of Labor's Employment Standards Administration that administers U.S. government contractors' compliance with various employment-related statutes, regulations, and executive orders.

Older Workers Benefit Protection Act (OWBPA). An amendment to the *Age Discrimination in Employment Act* (ADEA) that imposes special requirements for releases of ADEA claims.

open shop. A workplace that employs both union and nonunion employees.

oppressive child labor. With certain exceptions, employment of any child who is under the age of 16, regardless of the occupation, and employment of a child who is between the ages of 16 and 18 in mining, manufacturing, or other hazardous industries.

P

paid-time off (PTO). A plan that replaces various forms of leave traditionally offered to employees.

pass-through entity. An entity, such as an *S corp* or a *limited liability company,* whose income and losses are attributed to its owner/members and not taxed to the entity itself.

Patient Protection and Affordable Care Act (PPACA). A federal law imposing wide-ranging regulation of the health insurance industry. The PPACA includes shared responsibility provisions for *applicable large employers,* requiring such employers either to offer affordable, minimum essential coverage to their employees or, in certain cases, make a payment to the Internal Revenue Service. Sometimes called *Obamacare.*

peonage. A system, no longer permitted in the U.S., by which debtors or indentured servants are bound in servitude to their creditors until their debts are paid.

perma-temp. Slang for a worker who, despite long tenure on the job, is still classified as temporary for benefits or other purposes.

personnel manual. See *employee handbook.*

personal protective equipment (PPE). Equipment required by various *Occupational Safety and Health Administration* standards to be worn to reduce excessive exposure to workplace conditions that could cause personal injury. Employers are required to cover the cost of most PPE.

polygraph. A lie detector. Polygraph testing in connection with employment is prohibited in most circumstances.

predatory hiring. A campaign to hire workers away from a particular company to harm that company's ability to compete. Predatory hiring may violate anti-trust laws.

Pregnancy Discrimination Act (PDA). An amendment to *Title VII* of the federal *Civil Rights Act of 1964* that defines sex discrimination to include discrimination because of pregnancy, childbirth, or related medical conditions.

prevailing wage. The usual wage paid for a particular job category in a particular locale. An employer must obtain a prevailing wage determination as part of the process of applying for an H-1B visa. Some government contracts contain provisions requiring contractors to pay prevailing wages.

principal. The person on whose behalf an *agent* acts.

professional employment organization (PEO). An organization that, for a fee, jointly employs a company's employees to provide HR-related functions, such as benefit plan administration, payroll services, and workers' compensation coverage.

progressive discipline. A policy of imposing increasingly severe discipline for repetitive workplace misconduct.

project labor agreement (PLA). A multiemployer prehire agreement used on construction projects that requires all contractors and subcontractors who will work on the project to agree in advance to a master collective bargaining agreement.

protected health information (PHI). Information about employees and others that is subject to privacy regulations of the *Health Insurance Portability and Accountability Act.*

Q

qualified domestic relations order (QDRO). An order entered by a domestic relations court in compliance with the *Employee Retirement Income Security Act* that awards an interest in a pension plan to an *alternate payee* such as a spouse.

qualified medical child support order (QMCSO). An order entered by a domestic relations court requiring an employer with a group health insurance plan to enroll an employee's child (the *alternate payee*) if the employer's plan includes family coverage.

qualified plan. An employee benefit plan that qualifies for favorable tax treatment under the Internal Revenue Code.

qualifying event. An event that triggers an opportunity to elect *COBRA* coverage.

quid pro quo. A type of sex discrimination involving the exchange of sexual favors for tangible job benefits.

R

rabbi trust. A *deferred compensation* arrangement for select management or highly compensated employees. Employer contributions to a rabbi trust are not currently deductible by the employer and may not be includable in the employee's income if the trust assets remain subject to claims by creditors of the employer.

Racketeer Influenced and Corrupt Organizations Act (RICO). A 1970 federal statute, primarily aimed at organized crime that has been applied to employers that repeatedly violate immigration or other laws.

reasonable accommodation. A requirement under the *Americans with Disabilities Act* to protect persons with disabilities. Also, a requirement under *Title VII* of the federal *Civil Rights Act* to allow for employee religious practices.

Rehabilitation Act. Federal law that prohibits most federal contractors and subcontractors from discriminating against persons with disabilities and requires affirmative action to ensure equal employment opportunity.

respondeat superior. The legal doctrine that imposes *vicarious liability* on an employer for the negligence of its employees.

restrictive covenant. An agreement that restricts an employee from competing with his or her employer, using confidential employer information, or attempting to hire the employer's other employees. A restrictive covenant may also assign to the employer any intellectual property developed by the employee.

retaliation. Taking adverse action against a current or former employee for exercising rights protected by law.

reverse discrimination. Discrimination against members of a historically advantaged group, which results from treating members of a historically disadvantaged group more favorably. Quota systems and some *affirmative action plans* can amount to reverse discrimination.

right-to-work law. A state law that prohibits collective bargaining agreements from containing *union security clauses.*

S

safety data sheet (SDS). An *Occupational Safety and Health Administration* form used to communicate information about hazardous chemicals. Formerly called a materials safety data sheet.

salary reduction agreement. An agreement authorizing an employer to make payroll deductions from its employee's compensation to fund a Section 125 plan or other benefit.

salt. A person who applies for a job to unionize the workplace once hired.

say-on-pay rule. A requirement that publicly traded companies periodically disclose executive compensation and any *golden parachute* arrangements to their shareholders and allow shareholders an advisory (nonbinding) vote on those matters.

second injury fund. A special fund established under state workers' compensation laws. Second (or subsequent) injury funds share responsibility for benefits due employees who have pre-existing, nondisabling conditions and who become disabled through the combined effects of the pre-existing condition and a subsequent injury.

Section 125 plan. A benefit plan (also called a cafeteria plan) that offers cash, or a variety of benefits in lieu of cash, from which the employee may choose. Cash payments are taxable to the employee, but qualified benefits are not.

Section 1981. See *Civil Rights Act of 1866.*

seniority system. A system followed by management, either by custom or pursuant to a *collective bargaining agreement* with a union, under which an employee with greater longevity will be favored for promotion or reassignment over otherwise equally qualified candidates.

separation information. Information provided by an employer to a state unemployment insurance agency to assist the agency in resolving an unemployment insurance claim.

shop rights. In patent law, an employer's right to use an invention created by an employee on the employer's time and using the employer's money, property, and labor. A shop right is nonexclusive, meaning that the employer cannot prevent the employee from exploiting the invention.

slander. See *defamation.*

Social Security Administration (SSA). An agency within the U.S. Department of Health and Human Services that administers the Social Security Act.

special employer. An employer that has borrowed an employee from another employer (called the *general employer*) for a limited time period and has temporary responsibility and control over the employee's work.

spoliation. The destruction or alteration of documents or data that may be relevant to a pending or threatened claim.

State Workforce Agency (SWA). Formerly known as a State Employment Security Agency, a U.S. Department of Labor label given to the state government agency that maintains detailed information about local labor conditions and markets and performs a variety of functions, such as certifying individuals for the *Work Opportunity Tax Credit.*

statute of frauds. A provision in state law requiring certain contracts to be in writing to be enforceable in court.

statute of limitations. A provision in law that bars lawsuits that are not filed within a specified time period.

statutory employee. A person who, by law, is classified as an employee for income tax, workers' compensation, or other purposes, even though he or she might otherwise qualify as an independent contractor.

statutory nonemployee. A person who, by law, is classified as an independent contractor, even though he or she might otherwise qualify as an employee.

subrogation. The right of a person who pays a claim to seek reimbursement from the wrongdoer. When an employee is injured on the job by the negligence of a third party and receives workers' compensation benefits from his or her employer, the employer or its insurance carrier may be subrogated to the employee's rights and sue the third party.

summary plan description (SPD). A written description, required by the *Employee Retirement Income Security Act,* of the provisions of a benefit plan provided by the employer.

supremacy clause. The provision in Article VI of the U.S. Constitution stating that the Constitution, the laws of the United States, and treaties "shall be the supreme Law of the Land" binding in every state.

T

tax deferral. A feature of some employee benefit plans, such as qualified pension plans, that permits the employee to exclude plan contributions from gross income for income tax purposes until a later time, such as retirement.

teleworking. Also known as telecommuting, working using high-tech communications equipment from home or from a facility other than the employer's regular place of business.

tester. A person who applies for a job for the sole purpose of testing the employer's hiring practices for discrimination.

third-party administrator (TPA). A company that administers a health insurance or other benefit plan but does not assume any risk of loss that plan benefits are designed to cover.

time-off plan. An exception to the general overtime rules of the *Fair Labor Standards Act* that allows an employer under certain narrow circumstances to award compensatory time to nonexempt employees in lieu of time-and-one-half for overtime.

Tip Reporting Alternative Commitment. An agreement between the Internal Revenue Service (IRS) and an employer in the food and beverage industry under which the employer agrees to establish an educational program and reporting procedures designed to promote accurate tip reporting by employees, and the IRS agrees to assess payroll taxes based on tips as reported by employees.

Tip Rate Determination Agreement. An agreement between the Internal Revenue Service (IRS) and an employer under which the IRS and the employer determine and agree in advance on the rate of tips to be reported by employees.

Title VII. The sections of the *Civil Rights Act of 1964* that prohibit discrimination in employment.

top hat plan. See *excess benefit plan.*

tort. A wrongful act that causes injury or property damage. Tortious acts are classified as negligent, grossly negligent (reckless), or intentional.

trade secret. Business information, such as a customer list, formula, or process that has value because it is not widely known and its confidentiality is protected.

U

unemployment insurance. A federal/state system funded by employers, under which employees who have involuntarily lost their jobs receive temporary benefits.

unfair labor practice (ULP). Conduct by an employer or a union that violates the *National Labor Relations Act.*

Uniformed Services Employment and Reemployment Rights Act (USERRA). A federal law that requires service members on military leave to continue to be carried as employees for certain benefit and seniority purposes and to be reemployed when they return from military leave.

union security clause. A provision in a *collective bargaining agreement* that protects union membership or revenue. A union security clause may require that employees be union members to be hired (*closed shop*), that they join a union after being hired (*union shop*), or that, in the case of nonunion employees, they pay dues as if they were members (*agency shop*).

union shop. A type of union security arrangement under which employees are required to join a union within a specified time after hire.

U.S. Citizenship and Immigration Services (USCIS). Part of the U.S. Department of Homeland Security. USCIS is the successor agency to the Immigration and Naturalization Service of the U.S. Department of Justice.

V

variable pay. Pay, such as bonuses or commissions, that may vary in amount depending on productivity, company profitability, or other factors.

vested. Nonforfeitable. When pension plan benefits are vested, they belong to the employee, even if employment ends or the plan is terminated.

vicarious liability. Liability imposed on an employer for the negligence of an employee that occurs in the course and scope of employment.

Vietnam Era Veterans' Readjustment Assistance Act (VEVRAA). A federal law prohibiting most federal contractors from discriminating against Vietnam-era and disabled veterans and requiring affirmative action to ensure equal employment opportunity.

W

W-2. The federal tax form employers issue to employees and also send to the Internal Revenue Service to report wages.

whistle-blower. An individual who discloses fraud or other wrongdoing by an employer or U.S. government contractor.

white-collar exemptions. Exemptions from the overtime requirements of the *Fair Labor Standards Act* for persons employed in bona fide executive, administrative, or professional capacities or as outside salespersons.

window of correction. The opportunity an employer has to correct an improper deduction from the salary of an exempt employee and preserve the employee's exempt status.

withholding order. A court order in a domestic relations case, similar to a *garnishment*, requiring an employer to withhold and turn over a portion of an employee's earnings to cover the employee's family support obligations.

Worker Adjustment and Retraining Notification (WARN) Act. A federal law that requires employers with 100 or more employees to give 60 days' advance notice of a *mass layoff* or plant closing.

workers' compensation. A state statutory arrangement funded by employers, under which employees who suffer work-related injuries or occupational illnesses receive benefits while out of work or while limited in their ability to work. Death benefits are provided to dependents of employees who are killed. The statutes also typically provide for payment of medical expenses, funeral benefits, and vocational rehabilitation.

work made for hire. In copyright law, a work authored by an employee for his or her employer, the copyright in which belongs to the employer.

work-sharing agreement. An agreement between the *Equal Employment Opportunity Commission* (EEOC) and a state or local *fair employment practice agency* (FEPA) that allocates responsibility for processing charges of employment discrimination. Work-sharing agreements usually provide that a filing with the EEOC or the FEPA is considered dual-filed with both agencies.

work opportunity tax credit (WOTC). A federal tax credit allowed to employers that hire persons in targeted groups of hard-to-employ individuals.

workweek. A 168-hour period used in determining an employer's obligation to pay overtime.

wrongful discharge. See *abusive discharge.*

Appendix:
Federal Statutory
Thresholds

Many, although not all, federal statutes require that the employer have a specified minimum number of employees before the statute applies. Listed below are some of the more significant federal statutes affecting employment, along with the statute's applicable threshold, if any.

Employers that fall below any particular threshold should keep in mind that parallel state and local laws may nevertheless apply to them. In addition, the thresholds in most cases are *not jurisdictional*, meaning that unless the employer affirmatively raises a defense that it lacks the requisite number of employees, a court or administrative agency may proceed to hear a complaint brought under the statute.

Americans with Disabilities Act (ADA)—*15 or more employees.*

Age Discrimination in Employment Act (ADEA)—*20 or more employees.*

Drug-Free Workplace Act (DFWA)—*federal contractors and grant recipients.*

Electronic Communications Privacy Act (ECPA)—*all employers.*

Electronic Privacy Protection Act (EPPA)—*all employers.*

Employee Retirement Income Security Act (ERISA)—*all employers with employee benefit plans.*

Fair Credit Reporting Act (FCRA)—*all employers.*

Fair Labor Standards Act (FLSA)—*employers with annual sales or business of at least $500,000* (enterprise coverage); *employers whose employees are engaged in interstate commerce* (individual coverage).

Family and Medical Leave Act (FMLA)—*50 or more employees.*

health insurance continuation provisions of COBRA—*20 or more employees.*

Health Insurance Portability and Accountability Act (HIPAA)—*all employers.*

Immigration Reform and Control Act (IRCA)—*all employers as to eligibility to work and Form I-9 requirements; four or more employees as to nondiscrimination provisions.*

Occupational Safety and Health Act (OSHA)—*all employers as to compliance with health and safety standards; 11 or more employees as to record-keeping, posting, and reporting requirements.*

Patient Protection and Affordable Care Act (PPACA)—*50 or more employees.*

Section 1981, Title 29, U.S. Code—*all employers.*

Title VII—*15 or more employees.*

Worker Adjustment and Retraining Notification (WARN) Act—*100 or more employees.*

Index

blacklisting (Fair Pay and Safe Workplaces) rule, 400

bloodborne pathogens standard, 245–246

bona fide occupational qualification (BFOQ) defense, 266, 290, 307, 450

bonuses, 106, 126, 135, 184

breach of contract, 13, 364–365

break periods, 89, 108

bring your own device (BYOD) policies, 339, 450

building owners and safety in the workplace, 256–257

Bush (George W.) administration, 399

business owners
    bonuses for, 126
    employment status of, 18–22
    white-collar exemption for, 100

C

C corporations, 22, 125–126

Cadillac plans under PPACA, 194–195, 450

cafeteria plans (Section 125 plans), 146, 197, 200–201, 214, 461

case law
    AT&T Mobility LLC v. Concepcion, 18
    Browning-Ferris Industries of California, Inc., 8
    Burlington Northern & Santa Fe Railway Co. v. White, 72
    Burwell v. Hobby Lobby Stores, Inc., 274
    Clackamas Gastroenterology Associates, P.C. v. Wells, 269–270
    Czyzewski v. Jevic Holding Corp., 111
    District of Columbia v. Heller, 255
    Hively v. Ivy Tech Community College, 302
    Hoffman Plastic Compounds, Inc. v. NLRB, 391–393
    Lawrence v. Texas, 301
    Meritor Savings Bank v. Vinson, 301
    NLRB v. Catholic Bishop of Chicago, 416, 423
    NLRB v. Murphy Oil USA, Inc., 18
    Obergefell v. Hodges, 133, 301, 302
    Oncale v. Sundowner Offshore Services, 301
    Price Waterhouse v. Hopkins, 301
    Purple Communications, Inc., 425
    Salinas v. Commercial Interiors, Inc., 8
    Spokeo, Inc. v. Robins, 349
    Sure-Tan, Inc. v. NLRB, 391, 392
    U.S. v. Windsor, 301

Zarda v. Altitude Express, Inc., 302

cash balance plans, 169–170, 450–451

cash or deferral arrangements (CODAs), 171, 451

casual employees, 219, 451

cause, employees quitting or leaving work for, 234

cause, termination for, 66–67, 80, 451

CBAs (collective bargaining agreements), 420, 432–436, 451. *See also* unions and labor relations

CBR (chemical, biological, or radiological) attacks, 257

Centers for Disease Control and Prevention (CDC), 256

certifications
    fitness for duty certifications, 144–145
    medical certification for FMLA leave, 152–153

CFAA (Computer Fraud and Abuse Act), 357

CGL (comprehensive general liability) insurance, 286

Chapter 13 bankruptcies, 119, 451

charitable organizations. *See* nonprofit organizations

chemical, biological, or radiological (CBR) attacks, 257

child labor laws, 109–110, 451

children and parents
    maternity and paternity leave, 150, 290, 291
    pregnancy and childbirth, health care protections for, 203–204, 289–290, 460
    QMCSOs, 204–205, 360, 450
    school activities, parental leave to attend, 164

choice-of-law and choice-of-forum provisions in employment contracts, 11–12

church plans, 413–414

Circular E (IRS Publication 15), 132, 451

citations from OSHA, 248–250

citizenship or national origin discrimination, 283, 388–389

Civil Rights Act of 1866. *See* Section 1981

lie detectors, 340–341
mail, 346–347, *347 (fig. 18.2)*
marijuana use, 344–346
off-duty behavior, 334–335
personal use of employer equipment, 338
places generally considered private,
330–331
police search of office, employer consent
to, 331
relationship policies and love contracts,
298, 458
sensitive records, 332–334
social media policies, 347–349
substance abuse testing, 321–322, 341–343
surveillance, 334–335

privileged statements, 76–77

probable cause findings by EEOC, 280–281

probationary periods, 35

professional codes of ethics, nondiscrimination
clauses in, 285

professional corporations (PCs), 21–22,
269–270

professional employer organizations (PEOs),
380, 460

professionals
NLRA coverage/NLRB jurisdiction,
422–423
white-collar exemption for, 100, 464

profit sharing plans, 171

progressive discipline, 55 *(fig. 3.2)*, 460

project labor agreements (PLAs), 432, 460

protected health information (PHI), 333–334,
460

PTO (paid time off) plans, 145–147, 148, 401,
459

PTSD (post-traumatic stress disorder), 321

publicly held corporations, deduction limits for,
127–128

punitive (exemplary) damages, 119, 262, 282,
296, 356, 414

Q

QDROs (qualified domestic relations orders),
180–181, 449, 460

QMCSOs (qualified medical child support
orders), 204–205, 450, 460

QSEHRAs (qualified small employer HRAs),
200

qualified benefit plans, 167, 460

qualified disability, 160

qualified domestic relations orders (QDROs),
180–181, 449, 460

qualified individual with a disability, 314

qualified medical child support orders
(QMCSOs), 204–205, 450, 460

qualified medical expenses
for health FSAs, 199
for HRAs, 200
for HSAs, 196–197

qualified small employer HRAs (QSEHRAs),
200

qualified transportation fringe benefits,
214–215

qualifying events under COBRA, 201–203,
460

qualifying exigency, under FMLA, 151–152

quickie election rule, 428

quid pro quo harassment, 292, 360

quitting. *See* termination of employment

R

rabbi trusts, 183–184, 460

race discrimination. *See* discrimination; Title
VII of Civil Rights Act of 1964

Racketeer Influenced and Corrupt
Organizations (RICO) Act, 383, 460

reasonable accommodation
defined, 461
of disability, 317–321
of religious observances and practices, 272

reassignment. *See* job reassignment

record-keeping and reporting requirements
deductions from wages, 108
EEOC requirements, 285–286
employee privacy and sensitive records,
332–334
personnel files, 48–52
safety in the workplace, 247–248
tax payments, 140–142

recruitment and hiring. *See* hiring

reduced work schedule under FMLA, 155

reductions in force (RIFs), 82–84

references, 77–79

trade secrets, 355–356, *356 (fig. 19.1)*, 463

training
anti-harassment, 297, 298
in nondiscrimination policy, 267
safety in the workplace and, 227, 241, 242, 243, 244, 245, 255, 259
for unpaid interns, 87
WARN Act, 83–84, 458, 464, 467

transgender persons. *See* sexual orientation and gender identity

transportation fringe benefits, qualified, 214–215

Trump administration, 8, 190, 285, 302, 345, 410

trust fund penalty for failure to deposit taxes appropriately, 140–141

Twelfth Amendment, 2

two-weeks-notice period, 65–66, *66 (fig. 4.1)*

U

ULPs (unfair labor practices), 436–438, 463

undue hardship, 318–319

unemployment insurance, 229–237
base period, 231–232, 450
benefits, 237
cause, employees quitting or leaving work for, 234
claims procedure, 235–237
coverage and eligibility, 232–233
defined, 463
employer contributions, 230–232
FUTA and, 230, 455
misconduct, employees fired for, 233–234
nonprofit organizations, 414
quitting employees, 233–234
separation information, 235, 461
strikes and, 234, 441

unfair labor practices (ULPs), 436–438, 463

Uniform Trade Secrets Act (UTSA), 355

Uniformed Services Employment and Reemployment Rights Act (USERRA), 53, 160–163, 463

unilateral self-help, 250

union security clauses, 438–439, 463

union shops, 438, 463

unions and labor relations, 419–442. *See also* National Labor Relations Act; National Labor Relations Board

abusive and threatening language in representation elections, 429–430
agency shops, 438, 449, 463
antitrust law and, 427
card check representation, 430–431
card checks, 427–428
CBAs, 420, 432–436, 451
closed shops, 438, 463
collusion between employer and union, 438
concerted activity by, 338, 423–427, 451
conflict of laws, 434–436
duty of employer to bargain, 431–436
duty of union to bargain, 441
electronic communications used for concerted activity, 338
employee committees, company-dominated, 436–437
employee handbooks and, 426–427, *427 (fig. 24.1)*
EO 13201 and 13496 on notice posting requirements, 399
health care institutions, strike restrictions on, 442
impasse, bargaining to, 432, 440, 441, 442, 457
independent contractors, 421–422
laboratory conditions requirement for representation elections, 429
limits on right to strike, 441–442
management rights clauses, 433, 458
managers and supervisors, 422
mandatory versus permissive subjects of bargaining, 432–434
nonunion shops, 425–426
no-strike clauses, 441
outside organizers, 424–425
picketing, 439
PLAs, 432, 460
professionals, 422–423
quickie election rule, 428
refusal to work due to safety-related conditions, 441
religions forbidding union membership or support, 416
religious institutions, employees of, 416, 423
replacement workers, 440–441
representation elections, 427–431
right to work and union security clauses, 438–439, 461
salts, 437–438, 461
secondary strikes, 441
seniority systems, 308, 320, 321, 434, 441, 461

Additional
SHRM-Published Books

View from the Top: Leveraging Human
and Organization Capital to Create
Value
Richard L. Antoine, Libby Sartain, Dave Ulrich,
Patrick M. Wright

California Employment Law: An
Employer's Guide, Revised & Updated for
2017
James J. McDonald, Jr.

101 Sample Write-ups for Documenting
Employee Performance Problems: A Guide
to Progressive Discipline & Termination,
Third Edition
Paul Falcone

Developing Business Acumen
SHRM Competency Series:
Making an Impact in Small Business
Jennifer Currence

Applying Critical Evaluation
SHRM Competency Series:
Making an Impact in Small Business
Jennifer Currence

Touching People's Lives:
Leaders' Sorrow or Joy
Michael R. Losey

From Hello to Goodbye:
Proactive Tips for Maintaining Positive
Employee Relations, Second Edition
Christine V. Walters

Defining HR Success:
9 Critical Competencies for HR
Professionals
Kari R. Strobel, James N. Kurtessis, Debra J. Cohen,
and Alexander Alonso

HR on Purpose: Developing Deliberate
People Passion
Steve Browne

A Manager's Guide to Developing
Competencies in HR Staff
Phyllis G. Hartman

Tips and Tools for Improving
Proficiency in Your Reports
Phyllis G. Hartman

Developing Proficiency in HR:
7 Self-Directed Activities for HR
Professionals
Debra J. Cohen

Manager Onboarding:
5 Steps for Setting New Leaders Up for
Success
Sharlyn Lauby

Destination Innovation:
HR's Role in Charting the Course
Patricia M. Buhler

Got a Solution? HR Approaches to
5 Common and Persistent Business
Problems
Dale J. Dwyer & Sheri A. Caldwell

HR's Greatest Challenge: Driving the
C-Suite to Improve Employee Engagement
and Retention
Richard P. Finnegan

Business-Focused HR:
11 Processes to Drive Results
Shane S. Douthitt & Scott P. Mondore

Proving the Value of HR: How and Why
to Measure ROI, Second Edition
Jack J. Phillips & Patricia Pulliam Phillips

SHRMStore Books Approved for Recertification Credit

Aligning HR & Business Strategy/Holbeche, 9780750680172 (2009)

Becoming the Evidence-Based Manager/Latham, 9780891063988 (2009)

Being Global/Cabrera, 9781422183229 (2012)

Best Practices in Succession Planning/Linkage, 9780787985790 (2007)

Calculating Success/Hoffmann, 9781422166390 (2012)

Collaborate/Sanker, 9781118114728 (2012)

Deep Dive/Horwath, 9781929774821 (2009)

Effective HR Management/Lawler, 9780804776875 (2012)

Emotional Intelligence/Bradbury, 9780974320625 (2009)

Employee Engagement/Carbonara, 9780071799508 (2012)

From Hello to Goodbye/Walters, 9781586442064 (2011)

Handbook for Strategic HR/Vogelsang, 9780814432495 (2012)

Hidden Drivers of Success/Schiemann, 9781586443337 (2013)

HR at Your Service/Latham, 9781586442477 (2012)

HR Transformation/Ulrich, 9780071638708 (2009)

Lean HR/Lay, 9781481914208 (2013)

Manager 3.0/Karsh, 97808144w32891 (2013)

Managing Employee Turnover/Allen, 9781606493403 (2012)

Managing the Global Workforce/Caliguri, 9781405107327 (2010)

Managing the Mobile Workforce/Clemons, 9780071742207 (2010)

Managing Older Workers/Cappelli, 9781422131657 (2010)

Multipliers/Wiseman, 9780061964398 (2010)

Negotiation at Work/Asherman, 9780814431900 (2012)

Nine Minutes on Monday/Robbins, 9780071801980 (2012)

One Strategy/Sinofsky, 9780470560457 (2009)

People Analytics/Waber, 9780133158311 (2013)

Performance Appraisal Tool Kit/Falcone, 9780814432631 (2013)

Point Counterpoint/Tavis, 9781586442767 (2012)

Practices for Engaging the 21st Century Workforce/Castellano, 9780133086379 (2013)

Proving the Value of HR/Phillips, 9781586442880 (2012)

Reality-Based Leadership/Wakeman, 9780470613504 (2010)

Social Media Strategies/Golden, 9780470633106 (2010)

Talent, Transformations, and Triple Bottom Line/Savitz, 9781118140970 (2013)

The Big Book of HR/Mitchell, 9781601631893 (2012)

The Crowdsourced Performance Review/Mosley, 9780071817981 (2013)

The Definitive Guide to HR Communications/Davis, 9780137061433 (2011)

The e-HR Advantage/Waddill, 9781904838340 (2011)

The Employee Engagement Mindset/Clark, 9780071788298 (2012)

The Global Challenge/Evans, 9780073530376 (2010)

The Global Tango/Trompenaars, 9780071761154 (2010)

The HR Answer Book/Smith, 9780814417171 (2011)

The Manager's Guide to HR/Muller, 9780814433027 (2013)

The Power of Appreciative Inquiry/Whitney, 9781605093284 (2010)

Transformative HR/Boudreau, 9781118036044 (2011)

What If? Short Stories to Spark Diversity Dialogue/Robbins, 9780891062752 (2008)

What Is Global Leadership?/Gundling, 9781904838234 (2011)

Winning the War for Talent/Johnson, 9780730311553 (2011)